FRANCIS POULENC

'ECHO AND SOURCE'

Selected Correspondence
1915–1963

FRANCIS POULENC

'ECHO AND SOURCE'

Selected Correspondence
1915–1963

TRANSLATED AND EDITED BY

SIDNEY BUCKLAND

RESEARCH CONSULTANT: PATRICK SAUL

LONDON

VICTOR GOLLANCZ LTD

1991

First published in Great Britain 1991
by Victor Gollancz Ltd
14 Henrietta Street, London WC2E 8QJ

Publication of this edition has been made possible
by a grant from Les Amis de Francis Poulenc, Paris,
and the French Ministry of Culture.

A CIP catalogue record for this book is available
from the British Library.

ISBN 0 575 05093 4

Typeset at The Spartan Press Ltd,
Lymington, Hants
and printed in Great Britain by
St Edmundsbury Press Ltd, Bury St Edmunds
Illustrations printed by WBC Print Ltd,
Bridgend, Mid Glamorgan

Contents

List of Illustrations

Introduction

In 1951, Francis Poulenc received a copy of Paul Eluard's latest collection of poetry, *Le Phénix*. The inscription in the book read as follows:

A Francis Poulenc, écho et source. Paul Eluard.

Many of Poulenc's greatest songs and choral works were settings of Eluard's poetry, a poetry essentially of reciprocity. In his brief inscription, Eluard goes to the heart of Poulenc's inventive response to the poets who inspired his vocal music, to the heart of Poulenc's interchange with his many and varied friends. Nowhere is this interchange more evident than in Poulenc's voluminous correspondence.

Writing letters was an inseparable part of Poulenc's life. He wrote as he spoke, with a need to communicate, to confide and to share. The singer Pierre Bernac, describing what he called Poulenc's *culte de l'amitié*, said:

Francis had numerous friends, and friendship meant a great deal to him; he felt the need of reciprocity and mutual confidence. That is why correspondence held an important place in his life. He wrote with disconcerting speed, and his style was as alive, personal, unpredictable and spontaneous as his conversation. [*PB-FP* p. 34]

Poulenc the letter-writer is known mainly through a collection of his correspondence selected after his death by a cultured and music-loving friend, Hélène de Wendel, and published in 1967 by Editions du Seuil, Paris, under the title *Francis Poulenc – Correspondance (1915–1963)*. In selecting the letters, Hélène de Wendel was assisted by Pierre Bernac, Darius Milhaud (who also wrote the preface) and Henri Sauguet. The book has long been out of print.

In 1986, the English singer and teacher, Winifred Radford, having recently completed a translation of Poulenc's *Journal de mes mélodies* (published as *Diary of my Songs*), had the idea of translating into English Hélène de Wendel's selection of Poulenc's correspondence. Then aged eighty-five, Winifred Radford felt that she needed assistance with this task and asked me to collaborate with her. After initial discussions and combined preparatory work on a number of letters, Winifred Radford was unable to continue with the translation. It is my hope that I have brought this work to its conclusion in the spirit in which she meant it to be done. If it is fitting for a translation to be dedicated to anyone at all, then I dedicate this one to Winifred Radford, with admiration and with love.

In the early stages of my work I began searching for unpublished letters to and from Poulenc, in the hope of adding new material to that in *Correspondance*. Two important facts soon emerged. The first was that many of the letters in *Correspondance* were not complete letters. The second was that the letters in *Correspondance* represented only a fragment of Poulenc's epistolary output.

Letters written to Poulenc were relatively easy to trace (see under Sources of Letters). Those written by Poulenc, however, often posed serious problems. Many were in private and public collections in France, Switzerland, Spain, England and the USA. Many had been sold by auction and were dispersed in libraries and archives around the world. Poulenc's letters to Pierre Bernac, for example, were found to be divided between two major collections, the Frederick R. Koch Foundation Collection in the Pierpont Morgan Library, New York, and the Manuscript Department of the Bibliothèque Nationale in Paris. Whereas many collectors, both public and private, were generous in sending duplicates of letters they held, others had a policy of never making copies of the manuscripts in their collections. This meant several visits to distant places and transcribing the letters by hand. Only a small group of collectors were not forthcoming with material in their possession.

In comparing, wherever possible, Poulenc's original letters with those published in *Correspondance*, I discovered two main areas of expurgation. The first – understandable in the climate of 1967 – related to Poulenc's homosexual relationships. The second – less understandable – related to Poulenc's delight in his own achievement as a composer: 'The *Gloria* is without doubt the best thing I have done. The orchestration is marvellous (the ending, among other things, is astonishing)' (No. 325). 'I have finished *Les Ténèbres*. I think it is beautiful' (No. 337). The phrases underlined are examples of omissions in *Correspondance*.

Of the letters I have been able to check against the originals, those to Pierre Bernac and, to a lesser extent, to Simone Girard are shown to have suffered the most severe expurgation. When, as in the present volume, these missing passages are restored to their rightful context, Poulenc emerges as a far more honest and moving human being. In his compulsive confessions to friends, he writes frankly and openly about his innermost feelings and needs. Touching insight is gained into the intimate relationships he sought, most of them unassociated with the intellectual and social circles in which he moved in his professional life, yet inextricably bound up with his creative processes: 'If Raymond remains the secret of *Les Mamelles* and *Figure humaine*, Lucien is certainly that of the *Stabat* and *Les Carmélites*' (No. 265). 'My *Voix humaine* is opening in Paris on 6 February . . . I will send you the music of this atrocious tragedy (my own). It is a musical confession!!!' (No. 294).

The extra letters give us a deeper understanding of the nature of Poulenc's breakdown in the 1950s. The severe depressions from which he suffered at this time, usually ascribed to copyright problems concerning his opera *Dialogues des Carmélites*, are revealed as due in no small measure to the dissolution of his relationship with a young man from Toulon.

Curiously, no letters from Bernac to Poulenc appeared in *Correspondance*. It is widely assumed that this was due to Bernac's legendary modesty. Ten letters from Bernac are included in the present volume. They show unequivocally the true nature of the relationship between Poulenc and Bernac. As the distinguished English accompanist and Poulenc exponent, Graham Johnson, has written: 'For twenty-five years Bernac was Poulenc's counsellor and conscience; without being in any way lovers, the two men loved the artist in each other.'* Bernac's role as counsellor and conscience is nowhere more evident than in these letters. Nowhere more explicit is Poulenc's reliance on Bernac for advice and guidance, not only in his song-writing but in such diverse works as *Les Mamelles de Tirésias*, *Dialogues des Carmélites*, and the *Gloria*.

A significant aspect that emerges from the previously unpublished material is Poulenc's reciprocal concern for Bernac. Passages relating to Bernac in the letters to Simone Girard – among some of the most affecting in the correspondence – add a valuable dimension to our perception of Poulenc the man: his solicitude for Bernac; the care with which he designed their later recitals to accommodate Bernac's advancing years and altering voice; the depth of his understanding of Bernac's own vulnerability.

Among the newly-uncovered letters are many gems, including Rostropovitch's plea for a cello sonata by Poulenc, Stravinsky's last postcard to Poulenc and Edward Sackville-West's eulogy on *The Carmelites* at Covent Garden. Notable, too, are Poulenc's communications to the American singer and patron, Alice Esty, which throw new light on the background to the song cycle *Le Travail du peintre* and offer a fascinating glimpse of Poulenc the businessman. The letters to Benjamin Britten and the exchanges with Manuel de Falla are of touching interest, as are

---

*From *Homage to Pierre Bernac*, programme notes by Graham Johnson for a recital to mark the 90th anniversary of the birth of Bernac, given by the baritone, Richard Jackson, accompanied by Graham Johnson, at the Wigmore Hall, London, on 12 January 1989.

Poulenc's outpourings to his friend and confidante, the singer Rose Dercourt-Plaut.

There are many hundreds of letters to and from Poulenc in existence. The present volume comprises 350 letters, 225 from *Correspondance* (many of them restored to their original form) and an additional 125 letters, 102 of which have never been published before. The aim governing the choice of letters has been to provide fresh insight into Poulenc's compositions and creative processes, to illuminate the main events and relationships in his life, and to show the wide range of his activities and friendships. The letters are presented in chronological order. Read in sequence, they form a coherent narrative of Poulenc's life.

Both Poulenc's life and his letters seem to fall into three clearly-defined periods, each period marked by a decisive turning-point:

1915–1935 This period covers Poulenc's studies with Ricardo Viñes and Charles Koechlin; his early compositions, marked by a predilection for wind instruments and voice; the forging of friendships with poets and musicians who influenced the rest of his life; his service in the First World War; his association with Les Six and with Diaghilev's Russian Ballet; his introduction into the great salons of the twenties and thirties, and the compositions that resulted from commissions by these patrons; the formation of the Bernac–Poulenc duo in 1935 and Poulenc's first settings of poems by Paul Eluard.

1936–1953 A new dimension enters Poulenc's life in 1936 after a mystical experience at Rocamadour, from which stem the great religious works and choral writing. This period also sees the rise of the Bernac–Poulenc duo and the composition of many of the finest songs; the difficulties of the Second World War; the discovery of Denise Duval, who became Poulenc's favourite leading lady; and a series of international tours with Bernac including three to the USA.

1953–1963 A new turning-point is reached in March 1953 with the commission for the opera *Dialogues des Carmélites*, which occupies Poulenc for the next three years. This final period embraces the last great song cycle to poems by Eluard; Bernac's retirement from the concert platform in 1959; the setting of two texts by Cocteau for Denise Duval; European and USA tours with Duval; the last religious choral works, and a return to an early love, the woodwind sonata, with the completion of those for clarinet and for oboe shortly before his death in 1963.

It has been said many times of Francis Poulenc that his music was the very expression of his being, that for him composing was never an intellectual exercise, but always an act of love. His letters bear moving testimony to the indivisibility of his life and his music, and of his music and his loves. Constant in his correspondence is his great gift for friendship. As Tony Mayer aptly said, introducing Francis Poulenc at the 1956 Aldeburgh Festival:

> And who can count so many friends, both humble and famous, sharing equally in his likeable gifts and his need to be liked?

A Note on the Text

Except where the provenance of a letter is listed as *Correspondance*, *Les Lettres françaises*, or *L'Avant-Scène Opéra* (see under Sources of Letters), translations have been made from the text of the autograph letters. Only a very few passages have been omitted, in cases where, for example, information is inconsequential or of a private nature unrelated to Poulenc. These omissions are indicated by [. . .]. In the case of letters from *Correspondance*, *Les Lettres françaises*, and *L'Avant-Scène Opéra*, it has not been possible to verify whether these are complete letters.

Poulenc rarely dated his letters other than by the day of the week, or at best, the month. Dates between square brackets are editorial suggestions. Where a date has been changed from that in *Correspondance*, this is indicated and reasons are given in the Notes.

Words in round brackets are Poulenc's own words; those in square brackets are editorial additions. Words that Poulenc stressed by underlining are represented by italics.

The familiar form of address *tu* occurs in the correspondence between Poulenc and Stéphane Audel, Jean Cocteau, Doda Conrad, Louis Durey, Denise Duval, Arthur Honegger, Max Jacob, Marie Laurencin, Brigitte Manceaux, Darius Milhaud, Suzanne Peignot, Raymond Radiguet, Louise de Vilmorin.

To assist the reader who may not be familiar with all Poulenc's correspondents, biographical particulars are provided under the heading Poulenc's Correspondents.

Numbers in the body of the text refer to explanatory information given in the section headed Notes.

Where recordings are mentioned in the letters, the number and make of the first issue only are given in the Notes. For recordings by Poulenc as composer, performer and speaker, see Francine Bloch: *Phonographie de Francis Poulenc*, Bibliothèque Nationale, Paris, 1984. For recordings of works by Poulenc issued after 1982, see George R. Keck: *Francis Poulenc – a bio-bibliography*, Greenwood Press, New York/Westport, Connecticut/ London, 1990.

Acknowledgements

This English edition of the correspondence of Francis Poulenc has been made possible first and foremost by the unstinting co-operation of Rosine Seringe, niece and godchild of the composer. In making available to me original letters and documents in her care and in permitting full use of this material without restrictions, she has contributed significantly to a deeper understanding of Francis Poulenc and his music. To Rosine and her husband Jean Seringe I offer my warmest personal thanks for the hospitality and friendship they have shown me.

I should like to express my gratitude to the Association 'Les Amis de Francis Poulenc' and to Flavie Alvarez de Toledo for the generous assistance they have given to this project.

The late Hélène de Wendel who, in 1967, compiled the original French edition *Francis Poulenc: Correspondance 1915–1963*, gave her blessing to the idea of this English edition in a letter written shortly before her death in 1986. Her support was much appreciated.

I should also like to thank Marie-Ange – for a heartwarming talk and for her kind encouragement.

I am especially grateful to Myriam Chimènes who gave me many leads in France and, with enormous generosity, shared her findings and her writings on the baritone Pierre Bernac.

My enjoyment in translating the letters was greatly enhanced by discussions with two people in particular. I thank Elisabeth Bruner Flash for giving me the benefit of her linguistic expertise and enlightening me on many subtleties in the original French. Douglas Gardner brought his long experience as a writer to bear and helped me to solve many problems in the search for a faithful and fluent English translation. For the counsel and courage he gave me, he has my deep gratitude.

Patrick Saul has put me under great obligation by scrutinizing the text in the light of his prodigious knowledge of French music of the era and by volunteering many valuable suggestions and additional information. Any errors or omissions are entirely my responsibility. I am also indebted to him for his contribution to the index.

My special thanks to Richard Wigmore for the close interest he has shown in this project from its inception and for his continued encouragement.

For the use of copyright material and for kind help given I thank the following individuals: Flavie Alvarez de Toledo, Denis Bertin, Hervé Bonnasse, Valentine Chagall, Doda Conrad, Rose Dercourt-Plaut, Edouard Dermit, Cécile Eluard, Alice Esty, Isabel de Falla, Robert Fizdale, the late Arthur Gold, the late Henri Hell, Madeleine Li-Koechlin, Eardley Knollys, Madeleine Milhaud, Suzanne Peignot, Pierre Poulenc, the late Georgette Rostand, Mstislav Rostropovitch, Lord Sackville, the late Henri Sauguet, the late Théodore Stravinsky, Daniel Swift, Pierre Vidal.

For making available letters and documents in their possession and for courteous assistance, my grateful acknowledgements are due to the following libraries, archives and their curators:

In France, the Archives Jean Wiéner; the Bibliothèque Littéraire Jacques Doucet de l'Université de Paris; the Bibliothèque Musicale Gustav Mahler; the Music Department and the Manuscript Department of the Bibliothèque Nationale; the Bibliothèque de l'Opéra and especially Martine Kahane; the Fondation Singer-Polignac.

In England, the Britten–Pears Library, Aldeburgh, and Rosamund Strode; the British Red Cross Society Archives and Helen Pugh; the Central Music Library, Westminster; the Institut Français du Royaume-Uni; the Royal College of Music Library; the Royal Opera House Archives and Francesca Franchi; the Theatre Museum.

In the USA, the Carnegie Hall Archives; the Music Division of the Library of Congress, Washington, D.C.; the Harry Ransom Humanities Research Center, University of Texas at Austin; the Museum of Modern Art Archives; the New York Public Library; the Pierpont Morgan Library; the Music Library at Yale University.

In Spain, the Fundacion 'Archivo Manuel de Falla', Madrid; and in Switzerland, the Paul Sacher Foundation, Basle, and Ingrid Westen.

My thanks, also, to the following individuals and publishers for their kind permission to make use of copyright material:

Rosine Seringe: extracts from *Francis Poulenc – Entretiens avec Claude Rostand*, Julliard, Paris, 1954.

Winifred Radford: extracts from her translation of Poulenc's *Journal de mes mélodies* (*Diary of my songs*), Victor Gollancz, London 1985 and from her translation of Pierre Bernac's *Francis Poulenc: the man and his songs*, Victor Gollancz, London 1977.

Richard Jackson: for his translation of Cocteau's poem 'Toréador'.

Editions de La Table Ronde: extracts from *Francis Poulenc: Moi et mes amis*, confidences recueillies par Stéphane Audel, © La Palatine, Geneva, Paris, 1963.

Editions Gallimard: Part I of 'Intimes' from *Les Yeux fertiles*, 'Les Excellents moments' from *Le Livre ouvert II*, 'A Francis Poulenc' from

Poèmes retrouvés, all by Paul Eluard in *Paul Eluard – Oeuvres complètes*, Bibliothèque de la Pléiade, © Gallimard 1968.

For permission to reproduce photographs from the collection of Francis Poulenc, I am grateful to Rosine Seringe (1–4, 6, 8, 11, 13–21, 25, 27, 28). Other photographs have kindly been supplied by Myriam Chimènes (9, 10), Winifred Radford (23), the late Henri Sauguet (24), Pierre Vidal (26), the Bibliothèque Nationale (7), the Fundacion 'Archivo Manuel de Falla' (5), the Musée d'Art et d'Histoire de la ville de Saint-Denis (22), and the Paul Sacher Foundation (12).

Though every effort has been made to trace copyright holders, the publishers will be pleased to hear from anyone not acknowledged here.

Abbreviations of Sources Quoted

AA	Jean Wiéner: *Allegro appassionato*. Belfond, Paris, 1978.
AG-J	André Gide: *Journal, 1889–1939*. Gallimard, Paris, 1948.
AH-JSC	Arthur Honegger: *Je suis compositeur*. Editions du Conquistador, Paris, 1951.
AM-GAZ	Adrienne Monnier: *Les Gazettes. 1925–1945*. Julliard, Paris, 1953.
AM-RO	Adrienne Monnier: *Rue de l'Odéon*. Albin Michel, Paris, 1989.
APOL	Francis Steegmuller: *Apollinaire, poet among the painters*. Penguin Books, Harmondsworth, 1986.
BIRS	*Recorded sound*. Journal of The British Institute of Recorded Sound (now the National Sound Archive), London.
CPC	Henri Hoppenot: Préface aux *Cahiers Paul Claudel III*. Gallimard, Paris, 1961.
COCT	Francis Steegmuller: *Cocteau – a biography*. Godine, Boston, 1986.
Correspondance	*Francis Poulenc – Correspondance 1915–1963*. Réunie par Hélène de Wendel. Editions du Seuil, Paris, 1967.
CR-FP	Claude Rostand: 'Francis Poulenc – hier et demain' in *Le Figaro littéraire*, 7 February 1963.
DMS	Francis Poulenc: *Diary of my songs (Journal de mes mélodies)*, English translation by Winifred Radford. Gollancz, London, 1985.
ECR	Francis Poulenc – *Entretiens avec Claude Rostand*. Julliard, Paris, 1954.
FP-ASO	*L'Avant-Scène Opéra*, No. 52. Paris, May 1983. Issue devoted to Poulenc's *Dialogues des Carmélites* and *La Voix humaine*.
FP-CAS	*Francis Poulenc par lui-même*. Recording of a talk given by Poulenc at the Club des Trois Centres on 10 January 1962, set of two cassettes issued privately by Les Amis de Francis Poulenc, Paris, 1988, with the collaboration of Pierre Vidal and Studio Voxigrave.
FP-MMA	Francis Poulenc: *Moi et mes amis*. Poulenc in conversation with Stéphane Audel. La Palatine, Paris-Geneva, 1963.
FP-MMLP	Francis Poulenc: 'Mes mélodies et leurs poètes', talk given on

	20 March 1947, published in *Conferencia – Les Annales* 36, 15 December 1947.
FP-MMMA	Francis Poulenc: 'Mes maîtres et mes amis', talk given on 7 March 1935, published in *Conferencia*, 15 October 1935.
FP-PG	Francis Poulenc interviewed by Paul Guth in *Le Figaro littéraire*, 17 May 1952.
FP-PJ	Francis Poulenc: 'Pages de journal' in *La Table ronde*, June 1950.
FP-PV	Pierre Vidal: 'Francis Poulenc chez les jeunes' in *Journal musical français*, 6 March 1963.
FP-ROC	*Poulenc et Rocamadour.* Tribute to Poulenc marking the tenth anniversary of his death. Zodiaque, Paris, 1974.
H à FP	'Hommage à Francis Poulenc' in *Bulletin de la Phonotèque Nationale*, supplément spécial au numéro 1. January–March 1963.
H à M-B	*Hommage à Marie-Blanche, Comtesse de Polignac.* (Includes tribute from Francis Poulenc.) Private edition: Jaspard, Polus & Co., Monaco, 1965.
HH-FP	Henri Hell: *Francis Poulenc, musicien français.* Fayard, Paris, 1978.
KD-FP	Keith Daniel: *Francis Poulenc – his artistic development and musical style.* UMI Research Press, Ann Arbor, Michigan, 1982.
LV	André de Vilmorin: *Louise de Vilmorin.* Seghers, Paris, 1962.
MAM	Hélène Jourdan-Morhange: *Mes amis musiciens.* Editeurs français réunis, Paris, 1955.
MGT	'Les Mémoires de Germaine Tailleferre' in *Revue internationale de musique française*, No. 19, February 1986. Editions Champion–Slatkine, Paris/Geneva.
ML	Flora Groult: *Marie Laurencin.* Mercure de France, Paris, 1987.
MLC	Catalogue: Exposition Marie Laurencin, Galerie Daniel Malingue, Paris, 25 April to 21 June, 1986.
MODE	Catalogue: *Paul Poiret et Nicole Groult – maîtres de la mode art déco.* Musée de la Mode et du Costume, Hôtel Galliera. 5 July to 12 October, 1986.
MVH	Darius Milhaud: *Ma vie heureuse.* Belfond, Paris, 1987.
PB-FP	Pierre Bernac: *Francis Poulenc: the man and his songs*, translated by Winifred Radford, Gollancz, London, 1977. French edition: *Francis Poulenc et ses mélodies.* Editions Buchet/Chastel, Paris, 1978.
PB-GM	Pierre Bernac interviewed by Gérard Michel for French Radio: *France Culture*, 20 November 1970–15 January 1971.
PB-IP	Myriam Chimènes: *Pierre Bernac – interprète et pédagogue.* Mémoire de maîtrise, Université de Paris, Sorbonne, 1971–3.
PE	Paul Eluard: *Oeuvres complètes.* Bibliothèque de la Pléiade. Gallimard, Paris, 1968

PE-LàG	Paul Eluard: *Lettres à Gala*. Gallimard, Paris, 1984.
PE-LP	Louis Parrot: *Paul Eluard*. Seghers, Paris, 1964.
QJL	Georges Auric: *Quand j'étais là*. Grasset, Paris, 1979.
RAD	David Noakes: *Raymond Radiguet*. Seghers, Paris, 1968.
RADIG	Keith Goesch: *Radiguet*. La Palatine, Paris, 1955.
REF	Léon-Paul Fargue: *Refuges*. Editions Emile-Paul Frères, Paris, 1942.
SAT	James Harding: *Erik Satie*. Secker & Warburg, London, 1975.

LETTERS
1915–1935

When I recall my childhood I see myself always
sitting at a piano.

Francis Poulenc to Pierre Bernac
[PB-FP p. 22]

It is more courageous to grow just as one is than
to force-feed one's flowers with the fertilizer of
fashion.

Francis Poulenc to Henri Sauguet
31 March 1931

1. DARIUS MILHAUD TO FRANCIS POULENC

L'Enclos, Aix-en-Provence, June 1915

Cher Monsieur,

Here is the autograph you asked for. I was sorry not to be able to have a longer talk with you on the day of the concert; I was so tired!

I return to Paris in September. Write to me around 15 September to arrange a meeting: I will gladly have a chat with you.

Mlle Tilliard[1] tells me that you compose a little, and you know how interested I am in what is being done by those younger than myself.[2]

Please be assured of my true sympathy,

D.M.

2. ERIK SATIE TO FRANCIS POULENC

Monday, 16 July 1917

Mon pauvre Ami. Yesterday evening Viñes[1] told me of the terrible misfortune that has struck you.[2]

I feel for you with all my heart, dear friend, and beg you to see in me your entirely devoted

Erik Satie

3. FRANCIS POULENC TO RICARDO VIÑES

My address is: 4, rue de la Muette, Nogent-sur-Marne (Seine),[1] *25 July 1917*

Cher Monsieur,

So sorry I missed you today.

I shall be very grateful if you will tell me on which day of your two visits I can see you. When we meet I would also like to settle my little debt to you.

Please accept my kindest regards.

Francis Poulenc

4. FRANCIS POULENC TO RICARDO VIÑES

26 September 1917

Very urgent

Mon bien cher Maître,

Today I had such a lamentable and stupid experience that I am going to describe it to you and ask for your advice.

Recommended by a friend of mine who is himself on very friendly terms with Paul Vidal,[1] I went to see the latter to talk to him about the possibility of my entering the Conservatoire.

At the beginning of the visit he was pleasant enough, asking who had been my teachers up to now, and so on. Then he asked if I had brought him a manuscript. I handed him the manuscript of my *Rapsodie nègre*.[2] He read it carefully, wrinkled his brow and, on seeing the dedication to Erik Satie, rolled his eyes in fury, rose and yelled these exact words:

'Your work stinks, it is ludicrous, it is nothing but a load of BALLS. Are you trying to make a fool of me with these consecutive fifths everywhere? And what the hell is this Honoloulou? Ah! I see you have joined the gang of Stravinsky, Satie & Co. Well then, I'll say goodbye!' And he almost threw me out. So here I am, high and dry, not knowing what to do or whom to consult.

Could you not give me a letter of recommendation to Ravel[3] or Gédalge?[4] They might perhaps help to set me on the right track. Otherwise, well, I suppose I will go to the Schola.[5] But all the same, what a rude man that Vidal is! You should have seen how he spoke of those perpetrators of wrong notes – meaning Strav., Satie, etc. It was enough to make you die with laughter.

I dare to hope, *bien cher Maître*, that despite the many calls on your time you will be good enough to suggest what steps I should take, or else give me a recommendation to Gédalge. I send you my sincere thanks in anticipation.

This business has, I assure you, so much upset my plans that I really need you and your advice.

With kindest regards,

Francis Poulenc

When will you be back in Paris?

5. ERIK SATIE TO FRANCIS POULENC

Saturday, 29 September 1917

Cher ami – I would like to see you. You seem to me lost but easy to find again. Let's meet.

Whoever has given you such strange advice? It is very amusing. Never mix 'schools': an explosion occurs – as you would expect.

And now, to give you any useful advice I need to know what you intend to do, and what you are able to do.

Your approach to Vidal was that of an *amateur pupil*, not that of an *artist pupil*. He has brought that home to you. He is one of the old guard and he has thrown you off course. Laugh it off, *mon bon!*

Yours,

E.S.

6. FRANCIS POULENC TO RICARDO VIÑES

14 October 1917

Mon bien cher Maître,

Thank you for your very kind letter and for the recommendation to Ravel. Thanks to you, perhaps I can at last be directed sensibly.[1]

I am also very happy because Madame Bathori wants to put on my *Rapsodie nègre* at a concert at the Vieux-Colombier.[2] I could not wish for anything better.

Not forgetting that I owe all this to you, *Maître*, I thank you with all my heart and remain respectfully yours,

Francis Poulenc

7. FRANCIS POULENC TO VALENTINE GROSS*

Thursday, 30 May 1918

Ma bien bonne,

I am in PRISON. Alas . . .[1]

I am as vexed as a peacock that I was caught for sleeping out of barracks. Could my talents be failing me . . . my tricks deserting me? I am trying to find others, but bigger and better ones. I shall need help . . . I have some great ideas at the back of my mind.

I shall not be set free again until Tuesday morning.

Wretched Sunday.

Anyhow, I will get down to some work.

A thousand apologies to the Brunhoffs[2] and, above all, a thousand regrets . . . Let Beaumont[3] know of my bad luck. He should not be surprised to be without news of me for a few days!

*Later Valentine Hugo.

Tell anyone you like about it; it's terribly funny! I sleep in a tent in the midst of quite wonderful country.

Regards, and hoping to see you soon,

Poulenc

It is by real sleight of hand that I have been able to send you this *pneu*.[4]

8. FRANCIS POULENC TO VALENTINE GROSS

2nd Trailer Section, 63rd Regiment of Artillery, Arnouville-lès-Gonesse, Sunday, 2 June 1918

Five francs for Satie to be delivered by hand.

Ma Pauvre Amie,

My punishment has been increased by order of the lieutenant, a most unpleasant gentleman. I will not be let out until Friday. Time drags, I can tell you.

Here are five francs for Satie. I sent ten francs to him directly on Thursday. I will send some more, again with your kind help, next week.

I hope to see you soon. I am dying of boredom.

Poulenc

If you want to be really kind, do write – it will give me something else to think about. Is Jean Hugo there?[1] Have you any news from Le Piqueÿ?[2]

9. JEAN COCTEAU TO FRANCIS POULENC

Le Piqueÿ, Gironde, 2 September 1918

Mon cher Francis,

I am sad to hear that you are on the move but the Muse is watching over you, protecting you and organizing a line of trams following you, looming into view and ending up at the Place de la Madeleine.[1]

Yes, everyone is talking about the gold and silver trombones of the Duroc negroes.[2] I'll soon be dark enough to play in the band myself.

I am adopting your *Jongleurs*. I like the percussion prelude very much. Agreed, then – I am counting you in: *Jongleurs* in our programme.[3]

Now I can't wait to get back to hear your work.

Do you know Meerovitch's address?[4] Silence. I wonder why. Perhaps she has found a piano at last. Here, at Monsieur Dumur's, the grocer, there is a wonderful mechanical piano player. You put in two sous and out come maritime operas: *La Riviera* – drums, shell-castanets, watery gurglings and marine tootings – quite a masterpiece.

Do you know the Bordeaux fair and the fake ships? Like the show at the Casino de Paris, only bigger and better. Merry-go-rounds spinning world upside-down velvet mirrors Louis XIV horses in glossy enamel rearing in a dentists' and concierges' paradise. Battleships from the Rosenberg boutique. Try to get there in your 60 h.p. Then describe it all, in music for the interval.

Your faithful
Cocteau

10. FRANCIS POULENC TO RICARDO VIÑES

2nd Trailer Section, 63rd Regiment of Artillery, Arnouville-lès-Gonesse, Tuesday, 4 September 1918

Mon bon Viñes,

I am writing to you from prison. Yes, from a prison, actually none too dismal, where I am confined for a week for having spent the night in Paris without permission. You see what a true soldier I am becoming. Or to be more precise, let's say that I am really beginning to feel the stupid, strict discipline of the army. To my great regret I left Tremblay on Friday 24 August to come here to Arnouville for three weeks' training before leaving directly for the front. Arnouville is an utterly lovely place made entirely insipid by army life, since one is not permitted to enjoy any of its charms. Besides, knowing that a forbidden Paris is a mere 15 kilometres away is simply unendurable. Having been unable to resist the temptation, I am now suffering the consequences.

Unfortunately, I do not have a single pleasant companion with me, which makes the isolation weigh even more heavily upon me.

In addition, the constant thoughts that bind me eternally to my friends in Paris consume me daily, to such a degree that I feel my entire spirit will fall prey to depression any moment.

Fortunately, I do not expect to be in this situation forever. My greatest wish would be to enlist as a driver for the Red Cross – Comte de Beaumont's organization[1] – but, patience. I keep hoping and feel confident that everything will happen in its own good time.

And you, *mon bon Maître*, what of you? I suppose that Madame [Princesse Edmond] de Polignac's presence must give an immense uplift to musical life in St-Jean-de-Luz and that there are endless festivals and tributes to the memory of Debussy. And I am told that Ravel is with you as well. So you must be having a quite marvellous time. Have you seen Madame Errazuriz in Biarritz, with whom Picasso and his wife have elected to stay?[2] And have you seen Madame Cocteau? Jean, by the way, dreading all the excitement and in search of rest, has retreated to Le Piqueÿ, as he did last year, with the Lhotes.[3] He writes enraptured letters to everyone.

It would be very kind of you, *mon bon Ricardo*, if you will send me news of everybody down there – what they are doing, what you are playing, what is being performed, and so on. This would be a truly good deed, I assure you dear friend, for great is my boredom. I am working a little on the *Jongleurs* number, parts of which we played when we last met. It is not progressing too badly.

Two days ago I received a letter from Edouard Souberbielle[4] who is working at the moment on a piece for piano entitled *Jeux d'enfants*. Before he left I heard bits of this work. I think it will be an extremely good piece.

Ah! *mon bon*, how it hurts me to speak of all that when any work seems quite out of the question for me now.

Hoping that it will not be too long before we meet again I end, *mon cher Viñes*, with one last appeal for letters and with my very best wishes.

Francis Poulenc

Kind regards to Ravel, Madame Sienkiewicz and everyone I know.

11. JEAN COCTEAU TO FRANCIS POULENC

13 September 1918

Mon cher Poulenc,

Come out of prison quickly. Here is your task for the Music-Hall–Colombier performance. To maintain an atmosphere of surprise, I am giving each of you a task without letting on what I have given to the others:

1. A Spanish song (enclosed) that I want you to set – without the slightest trace of humour – in the Spanish tradition of Bobino:[1] 'Carmencitaaa' 'Toréadooor' etc., cut short at the end of each line for the verses in '*e*'. It is essential that neither the poet nor the musician is aware of the flaw.[2] Do not bring in anything Italian; the musician must be entirely taken in. One ought to be able to sing the song seriously at Bobino, for example.

2. *Jongleurs* (with Prelude).

3. Background music for the interval.

Keep working. I am thinking of you. The winter will be very rich and victory will be ours.

J.C.

P.S. Do not show the song text to Anyone.

TOREADOR*

Refrain
Belle Espagno o le
Dans ta gondo o le
Tu caraco o les
Carmencita!
Sous ta manti i lle
Oeil qui péti i lle
Bouche qui bri i lle
C'est Pépita a.

1
Pépita reine de Venise
Quand tu vas sous ton mirador
Tous les gondoliers se disent
Prends garde toréador!

2
Sur ton coeur personne ne règne
Dans le grand palais où tu dors
Et près de toi la vieille duègne
Guette le toréador.

3
Toréador brave des braves
Lorsque sur la place Saint-Marc
Le taureau en fureur qui bave
Tombe tué par ton poignard,

4
Ce n'est pas l'orgueil qui caresse
Ton coeur sous la baouta d'or
Car pour une jeune déesse
Tu brûles toréador.

Refrain

5
C'est demain (jour de saint Escure)
Qu'aura lieu le combat à mort
Le canal est plein de voitures
Fêtant le toréador.

6
De Venise plus d'une belle
Palpite pour savoir son sort
Mais tu méprises leurs dentelles
Tu souffres toréador,

Refrain
Lovely Spanish girl
in your gondola
you twist and turn –
Carmencita!
under your mantilla
your eyes sparkling
your mouth glinting,
it's Pepita!

1
Pepita queen of Venice,
when you appear on your mirador
all the gondoliers say –
look out, toreador!

2
Nobody rules your heart,
as you sleep in the great palace,
and nearby the old duenna
watches out for the toreador.

3
Toreador, the bravest of all,
when in Saint Marc's Square
the bull foaming with fury
falls, killed by your dagger,

4
it isn't pride which caresses
your heart under your gold cape,
it's for a young goddess
that you burn, toreador.

Refrain

5
Tomorrow, St Escure's day,
a fight to the death will take place,
the canal is full of craft
in honour of the toreador.

6
More than one beautiful heart
flutters to know your fate,
but you scorn their beauty,
you are suffering, toreador,

*English translation: Richard Jackson.

7

Car ne voyant pas apparaître	because you haven't seen
(Caché derrière un oranger)	(hidden behind orange-blossom)
Pépita seule à sa fenêtre	Pepita, alone at her window,
Tu médites de te venger.	you start thinking of vengeance.

8

Sous ton caftan passe ta dague	Under your caftan is your dagger –
La jalousie au coeur te mord	jealousy bites your heart,
Et seul avec le bruit des vagues	and alone with the sound of the waves
Tu pleures toréador.	you weep, toreador.

Refrain

9

Que de cavaliers! Que de monde!	What gentry – what a crowd
Remplit l'arène jusqu'au bord	fills the arena to the brim –
On vient de cent lieues à la ronde	they've come from a hundred leagues around
T'acclamer toréador.	to cheer you on, toreador.

10

C'est fait il entre dans l'arène	It's starting, he enters the arena
Avec plus de flegme qu'un lord	cooler than a lord,
Mais il peut avancer à peine	but he can scarcely move,
Le pauvre toréador;	the poor toreador;

11

Il ne reste à son rêve morne	all that's left of his sad dream
Que de mourir sous tous les yeux	is to die in front of everyone,
En sentant pénétrer des cornes	feeling the horns penetrate
Dans son triste front soucieux.	his sad and grieving brain.

12

Car Pépita se montre assise	For he sees Pepita, seated,
Offrant son regard et son corps	offering her glances and her body
Au plus vieux doge de Venise	to the oldest doge in Venice,
Et rit du toréador.	and laughing at the toreador.

Refrain

(The *e* of *Venise*, etc. must be stressed at all costs: *de Veni* SE.)
(It requires castanets, tambourines, etc. It will be sung by Bertin.[3])

12. JEAN COCTEAU TO FRANCIS POULENC

15 October 1918

Mon cher Poulenc,

You have at last received 'Toréador' – Ouf! Yesterday, meeting at the V.C. [Vieux-Colombier]. Bathori and musicians. The performance has been settled. 'A Bientôt' for the finale – the grand finale of Music-Hall. I would rather see you doing that than things for the interval – the interval being devoted to background music. Reply quickly about this.

The song must not be as good as Chabrier – it must be *well done* but *bad* – with rapid crotchets at the end: *Veni ze mirado or*, etc. Anyway, do it as you feel, for irony would be out of place in a 'Homage to Music-Hall'.

Find out about the orchestra from [Louis] Durey – and tell Bathori and Straram[1] at once about your percussion prelude.

FINALLY, KEEP WORKING,

PEACE

IS WITHIN REACH

J.C.

13. FRANCIS POULENC TO VALENTINE GROSS

2nd Trailer Section, 66th Anti-Aircraft Artillery Regiment, Sector 5,
[Châlons-sur-Marne], 23 October [1918]

Ma chère amie,

How bad of you not to write more often. I keep hoping to hear from you but as nothing has come I have decided to send you a few details about my new way of life. As you may perhaps have heard from Jean [Cocteau], I have been in Châlons for about a month. It is what one might call 'the good life'. In fact, we are living ultra-quietly in a not unattractive little village.

With nothing to do in the way of duty, I am able to get through an enormous amount of work. A few days ago I completed the orchestral score of my prelude for percussion instruments which will precede the *Jongleurs* number for the Colombier music-hall performance. At the moment I am finishing the transcription for two pianos of *Jongleurs* and am quite pleased with the whole thing. But anyway you will be able to judge for yourself as I will let you hear this transcription during my next leave of absence, which will fortunately be quite soon.

Now I have a Sonata for piano, violin and cello under way. I am rather enjoying working on this composition.[1]

During my leave, two works which you already know will be given their first performance: the Sonata for four hands and the Sonata for two clarinets.[2] I would also like you to hear, in private, the Sonata for piano and violin which I have just revised.[3]

A lot of fine plans, don't you think? The only thing that keeps me going is the thought of all these, and of peace.

And you, dear friend, what is happening to you? Are you also working, and at what? These are the things I would like to know.

I also hope you have not been affected by this atrocious Spanish flu that is causing such havoc at the moment.[4] Talking of which, it was Spanish flu, wasn't it, that caused the death of poor Annette Chalupt? How very sad our poor friend must be.[5]

Really, we are living through such dreadful times at the moment. Nothing but distressing news comes from all sides. One day it is [Juliette] Meerovitch telling me about the death of her brother, the next day it is one of our friends who has just lost her husband at the front and who writes a heart-breaking letter. All this is not exactly good for morale, I can tell you!

From Fargue[6] – nothing. He certainly lets a lot of grass grow under his feet, and I say this without malice. Tell him off when you see him. And what of Satie? Can I send money? Give me news, too, of La Fresnaye, Jeanniot, Gallimard, etc. It will help to keep me in touch and it won't hurt, I assure you.

Meanwhile, *ma chère amie*, please accept my very best regards.

Francis Poulenc

They are playing my *Rapsodie* and the Stravinsky pieces on 3 November at the Colombier. If you are interested . . .

14. FRANCIS POULENC TO COMTESSE ETIENNE DE BEAUMONT

Anti-Aircraft Division, Pont-sur-Seine (Aube), Sunday night [1918]

Today, *chère Madame*, in the open air, in the shade of an octagonal Chinese pavilion, I read aloud 'Le Panama', 'J'ai tué', 'Profond aujourd'hui'[1] and four or five poems by Rimbaud.[2]

Since these attempts at poetry reading seem to amuse you, I venture to send you these few lines on the 'SÉANCE CENDRARS DE PONT-SUR-SEINE'.

As you see, *Madame*, the provinces follow the example of Paris. I wanted to do my very own Rosenberg here.[3]

My audience – a doctor, a lieutenant, a captain. The venue – a pagoda-like kiosk in the castle grounds, the walls bedecked with indescribable woven Chinese hangings painted in gouache and badly damaged by the damp. All very much like those hunting scenes used as window displays in delicatessen shops.

And this is where I read Cendrars.

Ah yes, *Madame*, how right you were the other day, when you said that Cendrars was the man of the moment. He is so much so that the captain without hesitation detected in 'J'ai tué' a certain something – rather like *Les Misérables*. Is this not quite incredible?

At 'Profond aujourd'hui', they smiled but did not cry shame, far from that. 'I do not dislike it,' said the doctor, 'although I find the whole thing *pedantic* – but at least it is French, the sentences are logical. It is not in verse but there is a *certain lilt* that justifies the title of poem.'

At 'Panama', they laughed quite openly, but that was all. My listeners had so far been well-behaved, but then came Rimbaud's turn.

Well . . . he was the one who received all the brickbats. Quite incredibly, they accused him of copying Cendrars and Cocteau, proving just how easily the public can mistake the master for the pupil.

'How old is the fellow?' asked the lieutenant. 'Is he one of your set?'

Dumbfounded, I closed the book and the meeting came to an end.

Really, *Madame*, don't you find all this quite staggering? Afterwards, I had a good laugh.

As you must have heard from Emmanuel Faÿ, my *Rapsodie* will be performed on Sunday at the Salle des Agriculteurs. If it interests you, I shall be very pleased if you can come.

Meanwhile, *chère Madame*, my respectful compliments to you and to Monsieur de Beaumont.

Francis Poulenc

15. FRANCIS POULENC TO RICARDO VIÑES

c/o Madame Berthier, the draper, Pont-sur-Seine (Aube), Wednesday [January 1919]

Do not forward: if M. Viñes is only due back in about ten days, send this to him under cover as quickly as possible. Urgent. Respects – Francis Poulenc.

Mon bon Maître,

You know I spoke to you the other evening at Adrienne Monnier's about some simple little *Mouvements perpetuels* for piano that I'd written, easy enough for a child to play. Well, this is a request for you to give the first performance of them on the evening of Saturday 9 February, at Peinture et Musique in the rue Huyghens.[1]

I am sure that, to please me, you will say yes.

In any event, you must reply *as quickly as possible*, either in the affirmative or in the negative, to [Félix] Delgrange, 8 rue de Stockholm, but it will be yes, won't it?[2]

Manuel is to ask you to play two or three of his pieces as well: *La Soirée de Viroflay*, etc.[3]

If you have not yet returned, I think you must be just about to return. Did you play my *Pastorales*[4] in Italy? Were there any reviews of your concerts? Please drop me a line.

I am writing from Pont-sur-Seine where I am quite all right, but I hope to be posted to Paris soon. I am working hard, orchestrating *Jongleurs*.

Thank you, *mon bon Viñes*, for the concert on the 9th, and goodbye for now.

I shall be delighted to hear from you.

Francis Poulenc

My friend Mlle Tilliard will bring you *Mouvements perpetuels* on Sunday. It is ultra easy.

16. FRANCIS POULENC TO JEAN COCTEAU

Chez Madame Berthier, lingère, Pont-sur-Seine (Aube), [12 February 1919]

Bon Jean,

A fantastic scheme – send me *urgently* a letter, signed Russels, Rally, anything you like provided it sounds American.

In it, say that you have just returned from London and that you want to see me about the edition of my *Rapsodie*, etc. . . . etc. . . . I leave it to your imagination.

With the help of this fake letter I shall try to get leave – in fact, I am sure I will get leave. So write *immediately* and don't give me away to the police.

I am working hard. 'Toréador' for voice and piano is already at the copyist's. So is 'Toréador' for voice and instruments. We can run through it on Saturday if I get leave, so write that letter quickly.

I am counting on you.

Your devoted Francis

17. FRANCIS POULENC TO SERGE DE DIAGHILEV

76 rue de Monceau, Paris, Monday, 28 April 1919

Cher Monsieur et Ami,

Thanks to Picasso I have your address at last and am now able to thank you from the bottom of my heart for all you have done for me.

Everything has been agreed between Mr Kling[1] and myself. What is more, he has written me a most charming letter, and in his prompt reply I sense the effect of your warm recommendations. This is why I really do want to express to you all my gratitude.

I had the pleasure of hearing through Jean-Aubry[2] that my *Rapsodie* is to be played in London. I am extremely glad to think that you will at last be able to hear it, as the piano version does not really do it justice.

I very often think of the conversation we had at Madame Edwards'.[3] How right you are to ban literature from all choreographic works. Experience proves this only too well, even when one is dealing with great poets. Only the other day Braque[4] said to me: 'Isn't it already a great deal to have to take three people into account, namely the choreographer, the painter and the musician; if you have to include a writer as well, then all unity is sacrificed.' Quite so . . .

It is really up to the choreographer to work out the scenario and that is why – if it does not put him out and provided he has the time – I should like to correspond with Monsieur Massine[5] to see what we could do.

I hope to hear from you both fairly soon, and send you my respectful compliments. Thank you once again.

Your very devoted
Francis Poulenc

18. ERIK SATIE TO FRANCIS POULENC

Thursday, 15 May 1919

Cher Ami – Thank you for your lovely card. It gave me the greatest pleasure. Absolutely.

On Sunday, *Parade* proved that my orchestration is no worse than anyone else's. Many people thought the work was only right for the piano. Legend!!!

I am pleased, dear friend, that a young musician such as yourself should find that it 'SPEAKS' a little. Delgrange was perfect. One can entrust a work to him. Do so.

Bonjour, cher Ami; à bientôt.

Erik Satie

19. FRANCIS POULENC TO RICARDO VIÑES

Friday [1919]

Mon bon Maître,

On *8 June, at 3 o'clock,* Léonce Rosenberg, the art dealer in the rue de la Baume, is having a gathering devoted to the works of Apollinaire, for the benefit of his widow.

The musical side of this production will consist of some of my compositions. Jeanne Borel will sing twelve songs which I have just written on *Le Bestiaire*[1] and they have included you for *Mouvements perpétuels.* I am sure you will do me the favour of accepting.

In any event please be good enough to reply *immediately* to Monsieur Léonce Rosenberg, 19 rue de la Baume, Paris 8e.

I hope to come and see you on Sunday morning. In the meantime, *mon bon Maître,* please accept my kindest regards.

Francis Poulenc

20. FRANCIS POULENC TO JEAN COCTEAU

Paris, 30 August 1919

Mon cher Jean,

    Cocardes, piano and voice version, is finished.[1] Ouff! I was terrified of upsetting the balance at the very last moment. Thank heaven this did not happen. I hope you will not be disappointed. I found a phrase of great gentleness for 'uniforme bleu' – is it all right?

    How lovely it is to collaborate with someone living![2]

    I am going to suggest to Chester that they take *Cocardes*, if you agree, dear poet, as I know via Casella that they are keen to have some songs.[3]

    I went to the cinema last night with Valentine, François, Michel de Brunhoff and his young brother.[4] Quite a good film (an American drama) spoilt at the end by some heavy-handed patriotism, amputated limbs of servicemen, and so on . . . You can imagine how ghastly it was; that kind of spectacle has already become unbearable, everything has aged so much in the space of a month.

    What are you doing in AHUSKY?[5] How is Louis [Durey]? Is he relaxing? Write to me, either of you.

    Satie, whom I saw the other day, is composing some very beautiful nocturnes for piano; one will be included in the collective album.

In haste, best regards.

Francis

    I do not know Koubitzky's address.[6]

    What would you and Durey think of this title for the joint album: 'DISQUES'?[7]

21. FRANCIS POULENC TO IGOR STRAVINSKY

83 rue de Monceau, Paris, 26 September 1919

Cher Monsieur et ami,

    Having just received from London[1] a few copies of my Sonata for two clarinets, I am hastening to send one to you in the hope that you will be pleased to have it.

    I cannot express how happy I was to meet you and how much I enjoyed hearing your *Rags*;[2] they are truly magnificent and I look forward to hearing them again soon in Paris.

    Hoping also to have the pleasure of seeing you again soon, I send you, *cher Monsieur*, my most affectionate admiration.

Francis Poulenc

22. IGOR STRAVINSKY TO FRANCIS POULENC

Morges, 1 October [1919]

Thank you, *mon cher Monsieur Poulenc*, for your kind note and for sending me your . . . *Two Clarinets*, which I like very much. I shall keep them forever, in memory of that charming evening at the Hugos.

Very sincerely yours,

I. Stravinsky

23. DARIUS MILHAUD TO FRANCIS POULENC

Kensington, Lennox Gardens [London], July 1920

Mon Cher Poupoul,

Your letter gave me immense pleasure because the dreadful doorman at the Coliseum who barks and spits gave it to me ten minutes before the curtain went up on the first night.[1] It made me feel somehow that you were there.

We spent some appalling days working with Jean [Cocteau]. Everything was done in ten days and this caused a lot of trouble. Fortunately the Coliseum is a vast music-hall with marvellous stage-hands. The fan[2] was set up for the first time on Monday at a quarter past twelve; we had never rehearsed with it before and yet everything went smoothly.

The audience, somewhat taken aback at the afternoon performance (the sort of people who come for the odd hour and munch chocolates all the way through, as they do at the cinema), was very responsive in the evening. House full all the time (4,000 seats).[3] Our poor little *Rats*[4] took five curtain-calls. I conducted the orchestra (!) and thoroughly enjoyed it. Jean left yesterday, I leave tomorrow. Increasing success. Last night was very good – the conductor really rose to the occasion, in a way I would never have believed possible! He is a delightful fellow who loves his little drink.

The director will send *Le Boeuf* on tour all over England; according to the contract, this was conditional on its London success. Great fuss in the press. Many *very intelligent* articles. A few violent slatings – which is excellent – as in *The Times*, for example.[5] The Coliseum has asked me for another sketch for next season!

I am lunching today with Diaghilev, which promises to be quite amusing. Am longing to hear your new songs. I am afraid I will miss you in Paris as I leave for Aix in a week.

Give my regards to Roussel.[6] I am glad you see him often; he is so nice, so sensitive and so understanding.

Your

D.M.

24. MANUEL DE FALLA TO FRANCIS POULENC

Tuesday, 4 September 1920

Mon cher ami,

My sincere thanks for so kindly sending me *Cocardes* and *Le Cortège d'Orphée* [*Le Bestiaire*].

I like them so much that after playing through them once, I immediately played them twice more, which does not happen very often, believe me! We must see that they are performed next season at the Sociedad Nacional.[1]

When *Le Tricorne* is published, it will give me great pleasure to send it to you, touched as I am by your interest in the work.[2]

In the meantime, all my very best wishes.

Manuel de Falla

25. JEAN COCTEAU TO FRANCIS POULENC

[Carqueiranne], 11 April 1921

Cher Francis, always quick to announce good news and to send precise replies giving pleasure. WERE IT NOT FOR YOU I WOULD NOT KNOW A THING ABOUT *Les Fâcheux*,[1] SIC.[2] Thank you. I was sure of Georges [Auric] and dream of hearing his orchestration.

Take care of everything, of *La Noce*,[3] etc. I will be back on the 15th, with a great number of poems – I dare say my best. You will see. Moreover, I am dedicating my next book to your group.[4]

Your Jean

26. RAYMOND RADIGUET TO FRANCIS POULENC

[April 1921]

Mon cher Francis,

I have not written to you because I do not write to travellers. 'Monsieur Francis Poulenc, Rome'?[1] Would my letter have reached you? I know how famous you are, but all the same . . .

I am bringing a number of poems back with me. I hope that amongst this lot there will be something you like. There are some very long ones. It would give me great joy if you set some of these to music, for if the principle of 'three poems set to music' is by now well and truly outdated, it is not the songs themselves that are at fault, is it? And as only such short ones are being done nowadays, it might be quite a good idea to set one as long as, say, *Le Promenoir des deux amants*.[2] In any case, you know about all that far better than I. If you like, we can discuss this when I return.[3]

> I embrace you,
> Raymond Radiguet

27. ERIK SATIE TO FRANCIS POULENC

Friday, 10 June 1921

Cher Ami – Caryathis writes that there is a rehearsal on Sunday morning at 9 o'clock at the theatre.[1] Naturally, I will not be there. What would I do there? Nothing, of course. I have asked Auric to take care of my 'THINGUMAJIG'. If he cannot come, will you replace him? You would be doing me a great favour.

Thank you, dear friend. Regards to your sister, please; and greetings to your nephew and to yourself – from

> Erik Satie

28. FRANCIS POULENC TO PAUL COLLAER

4 rue de la Muette, Nogent-sur-Marne, 12 July 1921

Mon cher Collaer,

Thank you for your very kind letter, I would say even too kind, too indulgent. It gave me great pleasure but, but . . . I believe you are the one who is mistaken. I am far from having found 'my orchestration'; and Inghelbrecht was right: *La Baigneuse*[1] has no impact whatever. It is neither 'brash enough' for the theatre nor 'subtle' enough for good music. *Le Discours*[2] is not bad, I grant you. *La Fanfare*[3] is good (I am certain of that) . . . but . . . there are better things. And how far I am from those better things! *Le Gendarme*,[4] let us not forget, is for small orchestra, which I do know something about.

You will understand the pessimistic tone of this letter when I tell you that I am 'suffering from an attack of Stravinsky-itis'. Have you read Ansermet's[5] article in *La Revue musicale*? It's incredible, and God knows how I usually hate those 'great studies' of 'great men', like the one on Falla in last month's issue. But in this case you immediately understand the craftsmanship of the man, you see clearly into his methods. Ansermet gives the key to everything.

The CRAFTSMANSHIP, that is what is admirable in Stravinsky. Just listen to Ansermet (page 17): 'For [Stravinsky] composition has always been a matter of craftsmanship'. And not in the way d'Indy[6] goes about it. With the Russian it is simply a process of refining; with our old stuffed shirt, it is the art of making something grand out of nothing.

For two days I have been immersed in *Renard*.[7] The counterpoint is extraordinary. The secret is that [Stravinsky's] contrapuntal writing is a superimposition of very apt 'themes' rather than the Wagnerian hair-splitting you find in Honegger.

But I suddenly notice, my dear Collaer, what a crashing bore I am. Why bother people with all this nonsense? I am working, I am beginning a 'string quartet' although I hate the notion. I simply want to find out – forgive my presumption – if there is not a way of getting more out of it than usual.[8] I am finishing the Max Jacob.[9] I think this time I have finally got it right. As for *Promenades*,[10] here is how I have resolved the problem of short pieces. The plan is this:

Prelude. 10 Promenades. Finale. I view the 10 promenades as 10 variations on 10 different themes (one for each promenade). The special technique used for each number will create in the end a sort of *trompe-l'oreille* [aural illusion] given that there will be one in thirds, another in repeated octaves, and so on. In this way I shall achieve a semblance of unity.

But how stupid to be writing all this.

I hope my uncle gave you the manuscript of *Cocardes*. I offer it to you with joy because you are one of the rare people who have understood this work – which, perhaps wrongly, I have filled with too many intentions, as I wrote it in the very midst of the people synthetically portrayed in it.

Are you hot? Here, it is 30° in the shade. I have bought some bathing trunks so that I can spray myself with the garden hose. Where are you going this summer? Write! A thousand best wishes to you all.

Francis Poulenc

I hope to come and see you next winter by aeroplane as the railway is too dangerous now.

29. ERIK SATIE TO FRANCIS POULENC

Arcueil-Cachan, 20 August 1921

Cher Ami – Is this how you reply to my note? Have you seen Diaghilev? That was my question. Well, he came here.

How are things? Received a very good letter from Auric.

I am working on *Paul et Virginie*[1] as much as I can. I would like to slip some of it into a Pierné concert[2] this winter. And you? What are you doing?

Greetings to your sister and to your charming nieces and nephew. Kind regards to your uncle,[3] please.

Sincerely yours,
Erik Satie

30. FRANCIS POULENC TO JEAN COCTEAU

4 rue de la Muette, Nogent-sur-Marne, Seine, [Summer 1921]

Mon cher Jean,

I heard about all your problems from your mother whom I visited for quite a while last week. I hope things are better now and that your teeth are no longer troubling you. All the same, what a bad start for your trip. Fortunately, the Bertins are good company for you; they are so kind and so helpful.[1]

Marcelle, in a card received this morning, tells me that you all laugh a lot. This would indicate that Auric has not yet arrived, with his embittered heart and his sulky mistress (!?). Anyway, I have not heard a thing from him since his departure.

I went, as agreed, to the Society of Authors where I had no difficulty in getting the 432 francs for *Les Mariés*. As soon as you give me a definite address I will send you a money order for your share.

I saw Darius, just back from Wiesbaden, not very pleased with his audiences. 'It was like playing for the Officers' Club!' he said. He is in Aix now. Nininka is about to leave for Burgundy. She is very tired and needs to look after her bronchitis.

How wonderfully calm I am here in Nogent! I am working hard in order to become a great musician one day. I am composing pieces for piano, a string quartet, and so on . . .[2]

Le Gendarme incompris (Overture, Madrigal and Finale) was performed during the interval of the Russian Ballet in London. Ansermet (very enthusiastic) tells me that there was a lot of booing, which was confirmed by one or two Arguses. I hope this induces Chester to take on the suite – I shall add the waltz 'Dans quel piège' transcribed for orchestra.[3] I am going to see Ansermet when he comes through Paris. Papa Serge, too.

I read a review called *Tunélon la Mélon* or something similar, by Pierre de Massot. There is a really ridiculous letter in it by Georges [Auric], in which he writes about the stamp of Fauré, etc. What a mania for writing! No doubt it is to document posterity on the state of his delicate constitution. For a man who claims to be heartless, what romanticism!

Any news of our great countess? I think she is in Villebois . . .

What a Maupassant-like atmosphere there is in the woods of Meudon . . . Beware . . .

Where is the blonde Irène?[4]

Well, write me a long letter, tell me what you are working on, what Bébé [Raymond Radiguet] is up to, and if you have heard from Lucien [Daudet].[5]

With much affection,

Francis

31. FRANCIS POULENC TO CHARLES KOECHLIN

Les Terrasses,[1] *Vaux-le-Pénil, Melun (Seine-et-Marne), [September? 1921]*

Cher Monsieur Koecklin [sic],

I do not want to wait until I return to Paris to express the very great desire that I have to work with you. Circumstances, and in particular three years of military service which I completed in January 1921, have prevented any sustained study until now. I have therefore been obeying my instinct rather than my intelligence. I have had enough of this now and wish to put myself *very seriously* in your hands. I hope that you will accept a pupil as self-educated as myself and that my ignorance will not repel you. With your help I would like to become a *musician.*

I shall be back in Paris around the 20th, at 83 rue de Monceau. If I receive a favourable reply from you – which I earnestly hope for – we can meet immediately to make all the necessary arrangements.[2]

I hope you have had a good holiday and have managed to work peacefully. I, too, will be bringing back a few little things, which I will show you.

Your very devoted

Poulenc

32. MARIE LAURENCIN TO FRANCIS POULENC

19, rue de Penthièvre, [September 1921]

Mon petit garçon
Am I going to surprise you!
This letter is from an admirer.

Since my return I have been humming your *Bestiaire* as best I can and you have no idea, Francis Poulenc, how well you have conveyed both the nostalgia and the singsong quality of those admirable quatrains.[1]

And what I find so moving is that you would think you were hearing the voice of Guillaume Apollinaire himself reciting those very lines.

Work hard and be good.

Your elder and your friend

Marie Laurencin

33. SERGE DE DIAGHILEV TO FRANCIS POULENC

Savoy Hotel, London, 15 November 1921

Mon cher ami,

I received your letter just as I had replied to that of Madame Bongard asking her to send me the scenario of the ballet *Les Demoiselles.*[1]

As I told her, this ballet interests me greatly and the details that you give me on the subject seem very amusing.

There is one point in your letter that I find disconcerting. You tell me that I will be able to have the piano score next October (?) and the orchestral score in December. As your letter was written in November, I can only presume that you are speaking of the year 1922; consequently it will be a year before you are ready, which is a long time and seems to be in contradiction to the letter from Madame Bongard in which she assures me that the costumes are already partly finished.

Have I understood you correctly; is there not some mistake?[2]

I intend to come to Paris before the Christmas holidays and will be very interested to see and hear what you have done. Since you so wish, I will not mention this ballet to anyone. This is also in my own interests.

I am happy to tell you that I now have an admirable new *maître de ballet* – Nijinsky's sister, la Nijinska, who works wonders.[3]

Cordially yours,
Serge de Diaghilev

34. BÉLA BARTÓK TO FRANCIS POULENC

Budapest 1, Gyopár u.2., 29 November 1921

Cher Monsieur,

Please forgive my belated reply.[1] During part of the autumn I was away from home and it was only on my return that I found your first letter and the music you sent me, both having arrived after some delay. I would gladly have replied immediately, but some very urgent work for the printer – and then the political troubles in Hungary, which cut us off from all contact with abroad – prevented me, until now, from thanking you most warmly for your letter of last August and for your compositions. Above all it is your piano sonata for four hands and the sonata for two clarinets that have interested me most keenly. I am already looking forward to the other compositions on a bigger scale which you promised in your letter, and which may perhaps have already been published? I would also very much like to acquaint myself with some of the compositions of Honegger and Auric, but for us here, alas, they are almost unobtainable.

I have asked my publisher why my compositions cannot be obtained in Paris. I have been told, rather surprisingly, that music dealers in France still show in spite of everything a passive, and sometimes even an active, resistance towards German and Austrian music! It is very sad, and the result is that the French cannot even obtain the latest works of Casella[2] or Szymanowski[3] – which have been published in the Universal Edition in Vienna – although each of these composers belongs to a country which is a friend of the Entente. In any case, these works, and mine as well, can be ordered direct from the publisher in Vienna (the complete list of my works is in the March issue of *La Revue musicale*). I forwarded your request to the publishers of Universal Edition, from whom I have received the answer that they would be glad to send you *Le Prince de bois*.[4] *Barbe-Bleue*, my opera in one act, has just been published; if this work interests you, you could send your order direct to the publisher in Vienna.

Le Prince de bois and Barbe-Bleue will be staged at the Opera in Frankfurt-am-Main at the end of January or the beginning of February. Would it not be possible for you to make a short visit to Frankfurt on this occasion as a special representative of some musical review or other? Frankfurt is near enough to Paris! I would be very pleased to make your acquaintance. M. Milhaud will learn, I believe with pleasure, that in February next year our Waldbauer Quartet[5] will play his second quartet in Holland – the one they have already played in Budapest.

Thank you again for the compositions you have sent me, and while awaiting others, I remain

Your very devoted
Béla Bartók

35. MAX JACOB TO FRANCIS POULENC

Presbytère de Saint-Benoît-sur-Loire, 1921

O mon petit Francis en or
*Je t'envoie ces rimes fragiles**

I do my utmost, and more, and am not very pleased with myself. I ought to have a bit of talent at my age; it's ridiculous. But what can I do about it? Accept these poems as they come, since you have asked me for some, and be assured of my love.[1] I am immersed in a novel and lead a very pious life. No movie star brightens my monastic existence. Lucien Daudet's book arrived this morning. I receive few letters, and these from no one in particular. I await rhymes from Radiguet, heralded by the boy himself. I am not bored – I suffer – enormously, distractedly.

I wish I had four hands so that I could clasp each of yours in two of mine.

M.J.

*'Oh my little golden Francis
  I send you these fragile rhymes'

36. MAX JACOB TO FRANCIS POULENC

22 December 1921

Cher Francis,

I received the programme for a concert on 7 January which, alas! I shall probably not attend unless . . . who knows? at that concert, my poems – enhanced by your ever cherished music! Now methinks . . . I should perhaps inform the Society of Authors, rue Henner, of the title, titles? So that your music brings me an income until the end of our days and those of our heirs (I have a nephew). I think that every time we are played I should be entitled to 0 francs 25 centimes. Be a pal and send me word to say that we do belong to the Society in the rue Henner, or to give me the titles of the poems.

I am continuing to play the recluse, which works fairly well for my health, my work and my general peace. I trust that my friends will not forget me, even those who live in the midst of cinema stars and other kinds of stars.

I send you my love and think of you often.

Max Jacob

– merci –

They are ringing for evening prayer; it's half past four. Latecomers are conspicuous. Let's not make ourselves conspicuous anywhere except at concerts.

37. MAX JACOB TO FRANCIS POULENC

2 January 1922

Cher Francis

The weather bodes ill for travelling, there is a wind on the plain (subject for a characteristic piece for piano),[1] there are potholes in the roads (another subject, this time for bassoons). What does it matter, you will ask, as the carriages are over-heated by the rails. But are they on heat, as you suggest? Incidentally, it seems I have just invented a system of central heating for trains and stations that no one has thought of before. I offer you the patent as your New Year gift. And as well as all that . . . to get from the station to the town and vice versa, one has to walk 4 (four) kilometres. This is quite difficult for the luggage and not much better for the pedestrian . . . You will tell me there is always the bus. What a laugh! The bus, Sir, the bus? Again, what a laugh! The bus is a myth, and not even a solar myth; it is a lunar myth. What am I saying? It is nothing but a phantom bus (let us not speak of ghosts). The bus neither comes nor goes if it conflicts with Monsieur Berthany's meal times. Berthany! Berthany! I have not yet done with this fatal name, as Victor Hugo used to say, and is still saying, the immortal being!

For all these reasons, as well as for others (for even if there *is* a 'bus', since you insist, this bus is not, and cannot, be heated, either by my system or by any other), on 7 January I shall not be at my, at your, at our première. Talking of buses, what would you say to a pretty little characteristic piece for piano, for one, two or three hands, entitled: 'The Lunar Bus'? You should think about it. The opening arpeggios conjure up an endless plain in the moonlight. In the distance gleam the windows of thatched cottages or some such. The bus is announced by breathless, rapid chords. It is glimpsed, it is there, it is gone . . . But the driver was blind. The music must express what happens in the heart of the traveller waiting in the wind for the fantastic, formidable meteor to hurtle by.

I had hoped to write you a serious letter but the evening wind that prowls around my basilica has swept away my plans and has left me – as you will have noticed without difficulty, O sensible Francis – with an empty, or almost empty, head. However, I am still able to say this to you:

I do not belong to the Society in the rue Chaptal but to the one in the rue Henner. I shall write to the Chaptal gentlemen to ask if I may join, being the author of an operetta and of certain *mélodies* set to music by you, by Roland-Manuel and, I believe, by *tutti quanti*. I shall write and then I shall make a declaration. After which I shall claim 0 francs 25 centimes, which is not to be scorned. If you have any ideas for collaborating, let me know; I am well placed to meditate upon them, and the Post – despite the efforts of Monsieur Berthany to compromise its efforts – the Post, I say, is there to be used, the Post is for us, indeed it is ours.

Give my regards to Milhaud, to my pale and silent friend Honegger and to Auric who, I am told, is taking part in the *Congrès moderniste*. He is fortunate. 'Allow yourself to be admired but not to be imitated!' I would say to him, in the words of some poet or other.

I love Francis and embrace him.

Max Jacob

P.S. I hear that they have just invented the 'dectet', a curious ensemble of out-of-tune violins. Once again, my congratulations to the inventor.

I read some marvellous poems by Jean [Cocteau] in *L'Oeuf dur*. Really! they are astonishingly subtle and full of surprises.

I failed to get the Thingumy Prize again this year. *Ce n'est pas moi qui suis le nègre.*[2] I'll keep trying.

38. JEAN COCTEAU TO FRANCIS POULENC

[Le Lavandou], 17 May 1922

Mon cher Francis,

Thank you for your excellent letter, but Marie's illness[1] is spoiling Le Lavandou for me.[2] I am frightened. It seems to be very serious.

You are right to avoid all who retard and deride your progress. I do not think I can be accused of that sort of mentality. I much prefer to suffer the ridicule of 'artistic movements'. It is this that always draws me so to Diaghilev. You'll see that Auric will fail with his *Fâcheux* thing out of sheer apathy and with the excuse of 'What does it matter?'

Gide sent me a very strange letter. How does he manage to find fault with all my ideas while at the same time claiming they are his own? Between you and me, I replied in four lines: 'You are right, etc. etc. . . .' No point squabbling. The NRF live on the moon.[3]

I am bothered by what you tell me about *Paul [et Virginie]*.[4] With Satie, one always underestimates the element of miracle. He is often right while appearing to be wrong. (Auric has never understood this.)

Auric's idleness really upsets me. Could he be another Fargue?[5] A treasure like his is not to be wasted. Yet his love of marginal writers of short works: Tinan, Toulet, etc. . . .[6]

[. . .]

The end of Radiguet's novel is superb. To think that we will see our Auric *dawdling* along with this book under his arm![7]

I am having a rest. Afterwards I will think about your comic opera.

Jean

P.S. If Diaghilev could see Satie, *Paul [et Virginie]* would get going more quickly.

39. JEAN COCTEAU TO FRANCIS POULENC

Le Lavandou – Var, 3 June 1922

Mon cher Poupoule

Well, and there was I saying: the only one from whom I will have any details about the Russians etc. . . . I sent a wire to Misia requesting her to ask you for a letter and programmes and . . . Am I dead to your hearts, all of you? Write – tell – write a long letter. Has Marie been saved? Satie? Absolute silence.

In spite of the sun which goes to my head and makes me gaga, I feel gloomy, cut off from the world. I draw, I do not write. I am going to see the Hugos in a few days.

I embrace you,

Jean

Monsieur Radiguet greets you.

Le Lavandou – Var
3 Juin 1922

mon cher
Poupoule   alors - quoi disais:
              moi qui disais:
              Le seul par qui j'aurai
          de détails sur les russes etc....
              je télégraphiais a Misia
              en la priant de te demander
                  un envoi et programmes et...

Monsieur Radiguet te salue   Suis - je mort,
                                  à vos cœurs ?

Écris - raconte - écris une longue lettre.
Marie est elle
        sauvée ? Satie ?
              Silence absolu
      Malgré le soleil qui me grise et me
rend gaga - je m'attriste, coupé du monde.
Je dessine
    je n'écris pas. Je vais voir les Hugo
                dans q.q. jours :
        t'embrasse
                      Jean

40. Francis Poulenc to Léon Bakst

83 rue de Monceau, Paris 8ᵉ [June 1922]

Cher Monsieur,

Forgive my indiscretion in writing to ask if you could possibly obtain for me *one admission* for *Le Martyre*,[1] either on Monday 19th, Wednesday 21st or Thursday 22nd; I am in fact consumed with desire to see your décor and to hear Debussy's wonderful music in full.

Not knowing anyone on the administrative staff of the Opéra, it occurred to me to write directly to you. Please do not hold it against me if the whole thing proves to be impossible.

Please accept all my thanks.

Respectfully yours,
Francis Poulenc

41. Marie Laurencin to Francis Poulenc

Ermitage de la Forêt de Sénart, par Draveil (Seine-et-Oise), July 1922

Mon petit garçon
Come whenever you like
Come early for lunch at midday.

Next Tuesday Suzanne Süe[1] is coming in the afternoon and Dr Sourdel as well;[2] I think they will stay to dinner. I prefer to be alone with you to chat about our things[3] – so any other day is all yours.

I am well and truly spoiled by Blanche,[4] and becoming normal again – with time, and the photos you sent. You know I love nothing better than photos.

Au revoir cher Petit
Je t'embrasse
Marie

My cottage is charming. Diaghilev might come. If you want to come by car, it is a thousand times more convenient.

42. Max Jacob to Francis Poulenc

Saint-Benoît, 10 July 1922

Cher ami,

I will write some other time. The pilgrimage is in full swing at St-Benoît. There are 98 people in the house: counts, countesses, abbots, bishops, famous doctors, famous professors, etc., generals.

Holy Garden Party,* pray for us!
It has such style!!!
There's no doubt about it, one cannot escape
from the 'elite'!

I sign in haste and with love. I am being called . . . in short, I am the one who does the receiving these days. I am no longer received.

Max

Recently, I even had a poet, a professor of pure mechanics and another of philosophy. The lot of them half-socialist, half-royalist and so pious! – also very badly dressed, as is fitting!

43. JEAN COCTEAU TO FRANCIS POULENC

[Le Lavandou, July 1922]

Mon cher Poupoule,

I am thinking of you, and if I do not write more often it is because I am working very hard. So you will forgive me. Opposite me Radiguet is writing a *stupendous* book[1] and behind him Auric, with a great red beard, is composing his mysterious ballet. But though he does not reveal either the theme or the title, the music blazes forth. It is a real surprise. Imagine *Chandelles romaines,*[2] only a hundred times better. A brio and style that never lets up for a second. Afterwards he will write the incidental music for *L'Epouse.*[3]

This [drawing] is a souvenir of the rehearsals for *Le Sacre.*[4] Try to find out what has happened to *Paul [et Virginie]* and report in detail.

Your friend
Jean

44. IGOR STRAVINSKY TO FRANCIS POULENC

Les Rochers, Biarritz, 22 July 1922

Mon cher Poulenc,

I enclose the errata for *Le Chant du rossignol*[1] which you can paste into your little pocket-score.

I am always delighted to hear news of you, as well as of your work, which interests me a great deal.

I forgot to thank you for your book of *Impromptus*[2] which I like very much. Thank you!

Very cordially yours,
Igor Stravinsky

Have you finished your article on *Mavra?*[3]

*In English in the original text.

mon cher Popaule je pense à toi et si je ne t'écris pas davantage c'est que je travaille beaucoup - Donc tu me pardonnes. En face de moi Radiguet écrit un livre prodigieux et derrière lui

avec avec une grande barbe rousse - compose son mystérieux ballet. mais s'il cache le thème et le titre, la musique éclate. C'est un vraie surprise - Imagine les Chandelles Romaines en 100 fois mieux. Un brio et un style qu'on ne dérobent pas une seconde. Ensuite il écrira la musique obscène pour "L'épouse"

Ceci est un souvenir de répétition à Paris. Tâche d'atteler ce qui est fait de Parade et raconte M. Les moindres détails. Ton ami Jean

45. FRANCIS POULENC TO IGOR STRAVINSKY

83, rue de Monceau, Paris, [31 July 1922]

Mon cher Stravinsky,

Thank you for your letter, which touched me deeply. Thank you, too, for the errata of *Le [Chant du] rossignol*. If I have taken so long to reply it is because I have been madly busy the whole week. I have been spending long hours in the Bibliothèque Nationale looking for song texts for my ballet.[1] I have found some excellent ones and will start work on them in earnest the moment I get back from Salzburg in the second half of August.[2]

I am sending you the latest issue of *Les Feuilles libres*, containing my article on *Mavra*.[3] I was allowed so little space that I had to do it in the form of a résumé. Such as it is, may it provide proof of my admiration for *Mavra*. I am also sending you an article by Maurice Brillant in *Le Correspondant*, which shows a certain good will. What do you think of Boris de Schloezer's[4] article in *La Nouvelle revue française*? We'll have a good laugh about it in five years' time. Have you heard from Hammond?[5]

I will write from Austria to let you know what is happening. In the meantime, please give my compliments to Madame Stravinsky and accept my warmest regards.

Francis Poulenc

P.S. I would be very grateful if you would tell me what pen you use to write music. I have a dozen different kinds on my table, all vile and blunt after one page. Is it impossible to find your stave-tracing device on sale anywhere? In Switzerland?

46. DARIUS MILHAUD TO FRANCIS POULENC

Aix-en-Provence, summer 1922

Mon cher Poulet,

The Hugos have just left and I am going to settle down to some work, as I have not done a thing so far.

My stay in the Camargue was wonderful. It is such an exceptional place (both geographically and in my heart, for I used to go there every year with my friend Leo Latil).[1] Nothing has changed. The place is still wild and untouched. But this time I gained more of an insight into the harsh existence of the people of Les Saintes[2] because I was able to have a horse and, with the Hugos, to lead the life of a bull-herd. The festivities were magnificent – you must have heard all the details from the charming little Peignots [Suzanne and Charles], who in fact saw only the religious processions of the gypsies. Afterwards there were the Provençal festivals,

and the sorting and branding of the bulls, their arrival and then the bull-
fights. The Casa Fuertes came several times.

Valentine and Jean [Hugo] are delectable in the country. I was delighted
to have them here and to go on so many outings with them. They will come
back to L'Enclos[3] in September and will take me with them to Fourques.[4]

What is astounding is Maggy Hugo[5] transformed into a *Saintine*. She has
bought a house in Les Saintes, dresses like an Arlésienne, speaks Provençal,
leads a tough, hard life among the bulls, drinks and dances with the village
folk, and rushes from one end of the country to the other in her Ford to
attend all the festivals. This place lives for its festivals, every Sunday in a
different location, to which the bulls have to be brought.

I have not seen a single paper and know nothing of *Mavra* apart from
what you have told me. I am delighted with all this, as it brings us closer to
Igor [Stravinsky], the only one who really counts.

I was pleased to hear your news of Marie [Laurencin] – I had heard she
was better through a letter from Morand[6] to the Hugos.

Tell me about the Beaumonts' garden-party with Chicherin, about the
Dimitri–Chanel marriage, *Le Roi Saül* and Germaine's Sonata.[7]

I spent the day at an exhibition with Louis Gautier-Vignal[8] and his
family.

I am still tired and weak. It is really getting me down. The slightest thing
leaves me exhausted. I stick to my diet very conscientiously.

Did you see the insane article on Germaine[9] by Médan in *Le Feu*?

Give some thought to my concerts in America, which look likely to take
place in December. I am very keen on having something for orchestra by
you. Otherwise I will perform only my own orchestral works. For when it
comes to conducting the works of friends, yours are the only ones that please
me, and if I do not have something by Poulet I shall dispense with all the
rest. I can always take your *Overture* with me (from *Le Boeuf* performance).

I so much want your *Marches militaires*.[10] I expect there will be a drama
over obtaining the three parts that form a 'Suite' from *Les Fâcheux*, and if
you don't give me anything, I am certainly not going to have a whole
festival of Arthur's [Honegger] music.

All this has to be thought through beforehand. Of course, I'm talking
about the concerts for full orchestra, because in the case of those for small
orchestra the difficulty is, fortunately, only one of choice.

We will go to all the Collaer concerts[11] together, won't we?

Your friend
D.

In the Camargue we lived in the midst of mirages, as in the stories of
Clapier.

Have you seen the Hoppenots?[12] If not, phone them if the fancy takes you. They are at 103 boulevard Malesherbes, staying with the Hoppenot parents.

47. IGOR STRAVINSKY TO FRANCIS POULENC

Paris, 9 September 1922

Mon cher Poulenc,

Rest assured that not a day goes by without my thinking that I owe you a long letter – as I am thinking at this very moment – but it is impossible for me to concentrate. You will excuse me: various problems are troubling me at the moment. But I will write when calmer.

Your article gave me *great* pleasure. Monsieur Brillant's is like Madame Manuel's.

The pens you want can be obtained in London. My stock is finished – I will try to procure a new box and send you half of it.

How is your work going? Mine went quite well in Biarritz. I shall be in Paris for a few more days, then back to Biarritz again.

Keep in touch, as I am always pleased to hear from you.

Very sincerely, your
I. Stravinsky

48. FRANCIS POULENC TO SERGE DE DIAGHILEV

Nazelles, Indre-et-Loire, 24 September 1922

Mon cher Diaghilev,

How difficult it is to contact you. I wrote to you in Deauville and at the Continental, but to no avail – both letters were returned to me. So I am hoping I can reach you through Stravinsky to let you know that a title for the ballet has been found: *Les Biches*. It has so far met with general approval – I hope it will have yours. It is absolutely Marie Laurencin.[1]

I am staying here until 20 December to do my work for you. I think you will be pleased with me. I have finished the *Introduction*, which is about two and a quarter minutes long. It is followed by the *Presto* (I). The song of the three men will be number II – I have put it here as it would not have stood out as number VII, being too similar in spirit to the *Finale* (VIII). So number VII will be the slow song of the two girls.

I have at last found my number III (solo for the star), but how difficult it was! I hope I have managed to avoid the 1830 waltz, the 1870 waltz, the Italian adagio, the 'wrong notes waltz' *à la* Casella, and the sad waltz (*Parade*).

In fact it is a dance in two-four time, very lithe, very *danceable* – and also *andantino*, beginning in B flat, then moving through the most unexpected modulations. I am sure this is what is required.

I am at the beginning of the *Jeu* now (IV). For the first few bars, the singers count *ams, tram, dram, pic et pic et colédram*, etc. Then the dancers divide into two sides and the game begins. A sort of hunting game, very Louis XIV.

The *Rag-Mazurka* (V) is terrifying. Tell la Nijinska that she can start thinking of some frenetic movements in triple time.

All that remain now are number VI (*pas de deux*), for which I am afraid my mind is a complete blank; the song VII; and the *Rondeau final* for which I have a few ideas.[2]

I am planning my orchestration (in threes) for a hall of the Châtelet-Mogador type. So I hope we will not go on at the Opéra. The same thing applies to Auric's orchestration [for *Les Fâcheux*].

What do you think of all this?

Write soon!

Kindest regards to be shared with Boris [Kochno].[3]

Francis Poulenc

Marie [Laurencin] is working too.

49. MAX JACOB TO FRANCIS POULENC

Saint-Benoît-sur-Loire (Loiret), 29 September 1922

Cher Francis,

Bravo! dear Francis, for the photos! They are first-class, true-to-life, perfect. Bravo and thank you.

Bravo, too, for *Promenades* and all the other things you played at the Daudets. Wonderful! You are my favourite musician. Don't tell the others.

The *Biches* idea is lovely and I have no doubt that you will make something extraordinary of it.

I am working on a one-act play for the Vieux-Colombier, Gallimard having taken on the scenario (he is the owner of the V. Colombier). I am in correspondence with Jean [Cocteau] who is bitter but still *Jean. . .til*. My painting is progressing as well. I am busy – rather late – becoming a real painter . . . horrible! Something between Corot and Monet – nothing modest. It's not my fault.

I am happy about the themes of my plays. All in all, this makes for a lot of suffering.

If you see the Daudets, remember me to them. Tell Lucien that I am not offended by his supercilious attitude: it is of no importance . . . He obviously does not do it on purpose.

Bravo again! Thank you again! Work well! Keep it up! We are on earth to work for others and to reap a fair share of ingratitude. They insult Jean in *Littérature*! Disgraceful!

With much love,
Max

My compliments to the very distinguished lady whom you accompanied to that lunch.

Man Ray gave me a marvellous photo of Jean. It is on my wall, where there is nothing else. I will put yours there if some day you take it into your head to send me one.

50. Max Jacob to Francis Poulenc

12 October 1922

Cher Francis,

Thank you for your letter! I am pleased that the dedication gave you pleasure. The poems are part of a burlesque book which until now no publisher has wanted. I have never been able to write others like them. It was a passing phase.

Saint Cecilia may well be your patron saint but if I were you I would invoke Saint Joan of Arc, who was born on 6 January and who consequently shares certain characteristics with you. What's more, she has not been a saint for very long: so she has not yet been abused. I have prayed for your ballet. If one day I produce a good libretto for an operetta, I shall give it to you . . . there is plenty of time! First take a look at Roland-Manuel's and see if you like it, although it's *passé*.

Yes! Jean [Cocteau] is being treated despicably. WE are used to that kind of success and I myself am lower than the lowest in certain circles. It brings luck! If only my hair would grow curly and my stomach did not have folds of fat. Enough! It all brings luck! I'm finishing a great farce in one act which hasn't managed to make me laugh. Dressmakers have a saying: 'To do and to undo is still all work.' Dear Jean! he suffers a good deal more than I do. I am superstitious, so compliments frighten me.

Thanks again for the lovely photos. I embrace you.

Max

51. FRANCIS POULENC TO CHARLES KOECHLIN

Nazelles, Indre-et-Loire, [Autumn 1922]

Cher Monsieur et Ami,

You must wonder at my silence, since you have not heard from me for more than a month. Please do not be angry – the only reason for it is that I have been away. I was delighted with my stay in Salzburg. The French have had a huge success there. Your Sonata in particular, admirably played by Fleury, deeply impressed musicians there, somewhat overwhelmed by so much music in so short a time and with such limited resources. After Salzburg I spent a week with my sister at Houlgate and finally arrived here ten days ago. I am working very hard at my ballet *Les Biches*, which I find enthralling. I hope I can make a success of it.

I cannot impress upon you enough how I have benefited from my work with you during the winter, from the point of view of counterpoint as well as harmony. I am impatient now to start on three- and four-part harmony, and fugue. I have so much to do, however, that I shall not be back in Paris until about 15 to 20 December. So it is around then that I shall contact you. Naturally, I will write to you frequently about my work.

My Sonata for clarinet and bassoon is finished. I'm rather pleased with it. The counterpoint is sometimes quite amusing. I am also finishing a Sonata for horn, trumpet and trombone.[1] And what about you? Are you happy with your new installations? Are you working at any new compositions? How is your wife?

You will give me great pleasure if you can find a moment to write to me with all your news.

In the meantime, I send you my warmest regards.

Francis Poulenc

52. IGOR STRAVINSKY TO FRANCIS POULENC

1 January 1923

Happy New Year, my dear Poulenc.

I did not see very much of you at the concert.[1] Your hasty departure afterwards and your rather despondent mood during the concert – what was it all about? Or am I being indiscreet?

As for me, I left the concert in utter disgust and despair. So did Ansermet. Actually, the rehearsal had promised quite a good performance of *Mavra*. And then you saw what the singers did to me. Apart from how my music is performed, there is a great deal to be said about where it is performed. Most places tend to be designed for dressed-up music, whereas mine – the kind I have been writing for the past two years – is naked. And then it finds itself in the hands of couturiers, against whom brave Ansermet struggles desperately. I am in a very bad mood, and with good reason.

Your Stravinsky

53. FRANCIS POULENC TO MANUEL DE FALLA

83 rue de Monceau, Paris, 29 January 1923

Cher Falla,

Yesterday I practically brought the house down with my applause for your *Amour sorcier*[1] which I ADORE. Could you possibly ask Chester to send me the score – I would be so thrilled to have it. Did I ever thank you for your *Fantaisie*[2] for piano? It is an exquisite work. I have scrapped the *Caprice espagnol* – it would not have been worthy of you. I shall dedicate another composition to you, something that I am entirely happy with.[3] I send you a thousand warm regards.

Francis Poulenc

54. MANUEL DE FALLA TO FRANCIS POULENC

Granada, 7 April 1923

Thank you with all my heart, my dear Poulenc, for your letter, which I did not answer earlier as I was overwhelmed with work, my latest composition (*El Retablo*)[1] having just had its first concert performance in Seville.

By now you will have received *L'Amour sorcier*, which I was delighted to ask Chester to send you.

I hear marvellous things about your *Promenades* for piano!

I hope to see you soon in Paris. Until then, my warmest regards.

Your
Manuel de Falla

55. RAYMOND RADIGUET TO FRANCIS POULENC

Piqueÿ, near Arès (Gironde), Friday [1923]

Mon cher Francis,

I am on the balcony. Beside me, Monsieur Auric, stark naked, is typing letters. Jean [Cocteau] is lying on the beach. Up until now I have been lazing around but from today I am going to get down to work. And what work! A long preface to the collection of my poems, soon to be published by Grasset. After that, the revision of my novel *Le Bal du Comte d'Orgel*, which is coming out in November. And I dare say a few short stories, unless I allow myself to be tempted again by the novel.

I told you that my brother joined the Ivry factory as a chemical research assistant.[1] Would you be kind enough to write a letter of recommendation to your cousin? My brother and I would be extremely grateful. May I count on that?

What are your plans for this summer? We all intend staying here until we've exhausted the supply of fine weather. And we all embrace you.

Raymond Radiguet

56. JEAN COCTEAU TO FRANCIS POULENC

Piqueÿ par Arès, Gironde, 24 July 1923

Cher Francis,

Send news of Paris. Here, nothing much. Auric is at the typewriter with his back turned to the scenery. Radiguet is dictating his novel to him.[1] Impossible to find a piano. Wonderful excuse. I have been left with *Le Pauvre Matelot* on my hands.[2] Auric finds the ending too dramatic and altogether not his cup of tea. He asks for another libretto. I resist; he sulks. I really cannot give him librettos to try on like boots.

Write me a long letter – ♡ – Jean

The Hugos are arriving tomorrow.

57. ERIK SATIE TO FRANCIS POULENC

Friday, 3 August 1923

Cher Ami – Sunday is not possible. Thank you all the same.

My 'Gounod' is not 'working' very well. It seems yours is 'stunning'. Good for you.[1]

I shall be at the Fontaines' on Tuesday. So, until Tuesday.

Regards to Sauguet, please.

Your old friend,
Erik Satie

P.S. Tomorrow I am going to Senneville to spend the day with [Jean] Wiéner. I will give him your regards, won't I? Yes, I will.

58. ERIK SATIE TO FRANCIS POULENC

Monday, 13 August 1923

Cher Ami – As I told you the other night, I shall not be able to come and see you on Wednesday. Please make my apologies to your dear uncle and give him my best wishes.

I received a very nice letter from Diaghilev. He is in Venice and will be here on the 20th of the month . . . This sends cold shivers down my spine. Yes . . . Work is pouring out of me, like a torrent, or even a deluge . . . Yes . . . It cannot be stemmed . . .

Ever yours,

E.S.

59. FRANCIS POULENC TO SERGE DE DIAGHILEV

[1923]

Mon cher ami,

I was very pleased with my two days in Paris. What joy that you like the whole of *Les Biches*! Now send me *La Colombe* quickly so that I can get shot of this bird.

Have you decided on the sets with Marie [Laurencin]? Let me know via Boris [Kochno] the *exact* date that Nijinska will be passing through Paris – I will come there. From Monday, write to me or phone me at the Hôtel du Lion d'Or in Amboise.

All good wishes.

Poulenc

60. FRANCIS POULENC TO CHARLES KOECHLIN

Nazelles, Indre-et-Loire, 3 September [1923]

Mon cher maître et ami,

Apologies for my silence. I do not write because I am working all out. Just imagine, on top of finishing and orchestrating *Les Biches* a most perilous piece of work has come my way – commissioned by Diaghilev. I have had to do the recitatives, often too long and eight in number, for a comic opera by Gounod, *La Colombe*, which will be performed this winter in Monte Carlo. Fortunately I am very familiar with the stage works of good old Charles, and so I have been able to draw on everything I know about the style – by the way admirable – of this too often disparaged musician. And, by adding all my meagre store of *savoir-faire*, I have given birth to quite a good little job. Again, the chorales have served me well.

Once this task was completed, I set to work again on *Les Biches*, which I shall finish this week and take to Diaghilev in Paris.

All this is to explain my silence. You are extremely kind to have written to me. I am looking forward to your two Sonatas for clarinet (my favourite instrument); in fact I am dying to hear them. I confess that I have again succumbed to my weakness and have sketched part of a quintet for string quartet and clarinet.[1] I hope to finish it this winter. I am enjoying this combination of instruments very much.

I shall come and see you in Méry in October to show you my orchestrations. But I will write to you before then. In the meantime, I send you my warmest regards.

Your faithful
Poulenc

61. JEAN COCTEAU TO FRANCIS POULENC

[Piqueÿ par Arès, Gironde], 1923

Waiting for *Les Biches* and *Les Fâcheux* is very trying. I love your works like my own daughters. Monte Carlo is our 'gentle offensive'. We must arm our tanks with honey and roses. I am putting spark to powder in an article which will precede *Thomas l'Imposteur*[1] (*Nouvelles littéraires*): I declare that musicians will give Gounod his rightful place as painters have done in the case of Ingres. Write again. Admit that the woman on the other side of this card deserves it![2] I envy your warm house here in my damp-timbered shanty.[3]

♡ Jean

Radiguet hauled Auric over the coals for his idiotic articles. Result: the enormous article that was even worse.

I have not had any news from Igor [Stravinsky] for two weeks. Is he ill?

62. ERIK SATIE TO FRANCIS POULENC

Tuesday, 11 September 1923

Cher bon Vieux – You are lucky to have completed your THINGUMAJIG.[1] As for me, I am finishing my second act. *Oui.*

I received two charming letters from your wonderful director. Unfortunately, my third act will not be ready for 1 October. I am crying like Croesus over it. *Oui.*

Come back quickly: there is nothing to see in the country . . .

Yes: our dear Auric's articles are becoming somewhat *ARRIVÉS*. Strange!

I greet you as the old friend that I am.

Do not forget me.

E.S.

63. FRANCIS POULENC TO IGOR STRAVINSKY

La Lézardière, Nazelles, Indre-et-Loire, [September 1923]*

Mon cher Stravinsky,

I am ashamed to have left you without news for nearly two months. Forgive me and do not hold it against me – I have been working very hard. I have completed and delivered to Serge [Diaghilev] my recitatives for *La Colombe.* I did the job meticulously, trying to avoid a pastiche or a lesson in harmony *à la* Reger.[1] (I hope you will not find this too unkind.) In ten days I will go to Paris to deliver the completed *Biches* personally.

And you, dear friend, what of you? I heard about your trip to Weimar through Robert Lyon[2] and then Auric. Was it not too dreadful in these times of political tension?

I suppose by now you are in Biarritz. Did *le bon gros Georges* [Auric] visit you? I might just possibly appear at Les Rochers[3] in November, if the weather is good.

And your work? What progress with the Concerto for piano and orchestra?

You know, I often dream of the beauty of your Octet; it is so magnificent, so sure and solid. Have you made arrangements for it with the Danes[4] – and for my beloved *Mavra*?

I hope you will be kind enough to send me a long letter with replies to all these questions. With best wishes to your wife and son, and to you, dear friend, very much affection.

Poulenc

64. IGOR STRAVINSKY TO FRANCIS POULENC

Biarritz, 12 September 1923

Mon cher Poulenc,

Thank you for your letter and the lovely photograph of your house,

---

*Poulenc enclosed a photograph of Mme Paul Liénard's ivy-covered house, La Lézardière, with the following note on the back: 'I want you to be one of the first to receive this photograph of my house in Touraine. May its appearance entice you to visit it some day. With much affection, Poulenc.'[5]

which gave me great pleasure. Last week I had Auric with me. He played me a duo he had just composed – very pretty! And you? What new things have you done apart from scoring your ballet? I think I shall be in Paris about 18 October. Will you be there?

With fond regards,
Your Igor Stravinsky

65. Manuel de Falla to Francis Poulenc

Granada, 19 September 1923

Mon cher Poulenc,

We are joyously singing your *Chanson à boire*[1] at the Alhambra! Come and conduct it for us. The weather is wonderful and the Sierra is covered in snow. You will be pleased both with our welcome and your visit . . .

Come and complete your *Fantaisie espagnole*[2] in Granada!

I was delighted to receive your *Promenades*, which I adore. Thank you!

A thousand good wishes from your
Manuel de Falla

66. Francis Poulenc to Igor Stravinsky

Hôtel du Lion d'Or, Amboise, [5 October 1923]

Mon cher Stravinsky,

How delighted I was to see the announcement of your Octet on the posters at the Opéra! You can count on my being in Paris on the 18th without fail. I was there four days ago to play the complete *Biches* to Diaghilev, who had not yet heard it. He was pleased, as was Auric. How I long to have your opinion, more precious to me than anyone else's. I am now orchestrating intensely and am not unhappy. Would you be kind enough – and this is the main point of my letter – to send me as soon as possible the address of the bookbinder who bound *Les Noces*[1] for you so quickly. Mine requires three weeks to do *Les Biches*. I simply cannot leave my manuscript with him for that long as I am orchestrating from it.

I hope to see you often during the week I am in Paris. Meanwhile, I send you my warmest regards.

Francis Poulenc

And the Concerto? How is it progressing?

67. IGOR STRAVINSKY TO FRANCIS POULENC

Biarritz, 6 October 1923

Cher Poulenc,

The address of my bookbinder, if I am not mistaken, is 24(?) rue Condorcet and he is called neither more nor less than Adam. I think his shop is between the rue Turgot and the rue Rodier.

Glad to hear that you have completed *Les Biches*. If you need me for any advice whatever, do not hesitate to come – you know the warm regard I have always had for what you are doing and especially for *Les Biches*, the rest of which I am very keen indeed to hear.

I will be in Paris towards the end of the week and look forward to seeing you. So, until then, *mon vieux*.

Your Igor Stravinsky

The Concerto is coming along well, thank you.

68. FRANCIS POULENC TO HENRI SAUGUET

Hôtel des Princes, Monte Carlo, [1923]

Bonjour Monsieur Sauguet, how is everything? I often think of you but have not managed to write because I've been working so hard. Thank goodness my orchestration is making progress.[1] I am not displeased with it. You may already have heard through Darius that I have had a marvellous surprise. The choreography of *Les Biches* is a masterpiece. It is ravishing from beginning to end and exactly what I wanted.[2] We are working solidly so that *Les Fâcheux* can follow on. Talking of Auric, I find his article perfect – it expresses *exactly* what I think of you. I dare say you may have found it unpleasant to be lumped together with me, my poor fellow. But never mind, you can be happy to have won unanimous approval from 'the musicians'. What are you working at now? What has happened to the Sonatina for flute?

Do please send me a really good letter to let me know what is going on in Paris. It is such a pleasure to hear from all my friends – and you are among the best of them. So be sure to send me some lengthy pages.

With warm regards,

Your faithful
Poulenc

I am delighted with Désormière's[3] success as a conductor. He deserves it.

1 The young Francis Poulenc

2 Eric Satie in middle age

3 Igor Stravinsky in 1925

4 Ricardo Viñes in the 1920s

5 Manuel de Falla in 1926

6 Darius Milhaud and Francis Poulenc in Aix-en-Provence in 1921

7 Jean Cocteau and Georges Auric at Le Lavandou in 1924

8 Portrait of Cocteau in London, with inscription to Poulenc

9 Pierre Bernac and Francis Poulenc in 1937, two years after the formation of their duo

10 Louise de Vilmorin with Pierre Bernac in his Paris apartment in 1947

11 Poulenc in uniform at Cahors, 1940

12 Igor Stravinsky, Madeleine and Darius Milhaud, and Nadia Boulanger in Santa Monica, 1942

13 Cocteau and Les Six sporting spectacles. A reunion in the 1950s. Standing: Francis Poulenc, Germaine Tailleferre, Georges Auric, Louis Durey. Seated: Arthur Honegger, Jean Cocteau, Darius Milhaud

69. HENRI SAUGUET TO FRANCIS POULENC

11, rue d'Orsel, Paris 18ᵉ, 20 November 1923

Mon cher Ami,

Your letter gave me very great pleasure and I thank you with all my heart. I was very touched by the kind words you accorded me. I did not know how you would take Auric's article and it is certainly you rather than I who might have been annoyed by the comparison. For my part, I am delighted by it and nothing could have pleased me more. So all is well.

I wish I could be with you in Monte Carlo, especially for the first performance of *Les Biches* and *Les Fâcheux* which I am so longing to hear in full production. I am already quite certain of the lavish praise that will be showered on you. In any case I send you my warmest good wishes.

In Paris nothing much is going on. There were the Wiéner concerts. The first one was entirely Stravinsky and included the Octet, which I had not heard before. The second was devoted to Milhaud and Falla, with *Le Retable* and two new things by Milhaud, one of which, his *Symphony with Voices*, sounded just like a 'first draft' of *La Création*[1] (one of the themes is there almost in its entirety). This symphony is in fact very fine – I liked it a lot. The oboe is used to clever advantage and sounds most effective. As for the Octet, I was not as 'carried away' as I would have expected to be. It is true that I had Koechlin next to me curbing and restraining my enthusiasm. I nevertheless did have the feeling of something 'very good' and I am sure it is a marvellous work. Apart from that, there are no musical events worth going out of one's way for.

I am working as hard as I can on my Sonatina for flute which you so kindly ask after. It is coming along nicely and the third movement, already begun, is so far working out as I wished. I think it will be played at the Wiéner concerts in the spring. At least, they have asked me for it. But will it be finished?

Milhaud is in London, where he is performing *Pierrot lunaire*[2] to the English. Good luck to you, Gentlemen! I have not seen Auric since the last Wiéner concert. He must be working. All the better for us. Neither have I seen Satie, who remains invisible and difficult to approach these days. His persecution phobia is assuming huge proportions. And, besides, I think he does not regard me very favourably. (I have absolutely no idea why.)

I think that is all the news, *Mon Cher Ami*. I am very sorry not to have more to tell you. But no doubt your work and Monte Carlo take up so much of your time that you have none left for getting bored. Send me word, and some news, from time to time. You have no idea how much pleasure your letters give me.

Your devoted friend,
Henri Sauguet

70. DARIUS MILHAUD TO FRANCIS POULENC

[Telegram received in Monte Carlo on 12 December 1923]

                                    Paris 703 14 12° 11:30am

Radiguet died during night. Poor Jean dreadful state. Darius.[1]

71. FUNERAL ANNOUNCEMENT OF RAYMOND RADIGUET SENT TO FRANCIS
    POULENC

You are invited to attend the Funeral and Obsequies for

Monsieur Raymond RADIGUET
Man of Letters

deceased in Paris on 12 December 1923, fortified by the
Rites of the Church, aged twenty years, which will take place
on Friday 14th at 9.30 a.m. in the Chapel of Notre-Dame de la
Cité Paroissiale de Saint-Honoré d'Eylau (66 avenue de Malakoff).[1]

72. DARIUS MILHAUD TO FRANCIS POULENC

1923

Mon cher Poulet,

   We have been through some very distressing days over the death of poor
Raymond [Radiguet]. Jean [Cocteau], exhausted from the period before the
death, did not have the strength to move afterwards. He could not face
seeing Raymond dead, nor could he bring himself to remain near him, or
even to go to the funeral. He took to his bed for three days. He is calmer now,
well looked after by a constant stream of friends.

   Perhaps it is just as well that he did not see that tragic, bloated face with
its gaping mouth and its head flung back.

   When I see you I will tell you – but only you – many distressing and
painful things about these sad days. On the day of the funeral, quite a crowd
of people and friends turned up at the church (it is so easy to sign a register to
prove your presence), but very few went on to Père Lachaise. There, it was
heart-breaking.

   When you can, give me the exact dates for January so that I can hear *Les
Biches, Les Fâcheux*, the three Gounods and the Chabrier in the shortest
possible time.[1] When is your première?

   I think Jean will join you all in Monte Carlo.

La Brebis caused a great scandal among the season-ticket subscribers during the first act. Police intervened, performance stopped. Wolff yelled at the audience; then, by the end of the second act, we 'had' them. Carré is going to publish the press criticisms of *Pelléas*. He is very good, but the Isola brothers are terrified.[2]

I embrace you.

Da.

73. MAURICE RADIGUET TO FRANCIS POULENC

15 December [1923]

Cher Monsieur,

We thank you very sincerely for the deeply felt lines you wrote to us on the death of our beloved son.

He was to leave at the end of this month to do his military service. He had been assigned to the artillery of the 75th at Troyes and had obtained a deferment in order to correct the proofs of his forthcoming novel.[1] But within days he was struck down by this appalling illness. The night before he died, while delirium alternated with rare moments of lucidity, he turned to Cocteau and said very calmly: 'You know . . . tomorrow I shall die.' When Cocteau protested, he added: 'Oh, yes! I know very well I shall die . . . I shall be executed by the soldiers of God.'

Poor child! So much youth and talent, so much kindness! And now he is no more.

His kindness! If only you knew with what joy he came to report that his brother Paul had begun work at the Poulenc plant,[2] saying to me: 'I am happy. In Poulenc the musician I have a good friend whose heart I know well. He will do everything he can to look after Paul.'

And he was so pleased to learn that a short time afterwards his brother had been promoted as a result of your intervention.

Thank you in advance, dear Monsieur Poulenc, for all your continuing help. My dear Raymond's good deeds will thus bear fruit in the future.

Please accept our deepest sympathy and all our gratitude.

M. Radiguet

74. MARIE LAURENCIN TO FRANCIS POULENC

12, rue José-Maria de Hérédia, Paris 7ᵉ   Tél: Ségur 12–33

Mon cher Petit,

I came back this morning from Switzerland and snow. I found your letters, and Blanche full of anguish because she did not know where I was.

Footsteps in the snow soon fade.

But, *mon bon petit*, of what use would I be in Monte Carlo? Music, dancing – there would be some point. But décor – nothing can be done if it's no good – if the pink is not pink.

You really do torment me. Jean [Cocteau] will represent me. I have so much faith in him. I am curious to hear his impressions. *You* have the enthusiasm of an enamoured balletomane.

I am hoping with all my heart for something charming. But I am frightened.[1]

> Your old grandmother painter,
> Marie

75. Francis Poulenc to Paul Collaer

Hôtel des Princes, Monte Carlo, Tuesday evening [7 January 1924]

Mon cher Collaer,

Here at last is my news, and good news. The première of *Les Biches* was, if I may venture to say so, a triumph. There were eight curtain-calls which is *rarissime* for Monte Carlo. One has to admit that Nijinska's choreography is of such beauty that even your old roulette-addicted English lady cannot resist it. It is the very essence of dance. And the *mise au point* is impeccable. Can you imagine, there were no less than 72 rehearsals – about 250 hours of work. That is the way to get results. The sets, the curtain, the costumes, are a total success. I am really longing for you to see it. As for the music, although it is not exactly modest to say so, I won't hide the fact that I am very pleased with my orchestration. It has a brilliance and, I believe, a very personal range of colour. Even Auric, difficult as he is, approves wholeheartedly. They are busily rehearsing his *Fâcheux* which opens on the 15th. The more I hear the music the more I like it, a fairly rare phenomenon for me. On Sunday the curtain will at last go up on Chabrier's *L'Education*, which had to be postponed owing to the illness of a singer. I very much hope that Darius will be there. What joy for me to see him again after three months. I was very upset that I could not go to Paris for the première of *La Brebis* but it was absolutely impossible as I was just completing the orchestration of *Les Biches*.

If you are kind and do not bear me a grudge because of my entirely unintentional silence, write to me at length giving details of the Stravinsky performance and the other Pro Arte concerts. Did they eventually play my Sonatas for wind? I am very distressed that they have not been published yet, although I corrected the proofs this summer.[1]

If you need them, ask Chester directly for a copy. As for *Les Biches* I have not yet signed up with anyone. I prefer to wait and get what I want.[2]

Satie came here for a few days for his recitatives in *Le Médecin malgré lui*. I think he was very pleased judging by the excellent mood he was in during his short stay.[3]

In your next letter, be good enough to give me Mesens' address.[4] Is he working? If he has published any new works in Brussels, tell him to send me something. Cocteau is with Auric and me at the Hôtel des Princes. We are trying to take his mind off things as best we can. What a terrible thing Radiguet's death was. I myself was completely shattered by it.

Hoping to hear from you, I send you, *cher vieux*, my best regards.

F. Poulenc

76. MARIE LAURENCIN TO FRANCIS POULENC

12, rue José-Maria de Hérédia, Paris 7ᵉ, January 1924

My dear Francis

It seems that *Biches*
  move
    the Rich
  of Monte Carlo.

It would be good of you to find out from the Boss what has happened to my drawings, especially the one I worked on for the curtain – and a framed watercolour and the dresses. It was agreed that they would be returned to me. In fact I would also quite like to be paid.

I am delighted by the success. But I am in no way responsible. Your music is.

The choreography haunts me, and so does that couch![1]

Au revoir Francis.
Je t'embrasse.
Marie

77. ERIK SATIE TO FRANCIS POULENC

Friday, 11 January 1924

Cher Ami – Good day. How are you? Bravo again and again for *Les Biches*. Allow me to advise you not to pay too great court to Sieur (Scieur) L.L.[1]

Oui. Beware of the fellow. *Oui* . . . Do not forget that you are a thousand times superior to him. *OUI.* Regards.

E.S.

78. IGOR STRAVINSKY TO FRANCIS POULENC

Biarritz, 3 February 1924

Mon cher Poulenc,

I have just sent a note to Auric telling him how happy I was to hear of the success you both had in Monte Carlo and asking forgiveness for my long silence and my non-presence in Monte Carlo. My desire to be there, I can assure you, was very great, but I was prevented from doing so by my two concerts in Belgium and then by a pile of work in Paris.

I am longing to see you again soon and to hear all the details about your music for *Les Biches*. The only person I have seen who was there, Benois, spoke very highly of it. (I was sure of this anyway, because *Biches* is a very beautiful score.)

But when shall I see you? From now until March I am here working on my Concerto, then I am going to Barcelona for two or three weeks where I am conducting three concerts of some old things of mine. Then back to Biarritz until the middle of April.

Where are you and what are you doing? Do keep writing.

Very sincerely,

I. Stravinsky

79. FRANCIS POULENC TO IGOR STRAVINSKY

Saturday [February 1924]

Cher ami,

A thousand thanks for your very kind letter which touched me deeply. You know that there is no encouragement that I find more flattering than yours. Yes, *Les Biches* went well. I cannot find words to do justice to the beauty of Nijinska's work. She really is a creature of genius. The whole thing was danced so perfectly. And special praise for Nemchinova,[1] adorable in the starring role. Since our return, Auric and I have come up against a lot of jealousy and ill humour – quite naturally. Monsieur Satie is particularly enraged. Having fallen out with Jean [Cocteau], Georges [Auric] and myself, he is telling the whole of Paris that our 'trumperies' are ignoble and that, in addition, we are 'swine', that we were responsible for the silence that greeted his Gounod recitatives, etc. etc. He published an initial article to this effect in the programme for *Les Indépendants* and a second will follow in *Paris-Journal*.[2] This is not very nice, is it, and very surprising from that otherwise admirable being.

After two weeks of shopping and errands, I am going to settle down to work. The *Marches militaires* will occupy all my time.[3] You cannot imagine how I am longing to hear your Concerto. You say that you are staying in Biarritz until 15 April. Perhaps I will come and see you. I'll discuss this with you later.

While awaiting the pleasure of seeing you again this spring, *cher ami*, I send you and your wife my warmest regards.

Your faithful
Poulenc

80. IGOR STRAVINSKY TO FRANCIS POULENC

Biarritz, 11 February 1924

Cher Poulenc I received your very good letter and the two (newly published) scores. Thank you. Your scores came out at the same time as my Concertino.[1] Unfortunately I cannot send you the pocket edition, as Hansen has sent me only one copy – the pig! With fondest regards,

Igor Str.

81. MAX JACOB TO FRANCIS POULENC

Saint-Benoît-sur-Loire (Loiret), 12 May 1924

Cher Poulenc*

Publishers, publishers
are people with no hearts.
On bended knees we may beg for a volume
but our groans count for less than the pen
that served the author to put ink to paper.
Kiss their knees, grovel at their feet
they are black rocks, men without souls.
'No! No! Francis Poulenc shall not have one tome!'
And this is why! this is why! you have not had my latest works.
I send you, however, by this same post,
The Man of Flesh and he of reflections
hoping to find at last on this earth
one reader to whom this novel will appeal.
I heard of your immense success in Monte Carlo
for entire newspapers are filled with your name.
More than of Deputies they speak, Francis, of you,
from the banks of the Ganges to distant Phlegethon.

*The original text is in rhyming verse.

Satie will calm down: it is a fit of bad temper.
I was subjected to such a one, four or five years ago.
All geniuses, apart from you, are not easy to live with and many take their
troubles out on those closest to them.
Yes, Francis! of your première I do know the date
and were I not overwhelmed with work
I would go in carriages and caravanseries
to applaud your great work from my seat in the stalls.
Two years have gone since I was last in Paris
and all I have felt deprived of is my friends.
    I kiss your dear and much loved face.

Thanks, thanks, thanks
for the precious manuscript
that a little-known Belgian was to have set to music
but confidentially – to be quite truthful –
I prefer it to be otherwise
not wishing to spoil my memories of your music, and the music of other
friends.

If you have the use of a car, come to Saint-Benoît.

                                                              Max

82. JEAN COCTEAU TO FRANCIS POULENC

Le Calme, Villefranche-sur-mer, August 1924

Cher Francis,

    Your *Biches* help me to survive. And that says not a little. Georges
[Auric] plays them to me and they work their spell on my poor aching
nerves. I assure you this is the best remedy for me.[1]

    You are the one who should do *Paul* [*et Virginie*]. I CONSIDER MYSELF
FREE. Do you want me to do a write-up for you? The result would be well
worth the effort required.[2]

    Give me all the news. I am deeply grateful to you for lunching with
Maman. Her life is sad, which adds to my anguish.

    I seldom write because my hand does not know how to hold a pen any
more.

                                                              Your

                                                              Jean

83. JEAN COCTEAU TO FRANCIS POULENC

Villefranche-sur-mer, September 1924

Cher Francis,

The photos broke my heart.[1] I knew them all except one, but not so well done. I suffer now as on the very first day. I am dragging out a meaningless life.

Work well. Be thankful every time you wake that you are able to give free rein to the creative forces of your heart. Think of your friend Jean who loves and admires you.

Your works[2] are the only things that keep me going and give me the curiosity to carry on living.

J.

84. MAURICE RADIGUET TO FRANCIS POULENC

11 September [1924]

Cher Monsieur Poulenc,

I have just received the enlargements that you kindly had made.

I cannot tell you how pleased I am to have them. I was particularly moved by the photo of [Raymond] on the swing, and especially the one of him with his two brothers – which brings back his whole childhood to me.

Thank you with all my heart. I would never have dared to ask you for more copies of these two photos, but since you offer I would like to have two more of each, as Paul and René would be delighted to have the photo of the three of them together. In fact – note how I take advantage of you – if at some stage you could send me, either as a group or separately, pictures of those who were closest to him in his last years: you, Cocteau, Auric, and others whom you would know better than I, I cannot begin to tell you the joy that this would give me. He used to speak about you all with such affection that the pictures would be an inseparable part of my memory of him.

After that, I will not trouble you any more.

With my deep affection and gratitude.

M. Radiguet

From all of us, our best wishes and our thanks.

85. FRANCIS POULENC TO CHARLES KOECHLIN

Hôtel du Lion d'or, Amboise, [Autumn 1924]

Cher grand ami,

Please excuse my deplorable silence. I am very contrite and humbly beg your pardon. May I say immediately that I *fully* intend to work with you, twice a week for one hour, starting on 15 January, which is when I shall be back in Paris. Until then I shall not be budging from Touraine, where I am completing various things. A Trio for piano, oboe and bassoon is almost finished.[1] My Concerto for piano and orchestra is well on the way.[2] I am not displeased with all of this. I hope you will not be too severe in your criticism.

No, I have not read your two articles in *Le Monde musical* as that journal is nowhere to be found in the provinces, but I shall certainly get hold of it in Paris, as I have a friend who is a subscriber.

You cannot imagine how I am longing to hear your works for wind instruments – that kind of combination is so dear to me. Can you tell me when your treatise on harmony will be published? Perhaps it has already appeared.

Please know that I think of you often and that I remain your faithful and affectionate

Poulenc

86. HENRI SAUGUET TO FRANCIS POULENC

56 rue de Passy, Paris 16ᵉ, 16 October 1924

Mon cher ami,

Thank you very much for your card, which gave me great pleasure. Your silence worried me. I was afraid we might have fallen out!

I am very pleased to hear that you have done a lot of work this summer. We will hear it this winter which will be an immense joy for you, and especially for me. I, alas, do not have such good news to tell you. I have done absolutely nothing. I feel very despondent and have been assailed by a heavy depression for more than a month now. My life in Paris has become so much of a problem that I believe the only possible solution is to go away. I have no idea of what I shall do but I think I will have to leave here at the end of the year. I am bored to death, I have lost heart entirely, so much so that I do not even go to the piano any more. You see how uninteresting I have become!

Last night I went to the Ravel Festival, given by the SMI [Société Musicale Indépendante], to hear *Tzigane* which is quite the most artificial thing Ravel has ever put his name to. It is poor – very unexciting indeed. The principles that motivate those pages are so out-of-date that I am astonished anyone can still believe in them. Wildly successful, of course, with the lorgnetted ladies and the portly gents. As a whole, the works that were played last night seemed very antiquated to me. Especially the Quartet. I understand more and more why Ravel has no time for the music of today. It must appeal to him about as much as his music appeals to us at the moment.

I hear frequently from Darius, who tells me he is working hard. I hear infrequently from Auric. That's all. Nobody, apart from Honegger – bearded at the moment like the early portraits of Debussy – has returned to Paris yet.

I shall be very pleased to see you when you come back. Do not fail to contact me. With all my heart I wish you many more fine days of work. No one will derive more pleasure from the results of your efforts than I.

With devoted affection,
Henri Sauguet

87. MAURICE RADIGUET TO FRANCIS POULENC

24 November [1924]

Cher Monsieur Poulenc,

I have just this minute received the photographs that you so kindly had printed for me. We are all deeply grateful to you for these precious keepsakes, but I was afraid I had taken too great advantage of you by asking for so many.

I am again beginning to relive the dreadful days that preceded the death of our poor Raymond. A year already! How much time will pass before my grief grows less . . .

Once again, thank you with all my heart.

Affectionately yours,
M. Radiguet

88. WANDA LANDOWSKA TO FRANCIS POULENC

On board S.S. Paris, 17 April 1925. At sea.

Your letter was forwarded to me in New York. How touched I am by your affection![1] A few days from now I shall be crossing the threshold of my house in mourning.[2] But come and see me, bring me the comfort of your friendship. Don't worry that my sadness is too great. I shall overcome it and envelop my friends with calm affection, without a trace of bitterness.

Why has Auric not written to me at all, nor Honegger? And yet they often came to 'our' home and my mother was very fond of them.

Goodbye, dear friend.
Wanda Landowska

89. RAYMONDE LINOSSIER TO FRANCIS POULENC

Telegram (Post-mark Vichy) 3/7/25

Francis Poulenc Hôtel Albert-1er Vichy Allier Paris 49225 22 3 12/27

Satie died night before last after day in coma without regaining consciousness. Regards. Raymonde.[1]

90. RAYMONDE LINOSSIER TO FRANCIS POULENC

Monday 6 [July 1925]

Cher enfant,
    Forgive me for not writing sooner to give you the details about poor
Satie. He was buried this morning in Arcueil, in a simple rustic cemetery,
where the coffin was lowered straight into the earth – a deal coffin stained
red to imitate mahogany.
    I saw the poor old thing on Wednesday, on the morning of the day he
died. I went into his room and found him asleep, with his face greatly
altered since my last visit and covered in flies that did not even wake him, so
sound was his sleep. Naturally, I did not want to wake him, and I left. Then I
spoke to the nun who was looking after him and she told me of the profound
change that had taken place over the last few days. While expecting the
end, she had no idea of just how close it actually was. It appears that he slept
the whole day and died in the evening – I believe without regaining
consciousness. The next day Madeleine Milhaud found his room empty.
    For some days he had been living on nothing but champagne and
paregoric. Now that he is dead I will tell you about that horrifying visit that
so upset me. Without any warning, I found myself in the presence of a man
whose mind had gone and who rambled on deliriously for two hours. This
disintegration of what had once been our *bon maître* was terrible to behold.
    He had been so happy to see me. [. . .] He wanted me to come back; but
because he was sleeping, I was unable to see him again.
    His brother [Conrad Satie] learnt of his death through the caretaker of his
factory who asked him if he knew the Monsieur Satie whose funeral
preparations were reported in the newspaper. [. . .]
    The burial in Arcueil was fine. No doubt many people were unable to
attend, and only the smart, leisured, homosexual set was well represented.
But the setting was pleasant and the good people of Arcueil – his café
companions and others – followed the funeral procession. It would have
been a pity to see Satie, after his death, taken over by that fashionable
milieu for which he always showed such contempt. Darius was there,
looking impressively upset. Auric, stricken, had the same hangdog expres-

sion he wore at the première of *Les Matelots*, and was very close to tears. Cocteau sobbed rather noisily. Valentine was made up to the nines. Forgive me, but I could not help looking at the ceremony through Satie's eyes.

As to the flowers, I did not ask Cocteau's advice, firstly because I did not understand your telegram about this and secondly because I could not see what advice he could possibly give me.

I feared, and rightly so, that people would not turn up because of the holidays and the remoteness of Arcueil. I also feared that the funeral might be a rather poor affair and I wanted *le bon maître* to be treated as a *maître* and not as a penniless musician. So I sent on your behalf a very beautiful wreath (salmon pink roses and hydrangeas in the same colour) and I must tell you that what came from elsewhere barely covered the catafalque and that your wreath and mine were the only decorations that graced the church, apart from a piece of black cloth behind the altar. The only official wreaths were from the Swedith Ballet – in as bad taste as their performances, from Rouart & Lerolle, and from Les Amis du Vieil Arcueil. There was also a touching artificial violet tribute costing about 25 francs with a ribbon bearing the message: 'To Monsieur Satie – the tenants'. He must have been greatly loved there. The *patissière* wanted to know all the details of his death.

To answer your questions – he had definitely been given the sacraments as he was at Saint-Joseph's, a religious hospital, where he had already taken communion, which enabled the nuns to give him the last rites.

As for the manuscripts, I don't really know anything. His brother arrived on Saturday and no one had gone into the room in Arcueil after the death. I will phone Darius [Milhaud] tomorrow to hear his news and to put your question to him.

These, *mon vieux*, are all the details I can give you. I was very sad at the passing of this man who was always so friendly – even affectionate – to me. The particular kind of tenderness he showed towards me right until the last moment, and from our very first meeting seven or eight years ago, touched me – I might even say flattered me – deeply. And there were many reasons for our getting on so well. I was struck by this thought this morning, seeing some of his friends from Arcueil.

Of course, there was your quarrel with him which, even if it did not exactly put a damper on things for me, certainly made things awkward. I would have gone to see him sooner had it not been for that. Yet it is true that if I had seen him sooner he would probably have sent me away before he died, as he did with so many of his friends.

Forgive me for this disjointed letter. No sooner was I back from the funeral than I had to give a law exam to some girls who did not know a thing, then discuss some business, then go out this evening. It is very late now and I have to get up early tomorrow. In any case, he was an old friend who had been very seriously on my mind for the past two weeks. And it is hard to give up running everyone down over a drink, with the inevitable umbrella between us.[1]

Go and see Eugénie.[2]

Fondly, your
Y.F.A.
to recall the past.[3]

91. DARIUS MILHAUD TO FRANCIS POULENC

1925

Mon cher Francis,

A few lines in haste: the seals have been removed at Satie's place.[1] No trace of *Paul et Virginie* (all that was found was the libretto, full of Satie's annotations, which I have not yet seen. Conrad told me about it). There is a lot of unpublished material and more may still come to light; there is such a mess in his room that heaps of things could yet turn up. But I wanted to let you know immediately.

Do a beautiful *Paul et Virginie* for us[2] . . . When will you be back?

Fond regards from us both.

Your
D.M.

92. JEAN COCTEAU TO FRANCIS POULENC

14 July 1925. Cocardes!

Cher Francis,

Yes, chunks of life collapse and leave us covered in plaster. Satie's house looks like a house of crime. That man was a Saint. Even we failed to appreciate him fully, for there was always something noble underlying his whims.

Nothing new concerning *Paul [et Virginie]*. I received a very good letter from [Satie's] brother.

Darius is better. He is out and about. He looked dreadful but one has to put that down to exhaustion from the trip to Egypt.[1]

As for me, I am going through a fit of unspeakable fatigue.

I embrace you,
Jean

I do not have the exact address of the Picassos. They are still at Juan-les-Pins.

93. JEAN COCTEAU TO FRANCIS POULENC

Welcome [Hotel], Villefranche-sur-mer, [September] 1925

Cher Francis,

1. My idleness comes from thinking of those I love whilst lying in the sun in my dinghy out in the bay.

2. Just imagine, I am working. I cannot wait for your *Marches*[1] and the *Caprice italien*[2] which Lucien [Daudet] raves about.

I correct proof after proof. I see a lot of Igor. I have seen the Picassos. Théodore is doing my portrait and Soukalski sports his spats and little ebony cane (shepherdess's crook) between Nice and Villefranche.

Surprise! I have finished *Orphée*. I think you will be pleased. I have illustrated *Le Grand Ecart* and *Thomas*. I have written a little book on religion.[3] What a pity you do not live on the coast.

Serge spent two days in Monte Carlo. Didn't see him.

I embrace you,

Jean

94. DARIUS MILHAUD TO FRANCIS POULENC

[Summer, 1925]

Mon cher Francis,

Things are a little better and I am gradually getting back to normal. I am undergoing X-ray treatment for nagging neuritis that keeps plaguing me. I am working a little. I have begun *Esther*.[1]

The weather is exquisite here and it is a great pity that you are having black skies and rain. Next week we might take a quick trip down to the coast.

Bathori spent two days here, on her way back from Chamonix to Cannet. The Collaers left Basle by bicycle, finally arriving in Nice, stopping all along the way. Terrifying!

I have done the four-hand version of *Cinéma* from *Relâche*.[2]

If you are too cold in your Touraine come and warm yourself down here.

We shall be returning at the end of September in the Citroën. If the weather is good and my health better we may drop in on you.

The Lunels arrived yesterday. I am going to see them in a short while.[3]

Let me know what you are doing. Where is Georges [Auric]?

Warmest greetings from us both.

Darius

95. FRANCIS POULENC TO VALENTINE HUGO

Nazelles (Indre-et-Loire), 25 September 1925

Chère Valentine,

How are you? I have been wanting to write to you for some time but you know my epistolary laziness, especially when I am working a lot. Were your ears not burning the day before yesterday, for we spoke a great deal about you with the chatelaines of La Roche.[1] Lucien [Daudet] is in charming humour this year and of rare cordiality, particularly where I am concerned. As for you, your fortunes are on the rise: '*Bonne Valentine* this, *bonne Valentine* that', 'Jean [Hugo] has so much talent', 'They are so nice' etc. I do not know if we are to attribute this good humour to Ferras who, as you can well imagine, is the blue-eyed boy of the house. Between you and me, I don't find him all that bright, but I do think he is very nice to Lucien and, above all, admirably amenable.

Madame Ferras came to tea at Nazelles with Lucien and Edouard. I hadn't met her before. She is a very worthy woman and not a bit affected. Méméia [Mme Alphonse Daudet] is delighted with the whole arrangement.

To give you an idea of just how relaxed Lucien is, one can speak about Drian in front of him again, and about Madeleine Le Chevrel,[2] and even about the de Meyers!!![3]

Talking of strained relations, I received a charming note from Etienne [de Beaumont] thanking me for writing when his mother died. I hope this puts an end to our misunderstanding.

As you must know from Auric I am working hard. I have finished a long piece for piano, *Caprice italien*, in the style of the *Bourrée fantasque*. I am rather pleased with it. Anyway, I think it is quite effective – as a test I played it to Lucien and he immediately exclaimed: '*Quelle évolution, quel épanouissement!*'* I hope he is not mistaken. I am finishing my Trio now, very much like *Les Biches* only better, and I am continuing with the *Marches militaires* MAINLY for you.

How lucky you are to have *le gros Auric* with you. I am jealous because I miss him very much. I dare to hope that this is to some extent reciprocal. Tell him to write to me quickly. *Les Matelots*, which I know TO THE LAST NOTE, makes him ever present.[4] Tell me about his ballet. Tell me also what you are doing. Has Jean completed his Ciné work, and is your Herculean task over?

Write to me soon and send me photographs, if you have any. I have not heard from Cocteau for ages. Perhaps you are more favoured than I. You know that Darius is extremely well now. I am expecting the Peignots on

*Literally, 'What development, what burgeoning.'

3 October for the weekend. When will you come to Nazelles? Waiting to hear from you, I embrace you, as well as Jean and Auric. My regards to your grandmother.

Votre Biche
Poulet

96. MAX JACOB TO FRANCIS POULENC

St-Benoît-les-Gouaches (Loiret), 30 March 1926

Francis,

I sent you *Le Pénitent en maillot*[1] [sic] but the Post is becoming rather Soviet, and of thirty volumes despatched by the publishing firm of Kra itself, barely twenty reached their destination safely (and for this the taxpayer pays). I will try again.

I would certainly come to Clavary if I were not submerged: gouaches, more gouaches, and that mania for illustrations that grips publishers – with commissioning me to do them. This is all the more ridiculous as I do not have the slightest idea of how to set about such work – need untransportable photos – a whole arsenal for combat. In addition to these plastic arts there are all the Gallimards of this world, and all the reviews, etc. So I shall not be coming to Clavary. And besides, one is too happy there – a bad thing for that Paradise I yearn to reach through the martyrdom of thorns. The thorns I yearn for are, of course, the thorns of St-Benoît.

I am going to Paris one of these days to marry off a convert of mine. I shall go back there in May, if you are there . . . You can come to St-Benoît where I will be locked in a *tête-à-tête* with a novel that has been dragging on for two years and that represents, at the moment, the very thorns mentioned above. You are extremely lucky to have so much talent. What I call 'having talent' is not having to tear one's guts out to write the least triviality. With the result that one no longer writes anything, so as not to catch enteritis, appendicitis or even peritonitis. What I call 'having talent' is being like the young peasant girl who gave such a bright retort to her suitor:

> The peasant: 'I swear to you, Marie, that I will not be unfaithful to you with any of the others.'
>
> The peasant girl: 'And I, Joseph, swear to myself that I will not be unfaithful to any of the others with you'!

Marivaux himself could not have thought of a better *marivaudage*.[2]

A hundred thousand regards, and my sincere compliments to Madame Liénard.

Max

I am sending you my copy, my very own copy, my only copy.

If you see Gouy and Greeley,[3] tell them that they are as dear to me as my own blood, my skin, my pen and Poetry itself.

97. FRANCIS POULENC TO SERGE DE DIAGHILEV

83 rue de Monceau, Paris, [June 1926]

Cher Diaghilev,

You must have heard through the grapevine that Madame Croiza,[1] Maestro Auric and I myself will be giving a prestigious concert on Tuesday 5 July (5.15 p.m.) at the home of Baroness d'Erlanger[2] – quite an occasion, don't you think? I will be playing the famous Trio that you have not yet heard. Needless to say, we are *absolutely counting on you* to give us some publicity. I am even going to ask you to do us a little favour which I believe to be well within your power. I am going to send you 300 to 400 publicity leaflets and ask you to slip them into your programmes or to distribute them in the theatre or whatever you like. If this is impossible, make a bonfire out of them and let's not mention it again.

Vr. Rieti[3] is delighted with London. We are due to arrive on the 2nd with . . . Monsieur Sauguet! A good opportunity for you to put on a French production on the evening of the 4th or 5th or 6th, using our combined names.

Also, what would you think of a number for the interval, in front of the curtain: *Waltzes by Chabrier* played by Messrs Auric and Poulenc (fee £15 for both of us)?[+] We could even borrow some of the costumes from *Les Biches* – Auric, Nikitina's and I, Sokolova's.[4] Anyway, think about all this and send me a *quick* reply to my multiple questions via Boris [Kochno].

Your loyal and ever-loving
Poupoule

Rieti tells me that you have put on *Les Biches* again in London. Thank you.[5]

[+] Auric says that £12 would be better as it is easier to share.

98. WANDA LANDOWSKA TO FRANCIS POULENC

Hotel Great Northern, 118 West 57th St., New York City, 19 January 1927

Bien cher ami,

How often have I thought of you recently during the rehearsals of Falla's Concerto![1] I have just given two first performances of it in Boston and a third in New York with Koussevitzky,[2] as well as two others in Philadelphia with

Stokowski.[3] Koussevitzky was marvellous – we are planning a Paris première of the Concerto in the spring.[4]

I am writing to you in haste, between rushing from one town to another. But this is what is happening: I have spoken to Koussevitzky about your *Concert champêtre*.[5] He is already very attracted to it and he wants to perform it with me next winter in Boston and New York. I would be very happy to do so, but . . . there is one condition! I would need to have the music in hand, or rather under my fingers, by the end of May or the beginning of June. I have suffered too greatly from the tortures of waiting, and from the resulting anxieties, to go through another similar martyrdom. Please reply to me as soon as possible in New York. I shall be back in Saint-Leu[6] at the end of April and we could then work through it together at the harpsichord and add all the finishing touches.

I hope you are well, and I send you, dear friend, my warmest thoughts.

Wanda Landowska

P.S. I am also writing to Honegger and Auric.

99. FRANCIS POULENC TO IGOR STRAVINSKY

Monday morning [30 May 1927]

Cher Stravinsky,

I could not find anything to say to you last night to express my enthusiasm.[1] I feel it will be the same tonight. Yet I desperately want you to know into what state of *superior* emotion I was plunged last night. Your art has reached such a height that it would need the language of Sophocles himself to describe it. Heavens, how beautiful it is! Allow me to embrace you. Which is a rare honour for me. Your faithful

Poulenc

100. FRANCIS POULENC TO MANUEL DE FALLA

Tuesday morning [Paris, 7 June 1927]

Cher Falla,

Forgive my silence but since the première of *Oedipe* I have been in bed with terrible tonsillitis, a burning throat and a raging temperature that have left me utterly exhausted. I have a great favour to ask of you. This coming Thursday I was due to accompany my friend Mme Charles Peignot in your *Chansons espagnoles* (she is the niece of the pianist whom you know).[1] This young woman – whom I think Robert Lyon introduced you to the other day – sings REMARKABLY WELL. She has given the first performances of several of Auric's works, of my poems by Ronsard, of Satie's latest *mélodies*, etc. Would you be good enough to accompany the *Chansons* at five o'clock at Mme Juge's – 45 rue de Beaune? Will you send your reply directly to: Mme Charles Peignot, 5 quai Voltaire (the house is jointly owned by her aunt) letting her know if you can rehearse with her on Thursday morning at about 11.30. I think you will be pleased to hear this very fine musician and she will certainly be extremely proud to sing with you.[2]

Thank you in advance, *très cher ami*. I cannot write any more as I am very tired.

Your faithful
Poulenc

Mme Peignot's telephone number is: Littré 22–69. This could save you having to write.

101. WANDA LANDOWSKA TO FRANCIS POULENC

Saint-Leu, 2 August 1928

Cher Ami,

Hardly had you gone than I began to study, to examine in depth, the first movement of your beautiful Concerto. I am longing to see you again, for there are a hundred and one things worrying me and we ought to spend days together at the harpsichord, discussing them. So I will expect you, as you promised, next week, not on Monday 6th which is the day of my class, but on Sunday 5th or Tuesday 7th. Please bring me not only the Andante but the Finale as well. It is essential that I have the entire Concerto, as Ansermet, who came to Saint-Leu last Sunday, told me that the dates of 26 and 28 October had been fixed.[1] This has caused me some anxiety, for since you told me that those two dates had been postponed till the end of November, I saw myself with enough time to compensate, in a way, for your unfortunate delay in giving me your Concerto, for which I have been waiting since May. Ansermet has to print his final programmes between 10 and 12 August. So I will barely have the time to familiarize myself with the two movements which I do not yet know.

Goodbye then, *Cher Ami*, until Sunday 5th or Tuesday 7th without fail. Please keep free several entire, consecutive days, so that we can work seriously.

Affectionately,
Wanda Landowska

102. WANDA LANDOWSKA TO FRANCIS POULENC

Saint-Leu, 5 September 1928

Cher Ami,

I have just this minute received the two sections of your Finale. I fell upon them voraciously, only to find that they are very difficult! *Mon Dieu! Mon Dieu!* Whatever shall I do? Why are you so late with it all?

I am filled with a mixture of eagerness and terror at the thought of that third section which you introduce by two bars, left suspended on a blank page . . .

I am busy fingering certain passages *that are perfect.* But, for goodness' sake, do not delay! Goodbye, until Saturday!

I am waiting, dear friend.

Affectionately,

W.L.

Herewith the confirmation that you requested in your letter of 20 August.

103. FRANCIS POULENC TO CHARLES KOECHLIN

Le Grand Coteau, Noizay, Indre-et-Loire, Tuesday [1929]

Cher Koechlin,

What joy your letter gave me, and if it has taken me this long to reply, only my epistolary laziness is to blame.

Believe me when I tell you that however much joy it gave me to read your news, so much greater would that joy be on seeing you. I think of you often. You have planted within me a seed that I am doing my utmost to raise in the best possible way. I have read your treatises, which are marvellous.[1] How many times while composing a bar of music have I not recalled the '*too much movement*' or the '*not enough*' from the time of our lessons.

I shall be spending all of May and June in Paris. I hope you will not be in America at that time. Wanda Landowska is to play my Concerto for harpsichord [*Concert champêtre*] with the Paris Symphony Orchestra on 3 May. In June there will be a performance of my *Aubade*[2] for piano and eighteen instruments. I would so much like you to hear these two latest works.

As I am incurring enormous expense at the moment with the refurbishing of my new house in Touraine,[3] I readily accept your offer to return the small sum it gave me such pleasure to lend you some time ago. You can send me the amount by cheque; but I do not *at any cost* want to hear you speaking about adding interest – that would hurt me *horribly*.[4]

I am much looking forward to seeing you again, and send you my warmest regards.

Francis Poulenc

104. WANDA LANDOWSKA TO FRANCIS POULENC

In the train to Boulogne [May 1929]

Mon Ami, your letter moves me deeply.[1] Be happy and *live* your happiness to the full. I am also very pleased to have contributed to your joy. Write to me at the Hôtel Plaza, Buenos Aires, until I can give you my definite address. Keep in contact with Saint-Leu and my two dear children, so alone.[2]

Your flowers are beside me, fresh and beautiful. Your beloved concerto resounds and reverberates within me.

I embrace you tenderly,

Wanda

105. HENRI SAUGUET TO FRANCIS POULENC

1 rue du Poids-de-l'Huile, Toulouse, 14 August 1929

Mon cher ami,

I have received your *Concert champêtre* and am extremely touched that you sent it to me. What madness, what hateful gossip could have made you believe that I did not care about you any more! We hardly saw each other in Paris this winter: neither of us was there, and if I was not present at the performance of your *Aubade*[1] it was because I had left Paris for Germany, drawn not by the Russian Ballet but by a tormenting and tormented love which I had to calm at all cost! But, *mon cher ami*, how can we possibly believe everything that is said about the other! I still feel for you the same attachment, the same loyal and deep affection that I have always had for you and I would be extremely sad to learn that I had ever offended or betrayed you. I know there has been much gleeful repetition of Diaghilev's words after the performance of the *Concert* [*champêtre*] by the Paris Symphony Orchestra when he declared that what had amused him most was how green with envy, jealousy and resentment Auric and I looked! . . . Is this what you were told? Alas! that wretched man has been able to sow discord and hatred around him his whole life: today, don't you agree, the venom of this beastly creature has been exposed and will not succeed in causing conflict between us. In any event, if our friendship might suffer from the rumours people love to spread, my devotion to your music will never be anything other than profound and entire: it touches me too deeply in the best parts of my heart and spirit for it to be otherwise.

Where are you at the moment, what are you doing? Have you succeeded in finding the inner peace you were seeking? I have not been unaware of the difficult and depressing times you have been through. With all my heart I hope that this is now no more than a bad memory and that good days have succeeded the bad. Are you working? At what? I'd be so glad to hear your good news and to see that our friendship has not suffered from a long separation and from the lies of certain people.

As for me, I am working here on *La Chartreuse*[2] and making headway very slowly – too slowly. I would also like to write for the piano, but here there is a secret to be discovered . . . and it is one that still eludes me. Besides, I am very troubled at the moment and it is often impossible for me to write for days on end.

I was very sorry not to have been able to hear your *Aubade*. But I suppose it will be performed again this winter? I believe it is extremely lovely and moving.

My dear friend, tell me that all these clouds have been dispelled. I think that Rouart-Lerolle and Co. have sent out *Le Plumet du colonel* and the 'Schillers'.[3] If not, I will post them to you immediately.

Please continue to believe in my deep and faithful friendship. And thank you with all my heart for the *Concert champêtre*. I shall try to recreate once again on my piano all the emotion and the pleasure I experienced when you first played it to me and then when I heard it this spring. I remain your friend,

Henri Sauguet

106. MANUEL DE FALLA TO FRANCIS POULENC

Granada, 26 September 1929

What joy, my dear Poulenc, to have your Concerto [*Concert champêtre*] – at last! I read it with the keen delight that your music always gives me.

Now I await the happy moment of hearing it and talking to you about your use of the harpsichord. You can imagine how much this will interest me, especially after hearing a good, complete performance of the work. OUR Trio,[1] by the way, has just had an extraordinary success here . . .

The records[2] certainly do the work justice. Everything can be heard with marvellous clarity. And what interpreters . . . beginning with your-self!

I hope to be able to find two good soloists for a *live* performance.

Affectionately yours,

Manuel de Falla

I presume you have received my concerto by now. If not, please let me know so that I can have another copy sent to you.

107. FRANCIS POULENC TO MANUEL DE FALLA

83 rue de Monceau, Paris, [March 1930]

Mon cher Falla,

I am delighted to tell you the good news: I shall be coming to Spain at the beginning of April to give – in *Madrid* – a lecture-concert in which I will play 'your' trio, some piano pieces, and my harpsichord Concerto (with two pianos). Can you do me an immense favour and suggest *by return of post*: a good oboist, a good bassoonist, and a good pianist capable of playing the orchestral part of the Concerto on a second piano.

Perhaps you have a pupil in Madrid who would do this for me, or who would approach the necessary people for me, and to whom I could then send the musical parts for distribution.

I shall also be repeating this lecture-concert in Barcelona and Bilbao. To whom should I write in these two places? Please brief me on all this as soon as possible as it is urgent.

Furthermore, I have decided to make the most of this trip to Spain and to stay on for a while in order to work. Naturally, I have chosen *Granada* for this so as to be near you, for you know that my admiration for you is equalled only by my great affection. I shall be arriving in Granada straight from Madrid on Saturday 12 April, and I hope to remain there for five weeks. Where do you advise me to stay – somewhere fairly close to you and where I will be tolerated with a piano? (I hope to be able to hire a piano fairly easily in Granada.) I would need *two rooms* as a painter friend of mine[1] will be joining me after Easter to share my working holiday. If you know of a private family who would rent us *two rooms*, that would be ideal. We will of course be eating out all the time.

Should the opportunity arise during my stay there (beginning of May), to play my new Concerto for piano and 18 instruments [*Aubade*] with the Orquesta Bética[2] – or anywhere else in Barcelona – nothing would suit me better as, being already on the spot, I could ask for a reasonable fee.

For all this I place myself entirely in your hands.

My dear Falla, I am sorry to put you to all this trouble but I am so happy at the thought of spending this time near you. I much look forward to hearing from you.

With many thanks, and warmest regards,

Francis Poulenc

What is most urgent is the question of *Madrid*.

108. MANUEL DE FALLA TO FRANCIS POULENC

Granada, 13 March 1930

Delighted with your news, my dear Poulenc, but at the same time I deeply regret that your stay in Granada unfortunately coincides with my absence for about two months from the beginning of April. But I hope to be still in Paris when you return, and this consoles me for missing the wonderful occasion of your visit here.

I have been unwell (seriously so) and am still subject to a very strict regimen of isolation and silence in an attempt to recover completely before my departure. My doctor has formally forbidden all correspondence and that is the reason for this *machinerie*[1] – as well as for the brevity of this letter and its *complément* by my sister, who will be writing to you about the steps I have already taken on your behalf, reported in my telegram of this morning.

Affectionately yours,

Manuel de Falla

We may perhaps even see each other in Spain (in Seville or in Barcelona). I do hope so!!

109. WANDA LANDOWSKA TO FRANCIS POULENC

Saint-Leu-la-Forêt, 24 August 1930

Cher ami,

We cannot understand your silence at all. Set our minds at rest immediately.

I am happy to be able to tell you that I have succeeded in arranging for the performance of your *Concert* [*champêtre*] in London, on 21 January 1931, at the Queen's Hall, for the BBC, the most important radio in the world.[1] As soon as I know who will be conducting, I will let you know. Negotiations with Spain are continuing. Pérez Casas' association is very hard up and I have written to Pérez Casas[2] to say that, in order to make Poulenc's concerto known, I would accept exceptionally modest fees. I advise you to take the necessary steps regarding Madrid and Barcelona (Casals' orchestra)[3] where I have been pressing for the *Concert champêtre* as well. It is also probable that I will play it in Amsterdam. I will keep you informed.

Have you not received my letter in which I spoke of my friend Pitts Sanborn, whom I have asked to do a study on you?

Write to me soon.

Affectionately,
Your Wanda

Embrace your delightful aunt for me!

110. WANDA LANDOWSKA TO FRANCIS POULENC

Saint-Leu-la-Forêt, [1930?]

Mon cher Ami,

I simply cannot understand your silence. Haven't you received any of my letters? (There have been at least four or five.) I would be worried if I had not heard through one of your lady friends who had just seen you, that you are perfectly well. But, my dear Monster, how can you be perfectly well, having forgotten me to this extent . . . ?

The first rehearsal went very well. Will you come on Sunday to hear a certain *Concert champêtre* that I adore? And do you know why I adore it? Because it makes me feel totally CAREFREE AND LIGHTHEARTED!

Quickly, a sign of life, if not of affection, for otherwise this is the very last time I shall write to you.

With my love,
Your Wanda

We shall be rehearsing again on Saturday and Sunday at 9.30 a.m.

111. MARIE LAURENCIN TO FRANCIS POULENC

1, rue Savorgnan de Brazza, Paris 7ᵉ, 1931

Mon cher Francis,

Thank you very much indeed.

What is more, after leaving you at Madame de Castries's, I went straight to *Il y a*[1] by Guillaume Apollinaire. Looking at your charming score I saw that you had also set to music the three poems of Louise Lalanne. Of these three poems two are by me, 'Hier' and 'Le Présent'.[2]

Eugène Montfort, at that time the editor of *Les Marges*,[3] had the idea of hoodwinking his readers by inventing a bogus poetess. Of course, Guillaume agreed, delighted by the whole idea. At the time of going to press, Guillaume – who was idleness itself – had done nothing; and I remember we hunted through my schoolbooks, naturally full of nonsense, and ended up by finding those two early efforts, 'Hier' and 'Le Présent', which are nothing at all out of the ordinary.

If I write this to you, Francis, it is not to vindicate anything. Guillaume Apollinaire only took himself seriously in little, inconsequential matters – cooking, small-talk – and never in matters of importance.

When it came to life and poetry he was sublime, and possessed such a gift of second sight that I often prefer to bury myself within my four walls rather than approach the subject of Guillaume – a man misunderstood even by his most illustrious contemporaries, who never ever cared a damn about him.

And there you have it.

I embrace you with all my heart, my dear Francis.

Your old friend
Marie Laurencin

112. FRANCIS POULENC TO SUZANNE PEIGNOT

Le Grand Coteau, Noizay (Indre-et-Loire), [5 March 1931]

Chérie,

I have just booked the Salle Chopin for a Poulenc Festival on the evening of 1 June.

Here is my programme:

I   Sonata for two clarinets.
II   *Cocardes* with instruments
      Suzanne Peignot.
III   *Quatre poèmes d'Apollinaire* for baritone
      Gilbert Moryn – First performance.[1]
IV   Sextet for piano and winds –
      First performance.[2]
V   Piano pieces
VI   *Trois poèmes de Louise Lalanne*
      Suzanne Peignot – First performance.
VII   Trio.

What do you think of it? Good, isn't it? As I require *ten* instruments to satisfy my orchestral needs you will understand that I cannot exactly cover you in gold for this performance, which I am organizing at my own expense. If you will accept 300 francs towards your travelling costs, that will be perfect. Besides, it will be a very good thing for you from every point of view as I am hoping to have a full house and an elegant one at that. From now on, I am taking care of *everything* myself.

Seats at 50 francs and 30 francs, *and no complimentary tickets.* I shall give you for your own use four tickets numbered in advance, which is much better as we are then certain of what we are offering. I shall do the same for the press and for one or two musicians. This is the only way of avoiding dissatisfaction while making sure of the takings.

As for the instrumentalists – only the best: Darrieux, Dhérin, Lamorlette, Cahuzac, etc. etc.

As you can imagine, this will not exactly work out cheaply but I thought it was the only way of adding glamour to my first performances.

In all my spare moments I am now addressing envelopes made with beautiful paper, which will be stamped at half a franc and sent to all the appropriate people. In this way I am in direct contact with my public.

I would like to recreate the atmosphere of that famous concert (Trio – *Gaillardes*) at Les Agriculteurs.[3]

Will you let me know immediately whether I can count on you. Contact me by telephone any morning around nine o'clock.

I hope that *everything* is well with you. As for me, I am keeping busy, working and enjoying the quiet.

Des millions de tendresses ma chérie.

Francis

---

113. HENRI SAUGUET TO FRANCIS POULENC

55 rue Nollet, Paris 17ᵉ, 28 March 1931

Mon cher ami,

I have just seen Jean Cocteau. He informed me that you have given up the idea of writing the music for *Paul et Virginie* and are leaving the libretto to me.[1] I was extremely touched and want to express my immense gratitude to you. Thank you with all my heart, my dear friend, for this mark of friendship and confidence which I greatly appreciate.

Jean tells me that the only fully corrected libretto is in your hands. Will you be good enough to send it to me, please. I will have it copied and will return it to you if you like, as you may be attached to it. But I would like you to send it as soon as possible as I want to start working on it immediately. I am leaving for Toulouse on Tuesday and that is where I would ask you to send it to me, at the following address:

1 rue du Poids-de-l'Huile.

Thank you again, *mon cher ami*. I shall be very happy to write the music for this *opéra-comique* and proud that you have assigned this magnificent job to me.

Your loyal friend,

Henri Sauguet

114. FRANCIS POULENC TO HENRI SAUGUET

Noizay, 31 March 1931

Mon cher Sauguet,

A thousand thanks for your very kind letter. I want you to know that it is with much joy that I bequeath *Paul et Virginie* to you. The libretto is full of memories, too full of memories, and this is one of the reasons that made me decide to distance myself from it.

You are the only one worthy of touching this sacred memento because you loved Satie and admired Raymond [Radiguet]. And only you, with your disregard – so rare today – for what is fashionable, will know how to create from this timeless libretto a score that is free from the '1931 tone' (in the worst sense of the word).

My dear Henri, I wish you luck with all my heart. How impatiently I await the first performance of this work which I have so long dreamed of. Rest assured that you will find no more zealous protector of your offspring.[1]

I am working hard. I will be giving a Poulenc Festival on June 1st at the Salle Chopin:

Cocardes with instrumental accompaniment and the Sonata for two clarinets will represent what I love of the past; my present trend will be represented in the first performance of two song cycles on texts by Apollinaire, a Sextet for piano and wind, and a series of pieces for piano. I am very pleased with my songs, veritable *Cocardes* of 1931.

What's more, I am feeling very much on form at the moment. I don't know what the musicians or the public will think, but I don't give a damn, for I know that *I am right*. It is more courageous to grow just as one is than to force-feed one's flowers with the fertilizer of fashion.

I have a profound admiration for Hindemith[2] but am wary of his *ricochets*.

In any case, you can be sure that if my latest works are lucky enough to please you *sincerely*, it will mean a lot to me. What does public opinion matter after that?

Work well, and do write.

Your most devoted friend
Poulenc

Please drop me a line to let me know that this precious envelope has arrived. I would in fact like to keep this copy of *Paul*. So have it typed and return it to me as you kindly suggest.

115. FRANCIS POULENC TO IGOR STRAVINSKY

Le Grand Coteau, Noizay, Indre-et-Loire, Holy Thursday [3 April 1931]

Mon cher Stravinsky,

I am sending you a short article I have written on your *Symphony*.[1] Accept it as I offer it – as a small testimony of my admiration and affection.

I am working hard. On 1 June (Salle Chopin) I am giving a concert of new chamber works. If you come, I beg a great deal of indulgence in advance.

Do not forget your promise to visit me here this spring. Lots of good wine and affection await you.

I hope your family is well. Thanks to your records, I am often with you.

I send you, my dear Stravinsky, my warmest regards.

Fr. Poulenc

116. IGOR STRAVINSKY TO FRANCIS POULENC

Nice, 6 April 1931

Mon cher Poulenc, very touched by your note and the article on my *Symphony of Psalms*. I could not have wished for a better Easter present. You are truly good, and that is what I always find again and again in your music. May God protect you.

I may be in Paris at the end of May. If so, I will certainly come to your concert.

Your Igor Stravinsky

117. COLETTE TO FRANCIS POULENC

La Treille Muscate, Route des Cannebiers, Saint-Tropez (Var), [Summer, 1931]

Cher Francis, what lovely notepaper you have! Write more letters like that to me, on a big sheet of paper all lined and dotted with music. Thank you. I do not have a piano here but I am applying myself to re-reading 'l'Anguille' and the other charming *Poèmes*.[1] Yes, I am thinking about 'l'Ombre'.[2] Can't you visualize it as a rather short cinematographic sketch? (I am an old professor from the provinces!)[3] One that begins in lounge suits in a bourgeois setting, then passes with a single leap into the realm of the fantastic when the young girl opens the garden door and her shadow, no longer projected on the wallpaper of the sitting-room, soars into the garden – becoming enormous, of course – and the young man follows her. Do you think we could have it in 1880 dress? Anyway, we will talk about it all when we meet.

The weather here is just as one imagines it to be in Tahiti. What confidence in the day and in the morrow and the day after tomorrow! The newspapers speak of nothing but rainstorms and tornadoes, yet since 12 July I have been in a golden blueness that seems likely to last forever. The bathing, the sand, the figs, the garlic – oh! the garlic! – and the mild, white, sweet onions, the aubergine, the basil . . . merely to name them is to make music.

There is a typographical error in '1904'.[4] The eighth line should read: 'Come Hébé *qui les dieux servait*' and not 'que les dieux servaient'.[5] Perhaps you have already corrected it.

My love to you. I shall be returning on 15 September (Hôtel Claridge). Maurice Goudeket sends you his love too.

Your old friend,
Colette

Think of the grape-harvesting.

118. MAX JACOB TO FRANCIS POULENC

Le Nollet 55, 11 December 1931

Cher Poulenc,

You know that I am really very flattered to have inspired you. I say this entirely sincerely and not just to be polite.

Call No. V quite simply 'Souric et Mouric'.[1]

Of course you may include 'La Dauphine' in *Le Bal masqué*.[2] I authorize whatever your precious fancy dictates, O Master. That my name will have appeared beside yours will be my only claim to fame.

A hundred thousand regards from your fervent admirer.

Max Jacob

I shall give your kind message to Sauguet and Rieti.

119. MANUEL DE FALLA TO FRANCIS POULENC

Granada, 5 January 1932

Très cher Poulenc,

My best wishes for a happy New Year and a great thank-you for the joy you have brought by sending me the score of *Aubade* and of the *Concert champêtre*, which now more than ever I long to hear.

Aubade is well suited to the instrumental possibilities of the chamber orchestra of Seville (Orquesta Bética), and I have warmly recommended it to them. Their only fear is of the financial difficulties in hiring the parts, as the orchestra has extremely limited means. I would ask you to kindly warn the publishers of this . . .

I cannot forget your rendering of your latest songs. I count this among the greatest of all the joys that music has given me of late. That and Auric's beautiful Sonata have brightened the dark days brought on by my recent eye trouble . . .[1]

Can you give me Auric's present address? I am not sure if he received the signed copy of my Concerto which I requested the firm of Eschig to send him.

Yours

Manuel de Falla

120. FRANCIS POULENC TO MANUEL DE FALLA

Le Grand Coteau, Noizay, Indre-et-Loire, 17 February 1932

Cher Falla,

Forgive my long silence but I have been travelling so much since the beginning of the year that I have constantly had to put off writing this letter, offering warmest good wishes for 1932. You cannot imagine my joy on seeing your beautiful handwriting. I immediately assume that your eyes and your health are much better; and I picture you at work, for our future delectation, in that adorable house, every detail of which springs to mind the moment I close my eyes.

You cannot believe how I yearn for Spain, and though various considerations may prevent my returning there this year, I shall not be able to resist going next winter. I must confess that of all the countries I know, apart from my own, it is the only one that affects me in this way. Your music, which I have always loved, evokes Spain so vividly for me (just as Debussy's does France) that often in the evening, to the sound of the gramophone, my thoughts wander towards the Calle Darro, the Albaicín and the Generalife gardens of Granada.

I am so touched by all you say about my songs. You will soon be receiving a new collection. I hope that the last one (the fifth song) will please you, as it is one of my favourites.[1]

I have spoken to Rouart about *Aubade* and they have promised to be very modest in their demands. It is a great honour for me to have my work played by the Orquesta Bética. I hope you will one day come and stay with me in Touraine, as I know you like this region. You will find a house full of sunlight and gentleness, *à la* Ronsard.[2]

May I ask you something very indiscreet? One day, but only when you have the time and the energy, will you be good enough to send me a page of rough work or a scrap of manuscript that I will then have framed to bring luck both to my house and to my work. This will give me immense joy. But only if it does not put you out.

Auric's present address is: St Bernard, Hyères, Var. He now has a house in that lovely region, where he goes to work.

Dear Falla, please give my compliments to your sister who will, I trust, remember me.

Your admiring friend
Francis Poulenc

I do not have the pocket scores of the three dances from *El Sombrero de tres picos* and of *El Amor brujo*. When you write to Chester's please ask them to send these to me. I dare not ask them myself.

121. FRANCIS POULENC TO PAUL COLLAER

Noizay, 1 October 1932

Cher Paul,

Thank you for your letter. I am always delighted when I recognize your writing on the envelope. Everything you tell me about *Aubade*, *Les Biches*, and the Max Jacob settings makes me extremely happy, but I am very despondent about *Le Bal masqué* as I was absolutely counting on performing it at the Pro Arte[1] concert on 8 December. I have not played [in Belgium] for three years and I was so looking forward to it. Can you perhaps include the *Gaillardes* in the concert for the new Society [Philharmonic Society of Brussels] and the *Bal* in the concert on the 8th? I need not remind you that the question of a fee is not important; I would do it for nothing.

Le Bal, very brilliantly orchestrated, is just as suitable for 30 musicians as for a chamber concert. It is a much bigger and more violent work than my piano reduction for two hands might suggest. From the point of view of sound quality, one could quite happily skip, for example, from the *Partita* to *Le Bal*. Try to organize it, as this little trip is something I was really looking forward to. I would also have liked to hear the Roussel quartet that is being performed, I think, on the 7th or the 9th at Le Boeuf's concert.[2]

I am delighted that my Concerto for two pianos[3] is already being talked about in Belgium. I'll admit quite immodestly that it did in fact stun everyone at the Festival. Even poor old Pruneton[4] in this week's issue of *Les Nouvelles littéraires* had to acknowledge that it got a 'triumphant reception'. You will see for yourself what an enormous step forward it is from my previous work and that I am really entering my great period. You will also recognize that the germs of this progression are in the *Concert champêtre* and in *Aubade*, which were two essential stages in my development. It is possible that, in these two concertos, my concern for technical perfection – especially in the orchestration – might have diverted me from the true nature of my music; but it was necessary, and you will see for yourself with what a 'precise' pen I have orchestrated *Le Bal* and the Concerto, which I assure you are absolutely pure Poulenc. I must pay tribute to Defauw,[5] who conducted quite remarkably, and to the Toscanini orchestra [Scala Orchestra] about whom there can be no reservations . . .

I have of course promised Defauw the first performance in Brussels, so the Radio will have to wait awhile for the Concerto, which has not been published yet in any case. There is no need to tell *you*, my friend of so many years, how much pleasure it will give me the day I hear it performed by you. I would so much like to have a good long chat about it all in Brussels. So do try to organize the matter of *Le Bal*, and let me know quickly what response you get, for I have a very busy winter ahead.

With warm regards to you and Elsa.

Francis

How happy I am that you like Georges' [Auric] Sonata [for piano].

122. FRANCIS POULENC TO COMTESSE JEAN DE POLIGNAC

Noizay, [1932]

Marie-Blanche,

I was so hoping you would come here, even if only for one evening! I am sad and upset that you chose the train rather than Poupoule's house. We could have discussed the Sextet which – as I understood on the telephone – particularly interests you. You know how I love to please you and how, had things been different, I would have dropped everything to finish this work quickly for the opening of the Salon des Antiques. Unfortunately, I have so many problems at the moment that assignments *must* come first. So please do not hold it against me if I continually put off completing a work for which I am certain not to find a publisher.[1]

Just imagine – no one at the moment is even interested in the Concerto of this summer, despite the press and the success.[2] I am well aware that one has to keep working for love of art but there are nevertheless moments when one has to think of the next bit of coal and the next pork chop. On the brink of a winter without any commissions, I find myself forced to 'write for piano' which is what all these 'Publisher-Gentlemen' want.[3] All this is not the best of news, but I wanted to tell you lest you should think it was not my wish to please you, which would upset me very much.

The Aurics came to see me last Sunday. I really adore them. You cannot imagine how enriching I find Georges' intelligence. He is going to come here for a month to work. I am greatly looking forward to this study break.

You will be seeing me in Paris around the 9th. I am in fact recording *Les Gaillardes* for Columbia. I shall be staying for three or four days with dear old *grand Georges* as opposed to *gros Georges*.[4] I also need to see your aunt to make the arrangements for the première of the Concerto.[5]

Ma petite Marie-Blanche, I embrace you and *le Comte Jean*, too.

Your
Poupoule

123. PIERRE BERNAC TO FRANCIS POULENC

[Salzburg, August 1934]

Mon cher Poulenc,

I have been asked to sing some Debussy in three days' time. Would you agree to accompany me? Handsome fee. Give me your reply quickly.[1]

Very cordially yours,
Bernac

124. FRANCIS POULENC TO SUZANNE PEIGNOT

Nazelles, Sunday [30 September 1934]

Mon trésor,

You are to me exactly what you say I am to you, and you are the *only* person in the world who is like a *sister* to me. I always open your letters with joy, and it is with even more delight that I watch the road for your arrival.

Since Salzburg I have thought of you a great deal, *in many different ways*, and I consider you now to be at a decisive turning-point in your career. This is why I want to help you and why I think that the Ronsards[1] will be for you what the Concerto was for Jacques [Février].

I have already orchestrated three of them and I am beginning the last two. I am sure they will be *very good* for although they are for a *large* orchestra I am trying not to drown the voice.

I have just suggested to Morel the first performance for Lamoureux. I have also written to Lyons and to Brussels.

I am hoping that next September we can organize a Promenade Concert for you in London (broadcast throughout the world).[2] We will also try Geneva. You see we have a lot on our plate.

Another thing you can do is to make good use of Ferroud, Schmitt, etc.[3] You will have to know the five *mélodies* as you once – and I emphasize 'once' – had to know your prayers.

I feel obliged to tell you that Madame Brisson who directs Les Annales preferred Modrakowska[4] to you for my lecture *solely* because of that bit of paper in your hand: 'Mme Peignot sings charmingly but don't you think,' she said to me, 'that what she does is more suitable for a drawing-room, and besides . . . she sings with the music.'

I know you will tell me that Lotte Lehmann . . .[5] Granted . . . but it is well-known that she sings for hours on end (*without music*) in the theatre.

I have found a spot for you in another lecture at the Vieux-Colombier (The Songs of Chabrier in our Time), on 17 January. We *must* have a good long talk about it all. Can you come to Noizay on Saturday 14th for the weekend, with Monique? I cannot ask you before that as I am staying with my aunt [Tante Liénard] at Nazelles until the 13th (because of grape-harvesting, servants, etc.). Write to me here immediately. I embrace you affectionately.

Your Fr.

Naturally Henri[6] is also invited for the 14th. The spring-bed is brand new.

125. FRANCIS POULENC TO CONTESSA MIMI PECCI-BLUNT

Paris, Thursday [April 1935]

Chère amie,

I am leaving on Saturday for Rome with the young Stravinsky. We will therefore be with you by Sunday for dinner. Above all, I do not want to put you out or inconvenience you in any way. I am sure you must have a full house. If by any chance you do not have space for me, will you be good enough to ask Rieti to reserve a room for me in a small hotel. I am looking forward so much to the concert in Rome – I have been practising conscientiously and hope to be equal to the task.

With kind regards.
Fr. Poulenc

126. MANUEL DE FALLA TO FRANCIS POULENC

Granada, November 1935

Cher Poulenc,

You cannot imagine how happy I was to receive your long awaited letter and your music!

But how deeply I regret the latest cause for your silence, knowing as I do through sad experience the intense pain of losing those we love.[1] We in fact delude ourselves by believing them to be eternal, which they may well be, but what we would like is to have them forever with us *in time*.

It is quite a while since we have seen each other, my dear Poulenc, so I am delighted with your plan to come to Granada on the occasion of your second visit to Spain. Since our meeting in Venice[2] many things have happened, gravely detrimental to my nerves as well as to my work which has nevertheless continued, but in the face of what obstacles! . . .

This is the reason for my long absence from Paris (as well as from many other things), having to put to the best possible use every available *scrap of time* so as not to lose the *thread* of my work. Hence my visits to Majorca and the return trips to Granada according to circumstances.

Thank heavens, only rarely do I lack courage and inner calm, an immense benefit in these harshly eventful times.

Your music brings me precious relief. How I love your Concerto, with its beautiful directness of expression and that lively sympathy (in the best sense of the word) that endows your music so admirably and so exceptionally. And how moved I am to hear that my own music often keeps you company!

Your note about *El Retablo* touches me deeply, and I am longing to hear Bernac's *Don Quichotte*, rehearsed with such distinguished guidance . . .[3]

Many thanks!

And now, compelled by that terrible tyrant, Time, I must once more put off completing this letter (it has already been interrupted several times) as well as sending you the promised despatch. But it will not be long now!

With all my heart, your very faithful

Manuel de Falla

LETTERS
1936–1953

It is really Eluard who has brought out
the best in me.

Francis Poulenc to Pierre Bernac
June 1944

No one will ever sing my songs better than Bernac.
He knows the smallest secrets of my music.

Francis Poulenc in conversation
with Claude Rostand
[ECR p. 92]

My faith is the faith of a country priest.

Francis Poulenc in conversation
with Stéphane Audel
[FP-MMA p. 15]

127. PAUL ELUARD TO FRANCIS POULENC

54 rue Legendre, Paris 17, Tuesday [1936?][1]

Mon cher Poulenc,

Here is the poem I told you about the other evening. It is made of words set to the whole medley of Spanish tunes heard in a month.

I very much hope to see you on your return.

Sincerely yours,
Paul Eluard

I think there will be others.

POÈME ESPAGNOL[2]

Tu glisses dans le lit	You slide into the bed
De lait glacé tes soeurs les fleurs	of iced milk your sisters the flowers
Et tes frères les fruits	and your brothers the fruits
Par le détour de leurs saisons	through the byways of their seasons
A l'aiguille irisée	with iridescent needle
Au flanc qui se répète	and edge that keeps recurring
Tes mains tes yeux et tes cheveux	your hands your eyes and your hair
S'ouvrent aux croissances nouvelles	open themselves to new growth
Perpétuelles	unending
Espère espère espère	Hope hope hope
Que tu vas te sourire	that you will smile to yourself
Pour la première fois	for the first time
Espère	Hope
Que tu vas te sourire	that you will smile to yourself
Sans songer à mourir.	without a thought of dying.

128. PAUL ELUARD TO FRANCIS POULENC

4 April 1936

Mon cher ami,

I am sending you *L'Amour la poésie* and *Capitale de la douleur*. I am also including *Facile* which I don't think you have.[1]

I cannot wait to hear this music you describe.[2] Contact me as soon as you come back to Paris.

With warm regards,
Paul Eluard

129. FRANCIS POULENC TO COMTESSE JEAN DE POLIGNAC

Thursday [May 1936]

Chère Marie-Blanche,

You wrote me a love of a letter and I would have replied immediately had I not been working flat out. The Concerto [for organ][1] is almost completed. It has given me a lot of trouble but I hope it is all right as it is now and that you will like it. It is not the amusing Poulenc of the Concerto for two pianos but more like a Poulenc en route for the cloister, very XVth, if you like. Granted, the other 15th also has its charm . . . Vaugirard, etc.[2]

Like a peasant taking his vegetables to the market, I am going to Paris today for two days, to unload on Durand seven pieces for unaccompanied choir [*Sept chansons*], written for the admirable Chanteurs de Lyon, on poems by Eluard and Apollinaire. I think they are rather good, and new for me. Our Biquette [Brigitte Manceaux] who has heard them, has been most encouraging.

You see how serious Poupoule is. I confess that work is the only thing that tempts me now. At Noizay I have grown into a stoutish monk, somewhat dissolute, tended by a new and excellent cook. To preserve the Parisian in me, my room in Paris is almost ready, at 5 rue de Médicis, where my Uncle Royer lives.[3] I shall be your neighbour. The style will be pure Flea Market. I have already acquired: a bed, an armchair, a piano-stool, a chair, all for 200 francs.

You must be happy to be at Kerbastic as it is a place where you can be utterly yourself.[4] You may count on me for this summer. I feel rather like the friend from the country who only appears in the summer. But that is more or less how it is. I have been in Paris so little this winter. The important thing is that you should love me very much, as I love you and embrace you both.

Fr.

The lack of gossip down here delights me but I shall certainly make up for it this evening as I am dining with Misia and Marie-Laure.[5]

130. FRANCIS POULENC TO COMTESSE JEAN DE POLIGNAC

Château du Tremblay, Evening of 15 August [1936]

Chère Marie-Blanche,

Would you believe that your Poupoule's heart is full of moss and melancholy? I have just spent ten days here all alone in a big house, not my own, in the pouring rain – and what rain! – thumping away on a piano that has more fungus than flats. Constantly have I thought of the times when I was the happy, spoiled darling at Kerbastic. Unfortunately this year 1936, which I am hating,[1] is now depriving me of what were once *my only real holidays*: I leave tomorrow for Uzerche where, between dear *Yvonne Gouvernante* and gentle *Pierre Gouverné*, I shall have to toe the line for a good two weeks.[2]

Piled up on the piano and 'to be studied' for the winter [concert season]: six Weber, four Liszt, eight Schubert, a cycle by Schumann, the *Ballades* of Debussy, the *Histoires naturelles*, etc. etc. Then I shall return to Touraine.

Marie-Blanche, it is too sad that I see so little of you, but between 15 March and 1 July I was scarcely in Paris at all. And I never dare to just drop in on you as I do with Marie-Laure [de Noailles] . . . this is the only reason for what might seem to you to be favouritism, for you know how much I love my Jean de Polignacs. You do believe me and you do understand, I think.

You know I have been working VERY HARD and we will see each other soon, I hope, with seven beautiful, solemn Chorales [*Sept chansons*], *Les Soirées de Nazelles* in print, and a grave and austere Concerto [for organ]. May you find all these to your liking. The Chorales and the Concerto show a very new trend, *Les Soirées* the end of the *Biches* period – that is, twenty minutes of music for piano *brillantissimo*.

Who is with you at Kekker, Marie-Blanche? I find myself hearing the crunch of the gravel in the courtyard under the car that brings the parish priest on his early morning visit . . . It is the evening of the 15th; Titillon[3] has her bow and her little posy; Jean in a velvet jacket has Pougine[4] on his shoulder; you are there, beautiful and with 'a look of surprise', as is fitting. I curse the hard times that make it necessary to play the piano in Carcassonne, and I curse Monsieur Blum[5] who terrifies publishers who bury themselves alive in their safes.

Marie-Blanche, I am not 'Popular Front'. Am I wrong? I am an old French Republican who once believed in liberty. I loathe Monsieur de La Roque[6] but I used to like Monsieur Loubet[7] well enough. For me, you see, the Republic was men like Clemenceau[8] whose maxim I think of so often: on your feet!!!!!

However, since yesterday I have made peace with the government and am ready to embrace (for once) Monsieur Zay for his judicious and intelligent appointment of Edouard,[9] which makes me jump for joy. At last, a tribute to competence, to taste and to intelligence.

To believe, Marie-Blanche, that I have no leftish leanings is to know very little about me. I thought I had long ago given proof that popular *fronts* are dear to me and I confess that what pleased me about *Le Quatorze Juillet*[10] was really the *audience*. All this is very complicated. Tell me that you still love me, Marie-Blanche, and write to me at the Hôtel du Commerce, Uzerche, where I may be made to copy a hundred times: 'I played a wrong note' or 'I replied cheekily to Yvonne', etc.

I embrace you very, very warmly, and also my dear Jean. Swear to me that this winter will be a winter of perfect and daily love.

Francis

Needless to say, I am adding a new song to the one due for last year.
I play the Intermezzo[11] all the time. It makes me weep.

131. LOUISE DE VILMORIN TO FRANCIS POULENC

[November 1936]

VERRIÈRES[1]

If only I knew
the date! All I
believe I know, but
I may be wrong, is
that it's the month
of November 1936. A
cat called Napoléon
who is sitting by my side
has just interrupted
his purring to
mew Tuesday. So
now you know: Tuesday
November 1936

Mon Francis chéri,

I have just this minute come back from Kerbastic where I spent a few days with Jean and Marie-Blanche [de Polignac]. You may think I benefited from the country, so lovely where they are, and that I feasted on their food, which is so good. Well, not at all! I remained shut up in my room where I did nothing but work for you. When I raised my eyes to the window I could only make out the countryside through a thick wall of smoke, thoroughly established and constantly nourished by countless cigarettes. At lunch, as at dinner, I could scarcely taste the delicacies that were offered to me, so anxious was my mind and so tight my throat! And, to crown it all, at night I kept counting my feet! And, I can tell you, it's not funny having only two feet when you feel the need for six, or even eight, ten or eleven. Anyway, you can see the problem.

You are responsible for this dismal disorder, the account of which will not fail, I hope, to trouble your conscience. You are the one, Francis, you are the one who first (and you have therefore become for me Francis I) had the idea of 'commanding' poems from me to set to music. It was you who decreed that I should be a poet. Your confidence does me honour and pleases me even more since I believe it to be imbued with the sovereign charm of illusion. At Kerbastic I was only able to write 'Le Garçon de Liège' and 'Eau-de-vie, au-delà', which I send you herewith. As for 'Chevaliers de la Garde blanche'[2] (which I enclose as well) I wrote it some months ago in the greatest secrecy at Fourques, the home of Jean Hugo, with him in mind. For me, it is less a poem than a prayer and an avowal.[3]

If ever I do become a poet it will be your fault and I wonder if I shall ever forgive you for having exhorted me not to stifle the sighs of my melancholy.

A big kiss nevertheless and with all my heart, too!

Your friend,
Loulette

132. PAUL ELUARD TO FRANCIS POULENC

2 January 1937

Mon cher ami,

I find that what you have asked of me is not all that easy.[1]

I very much fear that I have only been able to think of entirely unsuitable titles. Here they are in order of preference:

1. *Tout dire* [Saying it all].
2. *Tel jour telle nuit* [As the day, so is the night].
3. *Aussi loin que l'amour* [As far away as love].
4. *Paroles peintes* [Painted words].

Take your choice, or better still, think of a title yourself that is in keeping with your music.

In any event, let me know as soon as possible what you decide. I am interested to hear.

Forgive me for this lack of ideas.

Until Friday. With warm regards,
Paul Eluard

The fourth title, which seems to preclude music, might for this very reason create a quite striking effect.

133. FRANCIS POULENC TO SUZANNE PEIGNOT

[1937?]

What has become of you, my blonde angel?

I feel somewhat anxious, not having heard from you. What is going on in your heart and what are your plans at this onset of winter? I have been giving you a lot of thought and would like to speak to you seriously about your life.

1. If you wish to make the most of your singing you must work very regularly, just like a pupil. Pierre [Bernac] never goes about it any other way.

2. There is only one way you can succeed, but it seems a sure one to me, and that is to get together with the group Nadia, Derenne, Cuénod, etc.[1] In the first place, you will make some delightful friends and in addition, together with them, you will gradually get on to Radio. Only yesterday Cuénod was heard in the first performance of a cantata by Milhaud.

But you will have to tell yourself firmly that it will be a quite different life from the one you are leading now, it will be the life of a true artist and not of an amateur such as you have been living for several years. You will be very busy, from early in the morning until late at night, and you will not be able to use Henri as an excuse.

You will also have to relinquish all thoughts of self-importance and you must realize that you will not be there to steal solos from Marie-Blanche [de Polignac]. Although it might seem incredible to you, Marie-Blanche has worked far harder than you for the last two years. Should you need convincing, you have only to listen to her recordings of Monteverdi. Pierre was bowled over by them.

Gradually, you will get to the top again and, taking advantage of the fact that Marie-Blanche is not always free, you will do odd things here and there, with the others. In this way, Nadia is taking Cuénod and Doda [Conrad] to America. I assure you that this is more *certain* and more prestigious than some hypothetical engagement by Cendrars.[2] While great stars like Panzera[3] and Bernac already have difficulty making it, it would be stupidly naïve to believe that it would be possible in your case. Admit it, my love.

Think about all this and you will see that everything I am telling you is absolutely right. What I am suggesting is so attractive, so lively and appealing, and would take you out of yourself so well, that if I were you I would jump at the opportunity. Otherwise, continue making your hats, have your picture in *Vogue*, and go on living a life that I do not believe is right for you. You have better things to do. Only a well regimented Suzanne Peignot will *progress*, will become a star again and make us forget the poor little wounded bird. So there you have it. Phone me one morning. Loving kisses.

Fr.

If you were a free artist you would come here and talk to me about it all *this Sunday*. Your room is ready.

I have reread my letter; the tone is harsh but you know that I adore you and that I am *right*.[4]

134. FRANCIS POULENC TO MADELEINE GREY

Noizay, [December 1937][1]

Irascible diva,

I wrote to inform Enoch that it was all right for the beginning of January. I think he has already given you my reply.[2]

You know perfectly well that I love you very much, that I find you talented, extremely talented, with a difficult disposition, a great intelligence, much musicality, a volatile temper, etc. etc.

See you soon. I embrace you, Divine one!

Francis

135. FRANCIS POULENC TO CONTESSA MIMI PECCI-BLUNT

26 January [1938]

Ma chère Mimi,

Just before leaving Paris for my tour of Holland with Bernac, I saw Rieti. Naturally, we spoke about you. Dear Mimi, I have no engagements whatsoever in Rome this winter and will only go there if you revive the idea of the lecture project which was cancelled last year.

Bernac and I are giving recitals in Milan, Turin, Lugano, and will be in Florence on Friday 25 March. If you want us on Saturday 26 March and if that date suits you, we will be delighted; otherwise after Florence we will go back to Paris. That is the situation. Dear impresario, be so good as to let me know as soon as you can. Write to me in Paris, 5 rue de Médicis.

I send you and Cecil a thousand affectionate regards and Bernac sends his respects.

Very devotedly,
Francis

Our fee will be the same as last year, that is 3.000 lire.

DRAFT OF THE PREVIOUS YEAR'S CANCELLED LECTURE
MENTIONED BY POULENC IN LETTER 135:

Memories of my Twenties

    1. Introduction – Apologies.
       Early memories. Viñes. Satie.
       Vidal rumpus.
       Satie – friendship with. Arcueil.

La boutique du père Demets.
Our meetings – Elaborate.

Programmes:

Groupe des Six
Rue Huyghens – atmosphere

Pieces by Satie, Poulenc.

2. The Russian Ballet

Parade. Elaborate. Atmosphere of première
in 1917. Spirit of an era. Picasso.
Apollinaire readings.

I come to know
Diaghilev

Stravinsky. Meeting at Valentine Hugo's.
Commission for *Les Biches*.

Stravinsky's example

Memories of *Les Noces*
Première of *Mavra*
I write *Les Biches*
Music from my twenties
Marie Laurencin
I play *Les Biches*

136. FRANCIS POULENC TO JEAN WIÉNER

35 Wimpole Street, London W1, 3 March [1938]

Mon petit Jean,

My sister has *only today* sent me your wonderful, kind, far too beautiful, far too indulgent article on your old Poulenc. More than any other – and no other has ever had that particular tone – it moved me, because it was from you. Thank you with all my heart. Life unfortunately prevents us from seeing each other as much as we would like, but we are still just as fond of each other, are we not?

I am at the end of three weeks of concerts here with Bernac, after which I will be able to go and work peacefully in Touraine.

Please note that the Chanteurs de Lyon are coming to Paris. On the 1st [May], in the evening, they will be singing my Eluard choral settings at the Salle Gaveau.[1] On the 2nd, in the afternoon, they are giving the first performance of my symphony[2] at a Concert Colonne and, finally and *most important of all* (for me), on Sunday 3rd at 11.00 a.m. in the

Dominican Chapel at 222 Faubourg St Honoré, they are giving the first performance of my Mass.[3] What a lot of Poulenc!

Hoping to see you soon, and with my thanks once again.

I embrace you,

Francis

137. FRANCIS POULENC TO MADELEINE GREY

Le Grand Coteau, Noizay (Indre-et-Loire), 7 June [1938]

Ma chère Madeleine,

I was hoping to see you during one of my visits to Paris but I am stuck here with my nose to the grindstone. In a letter there is always the risk of being misunderstood and I would not want you to think for one moment, because of what I am about to say, that I do not admire you, since in fact I have always given you abundant proof to the contrary. Having made that clear, may I say that your recording is not worthy of you and that I do not advise you to allow it to be released. We are all victims of the treachery of the wax – this is the reason why six sides of Bernac–Poulenc in Fauré have just been put in the waste bin. No, quite frankly, the recording is not 'you'. What struck me most while listening *very carefully* to the test pressing is your lack of joy. If you had seen yourself in a mirror while you were making the recording you would have understood immediately that this was not the vivacious, *lively* Madeleine of the recital hall.

I think the microphone terrorizes you – only in this kind of music, naturally – and I am wondering whether we would not do better with some serious Poulenc, of the *Poèmes de Max Jacob* type.

Think about all this, while repeating to yourself that I remain forever your devoted and admiring (but of course!)

Poulenc

138. FRANCIS POULENC TO YVONNE GOUVERNÉ

Monday [1938][1]

Ma petite Yvonne,

I wish I could express what happiness your all too short visit gave me. Do not thank me for my friendship; if only you knew how *essential* yours is to me. I am afraid, *ma petite Yvonne*, that I turn to you far too often.

Gradually (I am in no hurry) I would like it to be said in Paris that my Mass is worth working on – with a little bit of faith in the composition itself and a great deal of faith in me. I think Vallombrosa – who wrote me a charming letter – will perhaps be able to arrange something at Saint-Eustache with you. In his letter, his intention was to speak to you about it.

I am also counting on you for a revival of *Sécheresses* next winter with Munch.[2] My first choice of hall would be the Salle Gaveau, perfect in size for this composition. I have just finished amending, revising and polishing it.[3]

My conscience obliges me to say that I was partly at fault. In the first place, for having given in to James[4] by including additional bars for the orchestra between the final cry '*hear me*' and the conclusion. The only technical thing of which I am more or less *certain* is my sense of prosody. Adding *artificial* bars between an imperative phrase and an explanation is as if a man, ranting and railing, were to yell '*listen to me*', then go into the room next door and emerge ten minutes later to explain himself. What I would never have conceded to Eluard or to Apollinaire – oh! irony – I conceded to James . . . because he paid me for the work. I wanted him to be happy. You saw the result.

I have also touched up the conclusion very considerably – both in the orchestral part and the choral part. I had dreamed of an unaccompanied choir simply *highlighted* by instrumental touches but I have come to understand that what this created was a watercolour effect in the corner of a painting done in oils.

I confess to feeling very bitter that at my age I am still prone to such errors of 'auditory vision'.

How hard it is to acquire skills when one is still trying to find one's way. I keep seeing this in terms of a ladder, straight and difficult to climb. May God grant me a few more years of health, wisdom and application, so that I may try to leave behind me a little more than the little I have achieved so far.

Believe me, the hours of doubt are dreadful, and the greatness of those I admire – Debussy, Ravel, Strauss, Stravinsky, Falla – must not be obscured by the mediocrity that generally prevails.

I am working feverishly on the Organ Concerto. Two or three songs for Pierre [Bernac] are coming along quickly and well. These flowers make me hopeful of truly beautiful fruits to come. Dear Yvonne, it is very pleasant indeed to be able to say exactly what one thinks about oneself. Believe me, I suffer neither from false modesty, nor from pride, nor from an inferiority complex. I simply try to see things clearly – that is all.

Whereupon I embrace you and send you these songs, more amusing I hope than my prose.

Very fondly,
Francis

My intention is to let Munch have the first performance of the Organ Concerto in thanks for *Sécheresses*. See how the land lies.[5]

COMMENTS ON SÉCHERESSES

I The grasshoppers

Orchestra:	entire opening section relentless
bar 17:	tenor attack very violent
bar 22:	burning hot
bar 30:	altos very sonorous
29–40:	very violent
	This whole opening section blind with sand, sun and blood.
bar 46:	Sudden transition. The thermometer leaps from +50 to −10. Everything becomes clear – the 'clear, lucid cold' of Mallarmé.
bar 60:	Revert to the atmosphere of the opening section.
bar 87:	very gentle
bar 91:	very lyrical
95–96:	very gentle and clear
From 107 on:	very gentle and clear
114–115 (and especially 16–17):	*harp very important*, a rush of lyricism – ending in the greatest calm.

II The abandoned village

Orchestra:	very delicate from 172 to 183
At 189:	altos and basses very sonorous

III The false future

At 220:	Above all, do not fail to press forward with the tempo *à la Schumann*.
At 239:	The tenors must on no account stress beats like a theatre chorus but should maintain a long melodic line.
bar 247:	exactly the tempo of 220
bar 255:	altos well marked – very important
bar 273:	Mephistophelean *pianissimo* fairly long silence before

IV The skeleton of the sea

bar 275:	calm and solemn
bar 288:	The accelerando must heighten the impression of mystery and anxiety (of anguish, to be more precise).

bar 303:	Bring out clearly the beginning of this *new stage* in the tempo. This is the start of the crescendo and the accelerando that extends to bar 333, at which point it runs abruptly into the lyricism of the conclusion.
bar 334:	Find a lovely sonority for the tenors, then the whole choir melancholy and tender.
	entire ending: orchestra *intense* but not loud
Orchestra:	
At bar 346:	Bring out the ascending scale clearly.
bar 354:	choir really dazzling
bar 356:	orchestra ditto

Many thanks.

139. FRANCIS POULENC TO COMTESSE JEAN DE POLIGNAC

Château du Tremblay, Neubourg par Evreux (Eure), Wednesday [1938][1]

Chère Marie-Blanche,

I do not know what the statutory time is for a *lettre château* but whatever it is, I have disgracefully exceeded it. Forgive me. Since I left Kerbastic I have done so many things that I feel quite dazed. The return journey was rather distressing – mainly because I would have liked to have stayed on, and also because my hand, in the heat of the train, began to look like a 1925 Picasso. Fortunately I did not come across dear Doda [Conrad] on the way. Did you pass on the request from the pianists [Gold & Fizdale]? Once I got to Tours I went to see a surgeon friend who cured me in 24 hours with hot poultices and applications of Synthol. So, by Thursday, I was in a fit state to play the Concerto [for organ] to your aunt [Princesse Edmond de Polignac]. I think she was pleased. Just between ourselves, I did not find her in very good health that evening. She had a slight dizzy spell leaving the Chaplins' home,[2] where we had dined. Before the dinner (Avenue Henri Martin, where I was alone with her) I had been loudly singing the praises of Nadia [Boulanger] of whom – you were right – she is a little jealous, particularly as she had not seen her for some days and as Solange had had her to lunch. In the end, everything came right when we sat down at the piano.

On Friday I dined at Marie-Laure's [de Noailles] with Auric and Eluard.

Now I am spending a week at my sister's. Then I shall go to Paris and after that to Anost, if Bernac's father is well enough to allow him to leave. The neighbour is here. On Friday we are going to have lunch at Antoinette's, together with Auric and Madeleine Le Chevrel.

Needless to say yet again how fond I am of Kekker and of you and Jean. The Breton Marie-Blanche is my favourite Marie-Blanche. And of course Bernac will come to Kekker, with wings and a big smile. He will adore singing duets with you, he said. So there. I believe you will be in Venice on 7 September. What joy! This is a very badly written letter – forgive me. Think of your Poupoule when you read Baudelaire.

Tell the Comte that I found him poetic and handsome.

As for you, dearest Marie-Blanche, I embrace you tenderly.

Francis

There is no reason, simply because we did not work on the Vilmorins together, for you to do the same thing when you are on your own. You *must* be *ready* for the coming season.[3]

Hélène is not too bad. I had dinner at her place.

140. PAUL ELUARD TO FRANCIS POULENC

'Maison grise', allée du Perruchet, Le Pecq (Seine-et-Oise), Monday [October 1938]

Mon cher Francis,

This is quite absurd. I am not writing a book, but a title. And yet for these two poems[1] – one about well-being, the other about suffering – I can think only of titles that are *anti-public*.

I am now living permanently in the country, where I have been for the last five days.[2] I have been knocking in nails, lighting fires, trying to sort out the disorder. This morning the earth is frozen; I shall not be doing much digging today.

I hope you will forgive my incompetence.

Affectionately yours.
Paul Eluard

141. PAUL ELUARD TO FRANCIS POULENC

'Maison grise', Tuesday 1 November 1938

You must not be angry with me, my dear Francis, for not having found you your title. Your music, had I known it, would surely have guided me and the title would have stemmed naturally from it.

Miroirs brûlants[1] had occurred to me. The meaning fits both poems. But the *miroir ancien*[2] that appears in the first poem makes it a bit awkward.

L'or et l'eau froide[3] is similarly awkward because of *mélancolie dorée.*[4] And, besides, it rings too greatly of *d'amour et d'eau fraîche.*[5] Although . . . In fact, what you have done is fine.

With warm regards,
Paul Eluard

To console you, I am sending you a little book which concerns you, in some obscure way.

142. FRANCIS POULENC TO HENRI SAUGUET

London [March, 1939]

Mon cher Henri,
I am wild with joy. I see in *Le Figaro* that your dress rehearsal[1] is taking place on Thursday. Can you imagine, I am coming home on Wednesday and leaving again on Friday. What great luck! I beg you to find me a seat, anywhere, but just find me a seat. I would die of fury if I couldn't get in. You can imagine how I am looking forward to this great day. Send the ticket to the rue de Médicis or tell Jacques [Dupont][2] where I am to sit.

I am delighted with my stay in England. We are giving the first performance of 'Le Chat'[3] at our recital in London on Tuesday night. I think we are doing it well now.

What exciting days you must be living through! I am thinking of you fondly, and I embrace you.

Francis

143. FRANCIS POULENC TO COMTESSE JEAN DE POLIGNAC

Noizay, Monday [Easter 1939]

Marie-Blanche,
Are you back in Paris? Do you know that when I think of what might happen I tell myself that one of the things I would miss most is not making music with you any more. Of course, I can see myself a-bristle with white briar, feet in the boggy mire, but actually I prefer to be at peace, in front of the keyboard of a piano.

I have come here for Easter. I am not doing much work here, however; it is well-known that the country only suits me when my mind is free. When things are not so rosy I am far more in need of my boulevard de Grenelle than the 'meanderings of the Loire'. I shall return to Paris on Saturday – hint for Sunday lunch.

I have kept some sad news for this page: the second proof of 'Garçon de Liège' is *worse*, so it has to be done all over again. But 'La Grenouillère' has at last been published.[1]

I hope to God that I shall be able to write other songs. It appears that my case is not entirely desperate and that I might perhaps become an almost-great musician. Tell Edouard that I am thinking more and more of 'Tempest'- or 'Pericles'-like music.

Keep loving me. I embrace you, and of course the dear Comte, too.

Poupoule

144. LOUISE DE VILMORIN TO FRANCIS POULENC

Hotel Crillon, 15 July (St Henry's Day) 1939

Mon Poupoul chéri,

Your letter gave me immense pleasure. I would have dedicated *Fiançailles pour rire*[1] to you if I had not married my Pálffy.[2] But my Pálffy married me and you did not! One day I shall have to tell you about my life at present. You who have always known me at Verrières, surrounded by my brothers and my sweethearts, can you imagine me in a castle, in Slovakia? The vast park fades into the forest, and the mountains of the Carpathians mark the bounds of my horizon. Come and see it all and come and have a look at me at the same time, if you feel so inclined. But that's not the question, or rather, I have not yet replied to the question which you put to me. You ask me why the text of the poem 'Eau-de-vie, au-delà', published by Gallimard in the volume entitled *Fiançailles pour rire*, is not the same as the original text which you received from me a long time before the publication of this volume. Well, I'll tell you. This poem, which I had written without the slightest improper wish or thought, caused Marie-Blanche [de Polignac] to tease me so much that I am still smarting from the onslaught. She convinced me that the poem was indecency itself and that it contained images and avowals fit to make the most broad-minded of confessors blush. And when I told her that she had taken it all the wrong way she replied that my thoughtlessness was not, in her eyes, proof of my innocence.

She laughed – can't you just picture her – but I tell you I was left with egg on my face, and herb omelette at that! In short, I was afraid to allow it to be published as it was. I altered it for everybody else, and if I did not change it for you it was because I had written it for you and because I knew that your music would have the power to bring out the innocence of its original form.

Forgive me for this lengthy explanation. I have a long-winded style. I would like to see you and to embrace you. I do so in thought today and am, with all my heart, your

Loulette

145. PAUL ELUARD TO FRANCIS POULENC

'Maison grise', Allée du Perruchet, Le Pecq, [1939]

Cher Francis,

    The other evening – in our solitude[1] – we had the joy of hearing your *Concert champêtre*. It is a great work. We hope to see you soon. Our best wishes and affection.

                                                                Paul Eluard

146. FRANCIS POULENC TO HENRI SAUGUET

Noizay, Tuesday [29 August 1939]

Mon cher Henri,

    How greatly I appreciate your friendship and your heart! You are the only one of my friends who has thought of writing to me. I am extremely touched by this.

    I am still at home but I may be called up at any minute now. I do not know where, or in what capacity. As I am merely a private, it will certainly not be very dazzling.

    Anyway, none of that is of any importance.

    As one who senses an impending storm, I have spent a bad summer.

    Because the inn at Pouldu was uninhabitable, Marie-Blanche [de Polignac] took me in for ten days, then I came here. Wanting to be ahead of events, I worked a lot, nothing new, as I have not felt much like it, but I have completely revised the whole of my Sextet for Chester (it's very good now) and corrected a great deal of music, etc. I had started working on *Les Mamelles de Tirésias*, enthralled by my libretto, only slightly modified.[1] You know that nothing in Apollinaire embarrasses me. Anyway, God willing . . .

    Fortunately, dear Henri, I know that you cannot be called up. If the worst happens, do not forget me. Write to me often – that is the best thing I could wish for. I embrace you. Let's pray and have faith.

                                                                Fr.

147. FRANCIS POULENC TO COMTESSE JEAN DE POLIGNAC

Noizay, Monday [September 1939]

Et voilà, ma petite Marie-Blanche. Things are not good, but what can one do?

    I am ready to leave, waiting to be called up at any moment. I know neither where I shall be nor what I shall be doing. I am not surprised at what is happening. I have had such a strong sense of foreboding since the beginning of

August that I could not help feeling nervous. Forgive me for being unable to conceal this from you. I shall often think of those last holidays at Kekker and of our two beautiful musical soirées. That last evening, when I insisted on hearing 'Tu vois le feu du soir', I *knew* that I would not be hearing it again . . . let's say for quite some time. Think of your Poupoule. Love his music. That is all I ask of you. And promise that you will write to me often. I think with heavy heart of all your nephews and of our dear Princesse Henri.[1]

Marie-Blanche, I embrace you very tenderly, and Jean, too. You know that you have always been the dearest of friends to me.

Votre vieux Poupoule

Write to me at Noizay. Mail will be forwarded.

148. Princess Edmond de Polignac to Francis Poulenc

Manor House Hotel, North Bovey, Moretonhampstead, Devon, 17 September 1939

Francis, cher, cher Francis,

I do not deserve any of the sweet things you say to me – it is I who owe you a great debt of gratitude, for so many wonderful hours of music, and for writing the Venice concerto for me, as well as the Paris one, whose profound beauty haunts me.[1]

My family has asked me to remain in England for the time being. I shall be staying near a niece of mine, close to where the 1870 war brought me in my early years.

My address for quite some time will be: Roseter Hotel, Torquay, Devon (England).

But as soon as it becomes possible I shall return to Paris. Thank you for your thought, dear Francis. May God protect us. I embrace you and assure you of all my loyal friendship and admiration.

J.P.

I saw our Audrey the day before yesterday. Her delightful home is near here. She drives an ambulance for the Red Cross.[2]

149. Paul Eluard to Francis Poulenc

Lieutenant Grindel,[1] Station-Magasin de Mignères, Gondreville (Loiret), 9 October 1939

Mon cher Francis,

You are an angel to write to me, for no matter how we try to knock ourselves out with the most exhausting work, we cannot prevent the blanket of wind, rain and fatigue from suddenly lifting to reveal that space in which we once believed ourselves to be. There are brief glimpses of almighty horror with, way below, rank absurdity and, high above, everyday reality, normal reality, our friendship, our music, our poems, all that gives us our direction.

My dear Francis, I am so afraid of not being strong enough[2] and of making a fool of myself. Your two cards, so like you, have given me heart. Write to me again. Help me to hold out. Nusch[3] joins me in sending you love.

Paul E.

150. Francis Poulenc to Agathe Rouart-Valéry

Noizay, October 1939

Ma chère Agathe,

I am full of joy because I received a lovely letter from Paul [Rouart]: what journalists refer to in tricoloured slang as a *chic lettre*.

I have been wanting to write to you for quite some time as I think of you often. What an era ours is! And what a youth! I say 'ours' although I am no longer one of the young. This has been brought home to me – quite pleasantly, moreover – by my mobilization instructions which allow me to stay here for the present.

I am working. I have just completed a song cycle on poems by L. de Vilmorin [*Fiançailles pour rire*]. I spoke to Paul about it this spring. For some time after that I puzzled over the direction of the cycle, and then, suddenly, the gravity of the circumstances – Loulou's exile, confined to her castle in Hungary – gave me the tone. It is melancholy and lyrical.

I am not leaving Noizay as I shall be called up from here. I am staying here with my Uncle Royer and Mariette Sully (who created the role of *Véronique*). At the beginning of the war we had a full house. But then this sort of 'Pont-aux-Dames'[1] foundered on the petty domestic squabbles between servants and employers. I am reading a lot. If we were not constantly aware of our minds, life would truly be a drudgery these days.

Will you stay long in that watery Normandy? I hope Martine's cheeks are being mistaken for apples and that you are naturally making sure she keeps well away from the cider press, poor darling!!!

Do drop me a line.

Warmest regards
Francis

Excuse my handwriting, even worse than usual – I have lost my pen in spite of Saint Anthony.[2]

151. FRANCIS POULENC TO ADRIENNE MONNIER

Académie de France, Rome, 14 February 1940

Chère Adrienne,

Solange gave me the precious notebook. I almost choked with laughter and then with shame. Needless to say, I dare not appear before Colette David ever again! This new war has so far – and I repeat so far – spared me all hovels without doors.[1] I awoke this morning in the bedroom of Catherine de Médicis in the Valla di Roma. I feel almost ashamed of such a privilege.

This afternoon I am accompanying Bernac. I don't have to tell you with what feelings I shall be doing so. I am told that I am doing good work by behaving in this way. Let's hope that this is true.

To get back to the notebooks: thanks to you I have relived a paradise lost. How I love hearing about my dear Raymonde [Linossier]! As soon as it is published, I will send you a recent *mélodie* dedicated to her ever-present memory. The poem is by Eluard. The title: 'Ce doux petit visage'[2] . . .

I shall come and see you soon.

In the meantime I embrace you and send you all my thanks.

Francis

152. FRANCIS POULENC TO PIERRE BERNAC

Anti-aircraft Division, 72nd Battery, Cahors-Lot, 10 July [1940]

Vieux Pierre,

What a brilliant idea to have written to me at Masse.[1] This very morning I sent out a second 'sounding-letter' to you in Paris, my first having gone to Chinon.

I make a most charming soldier, all in khaki. My little escapade was quite incredible – I'll tell you all about it when I see you. Thanks to the Marshal we were not taken prisoner in Bordeaux like the chaps from Lyons. We were left to retreat towards the south. After days of travelling in cattle trains we have now taken root in a heavenly village in Lot, 3 kilometres away from Cahors, where I sleep in a barn straight out of the Fables of La Fontaine. I have unearthed an old Philemon and Baucis couple,[2] with whom I eat every night, together with three pals of mine. Divine food, exquisite Cahors wine. Philemon is a former lion tamer who married his Baucis forty years ago in Turin where she charmed snakes. They adore me. I speak to them about Italy. In a word, I am *happy. Yes, I am.* 'I have my hands', which is what I keep telling myself all day long, joyfully. Paris is intact. I would readily sacrifice all of Noizay for it. It is in fact rather odd what little store I set by things. I have faith in the future and in our 'team',*

*In English in the original text.

and what is more, I feel full of music. I have found countless themes and the whole colour of my ballet.[3] The absence of a piano has even been salutary. I like these parts. The air is buoyant. I live with peasants who give me confidence. That is all my news. You will no doubt be astounded by my calm. I assure you that it runs deep. [. . .]

Your long letter from Paris truly gladdened my heart. From every point of view, what you tell me is a blessing. It will enrich your art even more. Write soon. I embrace you.

                                                                      Francis

I wanted to buy a house yesterday. What bathing there is for us in the River Lot! I am noting marvellous spots for our summers.

153. HENRI SAUGUET TO FRANCIS POULENC

1 bis, impasse Masséna, Auch, 26 August 1940

Mon cher Francis,
    When I came back with Jacques [Dupont] a little while ago for lunch and saw your letter on the table, I literally threw myself upon it, first to devour it, and then to read it. What pleasure your letter gave me: I knew you were safe, and in Brive, as Odette Joyeux and Brasseur have been here since yesterday and they told me. But to hear it from you and to read your words has done me the world of good. I want to reply to you at once since you tell me that you are about to go back. I myself have not yet taken the decision to leave this side of the world for the other: on the one hand we are told that it is ideal there, and on the other hand that it is infernal. Obviously I will have to go back at some time or other. But before I do I want to be sure that I do not have to fear being treated either as an undesirable (alas! what role will artists, and especially composers, have in the world of the future?) or as a pauper (how are we going to make a living?). So I am going to wait here a while with Jacques, who came to join me when the Imperials marched into Paris.
    Auch is a village full of charm, the surrounding countryside is sublimely beautiful (and Jacques is painting a lot, even if I myself have not yet written a single note of music). The famous cathedral is very beautiful and I play the organ on Sundays at mass, and during the week for my pleasure. It is a very fine seventeenth-century instrument, unfortunately in rather poor condition but very, very interesting. Our life is calm, provincial. Among those here are André de Richaud, Jeanne Léger and Roger Lannes. Jean Marais was here and left to join the poet [Cocteau] in Perpignan. I had a certain number of army friends here, junior officers and colonels: they too have left. Soon Jacques and I will be alone. Then perhaps we will decide to

go back to Paris, where our mothers are. No news from them, naturally. So if you go back to Paris, phone my place, where Fouquet is supposed to be living in order to keep the apartment occupied, and say that I am well, that we are both well, that we nearly went to live in Toulouse, but that we soon came back here. I saw a few radio personalities there: Bondeville, very charming, Charmy, Zadkine, Lélia Gousseau, Le Roy, etc. All these people are stuck there and bored to death. In Auch we feel more at home.

My tale of the war takes two lines to tell: I began it here on 16 April and finished it, demobilized, on 31 July. In that time, I learnt how to march in step, do an 'about-turn', assemble and dismantle a gun, etc. Meanwhile I conducted the battalion band. Yes! I even wrote a march, which will forever be played at the youth camps in this region . . . And that is all!

Practically all of our friends are safe. But *nothing* is known of Christian Dior or Jean Ozenne. Pierre Colle has been taken prisoner. Laporte is near Montauban. Honegger would be in Agen, or near there. It seems that Ibert never left: they say he is in Gers, not far from Auch. I have never seen him here. As for Da [Milhaud], I am extremely upset about his departure. I don't think he had anything to fear for the moment. The Jacques Meyers have gone back to Paris. Jeanson, it appears, is editor of *Paris-soir* for the occupied zone . . . Heavens, what a lot of surprises!

The Marquise [de Casa Fuerte] is urging us to join her in Marseilles. But we will not budge from here except to go home: in the first place, money is very tight (my mother has all mine and we cannot receive any of it, alas!) and, anyway, travelling is so uncomfortable.

Dear Francis, how I hope that Noizay is intact! I have thought of it so often. And of you! God grant that we may all meet again in the not too distant future, as we did for all those Christmases and Pentecosts whose memory perfumes my past life. Who knows towards what, or where we are heading? I am not even sure I want to become a composer again! Does it have a *raison d'être* now? If, at least, I were writing pastorals and country dances!!

Bon voyage dear, dear Francis, may Saint Christopher protect you. May we see each other again soon. And, who knows, even have beautiful Sérénade concerts this winter.

Much loyal affection. Jacques embraces you. And so do I!

Your friend
Henri S.

154. FRANCIS POULENC TO DARIUS MILHAUD

Brive, 9 September 1940

Mon petit Darius,

I am going back to Paris tonight – in a cattle train. Be grateful for your American sleeping cars! I want to send you these few lines before returning to that zone of mystery where I think writing will prove difficult for me. In any case, let's agree on one thing: we will write to each other via your *mother* and you will do so on notepaper with no heading. I hesitated about going back to the capital but Auric – back at home again – sent word that I should return without delay. After all, I suppose there are spiritual values to be defended.

My plans can be summed up as follows: to spend the whole winter composing in Touraine, if I can stand it there despite the cold, and then in June (but where will we all be in June?) to go to the Argentine with Bernac. I am making very good progress with my ballet on the fables of La Fontaine.[1] The orchestration will probably be completed by January. I might try to have it performed at the Opéra where Lifar is dancing again. Then I intend offering it to Balanchine or Nijinska for North America, if I manage to get there in '41–'42. As well as *Les Biches*, with Marie's décor which I will take with me. Try to let Nijinska know about this. And, of course, the new orchestration. These days one can only live on hopes and future plans.

Marcelle Dullin,[2] who had fled to Brive, has gone back to Paris. She sends both you and Madeleine her fondest regards. Rose Adler[3] has taken refuge in the same boarding house – the one where Rosine[4] is staying. How thankful I am to know that you are in San Francisco. Each day brings this home to me more and more. You would be amazed to hear how many *volte-face* there have been, often quite astounding ones. I know one has to find a way to survive. Jouvet[5] is doing *L'Ecole des femmes* again. After that he is due to put on something new. I am hoping that Sauguet, who is still in Auch, will participate.

Noizay is now free but was badly looted.[6]

I think of you with deep affection and embrace you, also Madeleine and Daniel.[7]

Ton vieux Francis

155. Paul Eluard to Francis Poulenc

Thursday 22 May [1941?][1]

Mon cher Francis,

For the Louise de Vilmorin–Eluard session, I leave things entirely to you and Marcel Herrand.[2] My only suggestion is that one or two unpublished poems of mine could perhaps be read.

As for your ballet, I can quite *clearly* see myself finding a title – and I would be happy and flattered to do so – if only it were not based on La Fontaine. When I left my childhood behind, together with those fables so harshly thrust upon me and so laboriously committed to memory, I wanted nothing more than to reject La Fontaine forever. The moral content of his fables is a prison which I do not wish to enter ever again.

Yet for all that, since the mind of man is such that he can *always* share the thoughts of another, especially one he loves, it would give me pleasure – if you will read your scenario to me – to help you find a title for your ballet.

My dear Francis, do not resent this resistance. Our friendship and the admiration that I have for you compel me to be as outspoken in criticism as in enthusiasm. Moreover, as the quality of your music does not depend on the subjects that you choose, be thankful – very thankful – for my frankness.

And I am certain that we still have a thousand and one things in common, a thousand and one reasons to work together.

When will you come and see me? One word from you and I will be waiting.

Affectionately yours,
Paul Eluard

156. PAUL ELUARD TO FRANCIS POULENC

Friday [1941?]

Mon cher Francis,

Before leaving for the country, I want to let you know the first titles that have come to mind. Rest assured, there will be others.

A la Lueur de l'homme [In the light of man]
Les Animaux modèles [Model animals]
Mouvements animaux [Animal movements]
A la Mode animale [Animal fashion]
Mille pattes [Centipede]

Marie-Laure [de Noailles] and Valentine [Hugo] and my daughter Cécile are all in favour of *Animaux modèles*; they can visualize it on the posters, full of meaning and easily retained by the public. With my usual bad taste, I like *A la mode animale*.

Write to me here. Do not be afraid to express your disgust.

I shall be back on 10 September.

With love,
Paul E.

157. FRANCIS POULENC TO HENRI SAUGUET

Tuesday [1942]

Of course it is all right, *cher Henri*, for 4 February.

Please let Marcel [Herrand] know immediately. He already has the lecture-talk, so this will give him time to sort himself out and as I shall still be arriving on Saturday 18, I shall be able to help with the publicity, if need be.

Delighted for you about the Jouvet–Basle thing, which you richly deserve.

I cannot get over the progress I have made with my ballet. I feel, thank God, in that same state of creative *gourmandise* as at the time of *Les Biches*. I hope that the twenty intervening years will show only in the technique. I also feel sure that my orchestration bears a very personal mark now.

I am most intrigued by your music for the stage. Why? *A bientôt, Pernelle!*[1] I embrace you.

Francis

158. PAUL ELUARD TO FRANCIS POULENC

Eluard-Grindel, Hôtel du Cheval Blanc, Vezelay (Yonne), 7 February 1942

Mon cher Francis,

Your message reached me too late for me to listen to your choral work. I am very sorry. If they do it again, let me know by telegram.

We are staying here until the end of the month. I am working. You will shortly be receiving the second volume of *Le Livre ouvert*, including your poem.[1] Vezelay in the snow is very child-like. And we are well wrapped.

Affectionately yours,

Paul E.

Do not forget the promised manuscript!!!

159. FRANCIS POULENC TO CHARLES KOECHLIN

Noizay, Indre-et-Loire, 18 August 1942

Cher Koechlin,

I must confess that I had been waiting very anxiously for your letter. Alas, my instinct did not deceive me – my sense of foreboding about your delay in giving me your opinion was unfortunately justified. Although I feel a very great tenderness towards *Les Biches* – great enough to have taken the trouble two years ago to reorchestrate the *entire* work – I am sad that you prefer it so unequivocally to *Les Animaux modèles*. I am also upset that in the latter work you seem to have been struck most by its burlesque aspects. You are one of the rare few who have not been touched by the death, the dawn and the midday meal.[1] Coming from you, these reservations hurt me a great deal. I am very keen for you to see the score, which I shall send within a week at the latest. I fear that the production, which was perhaps not to your liking (and I add quite openly that I was responsible for it in every smallest detail), may have influenced your impressions of the music. But thank you anyway for your frankness.

Since you like 'le Poulenc burlesque', you will be pleased to hear that I have decided to set Apollinaire's *Mamelles de Tirésias*. Everything will be sung, but treated as arias, duos and ensembles. I do not know if this quaint little work will ever be performed but the main thing is that I want to write it.

May I now defend Messager's orchestration of the Chopin.[2] Apart from the fact that Désormière – excellent in my music – conducted it like a military march, one has to take into account the present complement of strings at the Opéra: disastrous whenever the woodwinds are playing in threes. In the pit on 8 August there were precisely ten first violins, seven second violins, six violas, six cellos and five double-basses. I know there were the holidays to contend with, but as the desks left empty by prisoners or Jews have never been filled, the music has seriously suffered. All the same, *Boléro* was not all that bad.

Have you ever had my song cycle on poems by Eluard: *Tel jour telle nuit*? If not I will send it to you, as I am very fond of it.

When you have read the score of *Les Animaux* tell me frankly if you still hold to your opinion. I send you my very affectionate regards.

Fr. Poulenc

160. FRANCIS POULENC TO ANDRÉ SCHAEFFNER

Noizay, [1942]

Thank you, my dear André, for your letter, which gave me true pleasure. I wanted to write to you so often during the summer but I found it difficult to express my very complex state of mind. The undeniably GRRREAT success of *Les Animaux* has brought many things bitterly home to me. I have suddenly become aware that for all the twenty-five years in which I have been writing music, a whole section of the public has cared very little for what I have been doing. So many surprised, delighted hands reached out to me in the foyer of the Opéra that I suddenly thought: but what about *Tel jour telle nuit*, *Les Motets pour un temps de pénitence*, *Fiançailles pour rire*, my Mass, *Sécheresses*, and so forth . . . Does none of that count? The public is not entirely wrong, however: as the reorchestrated *Biches* has not yet seen the light of day, it is solely in the realm of chamber and choral music that I have earned my stripes. In this domain, a great deal more insight is required to gauge the exact weight of a work.

Perhaps I have waited too long to express myself symphonically. Yet I have no regrets about this as I am only good at things I really want to do. Besides, I am certain that, for those who love Apollinaire and Eluard, what I have composed in the way of *mélodies* will complement the poetry of our time. I shall therefore be only too happy to meet many of my critics some twenty years hence.

During my stay in the country I have been doing a lot of thinking, and replaying a lot of music composed between the wars. What worthless drivel in the main, and how the names that count are so clearly those that we had always predicted. Only the kind of mediocrity that prevails today could so easily brush aside Stravinsky, Prokofiev, Satie, Hindemith, Falla, etc.

Apart from Françaix[1] and Messiaen, all the young composers are quite happy with what was done before 1914. Have you seen Hubeau's[2] Sonata, just published by Durand!!! Dear Delannoy[3] never lets us forget Milhaud for a moment, nor does Arthur [Honegger], to be quite frank. I earnestly hope this is just a passing phase and that ideas – after this dreary purgatory – will forge ahead again.

After some weeks of silence (I was in fact suffering rather badly from a liver complaint) I have settled down to work again. I have revised and completed the rough draft of a Sonata for piano and violin. The monster is now ready.[4] It is not too bad, I believe, and in any case very different from the endless *violin-melodic line* sonatas written in France in the nineteenth century. How beautiful Brahms' sonatas are! I did not know them very well. One cannot achieve a proper balance between two such different instruments as the piano and the violin unless one treats them absolutely equally. The prima donna violin above an arpeggio piano accompaniment makes me vomit. Debussy, somewhat breathless in his Sonata, has nevertheless succeeded in turning it into a masterpiece by sheer instrumental tact.

I am also working on six songs for voice and orchestra, based on 'folk poems' by Maurice Fombeure.[5] Imagine a kind of *Pribaoutki*[6] from the Morvan. I think they will be rather good and very striking in style and instrumentation.

I am well aware that I am not the kind of musician who makes harmonic innovations, like Igor, Ravel or Debussy, but I do think there is a place for *new* music that is content with using other people's chords. Was this not the case with Mozart and with Schubert? And in any case, with time, the personality of my harmonic style will become evident. Was not Ravel long regarded as nothing more than a *petit maître* and imitator of Debussy? By pouring out my heart to you like this I am reacting to certain implied criticisms so often levelled against me. Besides, I know your way of thinking on this matter and that is why 'our' book is so close to my heart.[7]

I shall be returning to Paris on 4 November for the winter. We must see each other often. I am sending you four tickets for my concert on the 7th, for both of you and the Souvtchinskys.[8] You will see how well my *Chansons gaillardes* – already fifteen years old – have stood the test of time.

We are also doing *Histoires pour enfants* by Igor. It is slight but divine, and at least his name, for once, will appear on our programme.

Marie-Laure [de Noailles] will be in your box.

So, until the 7th!

Best regards to your wife.

I embrace you.

Fr.

Please give the tickets to Souv[tchinsky] on my behalf, as I do not have his address.

161. FRANCIS POULENC TO PIERRE BERNAC

Beaulieu, 17 August [1943]

Mon vieux Pierre,

This is my last letter from Beaulieu as I am leaving on Friday for Brive where I shall spend five days before going to Paris. I very nearly had nobody to do my cooking in Touraine, as Marguerite left me in the lurch. Fortunately Georgette Chadourne[1] has come to my rescue, letting me have her maid from 4 September. Raymond [Destouches][2] has gone again, looking very well after three weeks of holiday.

In the end I worked far better than I would have believed. The rough draft of my Eluard cantata is finished.[3] I think the eight sections hang together quite well. It is certainly the most powerful of my choral works so far. Three of the sections are for double choir. So about 200 people will be needed. Which means this work is destined for Belgium. The music really fits the words – which have suggested some curious modulations. You simply have to know the Eluard rhythm as I do to get the best out of it all. The final (double) chorus is made up of twenty quatrains of identical rhythm (excuse my wretched paper)* which begin like this:

> Sur mes cahiers d'écolier
> Sur mon pupitre et les arbres
> Sur le sable et sur la neige
> J'écris ton nom

*The original letter is written on ledger paper.

> Sur toutes les pages lues
> Sur toutes les pages blanches
> Pierre sang papier ou cendre
> J'écris ton nom
> etc. etc.

and work up to the final coda:

> Et par le pouvoir d'un mot
> Je recommence ma vie
> Je suis né pour te connaître
> Pour te nommer
> Liberté.[4]

You can see from this the kind of gymnastics required in the modulations and just how precise the inflections have to be. But I think I've got it now. In any case, there is a great sense of continuity due to the single direction of the poems.

After so much grandeur and nobleness I think I'll attack *Les Mamelles* – I have some amusing ideas for it. When I stop off in Paris I shall talk to Bébé[5] about it – I am sure he will put me on the right track.

The weather, thank God, is cooler. The countryside is ravishingly beautiful, but still nothing like the Morvan, which really inspires me. I shall certainly go next summer after an inspection in May. Write to me in Paris.

I have better news of Jean de Polignac.

[. . .] Papoue[6] is expected at my hotel on Saturday. She'll be delighted as the food is very good there – meat morning and evening, eggs, etc.

My colleagues have not given me a good press for the Sonata [for violin] but praise to the skies the *Chansons villageoises*. Fortunately there are violinists impatient to see the Sonata published.[7] The piano here was too bad to even think of the one for cello.[8]

I embrace you. Write,

Fr.

I cannot wait to get the title of the cantata.[9]

162. PAUL ELUARD TO FRANCIS POULENC

Poitiers, 23 August 1943

Mon cher Francis,

It is very remiss of you not to know my address (35 rue de la Chapelle, tel: Nord 26–40). If your letter – which has only just reached me today – had never arrived, you would have resented my not finding you any titles. I will give the matter some thought. For the moment, all I can think of is: *Je suis né pour te nommer* [*I was born to name you*]. Would that type of title be suitable?[1] You must not expect too much, as it is far more difficult for me to find a new title for an entire collection, including a text as different and important as 'Liberté', than it is for me to group together under one heading poems like those in *Tel jour telle nuit*.

My books are very carefully *put together*.[2]

However, rather let me speak of the joy and pride I feel in your venture.

Will you stay long in Brive? Make a note of my address, for we must keep in touch. Are you in fact still in Brive??

As for us, our short sojourn here on the banks of the Clain is proving to be very useful. We have been staying with Denyse Parrot[3] who sang *Tel jour telle nuit* in Clermont-Ferrand in the spring. We are going back at the end of the week.

And we embrace you very affectionately.

Paul E.

163. FRANCIS POULENC TO MARTHE BOSREDON

Nogent-sur-Marne, Wednesday, 5 o'clock [Summer, 1943?]

Gourgandine jolie,

I am writing from my home town, where I am spending a day of pilgrimage. Nothing is as melancholy as this kind of introspection into the past; yet I can never resist it. But where are the banks of the Marne of yesteryear, now with no open-air dance-halls, no accordion bands, no Bébert in his cap and Nini in her pink silk blouse! A whole side of my music can be explained by my suburban past: that part, 'tickling in all the right places', of 'Hôtel' and your latest song – which Marie-Blanche de Polignac, who is difficult to please, considers to be one of my best. So sleep in peace and wait patiently for a legible copy.[1]

By the way, you are an angel. Thanks to your card, I recalled a ravishing theme and the whole structure of a piece for two pianos which I first sketched in Cahors. This is very important for me. So, in fact, you are my Saint Antoine de Padoue.[2]

I shall not leave for Noizay until Sunday.

Excuse my disjointed style. I am writing from a beach full of boisterous bathers.

Write quickly to Noizay and tell me that you are happy. I *demand* this, and embrace you warmly.

Fr.

164. FRANCIS POULENC TO PIERRE BERNAC

Saturday, 24 June [1944]

Mon petit Pierre,

I am taking advantage of a lorry service to send you this long letter. I am taking further advantage of a slight lull in the domestic storm to tell you about things other than power failures, water cuts, missing keys, refugees, etc. It is not much fun, day after day, I assure you. A week ago I even reached the point of envying you your precarious nocturnal electricity while here we were going to bed in the pitch dark and fetching water from the bottom of the garden. And on top of all that, the house is full. After the bomb attack on Amboise I went to fetch old mother La Rochette[1] and then the group from Tours – Raymond's [Destouches] mother, father and sister. The old prima donna is at our table. The others eat in the outside kitchen. As I am taxed to capacity with four refugees I prefer it this way; but things are not going smoothly and the situation is fairly delicate, as always when the social levels are not the same. I am expressing myself badly – Raymond's parents are very nice and it upsets me to think that they are not eating at the same table as their son. I know you will instinctively understand what I mean.

I do not contemplate the summer with much joy but then these are such minor misfortunes compared with the disasters all around us. I dream of nothing more than a long cure of solitude after the war. But forgive me – when I began this letter I vowed I would speak about other things. So here goes . . .

I am working regularly. Time – and those like yourself who love my music – will tell whether it is good or not. I am concentrating on *Les Mamelles*. A week from now I think I will have completed the final draft of the Prologue and Scene I. I had a lot of difficulty overcoming certain pitfalls in the text and respecting each *word* as well as the *work as a whole*. The husband's aria has turned out really well, although for a week I could not think of anything at all. You have certainly played a part in this because after I received your letter enlightening me about the tessituras, I wrote the aria as if it were for you.[2] With the result that, on hearing a particular melodic curve, Uncle Papoum said quite spontaneously: 'Oh! I can just hear Bernac singing that!'

I had always believed I would write *Les Mamelles* during a happy summer. It has, alas, been nothing of the sort.

The first act is divided as follows:

Scene I – Tirésias's aria (with grateful thanks to *Manon!*).[3]
Scene II – Tirésias-Thérèse (coda of Scene I).

Scene III – Lacouf and Presto (comedy tenor and baritone) (duo of the boozers).

Scene IV – Funeral of the duellists (the people of Zanzibar, Thérèse and the husband).

Scene V – Duo of the gendarme and the husband.

Scene VI – The husband's aria (very lyrical and poetic).

Scene VII – Finale – everybody except Thérèse.

The husband's aria is essential because it determines the role. I am reserving my wildest follies for the second act so as to keep up interest. Not for one moment have I lost sight of my light orchestration.

What with my words, my tessituras, my instrumentation, you see what tortures I am suffering. Uncle Royer, a very old devotee of the Opéra-Comique, and oblivious of my anguish, declares himself content. This is already a great deal. Many of the scenic details have suggested the music to me. I think the situations will be enough in themselves, for in the theatre I never rely much on the power of words. It would be hard to imagine 'Fêtes galantes'[4] on stage. I have read with very great care the orchestral score of *l'Heure espagnole,*[5] with the piano reduction close at hand. What a miraculous masterpiece, but what a deadly dangerous example (like all masterpieces). When one does not have the magical precision of Ravel, which alas is the case with me, one has to plant one's music firmly on sturdy feet.

Raymond brought me a copy of the Cantata [*Figure humaine*]. The others are all waiting, ready and wrapped, at friend Paul's [Rouart]. How comforted I am by this work in my hours of despondency. I hope and pray that I will be allowed to hear it at least once in my lifetime.

When I received it I did not want – as so often happens with my other works – to revise it all the minute I set eyes on it. It is successful both in its inspiration and in its workmanship, and this gives me new strength. A pity it is so difficult to perform. But this is also one of its qualities. Paul E. [Eluard] mysteriously sent me a typed poem with, at the top, simply: 'My dear Francis . . . Paul'. The tone of the poem – very beautiful, moreover – and the succinctness of the style, touched me deeply. It is really Eluard who has brought out the best in me.

The two Apollinaire songs, 'Montparnasse' and 'Hyde Park', are almost finished, apart from a word here and there.[6] Given that, in some peculiarly prescient way, the second of the two is unsingable at the moment, there is no urgency now.

Despite days when I am dejected and weary, I am nevertheless full of hope [*espérance*] (why was I about to write *expérience*?). I know we have some fine years ahead which we must turn to good advantage. Beautiful concerts, like those in Brussels, are lying in limbo, just waiting for us.

Although letters take a week to get here from Paris, write to me at length. It will give me so much pleasure. Were it not for the wretched question of food I think one would be better off in Paris. Tours is disastrous, badly damaged, alas, and practically deserted. Marie-Thérèse M.[7] and a few other ladies from her area are the only faithful ones.

The troops head ceaselessly towards the north, without a trace of euphoria, I assure you, and with such a weariness on so many faces that one absolutely longs for 'a crowd at last united'.[8]

I think the Pléïade concert must have fallen through. The time really wasn't right for it. For some time now, and without being a prophet, I have been unable to imagine the spring of '44 any differently.

Give me detailed news of everyone. Did the Messiaen performances take place and did you hear his *Liturgies?*[9] I have been playing quite a lot of his music again. When he sticks to his own methods and vision, it is truly remarkable; in other more contrived pages the influence of Dukas is irritating.[10] There can be nothing worse – in fact, for any of us. Saint-Saëns' method could guide a Ravel, for example. But what Dukas uses is a method based on other methods.

What has happened to Yvonne [de Casa Fuerte] and Papoue [Geneviève Touraine]? (What will become of her son when???) Poor girl.

Have you seen Marie-Blanche [de Polignac]? The poor creature was not made for these times. How she must miss Jean [de Polignac]! Is Suzanne Peignot in Paris? If so, give her a kiss from me.

I have devised a programme for a Poulenc Festival of *mélodies* which I am submitting to you (this so as to take my mind off things and to give me hope). I have had this idea for quite some time.

I   *Bestiaire* (1919). *Quatre poèmes* Apollinaire (1932) – you.
II   5 Max Jacob (1932) – Suzanne Balguerie.[11]
III   *Tel jour* (1937) – you.
IV   *Fiançailles* (1939) – Suzanne.
V   Jardin d'Anna (1938) – you.
       Allons plus vite (1944).
       Montparnasse, Hyde Park (1943).
       2 Aragon.

Not bad, eh, with *Villageoises* as an encore, thereby paying homage to Apollinaire, Max [Jacob], Eluard, Aragon, Loulou [Louise de Vilmorin]. Festival of Songs by Fr. Poulenc with the participation of Madame S.B., Monsieur P.B. and the composer. Pretty poster.

And with that, I'll leave you. I feel better and embrace you affectionately.

Fr.

I have on my mantelpiece a photo of Autun[12] as others have of a beloved woman.

165. Francis Poulenc to Pierre Bernac

Friday 14 July [1944]

Thank you *mon cher petit Pierre* for your long and lovely letter. Of all the letters I receive yours are especially precious to me, for you and Auric are my two true spiritual brothers, the only ones with whom I can discuss my work quite openly.[1] I am not *at all* well, my rheumatism is spreading, my shoulder is hurting now. I have made up my mind to consult a doctor, a refugee from Asnières, whom everyone says is very good and who will come here tomorrow. The mediocrity, or indeed worse, of the quacks in Amboise has led me to make this choice. For the last three weeks I have not set foot beyond my terrace. You can imagine how low my morale is – and what this forced confinement is doing to the state of my nerves. Since yesterday I seem unable to play the piano, so I suppose that soon the only thing left for me will be reading. The rough draft of *Les Mamelles* is almost finished. There remain only the finales of the first and second acts and the entr'acte. I am letting them 'settle' so as to be able to view them more clearly when I eventually get down to copying them out neatly.

I am afraid that this might be the last journey of this lorry as they were caught in the act [of carrying mail]. Another local van that comes by regularly might be willing to do me a few favours, but it stops at a grocer's where I don't shop . . . you can understand the rest. Won't you go and talk to Dubois and ask him to see if he can possibly set something up for me? He could perhaps call in the driver, whose particulars are as follows: 'Driver of van 16 – T.A.M. – Garage rue Balard'. And give him instructions, so as to make things easier for me, bearing in mind the possibility of an eventual trip to Paris for me. Attend to this immediately and seriously for otherwise I shall be cut off from everything – I tremble at the thought . . .

Thank you for sending the Messiaen to me. I find it quite simply indescribable, which does not stop me from feeling that he has a lot of talent. Dukas and Dupré[2] are very responsible for its didactic tone, exacerbated by the gentleman's mysticism. I would like to speak to you at length about all this but cannot because the lorry is leaving.

I just have time to embrace you very affectionately,

Fr.

The old girl, Rochette, who really thinks she is the upper crust, is sometimes absolutely odious. It's all I can do not to yell at her. Raymond's parents are *invisible* and utterly adorable. They are the best things here.

166. FRANCIS POULENC TO PIERRE BERNAC

Saturday [1944]

Mon vieux Pierre,

As the 'postal-lorry' has still not returned I conclude that we will now have to make do without it. Having received two letters in three days through the ordinary channels, I hope that we will be able to write to each other normally again.

I have just spent a horrible fortnight from every point of view. After taking the treatment prescribed by Chiron that Charles[1] had brought me, and feeling less and less well, Rhus tox and Bryonia having no beneficial effect on me at all, I called in a doctor who had fled here from Asnières and who is *perfect*. Far from being against homeopathy, he diagnosed my condition (attack of acute arthritis) and I continued with the Chiron treatment for some days, plus Sulfur and a dose of Nux. As my temperature rose every evening (to 37.6) I decided to prescribe my own allopathic treatment and thanks to sulphanilamides I now feel a new lease of life. Since yesterday I have had no temperature but my general state of nerves still has to be watched. I have not stepped out of home for exactly *one month* now, the terrace being the furthest I have ventured. Not being able to get away from daily domestic troubles, I became the way you knew me at Pouldu. There was one *dreadful* scene – where I yelled at Charles (odious because he wanted to give all the orders) – that shattered my entire entourage. Fortunately I was put in the right by my poor old uncle, who paid dearly the following morning by having an attack, which upset me terribly. You, better than anyone, understand the seething ferment that results from ill-assorted people being forced to live together. The Daciers in Nazelles had to leave some close friends after only one evening in order to avoid a violent outbreak.

For the moment, calm has been restored but it is awful to feel that for various reasons one simply cannot get away from each other. Thank God the news is so much better now, and hope so much more specific, that the radio has become my best medicine. I have not done a stroke of work for a fortnight, and quite frankly this was the best thing to do. Yesterday I played through everything I had done on *Les Mamelles* and on Monday I shall start copying it out. I want to be on top form to attack the two finales and the entr'acte (which is all I have still to do) as they are as important to the whole as 'Liberté' to the Cantata. Looking calmly over my rough drafts again, I can only tell you that this is 200% pure Poulenc. In any case, I believe that from the Apollinaire point of view, there could not be anything more orthodox. More than ever have I paid attention to the mute letters and taken into account the major role of the liaisons, which singers too frequently neglect. Particular fast phrases will only be intelligible if the liaison is violently stressed. To say that this is 'new Poulenc' – well, not really, but it could not be otherwise because of the constant relationship between Apollinaire's lines and so many of his poems that I have already set to music. However, it is *crammed* with music, with agreeably little repetition of the numerous themes, and *above all, above all*, it is madly scenic. There is not one event on stage that is not directly connected to the music, which gave me a lot of serious problems. Two retorts held me up for more than a week. The more I think about it, the more I believe that it is not possible to write true arias unless based on a sequence of lines. Otherwise, the rhythm is far too broken. For the lyrical work I dream of writing, it has to be like this.

Jacques [Février] and Claude Rostand are coming (by bike) to spend two days in Amboise, which will be like a breath of fresh air for me. If things do not get worse, couldn't you come as well, and spend a week here? I could quite easily put you up and you know the pleasure this would give me. Think about it, won't you? The speed of events will perhaps make all of this mere child's play. I know that you must be feeling a new lease of life, as I do. As I have repeated to you so often, there are wonderful days ahead of us. [. . .] Tell me about your plans for the Conservatoire. Of course you must make sure that you will still be free to go on long tours. Mind you, with air travel these days, everything is so easy. [. . .]

I have heard from various quarters that Papoue [Geneviève Touraine] sang *Les Fiançailles* extremely well. [. . .]

Write soon. I embrace you very affectionately.

Fr.

167. FRANCIS POULENC TO COMTESSE JEAN DE POLIGNAC

27 July [1944]

Chère Marie-Blanche,

Thank you for your long letter which brought me a breath of tenderness. Touraine is killing me, you have said it. Every evening I become feverish, just as I did in Rome, which exasperates me. Between seven and eight at night I virtually suffocate, and the rest of the time, I rail against this place, against all my domestic problems and against my own anxiety. Consequently, for the past three weeks I have done no work, as all this is enough to curdle the milk of my *Mamelles*.

I do not know what to make of this composition and I prefer to let it rest. Of course, give me a room near Autun and some solitude, and inspiration would quickly return. But I suppose everyone has to pay his due and mine is pretty slight. I try in thought to escape from here. An album of photos of Paris charms and lulls me like a shot of morphine. I beg of you, never let anyone refer to me as *le musicien tourangeau*,[1] for I have ALWAYS worked here as if in a prison, dreaming of those magic landscapes – Monte Carlo, Nogent, boulevard de la Chapelle, etc.

Yes, July is the month I always used to spend at Kekker. If only you knew how constantly I think of this. The other day the sound of my neighbour's old iron staircase made my heart leap. I thought I was stepping out of your Britanny hall and instinctively sought the simultaneous sound of a horse's hoof on the gravel.

What an endless string of memories come crowding in: the fragrance of magnolias in the hallway near the rackets; your perfume in the first-floor corridor; the scent of thyme at the turning to your mother's room, and of greengages and peaches in my own. The sound of the wood in the boiler around eight at night; and you and Jean, *always late* coming down, the black velvet dinner jacket and your dear, lovely face. All this is so pleasant to recall that it is not even sad, you see. No one can rob us of our memories – they belong to us and we must live on them. Writing all this to you today is a melancholy but sweet escape. I find my surroundings less depressing and I pity only those who have not lived. To suffer loss is hard, but never to have had anything is worse. That is why, when I picture you in the evenings alone and unhappy, what comforts me is to have known you once fulfilled.

In a different domain, all the beautiful paintings I have seen throughout my travels (even the Tiepolos in Venice) keep me company for hours when I recall them to mind, alone in some room. That you have turned to music again fills me with joy. Yes, the andante of the *Jupiter* is the height of unbelievable perfection. It has everything: line, freshness, grandeur, and what orchestration!!! Try to follow the score so as to savour the writing for woodwind. After hearing that, one wonders why one bothers to compose at all. I have become so hard on myself that there are days when, had I total faith, I would close my piano and retire to a monastery.

Fortunately there is one work, and perhaps only one, that tells me I was right to compose music, and that is my Cantata on poems by Eluard. I have a secret copy of it here. I play it every day, and its underlying integrity and faith foil my foulest mood, my harshest self-criticisms.

I have interrupted this letter for 24 hours because Paul Rouart, my publisher (son-in-law of Paul Valéry), unexpectedly rang at my door, having cycled back from Angers and being in need of hospitality. His presence dispelled for a while the detestable atmosphere of Le Grand Coteau and provided a most precious relaxation for me. He will take this letter to you. So I shall cut it short. I showed him (chastely) a little of my *Mamelles*. He seems sincerely pleased, which encourages me.

If there is no lorry available, write to me by post. It eventually gets here. I hope you have been able to soften the lot of poor Fernand. Have you heard from Marya [Freund]?

I embrace you in haste, very affectionately.

Fr.

168. FRANCIS POULENC TO AGATHE ROUART-VALÉRY

[July] 1944

Chère Agathe,

Paul's [Rouart] visit is an immense joy to me. It has cheered me up, and I was in great need of that.

Naturally I miss you (this is not a mere cliché) and embrace you.

Francis

169. FRANCIS POULENC TO PIERRE BERNAC

Sunday [1944]

Mon petit Pierre,

A very nice Parisian refugee has kindly offered to take this letter to you, and once again, I am using you as my central distributor of news. In the first place, need I say how thirsty we all are here for news of you all, and of our dear Paris. The wildest rumours have been circulating. We were told that 100,000 had been killed in Paris alone. The improbability of this extraordinary figure was enough in itself to reassure me. We heard that the Opéra had burnt down, Les Invalides and the Gabriel buildings[1] entirely destroyed, the Luxembourg Gardens riddled with shells, etc. Regardless of whether this was a lot of boloney or the sad truth, I naturally had to hide it all from Uncle Royer. As we have been without electricity and radio for three weeks, news has only reached us on the grapevine. Here, we feared the worst might happen, but thank God we have been spared. The Americans, arriving from Rennes, Laval, very quickly liberated our zone, but the Germans had blown up all the bridges and we feared they might put up some resistance. Enormous naval guns at Saint-Avertin were aimed at the Tranchée de Tours, Route du Mans, etc. We expected a small-scale defence of Amboise. We believed, thanks to the common sense of the Americans and the local resistance movement, that the jerries would push off by themselves, which in fact they did on Friday, the day before yesterday.

When the Americans arrived, Raymond [Destouches] behaved marvellously. He was fishing on the banks of the Loire when the first convoy came past, heading for Amboise. Wild with joy he hung on to one of the tanks and followed them right to the bridge of Amboise. At that point the Germans, hidden all along the avenue, let off a volley of machine-gun fire that killed three American soldiers. Protected by the tank, Raymond was unhurt. The Americans immediately aimed their tank guns at Amboise. Raymond begged the commanding officer not to fire as there were only about fifty soldiers in the town, who were likely not to be hit because they were on a lower level than the embankment, and the town itself would get the worst of it. Because of Raymond's trustworthy look, and his certificate from the English Red Cross, the commanding officer agreed not to fire and instead marshalled his convoy along the roads leading down to Nazelles. He gave a radio transmitter to Raymond, who crossed the Loire secretly in a fishing boat and went to find the Mayor of Amboise. When they had made sure that there were no more than sixty to eighty Germans in Amboise, the Americans withdrew to Pocé, with two dangerous missions to accomplish, one of which was to free Loches, also occupied by the Germans.

Such was the good work done by our young man. Tell his friends all this *in detail*, please. [. . .] He will probably go back to Paris soon and will return later to fetch Uncle Papoum, deeply shaken by these events. As for me, I went through sheer anguish thinking of you all and, I must confess, equal anguish thinking of my Paris. You know my passion for that city, as much for what is beautiful in it as for its more humble rue de Belleville or rue de la Chapelle. I am suffering, too, from not being there while everything is being reorganized, not that I'm on the lookout for a job (I would refuse any offered) but to be able to make my voice heard in the way of justice, as everyone knows I am perfectly pure and independent. [. . .]

I have been feeling well only for the past fortnight. Before that I suffered intermittent pains in the joints, sometimes accompanied by a temperature. Now that autumn has settled in, I feel reborn. I shall remember this year's stay here for a long time; it's only natural that in one way or another I should be punch-drunk from the events of this summer.

I have copied out the first act of *Les Mamelles*, except for the finale. The second (completely written also except for the finale), is coming along well, too. The work is far longer than I had anticipated. At least fifty minutes. I really think it is very good and that there are no holes in it. What I like about it now is that it is difficult to find the places where either the prosody or the poetic sense were so troublesome. In the text, the word Paris keeps cropping up; perhaps this, together with my nostalgia for its streets, enabled me to capture that moving tone in the midst of all the typically Apollinairian larks. Regarding the tessitura, it could not be more precisely defined, that is all I can tell you. We can go through it together with a fine-tooth comb, if you like.

Give my news to Marie-Blanche [de Polignac], Marie-Laure [de Noailles], Jacques [Février], and very especially to Edouard Bourdet, Inv. 67–80, to whom I replied by the last mail and who no doubt has never received my letter. [. . .]

When I think that Noizay is so totally untouched I feel almost ashamed. I hope that *Figure humaine* and *Les Mamelles* will prove a sufficient tribute from a Frenchman. The people of Noizay have been very good to me. Some of them even wanted to make me . . . Mayor! What a farce! Tell Marie-Blanche to cheer her up. Actually, I am sorry I could not oblige because there is nobody suitable here; but, alas, what could I possibly do for them?

Try to send me some news.

I embrace you affectionately.

Fr.

Kindest regards to your dear mother.

The day the Americans arrived, I triumphantly placed my Cantata [*Figure humaine*] on the desk in the study, near my flag, at the window.

170. FRANCIS POULENC TO HENRI SAUGUET

Noizay, 28 July [1944]

Cher Henri,

It makes me very happy to hear from far and wide of the success of *La Gageure*.[1] Paul Rouart's first words when he stopped by here for two days were: 'You were right, Sauguet is a true musician.' I am particularly keen to repeat this to you as I think he has not previously been exactly warm towards you. Same enthusiasm in letters from Claude [Rostand], Jacques [Février], etc. etc. You have come out on top, that is what matters, and that is certain.

How right you were to want to have it performed even at the end of the season. You are now launched. I did the same with *Les Animaux*, and it worked really well for me. Happy as I am about your success, you can imagine how despondent I feel about not having been there, for you know very well, dear Henri, that I have been a Sauguiste right from the start. Congratulate Jacques [Dupont] as well. By the way, I heard sadly of his great loss and would ask you please to pass the enclosed note on to him.

When shall we see each other again? I hope soon, and in peace-time. I feel horribly trapped here, more so because for five weeks I was entirely *house-bound* owing to a violent arthritic attack. I am better now, thank God, but if you add to this my anxieties in particular (full house) and my anguish in general, you will take my word that I am not in brilliant form. Nevertheless, I have been working. *Les Mamelles* is complete except for the two finales and the entr'acte. It has given me a great deal of trouble. I am encouraged by Paul Rouart's response to the work, but trying to set this text of Apollinaire to music really was a 'gamble'.

By giving full weight to the poetic content of this work, I hope to ensure that this bizarre little play enjoys more than an initial success based merely on surprise. It is dedicated to Darius for his return. My intention is to have completed the whole thing, music and orchestration, before going back. Circumstances permitting, I hope it will be performed next spring. It would be nice to share the same bill.

Jacques [Février] and Claude [Rostand] are supposed to be coming to Amboise for a few days. This would cheer me up considerably – solitude only appeals to me if it is broken by visits from friends. Tell me something about *Les Mirages*[2] now. I have asked Bernac, my obliging messenger, to send me the score, as well as that of *La Gageure*. Your première was too recent for me to have heard any talk of it yet.

Write quickly. Letters are tortoises but, like those in the fable, they do eventually arrive.

I embrace you, dear Henri.

Fr.

171. HENRI SAUGUET TO FRANCIS POULENC

18 rue Truffaut, Paris 17ᵉ, 4 August 1944

Cher Francis,

Your letter gave me enormous pleasure. Thank you for your loving friendship. I was very distressed, believe me, that none of my musician friends were with me at the première of *La Gageure*: neither you, nor Georges [Auric], nor Darius [Milhaud]! I felt very alone braving my judges. In fact, the work met with great, spontaneous success at all three performances and this consoled me for the press which – more or less in general – was really quite unpleasant towards me, as always. Benign – if somewhat idiotic – at the beginning, they changed their tone after the publication of Vuillermoz's[1] articles. There were two of them: one in some paper or other, the other in *Je suis partout*. Then all those who had been holding back began to vent their spleen. So, of course, I was 'nothing more than an amateur', or else 'a pleasant and witty enough *petit musicien*', or else 'a distinguished writer of delightfully out-dated songs'. What is the best thing I can do in response to attacks of this sort? Continue to write this poor music to the best of my ability while keeping well out of the way. But it seems that I am much too discreet about using all the means at my disposal. I ought perhaps to make far greater use of some of the tricks that are in vogue at the moment (and which of course I employ when I need to, like everyone else!) to get my compositions viewed with more favour. Obviously, Rameau's precept: '*Cachez l'art par l'art même*'[2] is frowned upon these days, when 'beautiful' has become synonymous with 'difficult' or 'complicated'. No doubt the only people we are dealing with now are vain, cold souls. And as my music is aimed only at sensitive souls it is obviously of no interest at all to that lot. Anyway, it certainly is of interest to the public: three full houses, consisting not only of friends or people there on my behalf, have cheered me up considerably. For the audience listened to me and they appear to have understood me. And if it is true that the words cannot always be heard, nor the plot understood, at least my success is an essentially *musical* one – and what more can one ask for? And if it is true that audiences very often have poor taste, they can nevertheless discern what is deeply felt and uncontrived. I do not know if they are mistaken in liking my work, but what is certain is that I do not believe *I* have deceived either myself or anyone else in writing it. Having said this, I was mortified by the press and was ill from it for quite some days. Now I have got over it. But I was thinking of seeking refuge in religion, like Mademoiselle de la Vallière after suffering a broken heart . . .[3] And no doubt I would not even have been a very good monk!

As for *Les Mirages*, we were most unlucky. The entire supply of electricity for all shows – theatres and cinemas – was cut off on the Friday before the week of our first performance. We were due to share the same bill as *Boléro* on the 28th: I had requested this. Now it has been put off, no doubt until after the war, because I cannot see this electricity business being cleared up before then. On the contrary, I believe there will in fact be more interruptions if there is a continuation of the massive bombings that have been ravaging the surroundings of Paris since the day before yesterday. Whatever will be left of this poor country, what with the advance of the allied armies, the bombings, the resistance movement, the conflagrations? . . . May God put a stop to this tragic disaster as soon as possible and bring back Peace to this absurd earth – which in no way deserves it but to which, since we are condemned to live here, I for my part would very much like to see it restored. Life here is extremely difficult. One spends a fortune to have a little food and one earns nothing now that theatres and cinemas are closed.

Otherwise, dear Francis, not much news. The weather is hot. I am trying to get away to Coutras. It is practically impossible. Impractically, it can be done by changing trains five or six times (and taking one to two weeks over it) or going by road. But until now I have found only disreputable lorries demanding 10,000 francs to take me to Bordeaux, plus the return fare! It is astronomical and crazy. So I remain where I am. Upset because I would like to see Maman, who has had a bad winter and wants me near her. I am very hesitant about taking to the road the way things are these days!

I am longing to hear *Les Mamelles*. I have been hoping for such a long time (and particularly since *Le Bal masqué*) that you would set a theatrical work to music. Of course, the subject is precisely that which would have frightened me most in the world. But you are more daring, more modern than I am and above all you have mastered your art to such an extent that – through its intense musical colour and life – it transcends the subject and gives it quite a different dimension. I cannot wait to hear it.

I can only hope that 'events' will take a turn for the better and that the end will soon be in sight. At present I think things are getting worse and that the engine of war is taking us towards ever more dreadful hardships; for in the face of impending disaster war takes on its most horrific guise – that of the lost war. And I would not like to be in Paris to see it – the further away the better!

Dear Francis, thank you again, with all my heart. Please tell Papoum [Marcel Royer] how touched I was by his letter and give him my best wishes and my best regards. Thanks also to dear, faithful Raymond [Destouches]. Jacques [Dupont] is sending you a note as well. He has had a great deal of trouble and is not feeling very strong at the moment.

A bientôt. May God protect you during the coming weeks and reunite us all soon.

Your faithful friend,
Henri S.

172. Francis Poulenc to Darius Milhaud

London, 3 January [1945]

Mon petit Darius,

I have been in London since yesterday. You can imagine my joy, and what this represents in terms of freedom regained. I am sending you this letter immediately via an officer who is leaving from here for New York, as the mail from France to America is still very precarious. I have so much to tell you that I don't know where to begin. You cannot imagine how often I think of you and how much I miss you. You can guess what we have been through these last four years; what would have become of you had you stayed on here? Thank God you had the foresight to realize this. The number of people deported and killed is beyond measure.

Here is a list of the work done by some of us:

AURIC – four very beautiful poems for voice and orchestra on texts by Eluard, Aragon, Supervielle; six ravishing works for unaccompanied choir;

an interesting Piano Concerto; an excellent song cycle on poems by Eluard; some very good film music.

SAUGUET – a very lovely string quartet; an *adorable* comic opera on *La Gageure imprévue* by Sedaine, unfortunately suspended for the moment at the Opéra-Comique owing to the purges among singers; a good many songs and, thank heavens, several films which have brought him new acclaim.

ARTHUR [Honegger] – a stunning symphony for strings; an *immense* Passion, not yet completed, for Switzerland; and various other works.

MESSIAEN – some first-rate compositions: quartet for piano, violin, clarinet and cello; organ pieces; a long suite for two pianos; litanies for choir and orchestra. Either one loves this music or one hates it, but it cannot be ignored any more than the paintings of Rouault. It has greatly influenced a whole generation of 25-year-olds, which is perhaps not so fortunate, as they are becoming systematized.

MYSELF – *Les Animaux modèles*, ballet based on fables of La Fontaine for which I have written the scenario, with décor by Brianchon. The choreography is by Lifar and as a consequence the work has been suspended, Serge having been childishly careless through his taste for publicity;[1] *Banalités*, song cycle on poems by Apollinaire; *Fiançailles pour rire*, song cycle on poems by Louise de Vilmorin; various song settings of Aragon and Eluard; Sonata for piano and violin (to the memory of Garcia Lorca); *Chansons villageoises* (Fombeure) for voice and orchestra; *Figure humaine*, cantata for double choir *a cappella* on marvellous poems by Eluard, one of which is 'Liberté'. De Vocht[2] is conducting this work – generally considered to be my best. It was printed clandestinely in May '44 by Paul Rouart and lasts 25 minutes.

Lastly, I wrote *Les Mamelles de Tirésias* this summer, an opéra-bouffe in two acts on a text by Apollinaire, which I have dedicated to you for your return to France.

We are all waiting to celebrate your return, but you are right not to rush back as your loved ones are alas no longer here. In '42 I went to see your mother. I spent a deeply moving day with her in Aix. Admirable in her courage, she kept repeating to me: 'I am happy that my Da is out of danger.'

Here in London, I have tried in vain to obtain your latest music. Try to send some to me at the French Embassy in London, c/o Louis Roché. It will be forwarded on to me. Please give our news to all our friends there.

While I am here, I am playing my Concerto for two pianos with Britten,[3] who has written some very good new works. Did you hear about the death of Jean de Polignac?[4] I have been very distressed about it. Their house in Britanny was ransacked. I am fortunate to have Noizay intact.

Write me a long letter, c/o the French Embassy in London. Give Madeleine a kiss from me, and Daniel too. I embrace you with all my affection.

Ton vieux Francis

Kindest regards from Bernac.

173. DARIUS MILHAUD TO FRANCIS POULENC

Mills College, Oakland, California, 5 January 1945

Mon si cher Francis,

Have you received my cards, my letters? If only you knew how I am longing to hear from you, at length and in detail. Tell me about your life throughout these last appalling years. Tell me, too, about everything you have written. Give me news of your family, your uncle, your sister and her family. Give Brigitte [Manceaux] my fondest regards.

I received a letter from my brother-in-law Etienne who tells me that he saw you.

Give me news of our musician friends – Georges [Auric], Henri [Sauguet], Déso [Désormière], Arthur [Honegger].

Over here, I have been working.[1] I am better this year but from January to September '44 I was seriously afflicted and thought that I would never walk again.[2] And I need my poor old legs to come and join you when transport conditions improve. I do not think this will be possible before the end of the war in Europe.

Did you see Menuhin when he played in Paris? I would love to receive some of your music. Perhaps through Foreign Affairs you might be able to send something?

And Deiss?[3] I would like to know whether he is all right. I left quite a few unpublished manuscripts with him (*Ronsard, Adages, Carnaval de Londres, Annonce faite à Marie, Pan et Syrinx* – goodness knows what else).

I will write to you regularly. Please, *cher petit*, do the same.

Daniel is a big boy now. He is doing some military training but mostly he paints and will, I think, become a painter.[4]

We have talked about you such a lot with Igor and Vera Stravinsky who came and spent two days here with Nadia Boulanger. Igor gave a lecture at the College and played his latest works for two pianos (Sonata, *Scherzo à la russe, Circus Polka*) with Nadia. It was a great event for us as we are quite a distance away from our European friends who are either in New York or Hollywood, and Hollywood is after all 700 kilometres from here. And, anyway, travelling is very complicated at the moment and one cannot find anywhere to stay. In March, Tansman and his wife[5] are coming here to give a lecture and a two-piano performance. I generally go to New York at Christmas and it is always wonderful to see the Rietis again, Yvonne [de Casa Fuerte], the Chareaux, the Claudel children, André Maurois and his wife.

Poor Vittorio [Rieti] heard that his mother had been deported from San Remo, with her blind sister and a brother, all of them over eighty years old.

Germaine Tailleferre is near Philadelphia. Monteux[6] and his wife are in San Francisco and we see them now and again. But this year I have had to forgo my trip to the East Coast and my concerts there, as I have to be careful about my health.

Mady sends her love. So do I.

Your D.

We often listen with emotion to the recording of your Mass, which we managed to obtain, and also to *Aubade* and your Trio which are in the College Library.

174. DARIUS MILHAUD TO FRANCIS POULENC

Mills College, 17 February 1945

Mon petit Francis,

At last I have received your long-awaited letter from London! Thank you for all the details about our musician-friends. It is admirable that you have been able to produce so many fine works during the past four years, in such atrocious and inhuman conditions. How I would love to hear your new compositions! I will send you a parcel of music soon through the Embassy in London, or perhaps through Washington (if I can send it directly to Paris in the diplomatic bag).

I learnt with intense sorrow of the deportation of Deiss.[1] What happened? Was he in the Resistance? It is heartbreaking.

I was very seriously ill for ten months and now that I have come through it I can barely walk 50 to 100 metres a day and am still very debilitated. In addition to my usual arthritic miseries I suffered an acute decalcification of the bones in the feet and knees, and after being bedridden for three months I languished in a wheel-chair for a further six. I shall have to wait until transport and living conditions are back to normal [before coming home].

We live in the country, in the park attached to the College. Naturally, we feel terribly isolated and cut off, but this place has been a refuge beyond all our hopes and we are somewhat ashamed of having benefited from such physical comfort while you have all suffered so much.

My teaching job keeps me amused – it is even quite exciting. And I am able to do a lot of my own work as I only teach for two hours in the mornings.

You will be receiving letters and cards that I wrote as soon as the postal services resume, with news of my compositions.

Stravinsky is in Hollywood but we are not able to see him much. Hollywood and San Francisco are about as far apart as Paris and Marseilles. He came here with Vera for three days. He gave a lecture at the College and, with Nadia [Boulanger], played his new Sonata for two pianos, which is delightful, a *Scherzo à la russe* (very *Petrushka* 1944) and his Polka for the elephants of Barnum Circus, which I do not like. He has written a wonderful Symphony, an Ode in three parts – also very beautiful – and two charming ballets. In Hollywood there are also the Tansmans and their two little girls. He has developed a lot and I heard a Symphony and a Quartet of his that were extremely moving. He did the music for a film two years ago and for another one this year. I myself have not been able to do anything in Hollywood. It is dreadful there, you have to be on the spot all the time and relentlessly on the go. I much prefer my modest College and the peace of the parklands bordered with eucalyptus trees all along the side of the house.

Rieti works at the Office of War Information in New York, doing Italian translations. He has had a great many difficulties musically. But at last Golschmann has performed one of his pieces; the admirable Budapest Quartet has played his second Quartet, which is charming; and the Ballet Theatre has devised a divertissement to a suite of waltzes by him.

Fabio[2] was mobilized, underwent a serious operation on his arm and was discharged from the army afterwards. He is due to come here with Elsie this summer, which will relieve our solitude and which makes me very happy for Daniel's sake, because Fabio paints and is talented and Daniel lives only for his painting and will be able to work solidly with Fabio.

Thanks to Kurt Weill, Yvonne [de Casa Fuerte] has at last been able to get into the orchestra at the theatre that puts on all Kurt's musical comedies, tremendously successful here.

Jean[3] is in the army, in Algiers for his military training.

Of the other musicians, Hindemith is at Yale. His music is very beautiful (Symphony). He has written an astonishing work on themes by Weber. Bartók is at Columbia University doing research on folklore. He is very ill.

Schoenberg is seventy and in retirement at the University of Los Angeles. He has three children, the youngest of whom is four. He came here for a few weeks, with his wife and his eldest daughter of twelve, to conduct his *Verklärte Nacht*, set as a ballet with miraculous choreography. There is an Englishman, Anthony Tudor, who is a choreographer of genius. He has brought a new element into the dance form, an acutely aware psychological element, sensuous, unbelievable in its intensity; but he generally uses impossible music. His masterpiece is a *Romeo* with music by Delius and wonderful scenery and costumes by Eugene Berman who is becoming a really *first-class* painter. He has done some marvellous stage décor for Stravinsky. Of the painters, Fernand Léger is still in New York, as cordial and affable as ever. He sells well. André Masson lives in the country – I haven't seen him at all. Berman lives in Hollywood and sees Igor constantly. Nadia [Boulanger], after teaching on the East Coast, is now living in Santa Barbara near Hollywood, with friends of hers called Sachs.

Dali enjoys a prodigious success here, which he maintains through constant extravaganzas. I came across him once at Carmel (a small beach not far from here). He was with Edward James, still the same as ever, charming and slightly dotty. Dali was very nice to Daniel, who was twelve at the time, and gave him lots of advice for his painting. Daniel as artist *tickles me pink*. Thanks to the wonderful university libraries here, he has been able to study in depth, through reproductions, the entire history of painting. He knows *everything*. He is only sorry not to have lived during the Renaissance! He has visited some very fine museums here, in New York and Chicago, and some magnificent exhibitions. Since the age of ten he has been painting constantly, and what he does stems directly from Dali, Bérard, Tchelitchev, and especially from Berman. How mysterious the sources of a painting are! He copies a lot of Italian drawings from the Renaissance. Physically he has developed very well and has turned into a charming youngster. He knows *everything* about music thanks to radio, records and concerts. He adores Francis, Stravinsky, Prokofiev and Tchaikovsky! As for my own music, he knows it by heart practically the moment it is written down. He is also in the cadets at his school.

Kurt [Weill] and [Lotte] Lenya have an old house in the country near New York. He is still as immensely kind as ever. He is the sort of friend one can always count on when things go wrong.

During the summer, here at Mills, we have a six-week session complete with 'Maison française'. Mady [Madeleine Milhaud] teaches diction and the history of theatre, and puts on a French play. Unfortunately her activity in this area is limited to the summer. For the rest of the year she is mostly housewife, cook, and driver, as the problem of 'servants' does not exist here: there simply aren't any! Or only for millionaires, and even then . . . The libraries here are her salvation as she reads a great deal, and she works in San Francisco at the American Relief for France, helping with the dispatch of clothing. And we always have one or another writer coming to the 'Maison française'. André Maurois has been twice, and also Julien Green. We are very fond of them both.

Among our virtuoso friends, Robert Casadesus enjoys an enormous success. He plays divinely. He is the greatest pianist here. Horowitz hardly plays any more due to ill health. Francescatti is also very successful. I heard him on the radio playing the Paganini. Szigeti gave a recital with a new Sonata by Prokofiev (originally written for flute and transcribed by Prokofiev himself specially for Szigeti). It is an enchanting work. But the musician with the most prestige here is Shostakovich. He is like Brahms: everywhere and all the time. The latest symphonies are execrable. On the other hand, the 5th and 6th are full of interesting things.

Among American composers, Aaron Copland outclasses them all. His latest works, tender, limpid, earthy, are very appealing. But his earlier works are also *very good*. His ballets, *Billy the Kid* and *Rodeo*, his piano sonata, and his piano and violin sonata – all have the stamp of an authentic personality. Amongst the young composers there are great talents and great hopes, but only time will tell!!

I think I have given you news of just about everyone. Show this letter to Henri [Sauguet] and to Roger [Désormière]. I have written to them several times. I have had a card from Roger, nothing yet from Henri.

I embrace you wholeheartedly, *mon Poupoule*.

D.M.

Regards to Bernac. I am going to write songs for you both, with all my heart.[4]

175. FRANCIS POULENC TO DARIUS MILHAUD

London, 27 March 1945

Mon petit Darius,

What joy to receive your immense letter full of details! It is so good to hear how you are living and what work you are doing. Regrettably, I see that your health is still not good. I hope that through proper care and *real* food, you will soon improve. You are right not to think of coming back, with things the way they are at the moment: food in Paris is still very uncertain, the weather has been bitterly cold, and there is no means of transport.

I am writing from London where I have come for a month, with Bernac.[1] We have given lots of concerts and the BBC gave the first performance of my Cantata based on poems by Eluard [*Figure humaine*]. Admirable rendering but in English, which threw me a little despite an extraordinary translation by Rollo Myers.[2] I think the general impression was good, though. Déso [Désormière] and Ginette Neveu were also both here. Déso conducted a marvellous performance of your *Suite provençale* which made the English yearn for the South of France. Georges [Auric] will be the next to come to

London – to do the music for two films. They suggested I should take one on but it did not tempt me despite an enormous fee.

In Paris, musical life – seriously embarrassed by the purges – is beginning to pick up again as best it can. There is also a terrible crisis at the Opéra. We are all so sorry about Rouché's departure.[3]

The rise of Messiaen has been the most important musical event. In fact you will find a fanatical sect surrounding this musician who, for all the impossible literary jargon, is nevertheless remarkable. The Messiaenistes are very much against Stravinsky's 'last period'.* For them, Igor's music ends with *Le Sacre*. They booed *Les Danses concertantes*, which I adore. But this makes things lively. This is what it is all about.[4]

Henri [Sauguet] is well. He has just done the most perfect ballet with Bébé. Title: *Les Forains*. Setting: travelling fair on a winter's night in the Paris slums. From beginning to end the music is inspired and the staging is astounding.[5] The Bourdaria concerts are the only ones that count. On 27 April, with Bernac and Balguerie, I am giving a festival of my songs at Salle Gaveau. This musical exhibition causes me much amusement. There are some interesting new songs, I think.

How can we send each other our music? I have not been able to find anything by you in London, nor by Igor. Only a few Hindemiths, at Schott's. See what you can do. You can go on writing to me in London, c/o the French Embassy, which I think is better than writing to Paris.

At last the war is over. What joy it will be to meet again! I am sure we will all have been in some way enriched by this appalling experience.

I embrace you, and Madeleine too, very, very fondly.

Francis

I am writing . . . a string quartet . . . no less!!![6]
Collaer is very well. He is doing fine work.

176. CHARLES KOECHLIN TO FRANCIS POULENC

27 April – Midnight [1945]

Cher ami,

First of all, forgive me for not having come to see you after the concert to congratulate you on your fine success – so well deserved.[1]

There were too many people, it was late, and I wanted to get home quickly to my dinner. So I am writing to let you know all the pleasure it gave me to hear your music. Primarily, it brought home to me how greatly compositions gain from being presented in a concert *devoted to a single*

---

*In English in the original text.

composer (which I have very often noted in relation to exhibitions of paintings as well). The *festival* is really the best and most logical of concert forms, with all due respects to Machabey who said with regard to me: 'A composer has only "one style", which is why festivals are often so monotonous.'

I do not know whether you have one style or several, but I do know that your works were set off to advantage by their very proximity to each other, whether or not there were contrasts (in fact, I loathe those symphony concert programmes where they switch for no reason from Beethoven to Debussy). Moreover, when presented with works by the same musician, one gradually becomes aware of the personality of that musician; and one realizes that there is in fact a *Poulenc style*, and that you know how to be, sincerely and simply, *yourself*.

You prove, by several of these pieces, that one can compose lively, sensitive, moving and personal works using a musical vocabulary that is common to everyone. I am happy to see thus confirmed a theory that I have always maintained.

If perhaps I do not like everything equally in that collection of songs, *I conclude with pleasure* that one always knows they are *by Poulenc* and that they are above all *music*. Which gives me much pleasure in these fleeting times. I particularly enjoyed the first collection, and above all the third, then the latest works (those performed for the first time), and lastly the intense and noble emotion of 'Les Ponts de Cé' in which breathes the very soul of our wounded Fatherland. I must add that Bernac was incomparable, as were you in your role of accompanist. Mme Balguerie has a beautiful voice and is very gifted, but there is in Bernac, together with a prodigious diversity of vocal colour, a precision of accent, an impeccable diction, a discreet mastery which I find clearly superior.

I could have said all this to you in two words in the middle of all the crowds, but I wanted to write it to you, however hastily. Once again, my congratulations, and believe me to be your affectionately devoted

Ch. Koechlin

177. FRANCIS POULENC TO CHARLES KOECHLIN

Noizay, April 1945

How kind of you, dear friend, to have sent me that good letter after my recital. Everything you said has been of such great comfort to me, for after an experience of that kind, one always wonders if one has not been too presumptuous. I agree with you entirely – a view of the *whole* of one's output is the best way of judging it, but it is also very onerous.

I am writing to you from the country where I am orchestrating my opéra-bouffe [*Les Mamelles de Tirésias*]. The quietness does me so much good!

With a thousand devoted and affectionate regards.

Francis Poulenc

178. PAUL ELUARD TO FRANCIS POULENC

[Spring, 1945][1]

À FRANCIS POULENC

L'oeil ouvert à l'aurore et sa première feuille
Comme au printemps la bouche et sa fleur de pêcher
L'oeil à peine éveillé mais sur le point de rire
Tient entre ses paupières
La grande nuit le petit jour
La lampe éteinte et chaude et la première eau claire
Le premier rêve et le premier réveil

La nuit le jour sont renversés
Sablier du plaisir pour le doigt de la soie
Sablier du désir comblé par le délire
Et par le lourd devoir de la matière

Source solide broderie en profondeur
Un seul corps pour le jour et la nuit un seul corps
Pour la vie et la mort.

Francis je ne m'écoutais pas
Francis je te dois de m'entendre
Sur une route toute blanche
Dans un immense paysage
Où la lumière se retrempe

La nuit n'y a plus de racines
L'ombre est derrière les miroirs
Francis nous rêvons d'étendue
Comme un enfant de jeux sans fin
Dans un paysage étoilé

Qui ne reflète que jeunesse.

TO FRANCIS POULENC

The eye open to the dawn and its first leaf
As the mouth and its peach blossom to the spring
The eye barely awake but on the point of laughter
Keeps between its eyelids
The deep of night the morning twilight
The lamp dimmed and warm and the first clear water
The first dream and the first awakening

Night and day have been inverted
Sandglass of pleasure for the finger of silk
Sandglass of desire overcome with rapture
And with the heavy duty of matter

Solid source embroidered depth
Just one body for day and night one body
For life and death.

Francis I did not listen to myself
Francis it is through you that I hear myself
On a pure white road
In a vast landscape
Where light is renewed

Night has no more roots there
Shadows hide behind the mirrors
Francis we dream of expanse
As a child of endless games
In a starry landscape

That reflects only youth.

Here, dear Francis, is the promised poem. I have put all my heart into it.
What do you think of it – very sincerely? And what will Mr Wild think, to
whom I have sent it?[2]

Nusch joins me in embracing you affectionately. And come back here
quickly!

Paul Eluard

Thank you for the cheque.[3]

179. FRANCIS POULENC TO PAUL ELUARD

Noizay [Spring, 1945]

Mon cher Paul,

Thank you with all my heart for the *marvellous* poem – it delights me,
moves me, and utterly confounds my sense of modesty.

If Monsieur Wild[1] is not happy with it . . . *Oh! alors* . . .

I will have it reproduced in the programme for the first performance in Brussels of *Figure humaine*. I also hope, for my future glory, that it will take its place in one of your forthcoming collections of poetry.[2]

I am orchestrating *Les Mamelles* at the moment and enjoying it very much. I shall be back in Paris at the beginning of June. I will phone you the minute I arrive. Once again, many, many thanks.

I embrace you affectionately, and Nusch, too.

As ever, your composer
Francis

180. FRANCIS POULENC TO PIERRE BERNAC

Noizay, Wednesday [Spring, 1945][1]

Mon petit Pierre,

Thank you for your letter. I am devastated by the decisions in Brussels. I have in fact written (precisely the way you wanted me to write) to Cuvelier[2] and Collaer. You would think that fate was hell bent on destroying me as a composer. The days of happiness that I am living at present – far superior to any nights of love, I assure you – are due entirely to my work. It is with true joy that I am orchestrating *Les Mamelles* and I think this will be very audible. My instrumentation is happy in every sense of the word and the whole work is really *excellent* (I am certain of this now, on reconsidering it coldly while going through the proofs) and so poetic that it must succeed. The work might have been outdated in 1932 but it now has its place in time.

Once again, I am finding time to read, to reflect, to be less stupid. It is because I know myself so well that I bought this house in '28. It was the joy of a solitary April here that inspired *Sept chansons* – to quote only one instance. Unfortunately, next winter I will not be able to even think of coming in January because of the coal shortage; wood is of no avail, the water would freeze in the pipes and the corridors would be deadly.

Working around the rehearsals for *Les Mamelles* I would like you to plan our concerts for January and March. I shall be spending February with Jean Hugo at Fourques, where I will have a quiet, warm room with a piano, unless I go to Switzerland – I have already discussed this with the very kind Gérard Bauer who knows of something perfect for me there. I will be back here during April and May.

I am returning on Thursday 7 June. They have asked me for five minutes with you on Saturday 9 at midday for 'Carrefour des ondes' on the radio. I have agreed. It means simply doing the two Aragons [*Deux poèmes de Louis*

Aragon]. If this does not suit you, could you arrange another date immediately with Mme X – I have already forgotten her name (ask the radio).

Gaston Gallimard very kindly sent me Tolstoy's *War and Peace* and I have been spending marvellous hours rereading this masterpiece which I first tackled when I was far too young.

[. . .] Try to organize a long holiday for yourself. You really need it. I am delighted at the idea of my summer in Brive. I shall probably leave at the end of June, 28 or 30, so as to go on my pilgrimage *first*.[3] I am feeling much better but am sometimes very tired. I need long days in the country. [. . .]

Confidentially, because of dear old Schaeffner, Claude is thinking of writing a book on me.[4] His very intelligent article has made a great impression on people like Lebec, Richet, etc., in other words, on people in general.

Tell Roland B. to write to me. I would be very pleased to hear from him. Give him my news. What you tell me about Teugels delights me.

I embrace you.

Francis

Eluard has just written a most beautiful poem on me (a commission from Mr Wild for a book on musicians or something). I have copied it out for you. It will be very valuable for certain of my programmes, etc.*

181. FRANCIS POULENC TO DARIUS MILHAUD

5 rue de Médicis, Paris, 1 July 1945

Mon petit Da,

You must really be wondering what has happened to me. My silence has been due, among other things, to my extreme anxiety about your parcel of music, addressed to 6 rue de Médicis. 'Postal Affairs' did not notice that there are only odd numbers in my street and so your precious despatch was sent from one obscure department to another in an apparently vain attempt to locate me. In the end, the parcel was returned to the diplomatic bag, from where, with great joy, I fetched it ten days ago. I devoured it, with my eyes and my heart, as you can well imagine, and then I shared it out as follows:

To Bernac: Bathori songs and Prayers.

To Monique Haas: piano pieces.

To Deiss: the three quartets, the two orchestral suites, the works for viola, for wind, organ, etc.

*In the original letter Poulenc includes a copy of Eluard's poem, 'A Francis Poulenc'. See letter 178.

I have drawn up a list covering all this, as well as the manuscripts not published by Deiss, which I have sent to Collaer for his radio series on Milhaud. I will have a copy sent to our radio as well.

Out of what you have sent me, my preference is for the three quartets and the *Jeux de printemps*. I find the 12th so beautiful that when the new season starts I am going to ask Calvet to perform it, with the Quartet by Fauré. For the rest, I will see how best to organize a concert of your works in November.

The trade union fees have put paid to chamber music societies like Triton, Sérénade, Pléiade, but we are hoping to start public chamber concerts for radio.

What Paul (Collaer) is doing in Brussels is admirable and ought to serve as an example. Rosenthal's orchestral concerts have brought in very good audiences. In spite of the cold, people have taken to coming every Thursday to hear modern music. With a few illustrious names as their patrons, young composers should be able to draw the same audiences for chamber music.

The spring has not been very brilliant musically, apart from two first performances of Messiaen, debatable but very remarkable. At the end of June, the Antwerp Chorale[1] was due to perform my Cantata, *Figure humaine*, and your *Choéphores*, with the Conservatoire Orchestra, but this did not take place. They are now talking about 4 November for this concert. De Vocht will give the first performance in Brussels at the end of October.

The Opéra-Comique revived, with growing success, your *Pauvre Matelot* and *La Gageure imprévue* by Sauguet (very lovely music, very lovely sets by Jacques Dupont). Boris [Kochno] formed a company again that put on four shows to packed houses at the Théâtre Sarah-Bernhardt. All very 1934 (Masson, Miró), with the exception of *Les Forains*, a total success by Bébé [Christian Bérard] and Sauguet.

I continue this letter, begun in Paris on July 1st, at Rocamadour, on the 8th.

I have come on a pilgrimage. As one has to go on foot from the station to the town (5½ kilometres in the blazing sun) pilgrims are few and far between and there is total quiet. I am leaving again tomorrow for the environs of Brive where I shall stay for two months in a divine spot on the banks of the Vézère. I hope to get down to some serious work as I cannot do a thing in Paris.

I shall finish the orchestration of *Les Mamelles de Tirésias*, the opéra-bouffe that I have dedicated to you for your return, and I will try to complete a certain quartet that fills me with horror.[2] In September, I shall spend six weeks at Noizay.

You have no doubt heard of the latest anti-Stravinsky campaign; I published a sharp reply in *Le Figaro* to Jolivet[3] who had written that modern French music owed nothing (sic) to Igor. It is Messiaen's pupils who are at the root of all this. He himself remains discreetly silent.

I interrupted my letter once more last night and when I got back to Brive this evening, I found a letter from Richard Chanlaire with official confirmation of the death of poor Raymond Deiss. He was condemned to death in '43 in Berlin, as we heard from a deportee who returned in May, but we kept on hoping. Now Richard writes that his grave has been found in Cologne. It is all very strange. Richard and Capdevielle[4] are trying to piece things together from various statements that have been made. Richard might go to Cologne. It is all absolutely heartbreaking. You cannot imagine how careless Deiss was. He really did everything to get himself caught by the Gestapo.[5] Naturally, the Will cannot be opened until after the official investigation. Capdevielle thinks as I do that Richard is the heir. But I do not have to tell you that no matter what happens, the [publishing] firm will look after your interests.

I almost forgot to tell you in the chaos of this letter that I did receive *one* parcel from you containing a beautiful pullover. Many thanks! In spite of the *immense* joy I shall feel on your return, I would advise you not to come back before May '46 as we will certainly suffer badly from the cold this winter through lack of coal. You must also make sure you have a car, and that lifts are in working order. Until you come back, I will take your place on the Opéra Committee. Déso's nomination is an excellent thing.

I am sending you this letter via the diplomatic bag, as well as a letter for you from Ibert.

Delvincourt[6] is waiting for you to return to give you a composition class at the Conservatoire. From a material point of view, we will all do everything we possibly can for you. Jaujard[7] is a delightful person, full of admiration for you. Forgive the disjointedness of this letter. I hope I have not left out anything important. I promise not to make you wait so long for news again. I embrace you very, very fondly, as well as Madeleine and your little artist.

Francis

Could you send me Horowitz's address?

182. Francis Poulenc to Pierre Bernac

Thursday 12 [July 1945]

Mon vieux Pierre,

I am glad to hear that you are taking a rest and having some treatment. There is no doubt that you need a cure this summer as your throat troubled you far too much last winter.

Are you perhaps staying in a hotel managed by the Buet sisters who own the Hôtel des Princes in Cannes where my dear old Tante Liénard died? If so, please give them my kindest regards.

As for me, I think I have discovered *paradise*. In a delightful little spot on the banks of the Vézère, I am living like a lord in a tiny little château that was transformed into a restaurant four months ago. There are only three rooms, the owner's, her son's and mine. Raymond [Destouches] sleeps in a small room in the farmhouse. Theoretically, the delightful dining-room (real wooden beams, real fireplace, enormous old tapestries) would be full of gourmets at meal-times, but only *yesterday*, the owner closed the restaurant for three months for some official reason. We were really on tenterhooks for two hours fearing she might ask us to leave . . . but then it transpired that – in Paris, in '26 – Raymond had known her late husband who owned the garage in the rue d'Armaillé. After an exchange of names of friends in common the owners now have us at their table, and I assure you that I am not losing weight. I have a room with small bathroom, and a ravishing view. The comeliest of toads sits at the foot of my bed. If inspiration does not come, *alors zut*!

Since arriving on Sunday night, today being Thursday, I have already orchestrated *forty-four* pages of *Les Mamelles* which I want above all to get shot of – while finishing *Babar* at the same time. Then it will be the turn of the Quartet. What a lot of work! Fortunately, I am feeling perfectly well, the last lot of treatment having cured all my complaints.

Raymond, as you can imagine, is delighted. He keeps me company very nicely and takes me for long drives. Like you, I was very pleased to get away from musicians, official waiting-rooms, etc. etc. I went to Rocamadour last week, all alone. It really calmed me down.

Write again soon. I embrace you.

Fr.

Gallimard is publishing Louis Roché's poems.[1]

183. FRANCIS POULENC TO PIERRE BERNAC

Larche (Corrèze), 22 July [1945]

Mon petit Nenfant,

As I have worked very well I have been granted a day of complete rest and [André] Lecoeur, Marthe Bosredon and I have come fishing for *écrevisses* in a landscape by Poussin. Naturally, I am not the one who is doing the fishing, so I am quietly making use of the time to catch up on my correspondence.

I am being a very good boy and working from morning till night. I am in the middle of the second act of *Les Mamelles* and hope to finish it in three weeks. I am enjoying it enormously and I don't think I would be telling you an untruth if I said that the orchestration is the best I have ever done. Imagine a *Bal masqué* for large orchestra. My main concern is lightness, so that the words can be understood, although I am also giving a lot of thought to the dramatic side, introducing new things constantly so as to keep the audience's attention. The entr'acte is astounding, punctuated with immense piano chords played by a virtuoso in a frenzy. With Bébé, we should have the audience at our feet.[1]

I have finished the rough draft of my *Babar*[2] which I am going to begin copying out. I think it will be amusing. The difficulty is to write not a series of little pieces but a kind of mosaic between the texts. At the beginning of September I will give you the words so that you can start practising. For concerts where more piano music is required this work could be quite fun.

I have sent Kiesgen[3] six projects for the Festival. I like the fifth one best. Think of songs that would go well with the rest and keep these projects in your archives. Some of them are very listenable. I am busy, on several fronts, trying to arrange something for Switzerland, where I want to spend the month of February. We have been requested for Rome but how can we be everywhere at the same time?

I am expecting to hear soon from Collaer about a definite date. I have also just written to Henri Hoppenot, our ambassador in Berne. I would very much like *Figure humaine* to be performed at the Lucerne Festival next year. Having completed everything else, I intend working on the Quartet in September at Noizay, and finishing it in Lausanne. That way, it could be performed in the spring.

I am, as always, delighted with my airy room and my very kind hosts. Raymond is as good as gold. Write soon. I embrace you.

Francis

The item for piano is the one I am preparing for the winter. I will get Jacques [Février] to check through it.

184. FRANCIS POULENC TO HENRI SAUGUET

Larche (Corrèze), 9 August [1945]

Mon petit Henri

I want to reply by return of post to tell you how saddened I am by your letter. You know that no one understands you better than I do since, like you, I am also subject to waves of doubt and sadness. The life of a musician is of course full of bitterness, but you must never let it defeat you.

Do not be unjust towards *Les Forains*, although I do understand your quite legitimate irritation when one thinks of *La Gageure*. The public always goes for what is most easily understood unless, like Messiaen, one lives entirely in the ether – often quite unbreatheable. *Boléro* might overshadow *Les Valses nobles*, but is none the less a success. Have faith, you have very true friends who now hold important positions: Collaer in Brussels, Déso at the Opéra. All this will stand you in good stead.

I am certain that ten months from now the question of publishers in Paris will all be settled, for reasons which I am unable to divulge to you. Do not worry that a Paul Rouart has approached you over *Les Forains*. That is all I am able to tell you. Go on composing music which you feel, and all will be well.[1]

I have known a time when Cubism overshadowed Bonnard, but he is none the worse for it.

You are held in far greater esteem than you think and when the question of State commissions came up both Delvincourt and Ibert were the first to support my proposal.

For the time being, have a rest. I intend staying here until 27 August. I have sent off my orchestration of *Les Mamelles* and my suite for piano, *Babar*, for which I have thought of the following sub-title: *Dix-huit coups d'oeil sur la queue d'un jeune éléphant.*[2]

Déso will be coming to Renaud de Jouvenel's,[3] ten kilometres away from here. His plans for the Opéra seem excellent. We are fortunate to have him there.

Apart from this, not much news from friends. Write and tell me that you are better.

I embrace you very fraternally.

Francis

185. FRANCIS POULENC TO PIERRE BERNAC

Monday 10 [September 1945]

Mon petit Pierre,

Our letters crossed each other.

1. If you want to do Reims before Brussels, agreed.

2. I am writing to Collaer about *Figure* [*humaine*], and to the radio as well.

3. I will take care of Dublin.

4. Agreed for Besançon and Mulhouse. Is Strasbourg working out? If not, phone Paul Rouart who has bought out the music shop, Wolf, and who will arrange it all. Then we will head for Switzerland.

5. Try and find a companion for Egypt.

6. Good idea for Algeria with Simone [Girard].

Concerning the last two items, we must discuss very seriously our plans for peace-time. About South America, as I have just explained to Kiesgen, from '46–'47 I want to go back to my pre-war timetable, particularly since by then I hope to have new supplies of coal at Noizay.

So:

October	:	Noizay
November	:	Concerts
December	:	Noizay
January	⎫	
February	⎬	Concerts
March	⎭	
April	⎫	Noizay
May	⎭	
June	:	Concerts (London, I suppose)
July	⎫	Holiday
August	⎭	
September	:	Noizay

In other words, five months of concerts, five of work at Noizay, two of holiday.

As I feel you should really get down to things without any delay, I think that, apart from our recitals, you should make two additional arrangements: one for the provinces, with Simone, for example, and one for all other engagements, with a pianist like Jacques Genty. Why not do South America with Jacques Février, who is pleasant to travel with and who could play the *M.G.* of Ravel?*

I told Kiesgen to make reservations for: England, Sweden, Denmark, Holland, Belgium, Switzerland, Italy, Spain. These last two countries must be included for '46–'47.

I am finishing my music for Salacrou.[1] From next week I shall devote myself entirely to the Quartet. Next spring I want to write a new Concerto for piano, ready for the winter of '46–'47.[2]

That is all my news. Here, everything is marvellous (butter excluded). Spirits are generally very high. Ouf!

I have been practising the Debussy and Milhaud accompaniments. *At last* I have found a *Faune* to my liking. How subtle Debussy is!

Let me know what you think of the text of *Babar*.

> With much affection,
>
> Fr.

---

*Concerto pour la main gauche.

186. FRANCIS POULENC TO MARTHE BOSREDON

30 December [1945]

Ma petite Marthe, très, très chère,
     Thank you for all the tenderness you show; thank you for the lovely gift –
from now on Nux Vomica is an addiction, assuming there is still anything to
eat in '46.
     As you can imagine, my life is churning with grief. While I was in Ireland
I learnt of the death of my dear uncle.[1] The pressure of work in England kept
me going but my return has been dreadful. From a distance I thought I was
strong. Fortunately, my uncle died in the space of a morning, very quickly
and without suffering. Now I am overwhelmed by all the material problems: tidying up, possibly moving home, and so on. And all this crammed
into an infernal winter of concerts.
     I think of you very often. For me you will always be the symbol of blissful
days in a part of the country that I adore.
     You will be receiving some Lanvin perfume, but they were out of the one
you like so I must ask you to have a little patience. I have taken the liberty
of sending some playing-cards to you for Pepete. Between ourselves, the
English cards are a disaster. I will bring some for you soon from Brussels,
where I hope to find some linen-backed ones. I don't suppose you are feeling
terribly happy. I hope so much that '46 brings you some peace. Suzanne
Lhote will send you an invitation in the spring, I know.
     Did you hear that Rosine [Seringe] has had a son? We are all ecstatic. She
is blooming and the little mite, although tiny, is very much alive.
     Nadia Boulanger will be conducting *Figure humaine* in Paris in May. If
you do not come for it, beware . . . beware. Give me all the gossip from
Brive. I would like to send you some cheerfulness but I am sorely in need of
some myself.
     Be content with a thousand tender kisses and the assurance of my fondest
affection.

Francis

     I have finally put the finishing touches to *Babar* with Bernac. It is all
holding together beautifully now.

187. FRANCIS POULENC TO IGOR STRAVINSKY

5 rue de Médicis, Paris, 28 December [1945]

Cher, très cher Stravinsky,
     I was delighted, dazzled – and in particular heartened – by the beauti-
ful parcel of music that I found waiting for me on my return from a long

stay in England. Once again, I felt your presence, your genius, your example.

How I have missed you these last six years, and how I have longed – not only for myself but for all of us – for your return to our bruised Europe, where there is still some music to be found. I have so much to tell you that I refuse to attempt it here.

In any case, you can be sure that I am among those to whom you bring the light. You must have heard of the polemics over your recent works.[1] Allow me to say how beautiful I find it, to be as misunderstood at sixty as at thirty.

I will not tell you about the work I have done since 1940. I have achieved what I could, but very often not what I wanted, because life – so difficult in every way – obliged me to give too many concerts, to compose two films, incidental music for the stage, and so on . . .[2] When you hear my recent compositions, I hope you will find that there is still some good wheat growing among the tares.

How often have memories of the past sustained me during the tragic times we have just lived through. It is comforting to think that one was twenty years old at the time of *Les Noces, Mavra, Pulcinella,* etc. . . .

When you have some new music published, try to send it to me. (I already have the *Danses concertantes*, Sonata for two pianos, *Circus polka* and, especially, *Scènes de ballet*, which I am *crazy* about.)

I embrace you affectionately, and Vera too, and send you my warmest wishes for '46.

Your devoted
Poulenc

188. IGOR STRAVINSKY TO FRANCIS POULENC

Hollywood, 10 January 1946

What joy, *mon très cher Poulenc*, to have your excellent letter. It has arrived just as I am about to leave for my concert tour. Hence this short note. Agreed, I will have some of my recently published music sent to you from New York, together with a few photostats of works not yet published.

Heavens, there are so many things to discuss, but when and how? When will we see each other again? I have no idea, bogged down as I am by continual work that permits of no *stoping* [sic].

You will soon see Nadia B. [Boulanger]; her departure from the USA (on 4 January) has left a void that will be difficult to fill. We saw a great deal of each other in recent years.

Very dear Poulenc, send me some of your own music, I beg of you; you know what loyal and tender feelings I have always had for your bewitching Muse.

Affectionately yours
I. Stravinsky.

New York, Boston, Baltimore, Havana, Dallas, San Francisco and . . . *back home** end of March.

189. FRANCIS POULENC TO PIERRE BERNAC

Sunday [August, 1946]

Cher Pierre,

I am sending you two little barefoot children[1] – be indulgent and affectionate towards them. It's a long story. In 1920 I tried to set this entrancing little poem by my poor Radiguet, but at that time I did not know how to go about writing a song that left me no room for modulation. Radiguet has been much in my thoughts again lately and, one rainy day, I rewrote this little song, pouring into it my experience and my memories.

I think the idea of the silence and the final, unexpected modulation is a happy one.

This song would make a possible second encore. At any rate, you cannot say that I am killing you with work at the last minute.

Can you send me, for my diary, the programmes of our Paris recitals in '43 and '44 and the one from the autumn of '45.

Much affection, in haste.
Fr.

Notice the effect a new poet has on my pianistic writing. Unfortunately, this is the only Radiguet possible.

190. DARIUS MILHAUD TO FRANCIS POULENC

Mills College, Wednesday, 15 January [1947]

Mon petit Francis,

I have just received your letter and have immediately had 1,000 cigarettes sent to you through an agency in New York. I hope they reach you. Let me know.

Madeleine will attend to your soap as soon as she gets back, as she has stayed on an extra week in New York to do *Perséphone*[1] on the radio, conducted by Igor. She leaves tomorrow and will be here by Sunday.

*In English in the original text.

I had to come back because of my classes, having already stolen five weeks from College time for the film in November.[2] To tell the truth, I found the trip to the East Coast very tiring. I conducted my second Symphony in Boston. What a miraculous orchestra! In New York, I conducted four Cantatas (*Pan et Syrinx, Adages, Amours de Ronsard, Cantate du Musée de l'Homme*) at the League of Composers, and the same programme at the Juilliard School. I conducted my first Symphony for the radio, and then recorded it for Columbia. I also recorded a limited edition of 2,000 copies of four of my little Symphonies,[3] which I greatly enjoyed.

But it is impossible for me to conduct standing up, and apart from this activity I stay mostly in the hotel and limit my outings to the bare minimum. We have seen a lot of François Valéry,[4] who is charming. Also Philippe Heugel,[5] who seems full of energy. The death of Salabert[6] is nothing short of a catastrophe. Given that he had taken over so many publishing businesses and, more especially, that he had the highly important New York agency, it is heartbreaking that he was not able to see his plans through. For he knew how to take risks. Mme Salabert phoned me to say that she would be taking charge of the business.

I was very pleased that you liked my final version of *Alissa*.[7] I would like to have it published. Do you think it would interest Dugardin?[8] Collaer could deliver the music to him. I think Bathori has it as well. That would be simpler. Would you be good enough to contact Bathori, and to discuss it with Dugardin, whom I do not know?

We will *definitely* be arriving in September. I was hoping to leave in the spring, but the administrative director of the Music Department of Mills has just lost his wife in highly distressing circumstances (long illness, cancer); he is taking six months' leave and has asked me as a favour to be here for the summer session. He has always been wonderful to me and I could not refuse. But I think I will come back here anyway in *summer '48*, to Berkshire where Koussevitzky has asked me to teach at the summer school.[9] I will therefore have almost a year to spend in France and to see how I react physically to the present difficulties, although things are much improved in certain respects. Heating is still a major problem – it makes us ill to think that over there, you are all freezing, whilst here there is gross overheating.

You will soon be seeing the Igors. He is younger than ever, funny, lively, delightful.

Daniel [Milhaud] is staying in New York for three months to work at his painting and drawing. He is an unbelievably mature boy, very appealing, but difficult because he is so independent, often unpredictable, sometimes quite childish, at other times like an old man. It is so worrying.

The important thing for me in Paris is to have a car. Otherwise, I cannot do A THING.

> I embrace you,
>
> Da.

191. FRANCIS POULENC TO DENISE DUVAL

Monday [1947]

Ma Denise,

You really are an angel, a treasure, to have phoned me this morning. I was going to phone but I was afraid of waking you. I am delighted with the good news about *Les Mamelles*. What luck to have a conductor [Albert Wolff] with experience of the theatre! I will drop him a line this very day. I am working like a slave; I will have finished everything, thank God, by my return on *Wednesday 22nd*. And then I'll make sure you really get down to work. I am so looking forward to spending a lot of time with you. I will think of you on Friday.

Do not forget 'i*dd*ole'. Equal weight to each note in the 6/8 time, but nuances in the mirror scene with accelerando.[1] Try to find some other shoes. Do not forget to have your blouse already undone by the time you attack the phrase on the high C. Aim for stability. Venus invisible yet present.

Bernard came for the weekend. We spoke of you continuously. The whole of Touraine, by the way, talks of nothing but *our* marriage!!!!!

I embrace you tenderly, my treasure.

> Francis

192. FRANCIS POULENC TO DARIUS MILHAUD

London, 11 June 1947

Mon petit Darius,

I needed the calm of London to find time at last to write you a long letter. My winter was horribly hectic because in the middle of all my concerts with Bernac I had to prepare *Les Mamelles*. After a great deal of trouble over the cast and the sets (Bébé [Christian Bérard] having let me down) everything turned out for the best.[1] I have an unbelievable Thérèse who is stunning Paris with her beauty, her acting talent and her voice. She is a new Heldy.[2] The press is marvellous. A part of the audience brings the house down with enthusiasm but the Puccini fans in the gods are outraged. This makes for very lively performances, which delights the management no end. Erté, whose programme cover you have seen, has done a very amusing *mise en scène*, in the style of the Folies-Bergères. Only one drawback: your absence.

I would so much have liked the performance of this work – dedicated to you – to coincide with your return.[3] Anyway, this will have to wait for the autumn, when I think we might be billed together.

I have come to London for a week. Saw and heard Hindemith yesterday – both he and his wife are very nice to me. Of course we spoke a lot about you. I like his *Variations for piano and strings* very much but his *Hérodiade* does not appeal to me at all. It seems to be 'always against Mallarmé'.*

You will find me this autumn settled into my new apartment in the rue de Médicis. It is small but very nice.[4]

Paul Collaer and his choir finally performed *Figure humaine* at the Pléiade concerts, with great success. I had a good spring this year. Now I am going to write a Sinfonietta for orchestra for the BBC's Third Programme.[5] I shall spend my whole summer at Noizay.

All our friends are well. Henri's Symphony went very well in Brussels.

Thank you for the cigarettes, received only on *12 May*, for the soap, received before that, for the marvellous photo of Milhaud father and son, for the beautiful pen drawing by Daniel, for all your letters, and your telegram for *Les Mamelles*. I assure you that we all await your return with immense impatience.

I am sure that combined with the sadness of returning you will feel great joy at seeing Aix and Paris again. For Daniel, it will be wonderful to discover an intellectual Paris; he will no doubt be enthralled by it, as it still reigns supreme in the realm of painting.

Auric continues to enjoy enormous success with his film music. The young composers – often quite disorientated between Messiaen and the outdated twelve-tone system – are expecting great things from your teaching. You will see what a splendid character Delvincourt is. The Conservatoire has gained enormously in standing.

What joy to say: 'See you soon!' I embrace you fondly, Mad and Daniel too.

Ton vieux Francis

Bravo for your rosette and for dear Madeleine's ribbon.[6]

193. FRANCIS POULENC TO PIERRE BERNAC

Le Tremblay (Eure), 18 July [1948]

Mon vieux Pierre,

I am longing to hear from you. Can you imagine that I have misplaced your summer address. So I have asked my brother-in-law, who is leaving for Paris tomorrow, to make some telephone enquiries for me.

*In English in the original text.

I have been here for a week and I have already done an incredible amount of work. Here, in spite of the gloomy weather, I have found again the calm of those beautiful Anost summers. Music keeps flowing out of me and is a constant joy. Very often my winter irritability is due to my lack of creativity. Let me quickly tell you a piece of GOOD NEWS: for our second New York concert[1] you will have a beautiful, brand new cycle, which I already love as much as *Tel jour telle nuit*. In *Calligrammes* I have really found what I was looking for.[2] What do I not owe to Apollinaire! I have already written four songs (two were vaguely sketched at Noizay in May); there will be seven altogether and I know exactly what they will all be like. Even more carefully constructed than *Tel jour*, this cycle has a true internal structure. All these poems of 1913–15 bring a flood of memories from my Nogent past and from the time of the 1914 war. Hence the dedication to all my childhood friends. The first, 'L'Espionne', about jealousy, is dedicated to . . . Simone [Tilliard]; the last, which I have already told you about, 'Voyage', to the memory of Raymonde [Linossier].[3] During my last few days in Paris I took my Muse off to the village – Vincennes, and so on – and, very gradually, during the course of my solitary walks, my song cycle took shape. Two *mélodies* like soldiers' songs will contrast happily with the rest. I can guarantee that you will have the whole cycle for New York. You can well imagine that if I undertake this responsibility it is because I am *sure* of myself. Whenever you like I will copy out the first four for you and you will have the rest by the beginning of September at the latest. They are made to measure for you, more in the lower than the upper register. As you are in charge of the programmes, here are the titles:

CALLIGRAMMES

seven *mélodies* on poems by Apollinaire

I	L'Espionne (F minor)
II	Mutation (E flat major)
III	Vers le sud (E major)
IV	Il pleut (B major)
V	La grâce exilée (E major)
VI	Aussi bien que les cigales (E flat major)
VII	Voyage (F minor)

As you can see, the keys are very precisely balanced, B major (IV) serving as the fulcrum.

Two movements of the Sonata for cello are complete and I hope to finish the finale this week. The first movement is still not quite right.[4]

I have sent my passport to Hegel for our visas. You should do so, too, as quickly as possible, as it takes a long time.

Write to me here immediately, or, from the 26th for a week, to Paris.

On the 16th, *Les Mamelles* had a veritable triumph at the Opéra-Comique before a full house of foreigners, women in evening dress, men in dinner jackets. Brigitte [Manceaux] was there. Denise [Duval] was given an ovation. July has been a very good month for her as she had a huge success in *Les Contes d'Hoffmann*, and *Le Carrosse* is already promising well.[5] She is on top of the world again. She has left the Grand Hotel and I have put her (figuratively speaking) into the Saint-James, in the rue Saint-Honoré. The more I see of her, the more attached I become to this girl.

I hope you are recovering and feeling better each day. A long letter soon!

I embrace you.

Francis

Suddenly America interests me, especially as it is only for six weeks and as everyone there is already writing me such nice letters.

Here is the programme for our performance at the League of Composers – very important:

I   *Bestiaire. Banalités.*

II   *Trio*

III 'Anna'. 'Allons plus vite'. 'Portrait'.
      'Feu du soir'. 'Belle jeunesse'.

Interval

IV *Bal* [*masqué*], conducted by Bernstein.[6]

Good, don't you think? They are discussing the date with Schang. Do you need money? I can.

194. FRANCIS POULENC TO BRIGITTE MANCEAUX

New York, Wednesday, 3 November 1948

Ma Biche aimée,

Everything is going marvellously. I am smitten by New York and divinely comfortable here. I have a two-roomed apartment at the Saint-Moritz with a piano supplied by Baldwin and a heavenly view over the Park. Imagine me at the Meurice! It is rather expensive but everyone advised me to do this and, anyway, I am so relaxed here that, in excellent form, I have been able to finish the hymn for Doda Conrad.[1]

I am leaving in ten minutes for Washington where our first concert takes place tomorrow. Sunday's concert here promises well. I am playing with Mitropoulos on the 11th, 12th and 14th.[2] I have chosen a very good piano. Lily Pons has been an angel to me. She sent flowers to my hotel. I have already dined at her place with Horowitz and on the 8th she is throwing a huge cocktail party for me. The young American music clique are all very nice to me. Saw Wanda Landowska. On Saturday I am going to the Toscanini concert. Horowitz is in superb form. He is definitely coming to Paris and will play in June. I will bring back some excellent recordings of the Concerto for two pianos conducted by Mitropoulos.[3]

Also a pleasant prospect to have some commissions. It would be very gratifying to make a living at last with real music. In Washington I shall be staying with Reine Bénard. This letter is for all of you. A thousand kisses in haste.

Francis

Good news from *ma divine* [Denise Duval].

195. FRANCIS POULENC TO BRIGITTE MANCEAUX

Boston, 10 November [1948]

Ma Brigitte,

Thank you for your letter. Your Poupoule is quite overcome, as much by the warmth of the American central heating system (inhuman: 25° here, with the window open) as by such a success that it leaves me somewhat dumbfounded. The New York recital was an *unbelievable* triumph. Full house. As we came on stage applause for three minutes, bows, re-bows. From the moment we began the Lully, the audience was ours. The main attraction of the evening was *Tel jour telle nuit* (seven calls). At the end people were positively yelling. Pierre and I were delighted but somewhat stunned. Yesterday, unanimous praise from the press. The only topic of conversation that night was our concert and Dior's inauguration. Meanwhile we were dining very quietly with Christian at a friend's. When you make it here, you really make it! Yesterday, endless phone calls from recording companies, publishers, etc. Fortunately, I had transformed my New York apartment into a fortress by cutting off the telephone and putting on my door 'don't disturb'. The recording of the Concerto for two pianos, conducted by Mitropoulos, is selling by the *hundreds*. let's hope the *Concert champêtre* goes well on Thursday. Don't worry, all this is not going to my head – you would have laughed to see two good old *Parigots* (Dior and myself) going home last night arm in arm. Clearly, the aim of our trip has been achieved. I can now earn whatever I like here – that much is certain. But please do NOT become the doting niece telling everyone about my 'delirious triumphs', etc.

Write to me with all the gossip from Paris. I devour the mail.

I embrace you very tenderly.

Your Poupoule

Go and see Denise [Duval] and give her some moral support as she is very depressed. She must be strong.

Paul Rouart wrote to tell me that the Sinfonietta went very well in London.

Pierre has been UNBELIEVABLE. He deserves his triumph.

196. FRANCIS POULENC TO COMTESSE JEAN DE POLIGNAC

New York, 21 November [1948]

Chère Marie-Blanche,

I awoke this morning in a great fit of melancholy. In spite of the view of Central Park in the sun, below my window, I am suddenly very homesick for my Place de la Concorde. I am delighted with my stay here but what joy it will be to return – who better than you can understand your Poulette. And yet, what a success!! I am quite stunned by it. The second recital last night was pure delirium. House full (Town Hall), seven recalls after the first performance of *Calligrammes*, five encores at the end of the concert – so, all in all, we took twenty-three bows!!! One needs a hall to seat 15,000 for the stentorian voice of Pierre, so rejuvenated by this success. You can imagine how pleased I am for him. I am constantly with Yvonne de Casa Fuerte, Rieti, Nathalie, Wicky and . . . with Horowitz (marvellously on form), dinners at the Milsteins, Francescatis, etc. Tonight we leave for two weeks in Quebec, Chicago, Los Angeles, and San Francisco where I will see Stravinsky and Milhaud. On December 11th the last concert in New York and on the 14th en route for Paris – Ouf!!!!!!

If you have five minutes, write to me airmail: c/o Milhaud, Mills College, Oakland, California.

I embrace you tenderly.

Your Poulette

197. FRANCIS POULENC TO ELVIRA VIÑES SOTO

10 March 1949

Chère Elvira,

Your letter, which was forwarded to me while I was away, moved me to tears. Thank you for the music, thank you for the photographs. I will do *whatever you want* in memory of my dear Viñes, whom I adored and to whom I owe EVERYTHING in my musical career, both as pianist and composer.

It will be a great honour for me to preface Monsieur Ignacio Sanuy's book. I shall write to him in Lerida. As I am leaving for Spain at the end of March and as I shall be there for two weeks, I may even be able to see him.

Concerning the records (naturally I will buy a copy of whatever is published), it is essential that the miraculous recording of *Poissons d'or* should be reissued first and foremost. Then Borodin's *Scherzo*, and the Falla record (in the hope that it will put many lost pianists back on the right track), and also *La Soirée dans Grenade* and *Torre bermeja*. After that my preference is for the Sonata by Scarlatti and the *Gavotte d'Iphigénie*, both played impeccably.[1]

You can write immediately to Monsieur Ploix, who has the record shop in the rue Saint-Placide, Paris (you will find his number in the Paris telephone directory) and to Monsieur Lévy-Alvarez, La Boîte à Musique, boulevard Raspail, Paris. Tell them who you are and that you are writing at my suggestion. I am sure they will give you a firm order for several records.

It will not be difficult to have something appearing in the press to coincide with the reissue of the records. I shall be very pleased if you can send me the tributes of Halffter and Mompou. Thank you for sending dear Ricardo's.

Unfortunately, I will not have the time to go from Barcelona to Lerida, to your uncle's grave. I hope that Monsieur Sanuy will be able to come to Barcelona. You can be sure that I will speak out loudly and clearly about all I owe to Ricardo.

Keep me informed of all your doings and know, dear Elvira, that it is always a great joy to hear from you.

Affectionately yours,
Francis Poulenc

198. FRANCIS POULENC TO LOUISE DE VILMORIN

Château du Tremblay, Evreux (Eure), 19 July [1949]

Ma douce Louise,

Do you know how many grey hairs you have given your old musician? I thought I would never find a way of setting to music all your *font, font, font*, and then suddenly it came to me and now I like my Mazurka a lot.[1] The atmosphere is very much the ball in *Le Grand Meaulnes*[2] – soft, melancholy and sensuous. I hope you will be pleased with it. I haven't allowed myself to cheat at all: all the *font* are there. I have simply inverted:

.... *font*
Tomber des mains l'aiguille

which becomes more euphonious like this:

.... *font*
Des mains tomber l'aiguille

because it avoids the *ont – omb*. Forgive me!

As I never see you now (alas) this Mazurka reflects the melancholy of a musician who nevertheless hopes to be forever 'your' musician. I was planning to come to dinner at Verrières on Tuesday 2 August. Will you be there at that time? I would play you my Mazurka as once I played 'C'est ainsi que tu es'.[3] Let me know if it is possible.

I embrace you tenderly.

Your Poupoule

We simply must find a title for the whole suite. *Keep trying*.[4]

199. FRANCIS POULENC TO DARIUS MILHAUD

[Château du Tremblay, Eure], 25 July [1949]

Mon Darius,

That I am a dreadful monster, there is no doubt; but as you are an angel, you will forgive me for my silence. Never do I find the time to tell you all that I would like to, and so I put off writing; this could make you think that I have forgotten you, which would upset me terribly.

I am at the end of a three-week stay at my sister's where I have been keeping my nose to the grindstone. I have done the Mazurka (Vilmorin) for Doda; it was diabolical but I think I have acquitted myself appropriately. And I have made some progress with my Concerto for Boston (first movement completed, second all planned).[1] This work fills me with anguish as it would not be particularly fortuitous to begin my second tour with a flop. I leave for America on 27 December and will remain there until 2 April; a bit much, but what can I do?

Although the spring in Paris has been very brilliant from a social and entertainment point of view, I cannot say as much with regard to music; as for ballet and theatre there have been nothing but repeats. They have been living off their old stock: virtuosos trotting out Chopin and Beethoven. Only your lovely town [Aix-en-Provence] is triumphantly in vogue. I am going there for the weekend (by plane) from Friday 29th to Monday 1st. Yesterday, Henri's second Quartet was given its first performance [by the Calvet Quartet]. I heard it on the radio. It is remarkable – the best of Sauguet.

Max de Rieux, who seems to get on marvellously with Léger, can think of nothing but *Bolivar*.[2] You can certainly give him credit for being ingenious and extremely adaptable. And with you present, I have no more fears. Only the question of the conductor remains. I saw Hirsch[3] again yesterday, at the selection committee of the Opéra. He asks that you write him a brief, precise letter in which you stipulate that you have made many compromises for *Bolivar* but that, regarding the conductor, you are adamant and YOU WANT Cluytens. Cluytens is remarkable for theatre performances.[4] Deep down I keep hoping for a Déso miracle when you get back.[5] Since his triumph with *Pelléas* in London his relations with Hirsch seem better. I was in London at the time. It was a resounding success. Extremely moving to see the gods crammed with kids of twenty yelling with enthusiasm at 'discovering' *Pelléas*. I was in England with Pierre Fournier, with whom I was unfaithful to Bernac this spring because of my Sonata. Recital at the Salle Gaveau for the first performance, with Igor's *Suite Italienne* and Debussy's Sonata played in such a special style (quite simply what is written) that it met with all the success of . . . a first performance.[6]

Auric has finished his ballet, *Phèdre*, an enormous score of which the little I know seems excellent to me (true Georges). Messiaen is lying low before taking off for America.

I took your class [at the Conservatoire] one day. Subject: 'Music in relation to the prosody of Apollinaire and Eluard'. All the pupils were adorable. The examples were taken from *Figure humaine* and *Les Mamelles*. I think my technical considerations interested them. It is so touching to see all those kids wanting nothing other than to understand. *They adore you and cannot wait for your return.*

I was supposed to deliver Henri's decoration[7] to him but the papers did not come through and so it has had to be delayed. Actually, you are the one who should do it this autumn.

I am going to spend the whole summer at Noizay. I hope I don't pass out from the heat. Saw Vittorio [Rieti] this spring, very charming.

Tell Madeleine that I never received the coffee, which is not important, but just so that she can advise her Italian. I would like you to bring with you in your luggage a small box of that divine tea, in the golden box.

I was in Spain for two weeks at the end of March. Particularly dead artistic climate except for Barcelona, where Halffter and his group are doing good work.

Apologies for delivering all this to you in one job lot. I am dying to hear your Quartets and your Octet. I simply cannot comprehend how anyone can achieve such a tour de force.[8] Philippe [Heugel] has promised me a pocket score. He really is a charming boy.

What a blessing to be seeing each other again soon! I send to you and to Madeleine my deepest affection.

Ton Poupoule

200. FRANCIS POULENC TO PIERRE BERNAC

[Noizay], Monday [September 1949]

Thank you, *mon petit Pierre*, for your lovely, long letter. *No*, you are not on the decline, thank God, and Chausson and Royaumont were clear proof of this.[1] I have *no fears* for our December concert, which must be publicized as follows: 'Only recital before their departure for America.' (The public always falls for this.) But what we must do is make sure the recital is superb. Your programme is *perfect*: English songs – Fauré – Schumann – Chabrier (yes, yes, yes, together with *lieder*) – myself – Ravel. I am going to work on his *[Trois chants] hébraïques*. By the way, poor Darius has had a relapse and is not sure if he will be able to come home on 4 October. It is very sad.

I am making progress with the Concerto. I only hope I make a success of the Finale. At any rate, the orchestration is very good.[2]

How right you are to go to Solesmes.[3] You must tell me all about it afterwards. Perhaps I will go myself one day.

I embrace you,

Fr.

P.S. Naturally, it is as composer and not as rival that I took you to task over Gérard [Souzay]. I was hoping that, after you, he would be a perfect interpreter for me but, unfortunately, his faults are those which I have always feared most for my music: too sweet, too smooth.[4]

201. FRANCIS POULENC TO BRIGITTE MANCEAUX

Boston, Tuesday evening, 3 January 1950

Ma bichette,

Well, that's it . . . this morning we played through the Concerto [for piano] for the first time. The orchestration is excellent and Charloton[1] is *delighted, delighted*. So am I. Of course I played like a pig – my attention being mainly on my orchestration – but I will rectify that in the morning. Naturally, the first movement changes the most (and for the better): the second subject is ravishing and the two orchestral tutti, soli – hopeless when played on two pianos – are on the contrary quite perfect. The Andante is as I had expected, the Finale very *amusing*. The whole bang lot is stunning. The orchestra was delighted. Thirty Frenchmen among them. Munch has conducted the Concerto for organ twice this autumn – it has had an incredible success here. It has been recorded and I am going to hear the test copies any day now.[2]

I am leading an austere life in this very puritanical town. Fortunately the museum is fantastic, as much for painting as for Egypt, Asia, Greece, etc.

Charloton is a treasure, and as French as Chevalier when one sees him in this environment. He lives in a charming country house, half an hour from the town. Naturally, Ginette [Neveu's] death was a most dreadful blow to him.

I rehearse every morning. Light, easy piano, very pleasant hall. By the grace of God. I eagerly await your news. Give mine to everybody around you. Pierre has just phoned from New York, delighted with his trip and entirely rejuvenated by his success.

On that note I leave you to go and rehearse.

A thousand tender kisses.

Fr.

202. FRANCIS POULENC TO SIMONE GIRARD

c/o Monsieur Schang – Columbia Artists, 113 West 57th Street, New York.
Montreal, 2 February [1950]

Madame,

I hope you still recall the two musicians who, in the autumn of '48, after an unforgettable concert, indulged in the outrageous luxury of going all the way back to Paris by taxi.[1]

These two maestros (I am one of them: Fr. Poulenc; the other is Pierre Bernac) are at present touring America with 'tremendous success',* which is success with tremolo. But, bearing in mind that they have also turned the hearts of thousands of English women, of Dutch women and of Italian women, and owing to the fact that Easter next year falls on 25 March, thus cutting short their usual three ecstatic months in America, they have decided to devote themselves to Europe. England in November; Holland in December; Italy from 15 January. Having heard tell of the rocketing success of your concerts and . . . your fees, these two stars imagine that you are well able to match their American scale, and so suggest arriving at the beginning of January '51. 'Do you like that'?*

Unable to stoop to such steps themselves, they also hope that as you have one foot (and what a ravishing little footsie!) in the flourishing society of Marseilles, you may be able to arrange something for them in that quarter as well. This, Madame, is what these delightful boys were wanting to tell you. They are at present in excellent health: pink, fit and plump.

Pray permit them, Madame, (the dear Doctor[2] permitting as well) to respectfully kiss the tips of your adorable fingers.

Il Maestro
Francis Poulenc

*In English in the original text.

203. WANDA LANDOWSKA TO FRANCIS POULENC

7 February 1950

Mon Francis que j'aime,

I think of our last lunch together. You were so adorably light-hearted. Your radiant goodness, the way you listen, are a source of happiness to me.

I embrace you tenderly.

Wanda

Whenever I play Grigny I shall always think of you . . .[1]

204. FRANCIS POULENC TO HENRI SAUGUET

New York, 12 February [1950]

Cher Henri,

Forgive my not writing until today but life here never lets up for a moment. I am taking advantage of a puritanical Sunday to give you some New York news. First of all: our Marquise [Yvonne de Casa Fuerte] – still exactly the same, adorable, faithful. Naturally we talk about you all the time. Vittorio [Rieti] nicer and nicer. His comic opera *Perlimplin* is delightful – among the best of Rieti. Virgil [Thomson] funny as ever and as feared as Stalin. The pianists [Gold and Fizdale] played me your very lovely waltz (*Valse brève*] which they have just recorded together with Auric's. I found the record of *Visions* [*infernales*] very good and that of *Mouvements du coeur* a bit dreary. Apart from your contribution (I say this quite frankly and Yvonne is of the same opinion) it is of very little interest.[1]

Thousands of concerts by great virtuosos with often identical programmes. Magaloff, who plays really well, played the *Variations* by Igor II.[2] That interested me enormously. Igor I is in California. Unfortunately, we will miss each other when I go there. The Concerto [for piano and orchestra] went very well, with varied fortune. Boston, certain public success, fairly good press. Washington, huge success, good press. New York, very respectable success, harsh press. But I must not complain compared with Messiaen who was unmercifully slated by all that lot and who was generally detested by the musical milieu as a whole. Thank heavens (vis-à-vis business) there was an *excellent* article in *Musical America* which is *the* sacrosanct paper of the concert societies of America. I am enclosing a little article about you from it. Menasce wrote a *very nice piece* on you in the *Musical Quarterly* which he says he has sent on to you. If you have not received it, let me know. I have the impression that Heugel is doing everything he can for you. What would be interesting to push here is your second Quartet and your ballet *La Rencontre*. Doda [Conrad] sings you a lot, and friends of mine from

Washington liked your *Visions* very much. I wish you could come here, for instance to see one of Balanchine's ballets. Agreed with Doda – I'll speak to Monteux in San Francisco about your prospective Concerto for voice.[3]

I would be deceiving you if I kept from you my joy at returning soon to Paris, despite the success of our tour. Bernac is in marvellous form. We have just been doing a lot of recording. I have made a long record of piano music, on one side Satie: *Gym[nopédie I]. Sarab[ande II]. Gnos[sienne III]. Descriptions automatiques. Avant-dernières pensées*, etc.; on the other side, Poulenc.[4]

I am going to record *Aubade* with Bernstein.[5] The new Sonata by Barber, first performed by Horowitz, is remarkable.[6] Menotti's new opera marvellous, terrifying, superlatively performed, with very little music.[7]

On the 17th, grand première of *Figure humaine* at Carnegie Hall by an admirable choir.[8] Alas . . . I shall be in Chicago.

If you write to me, do so c/o SCHANG – Columbia Artists – 113 West 57th – New York.

I embrace you.

Fr.

Impossible to find the cutting, which went as follows: 'Heugel has just published *Les Pénitents en maillots roses* by H.S. Admirably true to the poems, with that fine sense of prosody which the French possess, these songs, which will be given their first performance at the Mercury Concerts, make one want to know more of the work of Henri Sauguet, whose *Visions infernales* so impressed us last year at the concert given by Mr Conrad.'

205. FRANCIS POULENC TO YVONNE DE CASA FUERTE

Hotel Mark Hopkins, San Francisco, Sunday [1950][1]

Douce Marquise,

Thank you for your lovely letter. I am happy that you like *Figure humaine a great deal*.[2] I would have preferred you to like it *as much* as *Sept chansons* but I know that you are sentimental in the extreme.

Why, divine friend, does one set so much store by your approval? Many a tear has been shed because of this: I sense that you are as cold as marble when it comes to the Concerto [for piano]. But Aix will change your mind.

As for Stravigor, I agree; although I do not share your enthusiasm for *Orpheus*.[3] It is remarkable, but more deliberate than inspired, and somewhat contrived in its grandeur. Enough of mythology, of Greece, of antiquity, otherwise we shall be verging on 'the bombast of the seventeenth century, late Corneille'. The variation on Orpheus is a very poor theme, and the conclusion is not a patch on *Apollon*.[4]

This is why, at heart, I approve of the young Europeans searching for new emotion in the not yet ossified twelve-tone system, and why I find it lamentable that here [in America] they are still buzzing like flies around Hindemith and Igor, venerable though their old age may be. Take careful note of what I say (and believe me when I tell you that the young Europeans do not like me at all): once again, it is out of old Europe that new ideas will come.

Having said this, let me assure you that Igor remains my great passion, although I would rather have written the latest quartets of Bartók than Igor's most recent works.

Here, there is sunshine, which is divine after Chicago, snow, wind. I do not want to see another museum with 'the Renoir', 'the Cézanne', 'the Monet'; I want to see only landscapes by God.

Write to me again, beloved Marquise. At: Hotel Santa Rite, Tucson, Arizona (before 6 March).

I embrace you most tenderly.

Your Poupoule

206. FRANCIS POULENC TO DARIUS MILHAUD

Carmel, 28 February [1950]

Mon petit Da,

Forgive my dreadful silence, but you know what it is like to have twenty-seven concerts in two months. After a very successful concert in San Francisco I am in Carmel for three days, staying with a delightful old gentleman well disposed towards musicians. The Pascals [Pascal Quartet] played *very well* last night and it is our turn tonight.

San Francisco without you was somewhat sad. Had a long chat about you and Mad at the homeopathic pharmacy. We had a great success, an excellent press, and above all a Frankenstein[1] who keeps me amused vis-à-vis the Monteux [Pierre and Doris]. I don't know if I told you that [Monteux] did not want me for this winter. Frank writes that although the big concerts know nothing of me, in two song cycles I had rallied the whole of musical San Francisco and proved my importance. Wanting to be very polite, I telephoned the Monteux to give them my regards. Doris answered more than coolly. I did not want to seem to attach any importance to her husband's rejection.

I saw your very charming friends (from Berkeley, I think), she blonde, he with a dark beard, who both speak French so well.

Max [de Rieux] has written to me twice, unable to think of anything but *Bolivar*. I hope you are pleased with him and with everyone else. Anyway, I shall be there for the première. What joy!

Everything has gone well here. The Concerto [for piano] has appealed to pianists, to the public and to certain critics.

Total success for *Figure humaine* at Carnegie Hall. You are right – Hugh Ross is first-rate.[2] There are also many recordings that are giving me pleasure, especially of the Concerto for organ (excellent).[3]

Wherever I go I meet friends of yours. It is wonderful to see your influence on a whole group of young people (at the conservatoires and universities) whom you have released either from the twelve-tone grip or from Igor's neo-asceticism (possible only for himself).

What is rather terrible here is this need to classify everything. The slightest *mélodie* of mine is taboo, whereas my chamber music is accepted. They exaggerate like this with everything.

Bernac is as fit as a fiddle.

Not much news from Paris. I hear that Jolivet's Concerto for Ondes Martenot is a success. I also heard that you had been unwell again. I hope your attack has passed now.

I will not be back until 30 March as I am recording with Bernac during the last week of the month. I dropped in at Columbia. Lieberson[4] is really very nice and, as his wife is singing the first performance of *Léocadia* in New York next winter, things have worked out extremely well.

Really, what a divine place California is, and how well I understand your liking it so much.

Bernac sends you much affection. And I embrace you very fondly, and Madeleine, too.

Francis

Our Marquise [de Casa Fuerte] is exquisitely like herself.
The Piano Sonata by Barber is stunning. By far the best.
Menotti's *Consul* is a sort of music-less masterpiece.

207. FRANCIS POULENC TO YVONNE DE CASA FUERTE

Antlers Hotel, Colorado Springs, Colorado, 10 March 1950

Ma Marquise adorée,

Thank you for your long letter. Thank God, my return to New York is drawing near. I arrive at the St-Moritz on Tuesday 21 in the morning. Can you organize a dinner for the evening of the 21st? With the adorable Christian [Dior], to whom I shall send word.

I love discussing music with you because I love you, and also because I very often (not always) share your opinions. I will give you *Sept chansons* – Vittorio [Rieti] will make a violin version for you.

Of course I have a secret love for 'Belle et ressemblante', which burst from me one April day like a spring flower, but I also cannot help being moved by 'Toi ma patiente', which grew slowly one humid, tragic night in the summer of '43.[1]

My angel, if only you knew how well I understand your pain at being so far away from your two treasures.[2] If I do not mention it any more, it is in the hope of replacing your tears with laughter. I think there is no crueller word than *absence*. For all the frequency of their letters, my heart pounds with joy at the thought that in three weeks I shall once again be seeing my Denise and my Raymond, who really are like children to me.[3] You and I must see each other constantly during my week in New York. Keep the afternoons of the 25th and 27th free, as I shall be recording – with Pierre – lots of Poulenc, some *Chabrier*, some Satie and Debussy.

This second concert tour has continued to go very well; all in all, an unquestionable success. I am so happy for Pierre, as this is his only joy in life.

> I embrace you frenetically.
>
> Poupoule

You can write to me until the 17th at Birmingham (Alabama), Hotel Tutwiler.

208. FRANCIS POULENC TO PAUL ELUARD

5 rue de Médicis, Sunday [June 1950]

Cher Paul,

At last I have your address from our friend Scheler.[1] I must congratulate you on choosing the plateau of Gravelle – the cycling ground of my childhood![2]

Just imagine that yet again I am setting a Paul Eluard to music. This time, it is the poem 'Vue donne vie' [Sight gives life]. Will you forgive me if I ask you once again to think of a title that is more appropriate for a programme of music? I know this is a silly thing to ask of you, but I can't help it.[3]

Resounding success this winter in New York for *Figure humaine*.

It is sad that we do not see each other any more, particularly as I am told you have such a charming wife.[4]

You will find enclosed a little debt owing from *Les Animaux modèles*.

Please do not be cross about 'Vue donne vie', and believe, dear Paul, that I have as much admiration as affection for you.

> Francis

Has the poem on me appeared in any of your collections of poetry? One of our admirers has written asking me about this.[5]

209. PAUL ELUARD TO FRANCIS POULENC

Charenton, 3 July [1950]

Mon cher Ami,

My wife tells me that you authorize me to have my letters to you typewritten; she is training me to do things the easy way!

Thank you a thousand times for your letter and enclosure. The only thing I can think of as a title for the poem 'Vue donne vie' is:

FRAÎCHEUR ET FEU

I hope you will find it suitable.[1]

No, the poem about you has not been published in its entirety in any of my collections; I am considering including it, with the second part, in a forthcoming edition of *Le Livre ouvert*, in which only the first part was to appear.[2]

I am leaving tomorrow for Sarlat, in Périgord. It is a marvellous part of France and it is where Dominique comes from.

I, too, realize that we rarely see each other any more, which is a bit silly as it is not every day, or even decade, or century, that one finds a friend like you. I shall take my revenge when I return.

Affectionately yours,

Paul Eluard

And regards, too, from the (bad) typist, Dominique Eluard

210. WANDA LANDOWSKA TO FRANCIS POULENC

Lakeville Conn. P.O. 313, 17 July 1950

Francis, mon enfant chèri,

You overwhelm me! I was going to thank you for the score of your adorable *Suite française*[1] and now the *Figaro littéraire* gives me this marvellous surprise. And *la Table ronde!*

If I write only today it is because, by an unbelievable stroke of bad luck, the articles were addressed to me in New York, and as I had just given up my apartment, they were still there, waiting to be readdressed. It was our good friend Sam Barber who phoned one evening to read me your piece in *la Table ronde*. How to thank you? I wouldn't know where to begin. But know that every word I receive from you fills me with joy.

I have just finished, here in Lakeville, recording the second book of the *Well-Tempered Klavier*. It will be more beautiful, I think, than the first. Is this due to the wood panelling in the room with the harpsichord?

I embrace you and think of you with infinite tenderness. And thank you again, and for ever and ever!

Wanda

211. PAUL ELUARD TO FRANCIS POULENC

Wednesday, half-past midnight, [1950]

Mon cher Poulenc,

I want to thank you again for the evening spent with you and Pierre Bernac. Thank you for your clear, intelligent, intelligible music, thank Pierre Bernac for the infinite purity of his singing.

I hope to see you again soon.

In friendship and in admiration,

Paul Eluard

[Written on the back of this letter, in Poulenc's hand, is the note: 'on *La Fraîcheur et le feu*'.]

212. FRANCIS POULENC TO SIMONE GIRARD

Noizay, Indre-et-Loire, [Summer, 1950]

Chère Simone,

My cook and I have been living in a state of constant drama for the past month over a simple matter of olive oil. This is too silly and must be brought to an end. Save us from divorce (after twenty-two years!!!). She keeps producing bottles allegedly from Nice and they all smell of cat's pee in petrol. I beg of you, send me – *direct to the Noizay station* – a drum of five litres of *full-flavoured* oil. Pay for it and I will reimburse you immediately. Word of honour – I still have enough money in the bank.

I found Pierre [Bernac] in splendid form from every point of view. We'll try to turn up trumps in Edinburgh.

Millions of passionate kisses from the midst of atrociously rainy weather.

Francis

213. FRANCIS POULENC TO PIERRE BERNAC

[The beginning of this letter is missing. At the end of the letter is a note, written and initialled by Bernac, saying: 'I have destroyed the first page. 12.10.50 P.B.' See Poulenc's postscript.]

[October, 1950]

The *Stabat*[1] is finished, finished! I have just copied it all out, but the ten days of 'no man's land'* were indispensable. My nerves were so frayed by the end of it that I wondered if I wasn't deluding myself as to its merits. However, a cool assessment of it this morning has convinced me that it is good, because it is profoundly authentic.

I am writing all this to you because nobody understands my musical make-up better than you. I will always be indebted to you for inspiring the best of what I've written.

I also think that later on, people will come to realize that our 'team'* was not all that bad.

Whereupon I embrace you, and will see you on Thursday.

Fr.

Tear up this letter, in spite of the regrets of my possible future biographers!

214. DARIUS MILHAUD TO FRANCIS POULENC

Oakland, California, End of October, 1950

Mon cher Francis,

If you are in Paris won't you kindly stick a few pins into Marietti?[1] I wrote to him about the very remarkable English translation that Cushing (our friend with the goatee beard) has made of *Socrate*; as *Socrate* is out of print it would be good to republish it together with the English translation. There is a growing interest in Satie in the USA. Extremely important. Consequently, we are eagerly awaiting the recording of Satie's piano pieces that you made in New York.[2]

We are going to New York for ten days (*Choéphores* with the Philarm, 'Dimitropoulos' conducting and Madeleine narrating).[3]

I have a very advanced, delightful group of students this year.

I rest a great deal at the moment and this is doing me a lot of good. I have a difficult job ahead. Hirsch has asked me to lengthen all the interludes in *Bolivar*[4] to avoid those periods of silence. This proves that he intends to continue with the opera. It is very gratifying *for once* to have the last word over *ces messieurs de la critique*. Your letters to *Le Figaro* have helped a lot.

Write soon.

I embrace you.

D.M.

*In English in the original text.

215. FRANCIS POULENC TO DARIUS MILHAUD

Agadir, 6 March 1951

Darius chéri,

A dreadful monster is what I am. Will you forgive me? I hope so. You see where I am writing from. For various reasons (that will not interest you) I agreed to do Morocco and Algeria one last time with Pierre [Bernac]. Before this, I was in Italy, before that in Holland, and in November in England. Thank God from 20 March until 30 October I shall become a composer again.

As you have no doubt heard, they tore me to shreds over my Concerto in Aix[1] where the hastily rehearsed performance was indeed execrable. So I decided to defend myself by playing wherever I was asked. As I was asked a great deal I have been peddling my wares everywhere: Amsterdam with Klemperer, Rome with Clemens Krauss, Florence, Turin, Milan, Bologna, and so on.

In the end I acquitted myself with all the honours of war. You know what the currents of opinion are like in Paris. The three victims for this year are you, Hindemith, and myself. I am flattered and feel very fortunate in this company. With *Jeanne au bûcher*[2] at the Opéra, the 'classics' are in their element; the 'moderns' are in theirs with a few Schoenberg 'series' and the mediocre Viola Concerto by 'the marvellous Bartók' – a dreadfully trumped-up piece[3] but miraculously performed, one has to admit, by Primrose.

Messiaen is very well placed to do penance in the game of forfeits. He has been deconsecrated.

However, all this is of very little importance.

I am delighted with the success of *Les Choéphores* in New York. Everyone has been telling me about it. They say Mad was sensational (Yvonne, Surinach, etc., dixit).

The issue of *Le Coq*[4] that you wanted is in Noizay. Impossible, therefore, to look up the prophetic phrase for you before the month of May as I am staying in Paris for the whole of April to finish orchestrating my *Stabat*, which will be performed in Strasbourg on 19 June. I am keeping this work a secret so as to see all their faces when they hear these 45 minutes of choir and full orchestra, which Bernac considers my best work. As I am now wary of all these big shots (in Aix, with dear [Charles] Munch I had *one* rehearsal on the morning of the concert), I have chosen the Saint-Guillaume choir, the Strasbourg Orchestra and Fritz Münch; they are already working in an atmosphere of faith as de Vocht once did with *Les Euménides*.[5] 'Gros Georges' [Auric] is in great form: his ballet *Phèdre* is making a big impression at the Opéra.

Roland,[6] very important at Unesco, has really been a tremendous friend to us all. He was *incredible* at Aix. He got permission to speak about my Concerto during the interval of the concert – because he knew what sort of reception it would get from *ces messieurs*.

The death of Gide must have caused you great sorrow. It made me terribly sad. The French press was very laudatory; but fifteen years earlier, before Sartre, it would have been quite another story. That is the trouble with growing old for such a long time.

You must reply to me to prove that you forgive me and are still fond of me.

How are you and what are your plans?

Let me tell you that I love your music more each day; and prepare yourself for this: I now even love *La Création*, from which I used to feel quite estranged because of my phobia about jazz.[7] Now I see in it only very beautiful music. Also heard with joy your studies played on Radio Frankfurt. Fundamentally, we have far more talent than 'those gentlemen' decree.

Darius, I embrace both you and Mad very, very affectionately.

Francis

Do your pupils see me as anything other than Mooser's 'musical playboy'?[8] I hope so. Make them listen to my Mass, conducted by Shaw.[9]

216. FRANCIS POULENC TO SIMONE GIRARD

18 July [1951]

Secret

Chère Simone,

You wrote me an adorable letter after the *Stabat*; thank you. You will soon have our Pierre staying with you, and that is what I am writing to you about.

Disappointed by his last trip to America, which was not very fruitful, all he wanted was to give up singing immediately (sic). I persuaded him that from every point of view (and I am certain of it) this would have the most detestable consequences. People would say that he had no more voice, that he was finished, that Souzay had edged him out, and so on . . .

This winter we are going into our seventeenth season, which is not bad. So here is what I have persuaded him to do, and I am sure you will approve. Winter '51–'52 – Holland, Italy, America. At the beginning of the '52–'53 term, he will certainly be appointed to the Conservatoire[1] and will then have a pretext for giving up his big concert tours. As long as he can, he should continue with the small week-long tours, like those in Holland, and the Avignon concerts, and take his leave of the platform in this way, *imperceptibly*.

As regards Paris, he should start giving up recitals without seeming to do so and, to avoid comparisons with capacity-packed halls, he should appear once or twice each winter at the Salle Gaveau in easily found engagements. What could be wiser than this? Please back me up.[2]

As, on the one hand, I shall *never* be able to work with another singer,[3] and as, on the other hand, I shall have to continue going on concert tours for a while, I am telling you – *in the greatest secrecy* – that in '52–'53 the Fournier–Poulenc team will be in action. Not bad, but shh! shh! shh!

Have a good summer. Write to me about Aix.

I embrace you all.

Fr.

217. FRANCIS POULENC TO HENRI SAUGUET

Monday [1951]

Cher Henri,

I am so sad: our Poupet is dying.[1]

I go to see him every other day for five minutes as I am one of the few people he will agree to see. He is terrifyingly thin, with the eyes of a dying man, and I emerge totally shattered each time. Miraculously, he speaks of what he will be doing in a month's time . . . Germaine is wonderful and her husband as well. He really is royally treated. Louise [de Vilmorin] is kindness itself, so is Marie-Blanche [de Polignac].

Material help is all very well, but tenderness counts for a lot, too.

I am very heartsore for I have a great fondness for Georges, my country neighbour, and true friends are not easy to come by.

I am working hard. On Friday I am doing the recording with Jacques [Février] for my film.[2] It is not a bad work of its kind – popular dance-hall style, Max Linder silent cinema! I leave for Brive on the 14th until the 23rd, then I shall go to Noizay.

I hope you are seeing Denise [Duval]. Please try to cheer her up as she is very depressed over a deplorable love affair which goes on and on coming to an end. I am very worried, for you know that I think of her and Raymond [Destouches] as my children.

I have not been to a single ball as I do not enjoy these at all any more, ditto for cocktail parties. The Italian opera was sublime. The [Marguerite] Long competition incredible. Make sure you buy [*Paris-*] *Match* – you will have a surprise.

Dear Henri, I am extremely happy that you liked my *Stabat*. Rest assured, too, that Bordeaux was a profound joy both to my ears and to my heart.

I embrace you very affectionately, as well as Jacques [Dupont].

Francis

Work well!

218. FRANCIS POULENC TO HENRI SAUGUET

Noizay, 15 August [1951]

Cher Henri,

I am missing you. What have you been up to? The other night, as my sister was staying over, I put on the records of *Les Forains*. Never had I felt its melancholy more intensely, or delighted more in the patina of the work, which becomes more authentic from day to day. There is no denying, I *love* your music.

As you can imagine, I was greatly affected by Georges Poupet's death. I have lost a neighbour and, whenever I was away, an affectionate, attentive and very amusing correspondent. Detained in Paris by my film (completed, thank God, at the end of July) I was able to see him almost until the end. What is very sad is that he enjoyed life so profoundly.

I shall spend the summer here, except for a week in Edinburgh with Bernac. I thought I might pop over to Venice from London on 8 September but I have decided against it. It is ruinously expensive and anyway I must work.

I have just finished my *Thème varié* for piano, a serious work but I hope not boring. The coda of the last variation is strictly the theme backwards. You see, Mr Leibowitz, that we too . . .[1]

Christian [Dior's] collection is *unbelievably beautiful*. A quite stupendous sensation. I am so pleased for him and so proud for France.

Henri, let me hear from you. I picture you in your exquisite house.[2]

Francis

I haven't heard from anyone.

219. HENRI SAUGUET TO FRANCIS POULENC

Fargues, Coutras (Gironde), 20 August 1951

Cher Francis,

On my return from Paris last night I found your letter, which I read with a great deal of pleasure.

I left on Thursday night after hearing on the radio (and you can imagine with what emotion) that Louis Jouvet had died. I could not rest without going to see him. So arrived on Friday morning, going directly from the train to the Athénée where he had passed out on Tuesday evening, never to recover. In death, he was quite unlike the way we had known him. Poor Monique, who had not left him since the moment he had been struck down by this sudden attack, stood there before him, haggard, her hands clenched, her face no more than fifty centimetres away from his. So I saw him during the two days I spent in Paris, going backwards and forwards to that theatre that holds for me so many memories – of work on those five plays![1]

Crowds of people kept filing past him. The day after he died, his face was magnificent. I was truly overcome by this death. You know the faithful affection he had shown towards me for more than twelve years. And I returned this affection with, in addition, admiration and gratitude for having been associated with some of his finest productions. It was painful to see everyone's consternation. In the theatre there was a kind of havoc, a scuffling, and hustling and bustling, an extraordinary restlessness and overwhelming despondency: precisely what must happen in our arteries when the heart gives in and the blood races here and there in a panic.

I did not stay for the funeral, a very official affair, because I had left my house and my relatives, and I was expecting friends yesterday; and because this week I am at last leaving for Biarritz, to rehearse *La Voyante*, which our Denise [Duval] is singing on the 28th in a little production by Jacques [Dupont].

I saw Denise several times during her stay in Libourne: she came to have lunch here. We went to spend a day with her parents, who are adorable. She is like them, or they are like her. How charming she is, so inherently good and trusting. I understand why you are so attached to her.

[. . .]

I have heard from a few friends, especially after poor Georges [Poupet]'s death. I spoke about him a lot on the telephone to Geneviève (as I was not able to see her) and she told me all about his last days. His death, too, has affected me deeply: he was such a sensitive, loyal and true friend for almost thirty years. In the space of three months, we have lost three friends: Françoise in June, Georges in July, and now Jouvet. I am deeply upset. I have a photo, very beautiful moreover, taken during one of the last rehearsals of *Don Juan*: Bébé [Christian Bérard] and his dog Jacinthe, Jouvet and myself – and now I am the only one left. For how much longer!

Dear Francis, I sent you a loving thought from the train when I passed by your house at Noizay, shining in the sunlight – the light of your glory! A caress of the summer bestowed on your music and on you. One of the rare caresses of this particular summer, extremely wet in these parts! I pictured you at the piano. You were composing your *Thème varié*, but I did not know this. What a lovely idea, and how good it must be! You will play it to us in the autumn. But our ranks are declining, weakened by the loss of so many dear, rare friends. It is dreadful to grow older losing those we admire, those who can never be replaced. Who could possibly take the place of Bébé, for example, or Max, or Georges Poupet, or Jouvet . . . and so on . . . But we must keep going, learning how to love each other more. It really is worth while when one has the good fortune to have a friend like you, for whom one feels as much admiration as love! I embrace you, dear Francis, with all my heart. And so does Jacques. Much affection to Raymond.

Your faithful
Henri S.

220. FRANCIS POULENC TO DODA CONRAD

Noizay, 1951

Cher enfant chanteur et enchanteur,

You are very lucky to be rolling in the soft sand with a handsome American pianist. I, on the other hand, am living all alone, virtuous and turned in on myself (which attitude, rest assured, implies nothing of onanism). Nothing would be nicer than if you could come to spend the weekend of the 29th with me, to cheer me up in my hermitage. Take the train to Tours and, from there, the evening bus to Noizay.

What a lot to talk about – I look forward to it with delight! I have finished a theme and variations for piano which I am sleeping on before the final touches. Since then, I have lost all interest in my own music, which allows me to be very lucid about the music of others. Stravinsky's opera, which I love now that I've heard it (though not when I read it), is a marvellous lesson in dignity. Quite superb.[1] I hope that Madame, your illustrious mother [Marya Freund], did not leave Venice the night before!

Until the 29th, then? And, of course, I embrace you, my Dodush.

Francis
Maître d'Amboise

221. FRANCIS POULENC TO SIMONE GIRARD

[November–December 1951]

Chère Simone, présidente divine, you must excuse my silence, which quite belies what my heart is feeling for you. You cannot imagine how much and in how many ways I benefited from my little break in the Midi – to which you so *greatly* contributed.

I have never seen you so well, free as you were from all baritones and grey-haired *confrères*. And you have the ultimate intelligence – quite simply that of the heart (which of course I knew). You seem able to read between the lines, and this puts one so much at ease. If I were to dedicate to you a mere Carol in dialect, it would not be worthy of you, and so I shall instead dedicate to you one of the *Quatre motets pour le temps de la Nativité*[1] which I am now composing as a counterpart to the austere *Pénitence*. I think, the way things are going, that it will be very lovely. Something like a counterpart to 'Vinea Electa'.[2]

As soon as it is finished I will send it to you. You can have the parts copied and you can try it out under the gentle baton of Laugier.[3]

Unfortunately I am not as religious as I would like to be. Half of me remains quite the opposite. Though I am not totally impious, I am – alas! – as pied as a horse.

My hand is much better and I am preparing for America with our Pierre, who is *very much on form*, both mentally and vocally. Our old friendship makes the prospect of two months together in America seem very pleasant.

I shall probably go to Marseilles from Sunday night until Tuesday morning, in which case – if it is not inconvenient – I would stop by for lunch on Tuesday at rue de la Croix,[4] and would then take the Mistral.[5] Unfortunately I do not know if this plan will materialize, although my presence is certainly desired.[6] In any event, I shall let you know by phone before Sunday.

They are doing my *Stabat* at St Roch on 28 April. I am counting on you to come. Can you try to get Fleury to do it in Marseilles at the end of March? This would give me a marvellous pretext, when I return from America, for . . . a rest in the sun. Don't laugh at me. I have never had much sweetness in affairs of the heart, and when for once, after gadding around like a dirty old man, the right sentiment arrives, the wretched kilometres get in the way. Whereupon I shall return to my piano, but not without embracing you warmly, and the dear Doctor, too.

Fr.

Until Tuesday, let's hope.

222. FRANCIS POULENC TO SIMONE GIRARD

42 West 58th Street, New York City, [Beginning of 1952]

Ah! Some baritones have all the luck. They receive letters from *La Présidente*. I, poor soul, receive practically no mail at all from France and am abandoned by everyone, except, thank God, . . . Toulon.[1]

Ma divine, everything is going *marvellously* and, in the dashing rake sauntering down Fifth Avenue, you would hardly recognize the gloomy, grumpy singer you saw leaving from Les Invalides. Like a youngster, he gleefully consults his diary, packed with appointments until the day he leaves. We have a television appearance on Wednesday the 17th in the evening, which is the ultimate here, and then, as you know, we are leaving for Venezuela. He is doing recordings with Robert [Casadesus] and with me. What more could he ask for? Once again, Poupoule was right to get the better of his pessimism and force him to come on this trip.

Things are going very well for me, too. Great success in Cincinnati with the Concerto [for piano]. The admirable Robert Shaw Chorale will perform my *Stabat* on 27 April. What a pity I shall not be there, as it will be of an unbelievable perfection. We heard 'their' Bach Mass last night. There is no other choir like it in the world (except, of course, yours).

They like me a lot here. At last – a place where I am liked! I hope, all the same, that I am not too disliked in Avignon.

And, on that note, I place upon your august brow several kisses, I greet the dear Doctor, and I'm off to find our young scamp.

Francis

223. FRANCIS POULENC TO HENRI SAUGUET

New York, 25 January [1952]

Cher Henri, très cher Henri, mon Henri de toujours,

Last night I dined alone with our Marquise [de Casa Fuerte]. Her perfect sense of friendship led her to speak to me about a letter from you in which you were melancholy because of me.

I was terribly upset by this and for the last twenty-four hours have been able to think of nothing else. No, dear Henri, I am still as fond of you as ever; you are one of the rare people I simply cannot do without, first of all because I feel an infinite tenderness towards you and then because I have a very deep love of your music. I can see what may have caused you to believe that I have been aloof, and I want to explain myself to you right now, with affection and frankness.

If I have not spoken to you about *Le Cornette*, it is because I did not know how to do so. It has seemed to me that whenever a work of mine has not met with your approval, you have preferred to remain silent rather than to offer less than sincere compliments. This is why I have done the same in turn. And this should prove to you my utter sincerity when, after *La Voyante, La Chartreuse, Les Forains*, the Trio for reeds, the second Quartet, *La Rencontre, La Symphonie des Saisons*, and others, I shouted: 'Bravo Henri!!'

I may be able to use *passe-partout* phrases with other people, but I feel incapable of doing so with you.

Believe me, one does not stop loving a friend simply because one does not like one of his compositions.

Anyway, it is easier for me to tell you in a letter the reasons – no doubt bad ones – why I have avoided the issue of *Le Cornette*.

First of all, I find you too French for this specifically German text which, moreover, pales in translation. For me, your true romanticism is expressed quite naturally in *Visions infernales* and I consider a song like 'Régates mystérieuses' as a success which is quite rightfully your due.[1]

Besides, whoever the singer may be, it is extremely difficult to hold the attention of the listener for 50 minutes, especially when – as I believe is the case with *Le Cornette* – the orchestral part is better. In fact there are pages for orchestra that are remarkable and so typically you. With regard to the vocal line, I find it has neither your sensitivity, nor your usual precision (the success of the Menuet in *La Gageure*, for example, comes immediately to mind).

All these things together have caused me, I repeat, to avoid this work of yours. You must not hold it against me. No doubt I am wrong. Remember Manet saying about the portrait of the Sisley household by Renoir: 'If you put this picture in a warm place, it will melt!!' None of us is exempt from making errors of judgement.

And that, my dear Henri, in all frankness, is what I wanted to say to you.

Do not doubt my affection, my friendship, or my TRUE ADMIRATION.

I embrace you. Kindest regards to Jacques [Dupont].

                                                                    Francis

224. FRANCIS POULENC TO BRIGITTE MANCEAUX

New York, Saturday, 26 January 1952

Ma Biche,

Four days without a single letter from anyone – I was beginning to think I had been abandoned. Then this morning I got your letter (3), which bucked me up considerably. Delectably lazy week in my sumptuous suite at the Wyndham Hotel, bedroom, sitting-room with piano (only $8). It's ideal, rather like the hotels in the rue de l'Arcade. The owners adore me. They adore music.

Everything is ready for our departure for Venezuela. We are not going to Mexico as we have four concerts in Venezuela, which is superb from every point of view. I am playing the *Champêtre* with orchestra. We will be back in New York on the 7th (recital on the 10th). I want to find mountains of letters. Take note. Until my return my address will be: Wyndham Hotel, 42 West 58th Street, New York City. Spread the news.

Beautiful performance of *Salomé* at the Met. with [Ljuba] Welitsch. Tomorrow night Bach Mass by my beloved Shaw. Horowitz still away. The cadence of my *Thème* [*varié*] is now impeccable.

I see my exquisite Marquise de Casa all the time.

There will be an Elsa Maxwell supper on the evening of our concert.

Pierre [Bernac] continues to be on top form. He is giving a dinner for eight this evening at his place (Madame Beck's apartment, Edward's mother). Delighted that Roussin heard what I thought about *César*.[1]

A thousand kisses in haste.

Fr.

Phone Denise [Duval], Maillot 19-41, at about four o'clock and tell her she is a monster . . . a beloved one, of course.

225. FRANCIS POULENC TO COMTESSE JEAN DE POLIGNAC

Hôtel Potomac, Caracas, 4 February 1952

Ah! how deadly dull life is in Caracas, beautiful Countess! Picture Contrexéville[1] in July complete with little boutiques. But it is unjust of me to say this, as everyone has been very kind. I have been praised to the skies and I have made the acquaintance of a marvellous conductor, a Romanian, Celibidache.[2] He conducts the Berlin Philharmonic, and I have just performed the *Concert champêtre* with him. I feel in great *artistic* sympathy with him, and he with me. He wants to conduct my *Stabat* at the Maggio Musicale Fiorentino.[3]

Tonight and Wednesday recitals with Bernac, rejuvenated by 20 years, as he always is when he gets away from his humdrum Parisian routine. What is more, *he* had a *marvellous* press in Canada (at the beginning of the tour), which has given him a permanent lift. We return to New York on 7th, recital in Town Hall on 10th, followed by concerts and recordings until the beginning of March. All in all, a *very good* tour. I am in excellent humour and you should not read into my opening apostrophe anything other than a *surprise-épistolaire*.

I have received hardly any letters from Paris where it seems no one loves me any more, but never mind, I have both the Americas at my feet!!!

Elsa Max is giving a party after our concert. I very definitely enjoy being in New York. I have discovered a charming hotel on 58th Street (Wyndham

Hotel), behind the Plaza, where I have a little flat with piano. It is perfect for an old maestro. I had a great sadness before I left: I had to have my little dog put down. He couldn't go on any longer. I cried my eyes out when I kissed him for the last time, just before the end. I know you will understand.

We think we will be back on 5 March, unless . . . swept away by glory . . .

How is the Prince, the collection?[4]

Try to write. I embrace you very affectionately.

Poupoule

Have not seen Horowitz yet, on tour in Cuba.

226. FRANCIS POULENC TO COMTESSE JEAN DE POLIGNAC

Hôtel Potomac, Caracas, 6 February 1952

Countess, it's me again!

Yesterday I saw such a lovely house that I want to give you some interior decorating ideas, knowing that at this very moment you and Emilio are busy transforming the rue Barbet.[1] The richest banker in Venezuela (monthly income of 80 million) has just taken up residence on the top of a hill. Now the architecture here is *just right* – houses in Spanish colonial or modern style – but he has seen fit to change the tone drastically and build himself a Norman eyrie in Joan of Arc style. The all-marble interior, with its gilded cornices, rather resembles the Hôtel Régina, in the rue de Rivoli (the Louis XVI-Ritz would be too late an era) – rich furnishings, from the local auction rooms, great vases genre Marquise de Sévigné. Whence I come to the bedroom, which I suggest as a model for Madame's room. Walls hung with yellow satin. Immense boat-shaped bed upholstered in redcurrant red, with, instead of a headboard, a series of mauve-tinted smoked glass mirrors. Giant wardrobe of quilted satin with – to echo the mirror theme – a diamond (perhaps even a real one) studding each upholstery boss. Seats of gilded wood, one with golden canopy. And at this point I put to you an exquisite and not very costly idea for entering the boudoir: take a huge Louis XV-1900 wardrobe in three parts (I do believe I have seen one at Kekker painted mauve with threads of gold), place it against the wall, empty the central section, which will serve as a passage-way, do away with the door and replace it with a golden tulle curtain, veiled on each side with black Chantilly lace. And, at the bottom, do not forget a ruche of redcurrant red satin.

This, Countess, is what I suggest to you.

Upon your bewitching hands I bestow tropical kisses.

Francis

All the above can be certified true by the *sober-minded* Bernac.

227. FRANCIS POULENC TO YVONNE DE CASA FUERTE

Noizay, 21 April [1952]

Mon Yvonne,

My agitation is extreme. From morning till night, I can think of nothing but the concert on the 27th.[1] The première of the *Stabat* in Paris on the 30th is as nothing by comparison. How I would love to be there to hear the sublime chorale of my beloved Shaw. I only hope the soloist is good! I attach considerable importance to this première. I would like you to come away from it with tears in your eyes. Think of Bébé [Christian Bérard], think of the past, and of our poor Déso [Désormière], who is not getting any better – I am in despair.[2] I hope Virgil [Thomson] gives it a good press or, if he is conducting, that [Arthur] Berger will do so.[3]

I have come to Noizay for three weeks before the season begins. Is Vittorio [Rieti] coming? There are no seats left for any of the performances. I have just written two motets for Christmas, one of which is, I think, rather exceptional. With the one you already know, that makes three. I have only one more to write.[4]

I am also beginning a work for 'les boys' [Gold and Fizdale]. On the whole, I am in good form. If only you knew how much I love New York! I feel quite at home there now, and not to be going there next winter is barely compensated for by the prospect of going with Pierre [Bernac] to Bali – Java – Sumatra. Our success in America has given our old team a new lease of life.

How happy you must be to have Flavie with you again. Are you up to date with all our plans, secrets, and so forth?

I spent three unforgettable days of peace, happiness and sunlight in Marseilles. I am missing you. I have never loved you more than I have this winter. Write to me as soon as the *Stabat* is over, as I *cannot bear it any longer*. Write, of course, to Paris – 5 rue de Médicis.

Millions of kisses,
Fr.

228. DODA CONRAD TO FRANCIS POULENC

Philadelphia, 2 May 1952

Cher Maître-du-Stabat,

I wanted to write immediately after the Carnegie Hall concert but I was too busy with my departure from New York. I have sent you the programmes and a critique from *The [New York] Times*. The one in the *Herald* was unpleasant – signed Berger. He must suffer from a liver complaint, as he fills his pen with bile. Since he is a 'composer' and since the *Stabat* was *wildly acclaimed* (not only by myself who, I must tell you, shouted my lungs out), his reaction is rather flattering.

I, personally, was profoundly moved. Profoundly. And I am not sure that I do not even prefer the *Stabat* to the Mass. It seems to me, too, that Robert Shaw conducted the *Stabat* better – with more tenderness, less rigidity, less aggressive virtuosity – than in his first performance of the Mass, which I heard some years ago. [The *Stabat*] was very human, very humble, very beautiful in its emotion. The soprano had a lovely voice but seemed to be suffering somewhat from stage fright. They were called back eight times, which seems to me unprecedented for a work of this kind.

[. . .] Shaw has promised to send you the recording made during the concert. I thought his singers were absolutely dazzling. That marvellous accuracy and that melting quality, which perhaps comes from the fact that he does not separate his singers – sopranos, mezzos, tenors and basses – but intermingles them, which, for your music, is ideal. (I often wonder, though, how he manages to give them their cues, to stress nuances, to bring out different voices . . .)

I shall be back on the 20th. I hope to see you. [. . ,] I embrace you, and thank you again for the *Stabat Mater*.

Your old friend
Doda

Everybody *adores* you in America!

229. FRANCIS POULENC TO PIERRE BERNAC

Hôtel Beau-Rivage, Ouchy, Lausanne, Tuesday [January 1953]

Mon petit Pierre,

My set-up here is sheer paradise[1] – room on the fourth floor over-looking the lake; salon with grand piano nearby, part of a 'royal suite' and entirely sound-proof. There are about a hundred people in the hotel but 60% are royalty (King and Queen of Jordan and their entourage; sister of King Farouk; Charlie Chaplin and family). All these members of high society have their meals in their suites. The food is very simple but good. Sublime breakfast with an *extraordinary* Ceylon tea.

The gentlemen from the radio came to see me last night. Very kind, serious, deferential, 150% Swiss.[2]

Only one hitch: neither here nor in Geneva can I find the Horowitz recording of *Pastourelle, Toccata*.[3] As you know more about these things than Brigitte, will you ask Ploix to get it for me, charging it to my account and getting in touch with Stéphane Audel, 16 rue Delambre, 14ᵉ,

Danton 43–33, who will bring it with him when he comes here on the 14th. If Ploix does not have it and cannot obtain it for me, ask the radio people (rue de l'Université) if they can reproduce it for me, but I prefer a new record. I think there is one by Pathé-Marconi.

How calm it is here! It is doing me so much good. And what weather for working! Today I am beginning the Rostand interviews, which will be published by Julliard, like Darius's.[4] I have just written a long letter to Ströbel[5] about our recordings, giving him a detailed programme. A New Year card from him has made things a lot easier.

With much affection,
Fr.

It is *essential* to issue your recording with Robert![6]

230. FRANCIS POULENC TO SIMONE GIRARD

[Italy, March 1953]

Ouf! It's done – we have lost our virginity!!![1] But what a state we were in over that first concert for those dreadful Turin audiences. Listen to this: Rubinstein – one encore (execrable press); Robert Casa – one encore (good press); Gieseking – one encore (mediocre press). And so on. Thanks to twenty young people hidden amongst a lot of old crones, we got a second encore, but only because the hall was then deserted except for those twenty converts. Where are you, my Avignon audiences, and my Simone, and my Doctor Girard . . . ?

You cannot imagine how it constantly fascinates me to compare the two Pierres. Fournier is a *love*, a *real love*, but he is not my Pierre I (*our* Pierre, so as not to upset you). He is undoubtedly an admirable artist, the greatest cellist of our day, but he does not have all the multiple levels of my old Pierre, my irreplaceable counterpart. All the same, only someone with Fournier's stupendous class could make me take to a new duo. We caused a sensation with the Debussy, played the Schubert very well, the Schumann less well, the Poulenc quite well and the Stravinsky *very well*. Tonight, in Bergamo, everything should go quite smoothly. At any rate, it is very easy to play with Fournier. Like Pierre I, he never falters. I repeat that he is *adorable*. My confession is therefore ultra-secret. It does not bear recounting, even to the baritone.[2]

And the *Stabat?* I keep praying for hoards of loaded coffers to materialize miraculously in Avignon.

Keep writing to me and, above all, keep loving me. What a pity that Pierre I and I have no more than ten years ahead of us. In the realm of *mélodies* I am not afraid of anyone, and it is always a very pleasant thing to be in the lead.

Write soon. I embrace you tenderly.

Fr.

The duo Four–Poul is much in demand but it will be *rarissime* and very expensive.

LETTERS
1953–1963

Perhaps the heart of the matter is that the worst of
myself is the best of myself.

Francis Poulenc to Henri Hell
December 1953

Who will ever know all that lies at the secret heart
of certain works?

Francis Poulenc to Simone Girard
31 October 1955

Essentially, I am a man of song in all its forms.

Francis Poulenc to Pierre Bernac
Easter 1958

231. FRANCIS POULENC TO PIERRE BERNAC

Assisi [March 1953]

Mon petit Pierre,[1]

I am revelling in my 24 hours in Assisi, and that sceptic, Fournier, is excited beyond belief. We get on *perfectly* and I have a *great deal* of esteem and affection for him. We are beginning to play really well. The recording for radio is good, I think.

Happy Easter. A thousand kisses.

Fr.

Rome great fun and full of high society. Sam [Barber] is there. [Nicolas] Nabokov as well!!![2] Greet Le Grand Coteau for me and explain to Suzanne and André[3] that I will need very peaceful conditions for my work.

Now, sit down: La Scala has commissioned me to write an opera on . . . *Le Dialogue des Carmélites* [sic]. I said yes, and can think of nothing else. Performances guaranteed Scala, San Carlo, Cologne, Covent Garden, Berlin Opera . . . and perhaps even Paris. I had already thought of something along those lines but did not know exactly what. [Illegible] In any case, it is tailor-made for me.[4]

232. FRANCIS POULENC TO YVONNE GOUVERNÉ

Bastide du Roy, Antibes, Friday 3 April [1953]

Mon Yvonne,

I will never be able to thank you enough for the performance of the *Stabat* last night. It was quite simply *wonderful* – never before have I heard it like that. Everything was perfect: tempi, nuances, pauses. Say thank you to your choir very, very warmly. Rosenthal was stunning and Moizan, as always, so moving. I listened alone, in the night, in Marie-Blanche's big American car which had been left in the garden – so I was able to get the most out of the broadcast.[1] I did not know it was a public performance. There seemed to be a lot of applause. Were there any fellow-composers in the audience?

I am staying here until the 11th because on the 10th in Monte Carlo there is a Poulenc Festival: Sinfonietta – Concerto – *Aubade* – *Biches*. It is the first time this has happened to me. I am extremely touched. Very good tour in Italy with Fournier and also . . . but keep this a secret . . . I am doing an opera for La Scala based on *Le Dialogue des Carmélites* [sic]. Surely a fitting subject for me.

Happy Easter – again very fondly,

Francis

233. FRANCIS POULENC TO PIERRE BERNAC

Saturday, 22 August [1953]

Mon petit Pierre,

[. . .] I have begun *Les Carmélites* and literally *cannot sleep* because of it. I think it will be all right but there are so many problems. Expect to receive a flood of questions as I want it to be more than vocal. I have the mood of the great scene between the Prioress and Blanche, and a very good plan: calm at the beginning, fierce in the middle (rules of the Order), calm again at the end. If I am to succeed with this work it will only be through the music identifying absolutely with the Bernanos *spirit*. Very light orchestration to allow the text to come through.

Heard *The Rake's Progress* in Tours!!!! Excellently performed by some young Swiss, Germans, Belgians, English, etc. . . . so much more Stravinsky than with Cluytens. Nadia [Boulanger] had sent a busload of pupils (50) from Fontainebleau, who came and had a drink at my place.[1] *Everybody* has been telling me about your *extraordinary* concert in July.

That is all my news.

Write to me soon. Much tender affection.

Fr.

My gramophone is not lying idle. Operas, operas, operas.

234. FRANCIS POULENC TO STÉPHANE AUDEL

31 August [1953]

Cher enfant,

Just a brief line as Mother Marie[1] will not allow me the slightest distraction. I am working like *a madman*, I do not go out, do not see anyone, all the more so because, unfortunately, I have to go to Paris around the 12th for the recording of *Les Mamelles*.[2] I am absolutely counting on you for the weekend of 27 September. Before that I do not want to see anyone – not even you, and that says it all. I do not want to think of anything else; things are going (I might even say) too well. I am completing one scene a week. I hardly recognize myself. I am crazy about my subject, to the point of believing that I have actually known these women. You will see – scene 2 with the Prioress and Blanche is astounding in its calmness, severity, peacefulness and violence. Tell Cariel[3] that for Mother Marie all I can see is her. Pity she cannot sing!

[. . .] I am going back to my piano now, under pressure from Blanche. Very affectionately,

Fr.

235. FRANCIS POULENC TO PIERRE BERNAC

Noizay, 1 September [1953]

Mon petit Pierre,

It feels like a very long time since I have heard from you. It is true that because of the strikes one loses track of everything.

Prepare for a shock: in just two weeks I have drafted the first three scenes of *Les Dialogues*, which I will write next week. I cannot get over this. It just flows and flows, and it is like nobody but myself. It is madly vocal. I check each note and am careful to place the right vowels on the high notes. Not to mention the prosody; I do believe that every word will be understood. The essential phrases are almost without orchestra. The most beautiful scene so far is, of course, scene two (Prioress–Blanche) which has moments of great severity and a great nobility. How I long to show it all to you! Then you can tell me where there is a risk of it not working. For the Prioress I am keeping mainly to this:

In the case of Blanche, I know Denise[1] so well that I have given her only open sounds in the high register:

I am so passionately involved with my work that the briefest outing seems like a waste of time. If it goes on like this I will have completed Act I by December, which will give me a whole year for Act II, but where to in January???[2]

Great news, quite astounding:

Turn the page quickly:

Pathé-Marconi are going to record *Les Mamelles*!!!!!! with the Opéra-Comique and Cluytens. I am bowled over. They are beginning on 17 September! They are 'very keen to have such a typically French work'. I cannot help thinking that there is an American order behind it all as it bears no resemblance to the Challan Bourgeois indifference towards the *Stabat*. I am absolutely delighted, as there will always be someone to do the *Stabat*. Shaw, I hope.[3]

With *Sécheresses*, which Tzipane will do with Pathé-Marconi,[4] and the Sextet by Françaix,[5] my Parisian catalogue is beginning to look serious, as you see.

[. . .] My sister has just spent two weeks here. Brigitte will take her place from tomorrow. Apart from that, there is complete calm. Sublime weather, flowers ditto. Anna and Charles in good humour. All in all, divine summer. Rocamadour has a lot to do with this, I *know*.

I have prayed so many times for a libretto that the Holy Mother sent me this one to sing her praises with. Of course I am in love with Sister Constance. That lunatic of a Lulu, all those years ago, would have been exactly right for the role.

Only one character worries me a little at the moment, Mother Marie whom I shall meet in the third scene. I am going to make the role very Danco.[6] Do you think this will be right for the character? Although she is often present, she rarely sings alone; whereas the second Prioress, as well as having the aria in the first act, has a lot to sing in the prison scene.

While I see my second Prioress as the Balguerie type, I want Mother Marie very dry; that is why I think of Danco, as she has to sing *pp* in the high register.

Anyway, I am trusting in heaven to solve all this for me. And I mean it very seriously.

Write to me.

Much affection.

Francis

236. PIERRE BERNAC TO FRANCIS POULENC

5 September [1953]

Mon petit Francis,

Yes, I have received all your letters, almost at the same time, and I am happy to know that you, too, are satisfied with your summer, I mean with your working climate, and that *Les Dialogues* is going full speed ahead! Fortunately you will be able to take advantage of this momentum for another two months, and you will then approach the winter with a substantial part of it done. Couldn't you rent Suzanne's apartment in Cannes for January?

I have been giving a lot of thought to the characters in *Les Dialogues* and to the colour of their voices. The tessitura you have shown me for the First Prioress is excellent, but you can allow yourself some high As, if you prepare them carefully and if they are sung forte. Refer back to your scores of *Aida* and *Il Trovatore* and look closely at the roles of Amneris and Azucena: you will find the possibilities of a true Italian contralto quite edifying.

So the First Prioress will be the only true contralto. The problem then is to have enough variation in colour and tessitura between the Second Prioress and Mother Marie. I understood you were making the Second Prioress a lyric soprano: Aida, Mimi. Now you speak of making Mother Marie another lyric soprano, a little dry, something like Danco. That is all very well but, personally, I feel you will not have enough contrast with Denise's voice, which to my mind is also a dry lyric soprano. This is why I continue to hear Mother Marie either as a mezzo or as a dramatic soprano. Bear in mind that you are depriving yourself for the entire second act of any possibility of a low tessitura . . . These three women, all very different, will be singing in exactly the same tessitura. I cannot help thinking that Vhita would once have made a perfect Mother Marie, both physically and vocally, given a true high register.

It therefore seems to me that Mother Marie, if you do not want her mezzo, should be sung by a Tosca, by which I mean someone with great dramatic possibilities in the middle register, with a chest voice, and also possibilities in the high register, both forte and piano. You see things differently. That is a pity, for however much I try I cannot share your point of view. I am sure you will find that you lack a full-bodied voice in the middle register for your second act if you decide on three lyric sopranos. Bear in mind that you will not always be able to choose the voices yourself and that it is the tessitura of the roles that will determine the cast.

What good news about the recording of *Les Mamelles*! Aren't you going to Paris for this? It would perhaps be wise in order to tighten some of the screws. Cluytens is fundamentally rather slack – remember *The Rake*. You need to ensure that this recording is authentic and definitive. And you know as much as I do how important it is for things to sound alive on disc. We almost invariably choose slightly faster tempi than in public to avoid the impression that things are dragging. And it is essential for *Les Mamelles* to be performed con brio. I would almost have preferred Dervaux, who would probably do it in ten minutes less than Cluytens.

My holidays are coming to an end. Simone [Girard] has just left for Villeneuve, where I shall be lunching again on Tuesday, and seeing Denyse Cornu. I shall leave for Paris on Thursday or Friday. This depends on my friend from Berly, who is moving house and taking a number of things back to Paris and who wants me to give her a lift. Whatever happens, I shall be in Paris on Saturday at the latest. I will phone you and invite myself for a weekend at Noizay!

I am going to write to Georges Salles to give him my telephone number and to ask for a meeting next week. It is strange how entirely indifferent I feel about the results of that application . . . I suppose I had better go and present myself but I would be almost happy to wait another year and to take on Lapeyrette's class again. Paulet's louts depress me in advance . . . And what a mentality there seems to be behind it all . . . Anyway . . .[1]

The Thibaud plane crash is overwhelming after Ginette's.[2] I have not heard the details yet but Gérard [Souzay] must have returned to Paris last Wednesday.

I send my most affectionate regards to Brigitte, and embrace you.

P.

Or else make the Second Prioress a dramatic soprano and Mother Marie a lyric soprano. But if you are thinking of Tebaldi for the Second Prioress, you will not have enough contrast . . .

237. Francis Poulenc to Pierre Bernac

Friday [11 September 1953]

Mon petit Pierre,

As usual (and it gets to be quite irritating) you are right. Of course 'Mother Marie' must be written for a mezzo. So Act II will then have Constance – light soprano; second Prioress – lyric soprano; Blanche – soprano; and Mother Marie – mezzo.[1] What confused me at first was scene 4 (death of the Prioress) where contralto and mezzo come face to face. Apart from this scene – the only one where the two women confront each other – Mother Marie only has responses.

The first scene is completely finished, I am about to copy it out. I am relying on your coming here for the weekend of 20 September when I will play, I hope, scenes 1 and 2 for you. I am completely dotty about my subject. What with this and *Les Mamelles* the rosette seems rather un-important.[2] Confidentially, when I look at myself in the mirror with the decoration dear Dacier's wife brought to me, I do not like myself very much, as it ages me. Enough of the honours. What divine weather. Brigitte and I are living like landed gentry, with records galore, radio, and so on. If you have the recording of *Aida*, can you lend it to me?

I would like you to come on Saturday with Suzanne Peignot. Invite her for me.

I shall not be coming to Paris for [the recording of] *Les Mamelles*:

1 – because I have not been asked, 2 – because Berthe Schmitt will take care of all the details, 3 – because Mother Superior does not allow me to leave the cloister.

I embrace you.

Francis

Ring me please.*

238. FRANCIS POULENC TO DODA CONRAD

[Noizay, September 1953]

Hélas, dear Doda,

I am not going to see you before I leave as I never move from my table or the piano except to take the air on the terrace between two chords.

I am obnubilated (lovely word) by my *Carmélites* to such a point that I nearly called you 'Reverend Mother'!!! This whole venture is making me completely crazy. I can think of nothing else, I live for nothing else. Can you imagine that I will not even be coming to Paris on the 17th for the recording of *Les Mamelles*? Thank God (and it is truly God who must be thanked) my work is going well and when I come back to Paris on 15 October, I will definitely bring with me four scenes out of the seven that make the first act, perhaps even five. My familiarity with vocal music on the one hand, and with the mystical ambiance on the other, has so far enabled me to find the right tone. I think you will like it quite a lot. Without splitting hairs (or musical notes) I believe I have found a very special atmosphere. Obviously, people won't find it exactly amusing, but I think and hope they will be deeply moved.

As the weather is beautiful and I am absolutely alone, I have been able to maintain a good rhythm of work. Here is the whole story of my summer: after spending July in Normandy at my sister's – where I finished the Sonata[1] for Fzd-Gold – which I authorize them (by special dispensation) to play to you soon – I hopped over to Menton where I strummed away for Fournier and then, since 15 August, it has been Carmel at Noizay.

I have no special commission for America and my only regret at being tied to this task for so long is that it prevents me from flying off to New York. I hope to return there for a good while just as soon as I have finished *Les Carmélites*. Tell everyone there how much I love America – my best public. Tell Bernstein; tell Shaw[2] whom I adore (and even a bit more); tell Virgil [Thomson]. Regards to the exquisite Harrison.[3] In short, keep up the contacts which you were the first to establish, *I implore you*. I am thrilled

*In English in the original text.

about the recording of *Les Mamelles* with Cluytens, Duval, Giraudeau, etc. I hope it will go down well over there. I suppose it was an American suggestion, anyway.

You are my first letter this week as, unfortunately, I had to send off a few cards with 'thank you', 'how very kind', 'so touched'. But still no word from the Comtesse Blanche-Marie. Doesn't she love me any more? Embrace your august mother [Marya Freund] on my behalf and allow me to place upon your brow a very paternal kiss from your old maestro Poupoule.

239. FRANCIS POULENC TO MAURICE LEHMANN

Noizay, Indre-et-Loire, 22 September [1953]

Cher ami Lehmann,

I am told that you are *very* angry about my Italian *Carmélites*. This distresses me greatly for I have always had as much esteem for you as affection. The fault lies neither with you nor with me but with the French publishers.

Apart from the fact that it was Monsieur Valcarenghi who found the subject for me, when I had been looking for a libretto for years, he *commissioned* me, and at a *very good fee*, to write this work *for the publishing house of Ricordi*. Not only did the French publishers never have any such intention, but three years ago, one of them gave me to understand that if the eventuality should ever arise, I was quite simply not to count on him. Therefore . . . that an Italian firm should wish to reserve 'its commission' for an Italian stage . . . what could be more natural! *Aida*, before its première in Milan, first saw the light of day in Cairo.[1] Would you be even harder on me, who alas am not Verdi! To write this work I had to give up my concert tours in America, and one has to make a living. Unfortunately I do not think I would have found a way of doing so in our beloved Paris. That is the whole issue, in very simple terms.

Preserve for me your smile, your friendship and your trust.

Very affectionately,

Fr. Poulenc

Poor Louis B. What sadness, he who so dearly loved life![2]

240. FRANCIS POULENC TO YVONNE GOUVERNÉ

Thursday [1953]

Mon Yvonne,

Sanctity is difficult enough but sacred music of the *Carmélites* kind is terrifying. I go through alternating states of satisfaction and despondency for if this opera fails, it will fail dismally.

I am looking forward to *Sécheresses* on Monday. Wherever you are, so too is the spirit of Poupoule. I embrace you.

Francis[1]

241. FRANCIS POULENC TO HENRI HELL

Geneva, Friday [December 1953]

Mon cher Henri,

I was so bored at the concert of the Geneva Chamber Orchestra that I fled at the interval, hoping to find a train to Lausanne.[1] I have an hour to wait and am putting it to good use by writing to you while the orchestra plays . . . *Moulin Rouge*,[2] making two enormous women swoon with delight. There is nothing quite like a catchy tune and this one is certainly catchy. I came here to hear Stravinsky's Cantata with Cuénod and Mme Flore Wend singing. What a crushingly boring work it is and how awkward! It is one of the most Russian, most Oriental of Igor's compositions and has nothing at all in common with the Elizabethan poems.[3] Obviously there are moments of incredible musicianship, but on the whole the work is overwhelming in its sterility. It is terrifying to think that from now on Stravinsky will be composing in English and that his whisky will forever have a whiff of vodka. Oh! the dangers of America. In Paris he would have remained a cosmopolitan. It is sad. Cuénod sang extremely well but what can one possibly do with this Huguenot–Byzantine text?

I am delighted with my set-up in Lausanne, where I am living like a prince. I started working at once on Scene 4 of the *Dialogues*. I picked up the thread again immediately and am happy. This scene moves further and further away from recitatif. As the action is already underway and the exposition completed, the music can at last take over. This is why it is impossible to perceive the architecture of the work from the first scenes.

By the way, don't say a word to Ned[4] who wrote me an adorable letter about the Sonata [for two pianos], nor to Auric who would merely be irritated. Mum's the word, *I beseech you.*

Don't you think the recording of *Les Mamelles* is marvellous? I cannot stop thinking about it. It is one of the greatest joys of my *life* (sic). Definitely the work that is dearest to me, the one that at heart I prefer to all others. See how alive the orchestration is, how clear and varied it sounds, and how the vocal parts stand out well above it.[5] Anyway, people can judge the musicality for themselves. Cluytens is *sensational*. It explodes, sizzles, laments, grows taut, mellows . . .

Perhaps the heart of the matter is that the worst of myself is the best of myself.

I have been thinking mournfully that I would never be able to compose like this any more. True, in '44 I could not have composed *Les Carmélites*. When the records come out, is there anywhere you could write an article on the paradoxical coupling of the Mass and *Les Mamelles*? *Figaro littéraire*? Why not? Of course, silence from the critics about the Sonata. Obviously it is not *Gautier Garguille*!! by Sire Bondeville.[6] Not a word in *Les Arts*. In *Comoedia*, two silly lines, and from Claude [Rostand] a cautious article. Anyway, none of this is of any importance.

And to think that you will never write your book.[7] Monster! We could have had Denoël – Dobson in London, etc.[8]

Write to me. With much affection,

Francis

Beau-Rivage, Lausanne

Excuse my writing, I have the wrong glasses.

242. Francis Poulenc to Pierre Bernac

Hôtel Beau-Rivage [Lausanne], 19 December [1953]

Ouf! mon petit Pierre,

'She' breathed her last at seven o'clock last night, after a most horrible death-struggle![1] Mother Marie, more ambitious than ever, was unbelievably hard, poor Blanche completely crazed, and that great ninny of a doctor totally silent. As for me, I am exhausted but very relieved at having completed the entire scene here. It is *definitely* the most beautiful. You will see – with orchestra it will be *thrilling*, and vocally one can just let oneself go.

While the Prioress is in her death-throes, there is a small phrase of Mother Marie's (I use 'small' in the worst sense of the word) from which I am expecting quite a lot. The final note of the Prioress is a high A, fortissimo and very dry. Then it is all over. I am going to take a little breather before the fifth scene, so as to clear the air of all the rest. I am not allowing myself to look back, and I never replay the first scenes. The rhythm of the death of the Prioress will be the same as in the last scene of Act I but serene and celestial.

This is the crux of the whole play.[2]

Received a letter from Alexandria. Everything is going well. We need to be there for the 1st March, a Sunday. I think it will be best to take the Comet on Friday so as to have two days' rest. We have to stay until the 20th but will be wined, dined and lodged a great deal.[3]

I am trying to arrange a soirée through Jeanne Ritcher. Will you give some thought to a programme consisting of: Chabrier, Fauré, Debussy,

Ravel, Roussel, Satie, Milhaud, Poulenc. The title will be: 'French songs from Chabrier to Poulenc'. You can also include the Cannes Durey–Poulenc item. Of mine, *definitely Le Bestiaire* and some lyric songs.

I am still coming back on the 23rd. My liver has not settled down at all. It is true that the treatment!!!

With much affection.

Fr.

243. FRANCIS POULENC TO ADRIENNE MONNIER

Tuesday [December 1953]

Trés chère Adrienne,

On my return from Switzerland I found your precious book.[1] To say that it gave me immense pleasure is to grossly understate the truth. It *moved me to tears* for, of course, I turned immediately to page 63![2] The article on *Les Animaux modèles* is certainly one of the very rare *accurate* things ever written about this work.[3] For this, I thank you from the bottom of my heart. And I thank you, too, for all the rest: you have evoked my entire youth and all that was most precious about it.

Happy New Year. I embrace you fondly.

Francis

244. FRANCIS POULENC TO HENRI SAUGUET

Hôtel Majestic, Cannes, Thursday, February 1954

Cher Henri,

So here I am all alone on my grey, misty, rainy coast, without any help at all! I think it is those Carmelite Nuns who have exacted this austerity from on high. No complaints work-wise: I have only one more scene to finish my first act (1½ hours of music!). When I recall that I began on 15 August, I cannot get over it. Am I becoming Hindemith or dear old Da?[1] I know that you too are getting on with things. This is what Darius writes to me: 'Yesterday Henri played me the first act of *Marianne*. It is *adorable.*'[2] I am not a bit surprised, as I have always found you to have a great affinity with Musset.

I am staying here until 15 February. There is absolutely no one here and I suppose that the week of *Les Six* will play to empty houses.

Try to listen on Tuesday night to what I say about you.

How is Paris? Is it going all out to become dodecanised? The Carmelites, poor things, can only sing in tune. They must be forgiven.

I embrace you.

Fr.

245. FRANCIS POULENC TO HENRI HELL

Cannes, Sunday [14 February 1954]

Cher Henri,

I shall be in Paris tomorrow night (Monday). I have been working furiously and very well, I think. I have virtually finished my first act – 1h 25m of music. I have copied out six scenes which I will play on Tuesday evening to Brigitte. You would give me *immense pleasure* by coming to dinner as I am horribly sad, which I can say to no one but you. No doubt this anguished climate was necessary for my nuns. You will see – the atmosphere is terrifying and I think by the time the interval comes, the audience will have the shivers. I have found exactly the right atmosphere for the duo of the brother and sister: a mixture of anxiety and tenderness. I would never have believed that I could write a work in this style. I thank God for it, despite the suffering involved. And yet with all that suffering, I will still be known as 'the charming Poulenc'. I beg of you, put off everything else and come on Tuesday evening.

Reply by telephone. I embrace you.

Francis

246. FRANCIS POULENC TO DODA CONRAD

[Egypt, March 1954]

Doda, as soon as 'the concert'[1] was over I left for Egypt, hence this belated letter to tell you about the event. Your illustrious mother was more 'Freund' than ever, refusing to sit down at rehearsals: 'One does not rehearse *Socrate* sitting down,' said she, in a tone permitting of no contradiction. The performance went very well. At first, stage fright, like a young girl at her début recital. Then she settled down and the 'death' [of Socrate] was quite simply superb. I think she was very pleased. Etienne [de Beaumont] was delighted.

Do you know that I have at last heard the pianist Lili Kraus at Marie-Blanche's? I was *transported*. She really has great class. After Magaloff and Weissenberg, who played the same evening, she was sheer music after mere virtuosity.

I am now on tour in Egypt with Pierre [Bernac] after presiding at the examinations of the Conservatoire in Alexandria, in which the champion cyclist of the town – who looks like Soulima [Stravinsky] – obtained his diploma in *Solfège* and a gold medal for piano!!! In Alexandria, where I stayed for ten days, I finished my first act (1½ hours of music). I am longing to show it to you for you are *sure* to love it as much as our Countess [Marie-

Blanche de Polignac] wept over it. After Egypt I shall pop in to Rome for the Festival Nicolas Koka [Nabokov].

You seem to be staying in America rather a long time. What does this hide, blonde or brunette? Do you ever see our pianists [Gold and Fizdale]? Is there anything good on in New York at the moment?

[. . .] I am told that Sauguet's comic opera [*Les Caprices de Marianne*] is delightful. I am thrilled. Have you heard our new record in New York? *Les Mamelles* is due to come out any day now. I embrace you,

Francis

247. FRANCIS POULENC TO JACQUES LEGUERNEY

Cairo, 19 March [1954]

Charming Monsieur Leguerney, our journey is going well. Pierre [Bernac] is back on his camel again (twelfth-century Egyptian saying) and able to make the most of this trip that he so longed for. Our concerts in Alexandria went very well, as did the others. Our last one takes place tonight. On Sunday we leave for upper Egypt, complete with sun-helmets and fly-swatters. As Pierre told you, we are spending the weekend of the 27th in Athens, at the invitation of the Zeuses. We shall be in Rome on the 29th, delighted to meet up with you again. Our jaunts to little churches will be divine, with early morning carriage-rides and in the evenings Art with a very big A (too big, I fear).

Since you will be travelling by sumptuous sleeping-car may I ask you:

1 – to bring me the proofs of the sublime interviews [*Entretiens avec Claude Rostand*] which will keep you entertained en route. (Make notes of what shocks you.) Phone Claude for them, Auteuil 99–14.

2 – to bring me a record of *Les Mamelles* (I will reimburse Ploix), which will be my gift to the Contessa Pecci.

3 – to bring me the Chabrier waltzes for two pianos, which Jacques [Février] will send if you telephone, once he hears that Marcelle Meyer and I are going to record them.

4 – to get hold of the latest issue of *Disques*.

and, finally, 5 – if it is not too much of an imposition, to bring me my little overcoat that Anna (after you have arranged it with her by telephone) will bring to the train.

Let's be serious. Do you know that in Alexandria I finished my first act, with a duo that Pierre finds 'very good'* and which is sung no throats barred.

Till very soon. I embrace you while awaiting our Roman orgies.

Poupoule I

*In English in the original text.

248. ARTHUR HONEGGER TO FRANCIS POULENC

Schonenberg, Pratteln (Basle), 10 May 1954

Mon cher Francis,[1]

I have just received your *Entretiens*. I read them all at one go. Thank you. One thing I can tell you is that reading them has brought me incredibly closer to you. It has heightened the affection I have for you as a loyal friend and the admiration I feel for you as a musician, as a born creator of music, which sets you so much apart from so many others.

In the midst of the modes, the systems, the methods that the incompetent have tried to impose, you have remained true to yourself with a rare courage that commands respect.

We are, I believe, very different in temperament, but one thing I think we have in common is a love of music rather than a love of success. From dissimilar standpoints we express ourselves in a similar way.

You declare your love of Satie and your lack of understanding of Fauré. I personally began by regarding Fauré as an elegant salon musician, but now he is among those I admire the most. On the other hand, I consider Satie to be of excessively sound mind but devoid of all creative ability – 'Do as I say; above all, do not do as I do'. We both like the vigour of Strauss, we both prefer the successful *Louise* of Charpentier to the lamentable fiasco of Dukas' *Ariane* [*et Barbe-Bleue*]. You do not make the sign of the cross at the mere mention of Berlioz, who is admired for all that is detested in Beethoven, Wagner or Schumann. You realize how naïve it is to 'run down' Wagner in 1954 (like asking the Municipal Council to uproot the Eiffel Tower, one of the most flourishing attractions there is!) but you hope that you will never have to hear *Die Meistersinger* again. I, on the other hand, very much hope to live through it over and over. You do not like Van Gogh, for whom I would give all of Toulouse-Lautrec, whom I admire in the same way you admire El Greco.

All these differences, far from separating us, seem, on the contrary, to draw us closer together. Is not variety the most beautiful thing in life and in art?

Will you find me too presumptuous if I align myself with you to say: We are two 'honourable men'?

Je t'embrasse en fraternelle affection.

> *Ton*
> A. Honegger

Laura also sends you much love, and affectionate messages from the Sachers.[2] He conducted your Organ Concerto with my Symphony No. 2 in Zurich. I would like him to do your *Stabat* in Vienna.

249. FRANCIS POULENC TO JACQUES LEGUERNEY

Noizay, 26 May [1954]

Cher Jacques,

In Paris I took a quick look at your *Carnaval*. Now, a quieter reading has confirmed my first impression, namely that it is among *the best* of Leguerney. Everything about it is lively, sensitive and vigorously handled. In any case, these are precisely the kind of songs that lend themselves to orchestration, of that I am *certain*. Pierre [Bernac] agrees with me. I am sure it will sound *perfect* and that, orchestrated in twos, it would be exactly what those 'Gentlemen' want. Think about it.

I have been practising the piano non-stop, having put those Nuns into retirement in the cupboard behind my Paris piano. To tell the truth, I am missing them terribly, but it is better this way.

I embrace you.

Francis

It's extraordinary how people are going through the *Entretiens* with such a fine comb!

250. FRANCIS POULENC TO PIERRE BERNAC

Wednesday [July? 1954]

Mon cher, cher Pierre,

Thank you for your letters which, like Charlotte, I 'constantly re-read'.[1] They do me such an extraordinary amount of good and I cling to them as to a life-buoy. Your long postscript was passed on to me by the dear Doctor.[2] You know very well that you *can tell me everything* and that you *must do so* where my moral behaviour is concerned. Anyway, Delmas thought I ought to know what was in your letter, and how right he was! What a friend you are to me! You are the *only one*, Pierre, who can pull me out of this slough if there is still time. Since to be charitable is your lot in life, *take me in hand*. Above all, please understand that I have never been *indifferent* to you but, as I have said before, I have too much respect for you – as I had for Raymonde [Linossier] – to meddle in your emotional life. I have nonetheless followed a great many phases of your solitude with infinite tenderness. Just as I was never able to use the familiar *tu* with Raymonde, there is a certain moral *tutoiement* that I would find unworthy of you.[3] Many people would not understand me, but I know that you do.

Yes, you are right, I have indeed poisoned myself little by little. Too much introspection – emotional as well as intellectual – has been gnawing away at me for months. But can one prevent a lame man from limping? And yes, life has spoiled me in many ways, but do not forget a certain drama that has been *obsessing* me for the past eight years; my consuming love for Lucien, which far from abating only seems to grow more intense; my limitless affection for Raymond. When in April it became certain – something I knew and even wanted – that Raymond would soon move to the town of Noizay and when, in addition, I believed Lucien to be more distant, I fell into a blind panic that was not helped at all by worries about my liver, about my faith, about the von Le Fort Bernanos obstruction which means that I may be writing a work that can never be performed, and that I may not be able to sign up with Ricordi, etc. . . .[4]

I swear to you, my Pierre, since you write that it is all merely a question of *my morale*, that I will do everything to try to become myself again and, I hope, to better myself. Yes, my work is the only thing that will pull me out of this and, thank God, in that respect I have not lost my touch. In an extraordinary moment of emotion and turmoil (in Delmas' presence) the final moments of the *Carmélites* came to me, Blanche's arrival and her march to the scaffold. Looking at this music coldly, I honestly believe that it is overwhelming in its simplicity, in its resignation, and . . . in its peace. There is a modulation into the major key that is one of my best and that deeply moved the dear Doctor without his being able to explain why. Perhaps Father Carré is right and I will always be *Le Jongleur de Notre Dame*.[5]

Did I tell you how overcome I was by Lourdes the other day? I had never seen a pilgrimage before. It was at once atrocious and sublime. What moved me most was seeing all those young people, boys and girls, devoting themselves to the sick. Yes, you are right, charity should be something more than mere cheques.

Delmas follows my progress with extraordinary vigilance. He has done a series of medical tests in an attempt to get to the bottom of the intestinal problems troubling me over the past two years. The results of the tests are good, even very good, he claims. Obviously six weeks of near mad anxiety have seriously wrecked my nerves, and what this has done to the level of my uric acid is unimaginable. I have started gargling again as I have inflamed tonsils, which may well be the cause of all this mess. Remember my knee in '44, which was caused by my throat. You may be right: perhaps I will always suffer from the same little problems and persist in believing they are serious illnesses. Let's hope that's all it is.

Everything has been arranged with Delmas. I will arrive at Noizay on Sunday 8 August after going with him to visit my beloved Rocamadour, where they are expecting me, and his beloved Ligugé.[6] Raymond will fetch me by car from Poitiers. Can you believe that I who have never been all that keen on Noizay am suddenly becoming attached to it like the unfaithful and wounded husband who goes running back to his wife?[7] It is there that I shall be able to work again for I have always worked there and, besides, all my books are there, my music, my gramophone, my records, my radio.

What on earth would be the point of going into a clinic? I have asked Jeanne [Manceaux] to make the sacrifice of being at Noizay when I arrive there. May I now express my dearest wish: that when you return from your holiday at the beginning of September, you will come and spend *several* days with me to help me get back into our cherished work and to see my cure through to its completion. Mind you, I am playing the piano not all that badly; it has been mainly a matter of not wanting to.

I would like you to write to Richard [Chanlaire] (21 quai des Grands Augustins) and tell him everything that has happened to me (without details of Lucien, naturally). Tell him *firmly* that you know all about our row and that he is being ridiculous and is quite wrong to imagine what he did imagine. It is quite simply monstrous not to have believed me. Tell him how he has hurt me. Do not ask him to write to me – it is up to him to decide whether he should or not. Thank you in advance.

I am delighted to hear about your 'honeymoon' with Simone [Girard]. Have a good rest, relax, but most of all, write to me regularly and let me know all the concert gossip.

Forgive this too long letter. And thank you for everything from the bottom of my poor heart.

I embrace you.

Fr.

251. FRANCIS POULENC TO PIERRE BERNAC

Noizay, Tuesday [August 1954]

Mon Pierre,

[. . .] End of October weather here. The gladioli dare not show their heads. I feel a bit better. I must say that the shock of the Bernanos arbitration (too long to explain here) did not exactly help matters. Pierre, I am counting on you to do everything you possibly can to help me not to become a ridiculous old man. Everything you wrote to Delmas *is only too true*. [. . .][1]

The orchestration of the first scene of the C. will be finished tomorrow. Whatever happens, I shall continue with this work for I think Auric is right when he says that the sheer weight of a work forces doors to open. Reading through it again after a break, I am pleased with what I have done.

I am waiting for your arrival to play the piano again. Pierre, you must get me out of this. I feel so ashamed of myself at times but then when the anguish takes hold of me again, it is like a fever spasm.

Stéphane Audel will be coming to stay from 1–25 September. He is a tonic and (this goes for Brigitte's stay as well) it will be a good thing to have a third person to help both of you to put up with my lunacy. Delmas kept warning me that the recovery would be saw-toothed. Well, these teeth must be veritable canines. One day I feel as if I am reborn, the next, not a hint of it.

Of course I *want* to do the concerts in Holland, and those in Germany. It is a chance to become myself again and both Delmas and Lefort advocate it strongly. As we will be going by car it will be less tiring for me. [. . .]

I might have to go to Paris for the day to see Monsieur Lavery (author of the First Legion)[2] who holds . . . the von Le Fort copyrights. Perhaps I could come back with you on the 8th. I will keep you up to date on this thrilling adventure. The lawyer representing Lavery has married a friend of the Lecreus. This is already in our favour. God willing.

Seeing you again will do me as much good as it will give me pleasure. If only you knew what you have become to me. I embrace you.

Fr.

252. FRANCIS POULENC TO PIERRE BERNAC

Monday [September 1954]

Mon petit Pierre,

I am addressing this to you in Paris as I believe you will be home soon. Only bit of good news: I have orchestrated, and *very well*, half of my first act (will there ever be a second?). For the rest, Jeanne [Manceaux] will tell you everything better than I can. Phone her on Neubourg 72. Stéphane Audel is looking after me with touching affection and intelligence but it is you I am longing to see, you whom I have not seen for a thousand years. I rely on your tenderness, your strength of mind, your lucidity. I so much want to pull myself together but will I ever manage? My intestines, my digestive system too often cause me distressing thoughts.

All our trips pass in detail – and what minute detail – before my eyes. I so much want to travel again. I often did so with such bad grace but how wrong I was. One does not realize how fortunate one is at the time.

I embrace you with all my affection. And now, take charge of me – and what a charge to take!

Francis

253. DARIUS MILHAUD TO FRANCIS POULENC

Mount Angel Abbey (Oregon), 20 September 1954

Mon cher Francis,

Your few lines from Noizay made us very sad. I had so hoped that you would have benefited from your stay. But even so you have been able to work well and I am sure your orchestration is marvellous.

As we arrived in Mills with a week to spare, we have come to stay with the Benedictine monks of Mount Angel. For the past two months one of the Fathers who is in charge of plainchant (as at Solesmes) has been writing to me to try to persuade me to compose a Mass, with free polyphony alternating with Gregorian elements (as in the *Magnificat* of Palestrina and the Masses of Vittoria). I came here to see him and to explain that I simply *could not* write a Mass.[1] He pointed out that Bach, Beethoven and Stravinsky were not Catholics either. I explained to him that, nevertheless, although the polyphonic concept was enthralling, my particular faith prevented me from having the sentiment required. So we decided that I would compose Psalms of David for his abbey, on the same principle – plainchant alternating with free polyphony. But only certain ones, like Psalm 50, and the Miserere for the days preceding Easter. As for my religious conscience, I am entirely in my element with these Psalms.

This particular Father loves your music; he knows your Mass well, and your *Stabat*. I spoke to him at length about you and he promised to pray intently for your recovery. I, too, often pray for you but perhaps you will be more receptive to the prayers of a Benedictine Father than to those of an old Jewish friend who can offer you only his immense and deep affection.

This abbey is set in a wonderful landscape. It took us three days to get here by car (700 miles); we crossed vast forests of great redwoods, giant trees thousands of years old, tall straight columns, sentinels of time.

Mon Francis, I embrace you. So does Mady. We love you so much.

Da.

254. FRANCIS POULENC TO SIMONE GIRARD

Wednesday [September/October 1954]

'My' Simone (forgive me, Doctor, for using the possessive), I know that I am not being reasonable and that, despite some glorious times with a calm, relaxed Lucien, all this will only lead to renewed suffering; but really, yesterday morning I was simply unable to turn my back on him, in spite of the goodness of your hearts and your hands. Let's hope that I will soon be strong enough to do so. Unfortunately, saintliness is not quite yet my lot in life. I know that this is all lamentable, and how will I ever manage to pull myself out of it? Ah! if only I had some assurance about *Les Carmélites*.

Darling Simone, do not despise me. I will never ever forget what you have all done for me. You are my refuge. For me, Avignon represents salvation. I think constantly of Father Rigaud, of you, and of Vincent [Laugier]. Alas, I am no longer master of my will, of my poor nerves. I am all adrift. It is mortifying.

Francis

255. FRANCIS POULENC TO DOCTOR AND MADAME GIRARD

Friday [October 1954]

My Girards, I am writing from this beautiful 'Mistral' which used to so enchant me. Stuffed full of sedatives, I am holding out – quite obviously so to the old bag I passed in the corridor who exclaimed: 'Well, well, if it isn't Poulenc!' She should have said 'the ghost of Poulenc'. Ah! my dearest friends, what do I not owe to you – certainly this wretched life that I take back to Paris with me.

How ashamed I am to have involved you in this mortifying mental agony. You really must love me to have taken me so well in hand.

At least I have been able to catch the 'Mistral', which I do not think I could have done in Dijon. I have the comforting impression of a fourfold magnet supporting me from a distance – you two and the two saints. Which is not to insinuate that you are sinners!!!

It is all so easy when I am in your home. Nobody moralizes, not even your adorable daughters and sons-in-law, nobody harps on my break-down.

May I one day prove worthy of this help. Last night, listening to the concert, I was overwhelmed by a sense of shame for the musician in me. No doubt my Sacred Ladies have wanted to purify me by fire.

Unfortunately, the only thing that will blot out that face is another face.

Do you know my song 'Ce doux petit visage'? And the line in 'Belle et ressemblante' (*Sept chansons*): 'A face at the end of day, a face in the scales of silence'? I have always been a prey to faces. May that of Christ enlighten me one day. Excuse both style and *écriture ferroviaire*[1] (am not displeased at having found that term in my state of sedated limitation). What consoles me is that music is not very far away.

I think these terrible Nuns, before losing their heads, have wanted me to sacrifice mine. Which is not impossible.

14 Brigitte Manceaux,
Poulenc's niece

15 Poulenc at Noizay
in the 1950s

16 Wanda Landowska and Francis Poulenc in New York, January 1950

17 Bernac and Poulenc on board ship in 1949, returning from their first tour of the USA

18 Poulenc with the soprano Suzanne Peignot, one of his earliest
interpreters

19 Poulenc and the singer Rose Dercourt-Plaut in the 1950s

20 Francis Poulenc in 1953 with the American duo pianists Arthur Gold and Robert Fizdale, to whom he dedicated his Sonata for two pianos

21 Poulenc with Arthur Gold and Robert Fizdale in Marseilles, 1953

22 Paul Eluard in 1948 at the launching of his book *Voir*. Poulenc set seven poems from this collection in his song cycle *Le Travail du peintre* (1956). (Photograph by René-Jean Ségalat)

23 Bernac with Simone Girard and Yvonne Gouverné in Scotland, 1957

24 Henri Sauguet and his cat, Captain Mirliflore

25 Poulenc and his dog in 1950. The inscription is to his friend Marthe Bosredon.

26 Poulenc giving a talk at the *Club des Trois Centres* in January 1962

27 Poulenc and Cocteau at the time of their collaboration on *La Voix humaine* (1958–59)

28 Francis Poulenc and Denise Duval (Photograph by Poulenc's nephew, Denis Manceaux)

I am posting this letter in Lyons to overwhelm you with affection in your home where all is calm again and where Simone shows signs of fading away through lack of emotional turmoil. Anyway, nothing more to fear: the tornado is leaving for Germany.[2]

Fr.

256. PIERRE BERNAC TO FRANCIS POULENC

4 November [1954]

Mon petit Francis,

It may surprise you to find this letter from me on your arrival, especially as it holds no gentle or consoling words of the kind you have been subjected to far too often, and all to no avail. Instead, there are certain things I want to tell you before I see you again.

You are returning home after this cruel but necessary experience. It had to reach this point, and I am certain that after so much turmoil you will feel something akin to relief. The question is now settled. Unfortunately, through your lack of moral virility, you have worn down the affection of this loyal but not very interesting boy. I am sorry for you if you really love him as much as you think you do, something of which I am not entirely convinced. You loved the character you wanted him to play at your side. If you had really loved him you would have loved him for himself and not for you. But that was not the case. As proof I merely observe that before this break-up you would not have hesitated to form other attachments, yet you were jealous of any he might have made. In fact, what I would wish most for you now is to see you find someone else, if indeed you have honestly not yet succeeded in finding another formula for your time of life.

Be that as it may, the situation is now quite unequivocal, and I hope that there is no substance left to feed your obsession. Face the reality plainly and squarely and put up with it. You are neither the first nor the last to suffer a broken heart. It is too convenient, don't you see, to put everything down to illness. Your inclination to let yourself go does not date from today. What is more, there is human dignity to be preserved. I suffer so much to see you losing it completely in the eyes of everyone, not only your friends. Francis Poulenc, even on the human plane, is surely greater than this. Have no doubt that this feebleness will eventually make itself felt in your art. Life is not a matter of easy solutions.

What I want to tell you is this: with regard to myself – forgive me, Francis, but I am not a saint – although I thought I was fairly well balanced I have to say that you have made me lose that quality. I feel that you are draining me completely and I have on more than one occasion wept with nervous exhaustion on leaving you. I am naturally ready to listen at length to your stories and your thoughts when you return, but can we dispose of the subject once and for all? I *must* tell you this: if, every day and all day long during our coming concert tour, you talk to me about Lucien, I do not think I shall be able to stand it. I ask you to think hard whether you can get a grip on yourself or not. I am going to have to sing almost every day and, believe me, this is not the same as having to accompany. My responsibility is great in a different way, and in addition my instrument is myself. If you think you cannot react like a man – and I myself am certain that you can – then I must ask you to tell me now, for in that case I think we would do better to cancel the tour.

Forgive me for disappointing you like this. I am always ready to help you in the best way I can, which is not much; but when we are on tour there are certain things I fear I can no longer bear. I am tired, I have worked a great deal, and I am less master of my nerves. The proof is that some of your telephone calls have left me on the verge of tears. I tell you frankly, Francis: I am *afraid* of this tour in these conditions. Forgive me.[1]

257. Francis Poulenc to Marthe Bosredon

c/o Doctor Maillard, L'Hay-les-Roses, [End November 1954]

Ma petite Marthe,

I am in a clinic for three weeks in an attempt to get some sleep. I was not sleeping more than two hours and sometimes not even that. Delighted about your new apartment. Of course I will come and see you and with what joy. I am now sleeping 18 to 19 hours out of 24. Not much fun but there was no choice.

I had to cut short my tour of Germany. One day I will tell you *the reasons* (in the plural) for all this.

Millions of affectionate greetings,

Francis

258. Francis Poulenc to Simone Girard

Saturday [December 1954]

Ma chère Simone,

I am leaving on Monday for Cannes by plane to avoid going through places that my nerves could not endure. I refer to Marseilles and Toulon, for in Avignon your cherished affection far outweighs all the anguish. I am better, but still horribly on edge, and sleep still evades me. I hope this stay in the sun (mostly in Antibes at Marie-Blanche de Polignac's) will do me good. In any event, I can be sure not to encounter a certain person there. That is the great thing.

More promises and assurances about *Les Carmélites* but nothing in writing. This does not help matters at all, so you will have to forgive me if I am not quite yet on the road to recovery. Fortunately I have a marvellous neurologist who is getting me to unwind, but my system is still poisoned due to the barbiturates.

I hope you will have a happy festive season. I will send you my Christmas gift* at the beginning of January, which will comprise *Les Mamelles*, the Mass, *Les Motets pour le temps de Noël*, and *Les Biches*. I have not yet been able to attend to this. Actually, it is only a week since I left the clinic.

I hear through Pierre that you are rolling in money and that the concerts are going great guns. I knew it.

Dear, dear Simone, I send to you and the doctor and your dear ones far more than tender, affectionate good wishes. I apologize from the bottom of my heart for the tornadoes I have visited upon you, but if ever music begins to flow again in me you can tell yourself that without your help it would never have happened.

I hope that 1955 will bring me, if not joy, at least peace.

Embrace Laugier for me and give my very best regards to the dear Father. And of course embrace Antoinette.[1] I shall try to be on dazzling form for 2 February. Even if it kills me, I really want to.[2] Write to me at the Majestic, in Cannes.

Again with all my affection, dear Simone.

Francis

259. FRANCIS POULENC TO MARTHE BOSREDON

Antibes, 30 December [1954]

Marthe chérie,

I have just been trying to get you on the telephone. Impossible: you do not answer. May this card bring you my most affectionate wishes and my thanks for the truffles. Marthe, tell me quite frankly what you would like as a gift. My poor darling, if you knew from what black hole I am only just emerging – it has been atrocious. For months now I have been tormented by troubles, betrayed in my work (I still do not have the Bernanos authorization for *Les Carmélites*). I was in such a state of nerves that I had to abandon my tour of Germany after two concerts and go into a clinic. I am better now,

*In English in the original text.

but sleep still evades me and sleeping pills make me dopey. It is a vicious circle from which I only wish I could escape. Where is the joyous Poulenc of old? I beg of you, keep this secret deep inside your heart so that it does not snowball. On 6 January I shall be going home from Antibes, where I am at the moment. Then I am going to play in England.[1] On 2 February there is to be a concert, with Bernac, to celebrate our 20th anniversary. Then I will probably be leaving for Rome.

Marthe darling, I will definitely come and see you this summer. My handwriting should tell you a great deal about the state of my poor nerves. I embrace you tenderly.

Francis

260. FRANCIS POULENC TO BENJAMIN BRITTEN

[December 1954]

Happy New Year my dear Ben. I am better at last and will be arriving in London on 13 January for our rehearsals.[1] We will play from the music, which will be easier for my convalescing memory. You are doing the second piano part, aren't you? I am *so much* looking forward to this concert. It will be my return to the platform!! Agreed for Aldeburgh '56.[2]

I embrace you as well as Peter.

Francis

261. FRANCIS POULENC TO BENJAMIN BRITTEN

Hotel Majestic, Cannes, 5 May 1955

Cher Ben,

What joy to receive your songs this morning which I like more and more!

What I find remarkable, apart from the musical quality, is that you achieve such rich accompaniments by such simple means. Reading through the music, one is astonished that it is not 'blacker'.[1] This is exactly what I myself have always tried to do.

After Toulouse I came back here to watch – unfortunately from a distance – over my invalid who is in Toulon.[2] He is not much better but neither is his condition worse. The more time one gains, the greater the chances of a recovery. God willing, I am going back to Paris on the 12th for a recital with Pierre.

I wish I could express how happy I was to see you here. There were not many people in the audience but you gave *lasting* pleasure to a handful of true musicians.

With much love to you and Peter.

Your devoted
Poulenc

262. FRANCIS POULENC TO ALICE ESTY

Noizay, Indre-et-Loire, 2 June [1955]

Chère Madame,

I hope you have not forgotten that we are *working* and dining together on Monday. I am looking forward to it very much. Do not be afraid of me as I am a very kind composer when it comes to my interpreters. Moreover, as you sing my music very well – your record bears testimony to this – everything will go extremely well.[1]

Not having seen you alone so far, it has been difficult for me to thank you for your very generous gesture: the purchase of the manuscript of my Sonata which has enabled our dear pianists to settle their debt.[2] Pierre gave me $750 in two cheques. May I timidly make so bold as to say that Gold and Fizdale had mentioned a sum of a thousand dollars, which seemed to be confirmed by the fact that when you handed $500 to Bernac in January you said to him: 'Here is half of what I owe Poulenc.' If you think my request is justified you can settle the $250 either in dollars or in francs, as you like.

What a delicate thing it is to discuss money with a beautiful woman! I wish you could suddenly be transformed into an old man with a beard. And I still have to discuss *Le Travail du peintre* with you! Our friends, knowing that for a long time I have been wanting to compose this important cycle, thought you could perhaps commission it from me, which means that it would be dedicated to you, that you would get the manuscript and the first performance of it, and that I would gladly record it with you in Paris. You know I have not composed any *mélodies* for some time. I had just about had my fill, and what I need now is something quite exceptional to whet my appetite again. Before he died, I spoke to Eluard about my wish to create a counterpart for *Tel jour telle nuit* to the glory of painters, something I believe has never been done before.

Le Travail du peintre would consist of seven parts: 1 – Picasso, 2 – Chagall, 3 – Braque, 4 – Juan Gris, 5 – Paul Klee, 6 – Miró, 7 – Jacques Villon.[3]

If the thing interests you I could begin working on it this summer, when I have completed my opera. I would deliver it to you as quickly as possible, *without delay*, for, at this point in my work, it is important for me – for my own sake – not to botch the thing.

Only on receipt of the manuscript would I ask you for a thousand dollars, for I never accept an advance on a work I have not begun.

There is no hurry for your reply, just think it over and write to me later from America.

If you are good enough to accept my offer you will be doing me the very great favour of enabling me to compose a work quite out of the ordinary.[4]

Forgive this long business letter!!!

> Respectfully yours
> Francis Poulenc

263. FRANCIS POULENC TO ROSE DERCOURT-PLAUT

Evian, 2 July [1955]

Ma chère Rose,

Forgive my dreadful silence. Time and time again I have wanted to write, but so many things have happened in my life over so many months that I did not know where to begin. First and foremost, let me tell you that I am very well. And things will be perfect the moment I can get to sleep without having to take any more drugs. When we meet again – soon, I hope – I will tell you everything in detail. You heard, I think, that in November I went into a clinic in order to sleep for two weeks! After that, life took an odd turn. The boy who had caused me so much suffering became horribly ill. Thanks to my help, I hope he has been saved. So now suddenly the tables have turned, but all this is too complicated to tell you here. I have become so much my old self again – of years ago – that I am seeing everything in a new light.

Raymond and Céline are living permanently at Noizay. They are very happy, and so am I to see them like this. I spent two-and-a-half months in Cannes. It was marvellous for me. Now I am completing a cure at Evian. I am dividing July between Normandy and Aix-en-Provence. I have not yet decided what to do in the first three weeks of August. But after that it will be Noizay, where I very much hope to see you. Anna, who was *wonderful* to me during my illness, is expecting her daughter from Brazil. I don't know who will take her place in Touraine, as of course I cannot keep her from her children for twenty-four hours a day. Anyway, we will see.

Work is going very well. I have only two more scenes out of twelve to finish *Les Carmélites*. As far as that is concerned, thank God, things have finally come right. I do not think I have ever done anything as good. You will see – it is terrifying. When I play it to you, you will weep and weep. This summer I promise to compose a beautiful song for you.[1] You deserve it, loyal interpreter and beloved friend!

Fortunately I am no longer the demented wreck I was last autumn. Let's say no more about all that. I am happy to hear that you are still on form. We will do some work in Touraine – 'Rosemonde' and *Parisiana*, my latest offspring.[2]

I hope you and dear Plaut are well. [. . .]

Ma petite Rose, what a strange time I have been through! Anyway, as I have said, it is all over now. Sometimes these ordeals are necessary. No doubt my Carmelites have required this of me.

Till we meet, I embrace both you and Fred with all the strength of my old friendship.

Francis Poulenc

Two or three photographs of myself with my dear old doggie (postcard-size) would be very welcome![3]

264. FRANCIS POULENC TO ROSE DERCOURT-PLAUT

Tourrette-sur-Loup, Alpes Maritimes, 12 August [1955]

Chère Rose,

Thank you for your letters and for being an errand-running angel. I am writing from a delectable village 30 kilometres to the north of Nice where I am spending the month of August. The weather is exquisite as we are 400 metres up in the mountains. It is quite unspoiled here, unlike St Paul or Vence. I have a room with a piano, thanks to which my *Carmélites* are nearing their end. I shall be back in Noizay on 25 August. I am absolutely counting on you for a full weekend at my place. I will play you my opera (have handkerchiefs ready) and, I hope, your song. I have found the right poem, by a very talented woman.[1]

Don't saddle yourself with all my parcels – leave them with my concierge in the rue de Médicis. I will fetch them there on 15 August. Why don't you come with Fred for the weekend of 18 September? It would be splendid. I shall be going back to Paris on about 6 October. You can write to me here until 25 August and thereafter at Noizay. I am *perfectly well*. My menopause is over! I embrace you,

Francis

265. FRANCIS POULENC TO PIERRE BERNAC

Cannes, Friday [August 1955]

Mon vieux Pierre,

I am writing from the Majestic, where I have been since Tuesday. I had to bring Lucien down to Cannes again because a sharp rise in his temperature made me fear a sudden complication. Fortunately, after four days in a clinic, his temperature dropped. He had probably caught a chill. His poor system goes to pieces at such a rate that I feared seeing him stuck here for some time. But thank heavens after four days of rest at his friend André's he will be able to leave next Wednesday for Toulon. Fortunately for this simple, trusting being, *everything* has a natural explanation. He speaks only of the future, of what he will do next summer, and so on. I have entrusted him to my sixteen blessed Carmelites: may they protect his final hours since he has been so closely involved with their story. In fact I began the work at his side, in happiness, in Lyons in August 1953. After all the torment, which I need not describe to you, I have just finished the work, at his side, during the last days of his earthly life. As I wrote to you once before, I am haunted by Bernanos' phrase: 'We do not die for ourselves alone . . . but for, or instead of, each other.'[1] If Raymond remains the secret of *Les Mamelles* and *Figure humaine*, Lucien is certainly that of the *Stabat* and *Les Carmélites*.

Yes, I have completed my opera, apart from a few final touches. I intend to make the finished copy during the next week at Noizay. I was booked to go back on the 25th, but have managed to put it off until the 30th. So I shall be at Noizay on 1 September. If Lucien is still of this world in October I shall take a trip to Toulon around the 8th, determined this time to cross the maternal barrier. I have arranged everything with a decent family doctor and a good nurse. Here, Mantoux has been wonderfully humane, not torturing him needlessly, since nothing can be done. Richard [Chanlaire], who has been marvellous, will come down with me on the last day to help me. Actually, I myself am unbelievably well. My heart is aching but . . . that's human nature. Lucien has shown so much tenderness towards me over the last six months, and I have been able to make his life so much more comfortable and have him so well cared for, that this great drama of my life is ending in the most melancholy (dare I say it) happiness.* My morale vis à vis Lucien is very high and that is what is needed. In Tourrette, on the only occasion when he ever suffered five minutes' anxiety, he said: 'Oh! I know that if you had been worried you would never have worked so well.' And another time: 'You know, I have had two good hours of sleep. Your funeral march has been a blessing for me.' Strictly speaking, the final scene is not a funeral march but rather an intoned psalm. I think you will find it very beautiful – in any event, terribly moving. And that is all my news. It has done me good to be able to speak to you and to Brigitte – as well as to the *wise* Anna, who wrote me an extraordinary letter.

*In the original letter, the word *douceur* is crossed out in favour of *bonheur*.

Could you send me (at Noizay) the prosody of:

> Deo Patri sit gloria
> Et Filio qui a mortuis
> Surrexit ac Paraclito
> In saeculorum saecula[2]

I embrace you mournfully.

Francis

P.S. Adrienne Monnier, incurable, quietly committed suicide (sleeping pills), asking that her close relatives and friends be told of it only three months later.[3]

Quickly send a short, *optimistic* card to Lucien, 60 boulevard Carnot, Cannes, telling him that you are happy to hear that he is better, and the good angel of my work. Thanks.

266. FRANCIS POULENC TO MARTHE BOSREDON

Hôtel Majestic, Cannes, 27 August [1955]

Ma petite Marthe,

I put down the telephone feeling very sad and rather furious. I am really very *profoundly* unhappy and very *secretly* hurt, and when I ask for your help you speak to me about your cats. You are not being serious. And to think that at Noizay I shall have to act as if nothing were wrong. Believe me: to hear *Les Carmélites* in a comfortable armchair is well worth the scratches of your pussycats. Leave them in the care of friends and come and see me next Saturday the 3rd, at Noizay, where I shall be from the 1st.

Think about it, and if you still have any of your lovely heart of 1940, you will come running to my aid.

I embrace you . . . in spite of everything . . . with much tenderness.

Francis

Don't play *les Mères Michel* with me, or watch out![1]

I shall offer a ciborium to Roc. as an act of thanks, once *Les Carmélites* is finished.[2]

267. FRANCIS POULENC TO PIERRE BERNAC

Noizay, Friday [September 1955]

Mon petit Pierre,

I am working flat out. Your Schumanns – the Chabrier waltzes – *Babar*. So much for the piano. Obituaries on Adrienne [Monnier] and Madeleine Le

Chevrel. Homage to Cocteau. Introduction to the Sonata for 'les boys'.[1] Two articles for *Art*. A study for La Pléiade on the Russian Ballet.

End of the women, draft of the painters.[2] As you see, I do not have time to get my breath back. These women are driving me crazy. Sometimes I wish there were twenty of them, sometimes fourteen!!! It is horribly difficult to work out a *plausible* moment for the beheading of the poor nuns that does not coincide with the beginning and ending of phrases. I will solve it eventually, but it is like a puzzle. At one time I thought of taking as a guideline a certain number of bars, but that became too automatic. So I am now resorting to instinct. Do you know the admirable letter from Debussy to J. Durand: 'It is strange how two "parasitic" bars can demolish the most solidly built structure! Nothing alerts us to this, neither experience nor talent. It is instinct, old as the hills, that alone can save us.'

Will you time our two records for Véga as quickly as possible? Do you like the title: *35 ans de mélodies de Francis Poulenc*? Do you have a better one? I think it is quite striking.[3] There will be a double sleeve with the portrait of me by La Fresnaye on the cover. If the publishers are not too demanding, the texts will be reproduced.

RECORD A

1. *Bestiaire*. 'Jardin'. 'Allons plus vite'. 'Pont'. 'Montparnasse'.
2. *5 poèmes Eluard*. 'Feu du soir'. *Fraîcheur*.

RECORD B

1. *Gaillardes*. 'Priez pour paix'.
2. *Métamorphoses*. 'C'. 'Disparu'. 'Paul'. *Parisiana*.

I find this selection excellent. We have four sessions for the recording. Let me hear from you.

The 'war of the moustache' is underway; at the moment your army seems to be defeated. It is much better now (my moustache) than on the photo. At any rate, it makes me look younger and gives me a rather jaunty air!!!

I embrace you,

Fr.

I am trying to knock myself out so as not to think of you know what. Thank heavens my morale is high.

Here is the updated moustache list:

Against	*For*
Madeleine Bataille	Anna
Vicomtesse de la Rochette	Marie-Thérèse
Bernac	Denise (who would not have married Maurice if I had looked like this when she met me)

Bonnasse	Denise Bourdet
Mme Guignard	Nicole Champin
	Antoinette d'Harcourt
	Georgette Chadourne
	Simone Girard
	Jeanine B. de B.
	Richard (very much in favour)

268. FRANCIS POULENC TO ARTHUR GOLD AND ROBERT FIZDALE

Noizay, 17 September 1955

Chers amis,

You ask me to introduce my Sonata[1] to the American public. Do you know that this is terribly difficult to do, for what is in fact genuine simplicity can so easily be seen as false modesty.

However, since you so wish, I will try to relate the circumstances which prompted me to write this work and will attempt to explain what I wanted to do.

It is to you, dear friends, that I owe the birth of this work, for nobody plays my music the way that you do. Not content with being scrupulous interpreters of my music, you are able, with your insight, to divine that intangible essence which, however meticulous we may be, we poor composers always leave unstated between the lines of music.

After the Concerto for two pianos, I wanted to hear you play something else. That is why I decided to dedicate to you a Sonata for two pianos.

Do you remember that room in the Hôtel Beauvau in Marseilles where, in December 1952, looking out of the window at the activity of the port, I began the present Sonata? It was in that very hotel that Chopin had stayed with George Sand on his return from Majorca.

I began with the Andante, with the general architecture of the work already in mind. Framed by a Prologue, an Allegro Molto and an Epilogue, this Andante is for me the very core of the work. Here it is no longer a matter of poetic play before a portrait of Mozart hanging on my wall, as in the Andante of the Concerto for two pianos, but rather of a profoundly lyrical élan. Sometimes drawing inspiration from aspects of my choral music, I tried, at certain points, to achieve a great purity of line – for example, the bass notes in unison in the final bars of the Andante.

The first piece is conceived not as a first movement of a classical sonata but as a true Prologue. Its second theme, 'animé', is simply a rhythmic progression intended to bring out the lyricism of the *extremely slow* melody in C Major, which forms the central episode.

The Allegro Molto is a Scherzo, the main interest of which lies in the middle episode, *extraordinarily peaceful.*

The Epilogue is not strictly speaking a Finale but a recapitulation of the other three movements, preceded by a new theme.

I would readily describe the Concerto for two pianos as blithely bravura, whereas the present work has the gravity of a string quartet. The advance copies of the recording, which you let me hear, delighted me.[2]

Thank you for bringing such popularity to this work for which I have a great weakness.

As I have no audiences more loyal and more understanding than those in America, I feel sure it will not surprise them to know that at that point of my career – in 1952, before I had undertaken my opera on Bernanos' *Dialogues des Carmélites* – I was thirsting for music of a kind that was quite simply human.

Thank you with all my heart.

Francis Poulenc

269. FRANCIS POULENC TO SIMONE GIRARD

Noizay, 31 October [1955]

Ma petite Simone,

I think of you a great deal in these very sad times. So much water has passed under the bridge this last year – the dear doctor gone;[1] Lucien delivered from his martyrdom ten days ago, the final copy of *Les Carmélites* completed (take note) at the very moment the poor boy breathed his last.[2] I got up from the table and said to my faithful Anna: 'I have finished: Monsieur Lucien will die now.' Who will ever know all that lies at the secret heart of certain works?

Tell Vincent [Laugier] and Father [Rigaud] that I have not become a saint, but that they should love me all the same. I hope that when my time comes, I shall know how to die . . . as Blanche did.

I hope your apartment is nearing completion. One must live, my dear Simone. When I think of the nightmare I inflicted on you a year ago I ask myself if it was really *me*. Oh! the endearing anger of the beloved doctor that famous evening. You can be sure that in my prayers tomorrow, I will include these two beings whom we have both so much loved.

I have come here to spend ten days with my dear old wire-haired fox-terrier, Raymond,[3] in his exquisite house. He pampers me. Thank God, he has never suspected anything.[4]

I embrace you tenderly.

Francis

270. FRANCIS POULENC TO ROSE DERCOURT-PLAUT

[Paris], 24 December [1955]

Ma petite Rose,

It is appalling to be so lazy. I ask your forgiveness on bended knees. What a lot has happened since your departure! That famous day of the storm, and the taxi strike, etc. . . . I finished copying out the last scene of *Les Carmélites* at five o'clock, at precisely the time my friend from Toulon was dying! Is that not strange!!!! Although expected, this death has affected me deeply. It is too long and too complex to explain in a letter. A good six years of my life now well and truly in the past. What a lot of mixed feelings, and suffering too! But all necessary for *Les Carmélites*. I am finishing the orchestration now.

In the autumn, I gave a lot of concerts with Pierre [Bernac], made many recordings and completed my version for piano and voice for the printer. Now I am turning my thoughts to new music, and first and foremost to your song ['Nuage']. I might be coming to New York for a week at the end of October. Why don't I accompany you in a little recital for radio with 'the first world'* of this song? Anyway, we will see each other before then.

I am going to spend the New Year at Raymond's. I shall go again in February. I work very well there. I have had my upright piano moved there. Raymond finds the winter rather a trial but I don't mind it.

Brigitte [Manceaux] has not been well. She has been suffering from lumbago. She is better now.

Fred's photos arrived yesterday evening. What *incredible marvels*!!! Everybody exclaims on seeing them. It is *amazing*. I have never been so well photographed, and the ones of Brigitte are fantastic. I think she would be wild with joy to have two or three for herself. I have already given her one but I am keeping the other two (one for Paris, one for Noizay). I shall give the Destouches theirs on the 31 December.

I am crazy about my little radio, which works wonderfully. I take it with me on all my trips and, thanks to you, any depressing thoughts are banished from my hotel rooms. Anna and Charles are well. They send you their respects. Embrace 'my photographer', 'my engineer', 'my friend Fred', and let me tell you once again how precious your affection is to me.

A very fond embrace for you as well.

Francis

271. FRANCIS POULENC TO BRIGITTE MANCEAUX

In the train at Liverpool station, 28 March 1956, 8 a.m.

Biche rose,

Not having booked my seat and, thank God, not being like Sieur Bernac

*In English in the original text.

(who nearly made us miss the plane in Thessaloniki), I arrived very early and am making good use of this 'extra time'* to have a little chat with you. Very nice concert last night. Full house, reasonable acoustics, respectable conductor and orchestra. Jean Françaix and I played very well together. We are performing again in Cannes on 5 April. How glad I shall be to get back to 'my' Majestic, 'my' room and my orchestration [of *Les Carmélites*], which I am longing to finish.

Milan was enchanting. Sabata, who in one week knew the score by heart, is *very enthusiastic*. Everything has been ultra-arranged for January[1] and I was treated like Richard Wagner!! Exquisite evening at La Piccola Scala, a theatre seating 600, with Stravinsky's *Apollon*, *Le Retable* and a very successful opera. Vocal perfection. Sabata estimates that the orchestra will need 30 rehearsals for *Les Carmélites*!! Sounds like a dream.

Spent my time at the Biffi restaurant (in La Scala) with Karajan, Schwarzkopf and other small fry! I assure you that I am going to enjoy myself there. Having been forewarned about the hysterics, Machiavellisms and ultimately impeccable work, I am determined not to worry about a thing.

Rome was charming, very social. Grand dinners and luncheons every day. My reception at the Academy was very kind and very cordial. We are a great batch this year, replacing Furtwängler, Enesco, Honegger, etc. We have Britten, Frank Martin, Shostakovitch, myself . . . and Messiaen instead of . . . Charpentier. Britten, Shost and I were unanimously elected. The Academy was founded by Palestrina and is taken very seriously in Italy.

Marcelle [Meyer] is very well. As a special favour, she was allowed to be present at the reception, as well as Mimi Pecci. Usually women are not admitted, but with my reputation as an old Don Juan! Marcelle told me again how excellent our Chabrier waltzes are; I'll take her word for it.[2]

The new pressing of my Satie record is also excellent.[3] I am very pleased with it. Very interesting Marigny concert. The Boulez is remarkable. If the prosody had not been like the toothed edge of a saw, which made the text unintelligible, it would really have been first-rate. Intelligent as he is, I am sure that Boulez understood. What a delight such a gifted and intelligent being truly is![4]

Very beautiful Webern. There is a touching atmosphere at these concerts. Crowds of young people cram in together for standing room at 150 Fr. I do not understand how anyone can ignore a trend like this.

*In English in the original text.

When I think that poor old X sniggers and says: 'If there are mistakes in my material, they will think it's dodecaphonic.' It's as rich as 'My child could do better than that' as a response to a picture by Paul Klee. Having said all that, I shall continue to write doh mi soh doh and disapprove of Stravinsky – who has taken to wearing hats too young for his age.

And now, write to me in Cannes.

A thousand kisses for you and the others.

Fr.

272. FRANCIS POULENC TO ROSE DERCOURT-PLAUT

[Brive, Corrèze], 16 June [1956]

Chère petite Rose,

Excuse my dreadful silence but I have had an insane amount of work to do recently. I have just finished the orchestration of *Les Carmélites*. It will be produced in February at La Scala and in March in Paris. I have corrected the piano score, and prepared the concert and lecture that I am giving in Aldeburgh (at the Britten Festival on 24 June).[1] Now that the main work is over I am going to turn my mind to various other things, and primarily to your song ['Nuage'], for which I have already found two bars!!!

Here are my plans: from 26 June to 12 July – Evian. From 12 to 20 – Milan. From 20 to 23 – Aix. From 24 to 28 – American Conservatory in Fontaine-bleau, where I am giving a course with Bernac on my music. From 28 July to 14 August – Normandy, at my sister's. Then Noizay.

Couldn't you come to Fontainebleau from the 24th, before Enghien? Or could you make a weekend at my sister's in August (two hours away from Paris)? I am of course *counting* on a weekend in September at Noizay with my beloved photographer. I shall not be going to America this winter but certainly next winter. This winter I have my opera everywhere – Milan, Paris, Vienna.

Will you be an angel and slip into your luggage four pairs of socks for me, in nylon without elastic at the calf, two blue and two brown. (I take size 42 in France.)[2] A record of *Les Mamelles* and a cheque book which dear Paffrotti at Salabert's will give you for me. Naturally I will pay you back for the socks and record. What joy to see you again soon. I am marvellously well and am sleeping again without taking anything. Everything is fine with the Destouches. Brigitte [Manceaux] too. We cannot wait to see you. Do, do come to Fontainebleau.

I embrace both you and Fred.

Your devoted
Francis

Will Fred ask Goddard [Lieberson] for the Symphony in C by Igor. Many thanks.

273. FRANCIS POULENC TO SIMONE GIRARD

Wentworth Hotel, Aldeburgh, Suffolk, Sunday [24 June 1956]

Beauté céleste,

The Britten Festival is exquisite. This afternoon I gave a talk, and was very much on form.[1] And tonight I shall play in *Aubade* under the *Swiss* baton of Sacher. Not a conductor for you, not enough balls (keep this expression from Rochette and Vincent, your two old beaux!).[2]

Britten and Pears are sensational. They do everything here, and marvellously well. They played some Mozart for four hands adorably!!!

The weather is good for England, but one is freezing cold all the same.

I shall be in Evian on Tuesday, at the Splendide, where my lovely boyfriend* will join me. Then we leave together, by car, for Milan and Venice. We are going to the last night of *Don Juan* on Friday 20 July. I shall not leave again until Sunday 22nd. Try to come to the Italian concert on the 21st so that we can see each other for a while. I don't know where I shall stay. I have rejected the Negrescou on the pretext of its scruffiness, but in fact it is the spirit of poor old Lucien that I want to avoid in that hotel.

Everything is going very well for Milan. The Italian translation is marvellous.[3] The orchestral parts are being prepared and Wake[4] is starting the décor. I am going to have a lot of fun with it all.

Write to me at the Splendide in Evian.

I embrace you.

Poupoule

274. FRANCIS POULENC TO BENJAMIN BRITTEN

Hôtel Splendide, Evian, 4 July [1956]

Cher Ben,

I want to tell you once again what joy it gave me to be with you at your exquisite Aldeburgh Festival. It is all so much *you* – full of intelligence, finesse, and heart. And from your window, I 'saw' Peter Grimes;[1] and in London, I bought the fascinating records of *The Turn of the Screw*.[2] All this has drawn me even closer to you, for whom I have so much love and admiration. Thank you.

The other day I heard an air by Purcell that moved me to tears. It is a

---

*In English in the original text.

passacaglia sung by an alto voice. The continuo on the cello goes something like this:

If you recognize it, can you tell me exactly what it is so that I can buy it.[3] I embrace you, and Peter, too.

Francis

275. FRANCIS POULENC TO PIERRE BERNAC

[Château du Tremblay, Normandy], Friday, 17 August [1956]

Pierre, mon vieux,

Here is the good news: *Le Travail du peintre* is finished. I gave birth without any pain and without an anaesthetic. I am pleased with my work. It is the work of someone who knows what he is doing. Exceptional tessitura:

in fact – made to measure for you – and this is not the effect of mere chance, believe me, as I am going to *force* a recording on Pathé-Marconi (I will explain how later) at the end of next winter: *Tel jour – Travail – Calligr – Banalités.*[1]

On Monday I will take your test pressings back to Véga with a severe, record-by-record criticism. I am still hoping for an improvement if they do a new pressing, for it seems impossible that there can be such a difference between the tape and the wax.

The Satie record has come out: excellent recording, execrable pressing!!!![2] Fortunately there is one unadulterated joy: Marcelle's Chabrier is *fantastic* and our waltzes are perfect.[3] Forgive me if I say that, as far as style goes, it is unbeatable. Marcelle gave me a few tips, and I put lots of butter in the sauce.[4] As for her solos, I swoon. What music!! But what artistry, filled with secrets! There is an *Air de ballet*, same style as *Embarquement pour Cythère*, which makes me faint clean away. Marcelle plays all this with insolence, pearls on her fingers, and great flair. It is marvellous.

I am nearing the end of my stay. I leave on Sunday evening for Paris where I will spend Monday and Tuesday. Important meeting at the Opéra with Hirsch and Bondeville. On Wednesday I leave for Noizay with Brigitte, who will stay for four days, and Henri Hell for ten. He intends to finish his book about me at all costs. He has just written a remarkable article in *La Revue de l'Opéra* on *Les Carmélites* which has galvanized a lot of people at the Opéra. Giraudeau immediately asked me for an autographed photograph. Last Sunday in Deauville I saw Denise, who understands perfectly about Milan.[5]

Talking of Milan, they are busy *making* the sets for the first act and preparing the others. Wake went to see Wallmann in Venice.[6] I have not seen any of it but it is better this way. I have decided to agree to everything with my *eyes shut*, so to speak. I still do not know who is singing but I'll leave it to them.

Quite enough to keep me busy with the Paris production. Albert Béguin warmly recommends Balachova as the person to produce it. In any event not Tassencourt, who does not know a thing about music. That is as far as I have got.[7]

I am enclosing [Griffith's?] letter for your file. Keep it if it interests you – I don't want to think about any of that any more, particularly as I am in a total spiritual desert right now. I am bored stiff at mass and I wait for the *Ite missa** as I used to wait for the bell at the Lycée Condorcet. It is sad, but what can I do?

I beg of you, pray for me in Assisi, that I may meet a simple, good priest (like the dean of Rocamadour) who, wafer in hand and wine before him, will be able to do something for me.

During my peculiar illness, I noticed that whenever I encounter an *intelligent* priest, he soon becomes my worst enemy. I could willingly have insulted and clouted the priest in Avignon, for example. I know you understand what I mean. My desire for everything to come right shows that deep down I have an atavistic, very real need, a craving, for something.

Claude is well. What a poor, tortured boy he is![8] Naturally, my thoughts often revolve round Lucien and, although I have made total peace with his memory, the notion that he may have died in my place, and from what I believed I was suffering from, troubles me deeply.

I have had a most pleasant stay here. The Manceaux are very much on

*The Latin dismissal formula at the end of the mass: *Ite, missa est* (Go, the mass is ended).

form. Brigitte has rented a house for September in St Tropez. They tell me
that Noizay looks extremely beautiful. I am expecting you there at the end
of September.

Warm regards to the lady [Simone Girard].

I embrace you.

Fr.

Write to me at Noizay.

I heard Gérard [Souzay] in Toulon. Not good. *Les [Chansons] Gaillardes*
too slow, too virtuous.

Do you approve of this for the Danco-Poulenc record:

A – *Airs chantés; Max Jacob*

B – *Trois Lalanne;* 'Doux petit visage'; *Trois Vilmorin*

Tell me frankly. If you have another idea, let me know. I cannot help it –
for my own part, I love this kind of song.[9]

276. FRANCIS POULENC TO ALICE ESTY

Noizay. Indre-et-Loire, 26 August 1956

Chère Madame,

Here is some good news: your songs are finished and I am very pleased
with them. Won't you come and fetch them in Paris in October? I would
prefer to play them to you rather than send them.[1]

I will check the vocal score with Pierre at the end of September.

Have a good summer.

With kind regards,
Francis Poulenc

277. JEAN HUGO TO FRANCIS POULENC

Mas de Fourques, Lunel, 30 October 1956

Cher Francis,

It is with a heavy heart that I write to you. The libretto of *Dialogues
des Carmélites* is wonderful and I am sure you have made of it one of your
finest works. But I cannot design sets any more. I feel absolutely incapable
of a single theatrical idea. Perhaps I have been living away from it all for too
long. I would only produce something unworthy of both you and Bernanos. I
am in despair, dear Francis, at having to say no to you. To collaborate with
you, to see you again often, would have been so good.

I embrace you.
Jean

278. Francis Poulenc to Claude Rostand

[Milan], January 1957

Cher enfantelet,

I am calm, calm, calm and happy. My orchestra sounds marvellous, my voices too, and what voices!!!![1]

Everything is going wonderfully and think you will be proud of me. Come on the 26th at dawn, all of you: if it opens on the 28th you can attend the dress rehearsal on the 26th, if it opens on the 30th (not impossible), come on the 28th in the morning (same thing).

We are rehearsing morning, noon and night. There will be about 40 rehearsals in all, of which THIRTY *à l'italienne* with orchestra!!!

I think you will weep. What a theatre, what workmanship. Never anywhere has the production of a work of mine been so PRECISE. Just like Verdi before *Otello* (unbelievable at his age!!!).[3] I have been able to check every little detail.

Perfect article by [Jacques] Bourgeois who had anyway lunched chastely 'at home'.* See you soon.

Fr.

279. Francis Poulenc to Claude Rostand

Milan, 2 February 1957

Ange adoré, thank you for the beautiful article, which overwhelmed me, especially coming from you for you know of my growing and *secret* weakness for my Claudichon. I am dead tired!! I am staying for the 4th performance. The 2nd (Pederzini ill and replaced) was lousy but the 3rd was *sublime*!!! I was shown the ultimate in electronic music at the RAI [Italian Radio]. Madly Goncourt but interesting. Big kisses to you both.

Poupoule

280. Francis Poulenc to Henri Hell

Milan [February 1957]

Cher Henri,

Thank you for the fine and splendid article. The one by Claude [Rostand] in *Le Monde*, also gave me great pleasure. This time he is clearly taking a stand. The wiles of [Jacques] Bourgeois, on the other hand, appeal to me far less. Yesterday I spent the day at the RAI listening to a lot of electronic and serial music. Very beautiful sonata for flute and piano by Boulez although a

*In English in the original text.

little too long, but by a *true* musician. Compared with that, what a lot of twelve-tone *old hat* from so many *young* musicians!!!! There is already so much clichéd stereotype in the genre. The instrumentation of Puccini's *Manon Lescaut* last night was more rich in surprises.

I am worn out: breakdown* looming. How glad I was to have you near me, dear Henri, very dear Henri! Perhaps, for the benefit of *ces messieurs de Paris*, I should include fifteen Chinese gongs, eight vibraphones and ten xylophones. No! May God protect me from the angel of the bizarre! I shall be back on *Thursday 7th*. Come to lunch.

I embrace you affectionately.

Francis

281. FRANCIS POULENC TO ROSE DERCOURT-PLAUT

[Paris], 1 May [1957]

Ma chère petite Rose,

Forgive my long silence but writing is not my forte, as you know. Fortunately others do it for me, and so you know all about the outcome of *Les Carmélites*. It will be opening in Paris on 21 June. I hope you will be there. I think it will be wonderful. Milan was superb but Paris will be overwhelming. The entire cast is marvellous and Denise in the role of Blanche is superb.[1] She really is a great actress and Bernac, with whom she has been working over the last six weeks, has done marvels with her.

My morale is high, as in Cannes in March I met a love of a career Sergeant (29 years old and as kind as he is handsome) which has brightened up my life considerably after all the disappointments of the last few years.[2]

At the moment I am finishing a Sonata for flute and piano for the Strasbourg Festival.[3] As for America, nothing is definite yet. I am due to go on tour with Duval in '58–'59.

Will you make enquiries and tell me whether Herbert Barrett, 250 West 57th Street, is a serious agent? He is the agent for Backhaus, Kirkpatrick, Moiseiwitsch, Tourel. He was very taken by Duval and has written to me about a proposed tour.

They are doing *Les Carmélites* at the Met in '59 but not in French. I prefer it that way.

The Destouches are very well and Raymond is working. My sister is delighted with her new apartment. Brigitte is in top form. We often speak about you, I can assure you. I am pleased that your singing is going well and

*In English in the original text.

that your song ['Nuage'] has been well received. There is a new one on a poem by Desnos that will suit you perfectly.[4] What joy to be seeing each other again soon.

I embrace you fondly.

Fr.

For Fred

Beloved photographer, your photos are FAN-TAS-TIC and never have I had better ones. Many thanks. Could I have, in the small size, a few of the one where I am in the armchair with my legs crossed. That is the one – if you agree – that will go at the beginning of Henri Hell's book on me. Come quickly and see *Les Carmélites.*

I embrace you.

Poupoule

282. FRANCIS POULENC TO ROSE DERCOURT-PLAUT

[Noizay], 9 June [1957]

Ma petite Rose,

Here I am in the throes of final preparations for my grand première, for as far as I am concerned, this is truly 'my' première. In Milan they worked for me. In Paris *Les Carmélites* will be *exactly what I imagined.* Everything pleases me: sets, music, production, cast. Denise is sublime. What an actress! Blanche, so much a part of me for so long, is at last springing to life. Think of me on the 21st. On the 18th I am playing my Sonata for flute and piano in Strasbourg. This is a very full month.

As for matters of the heart, things are also going very well. My Sergeant is a love. I am writing from Noizay where I came for the two days of Pentecost. I have my meals with the Raymonds who send you their love. Great news. Brigitte has bought a plot of land in St Tropez and is busy building. She is wild with joy.

Of course you will see *Les Dialogues* when it reopens.

[. . .] Thank you for the marvellous photos. I embrace both you and Fred very fondly.

Fr.

If I go to New York it will be in February. *Les Carmélites* is due to be shown on television then.

283. Francis Poulenc to Pierre Bernac

Touring-Hotel Bristol, Cologne, 12 July [1957]

Mon petit Pierre,

This is a good sized paper to keep my 'bather' entertained. I am *very happy* with the performance of *Les Carmélites*.[1] Firstly, I have fallen madly in love with Mother Marie, a tall thin German (aged forty) with the chic and dash of a Dorziat,[2] who is quite simply marvellous both *vocally* and *scenically*. In Munich she is singing Verdi's Lady Macbeth. You can picture the sort of character. My First Prioress is an Alice Halphen at thirty, slightly hunch-backed both in front and behind. Without the costume it is a bit outrageous to see this Rebecca thrashing about on a Carmelite death-bed, but with the nun's habit it somehow works. She is much liked here. Very good voice, but she makes too much of it for my taste. Second Prioress excellent and very much in the role (Colette Siry only less pretty). Very good Constance who sings Despina etc. . . . Fairly ordinary Marquis, and Chevalier somewhat old but very suitable. Sensational First Commissioner, a great thug who whistles through his fingers (this is how the Germans see us). Priest definitely the weakest of all, small and timorous (their view of him is of an old clergyman as in *On ne badine pas* . . .).[3]

The production is *perfect* in more areas than one. There is a most thrilling stir in the crowd after the death of Blanche. The tone from beginning to end is more ferocious than moving. Blanche is excellent in every way, lost and haggard in the midst of all these tough men and women.

The stage director consults me about everything and lets me add all the finishing touches, with charming good grace. Which I put to good use. The sets, very schematic and quickly changeable (motifs on black velvet) are highly ingenious and striking. Imagine the *tricolore* of Paul Colin[4] only more sombre.

Good orchestra but not enough strings. They are adding more this morning.

You cannot imagine how kind everyone is to me. Claude[5] finds that German changes my music far less than Italian does. Having seen all three of them, he is delighted. He is a very sensitive boy from that point of view. But what a poor lost child when it comes to life, and yet . . . the directors of the car firm for which he works in Paris have chosen him out of countless applicants for a sub-managerial post in France. The split personality of certain beings is truly incredible. Have you noticed how some people give themselves away in their sleep? I went into his room the other morning without his knowing. He was curled up, like a pathetic little child. A far cry from the splendid sleep of Louis who, with his arms lifted in an imaginary crawl, smiles out at life with all his being. It will be a tonic for me to see him again in a week's time. Claude's joy at going to the opera every night compensates largely for the gentle monotony of our daily existence. Very close, unhealthy, unpleasant climate here – colic is apparently a summer tradition. 'Enterovioforme' is our salvation.

There is only one more *Carmélites* before the summer; further performances in September (the Opéra closes on the 16th). So we are going to spend two days with Hervé [Dugardin] wallowing in the dodécaca[6] of Darmstadt. There is only one good programme with a new Sonata by Boulez. I will be at La Mule noire in Aix on the 19th. Make sure I find a long letter from you. Take care of yourself and, above all, have a good rest. That is by far the best treatment for you. You sing *Le Travail* [*du peintre*] WONDERFULLY but Jacqueline [Robin-Bonneau] plays really far too delicately on top of the keys – it becomes a sort of lady's fancywork. This has also struck Claude, who had tears in his eyes when he listened to your Schumann.

Has Gérard [Souzay] heard *Les Carmélites*? I have not seen him. I embrace you.

Fr.

Incredible mail concerning *Carmélites*. Very touching! Wild enthusiasm for our Saint Suzanne [Lalique]. What do I not owe to you in life!

284. FRANCIS POULENC TO BENJAMIN BRITTEN

1 August [1957]

*Ben, my dear,**

Apologies for my dreadful silence but as soon as Paris was finished I had to go to Cologne for the German *Carmélites*. YES, YES, YES, with joy, for *Les Mamelles*, both of them. I want Peter as the husband (there is a tenor version). I shall try to make a brilliant transcription!!!![1]

I say yes, by this same communication, to your secretary and embrace you, wishing you 'Happy Holidays'!

Francis

285. MARC CHAGALL TO FRANCIS POULENC

'Les Collines', Vence (A.M.), 3 October 1957

Cher Monsieur Poulenc,

I am both flattered and delighted to receive your songs on painters – myself included – based on poems by our very great friend and poet Paul Eluard.[1]

*In English in the original text.

It is true that, as I am only a lover of music by ear, I cannot read your music with my eyes; but I hope I shall have the opportunity of hearing it on the radio.

When you are in the South of France it would give me great pleasure to see you in Vence.

I was present at the first performance of the Russian Ballet's *Les Biches*.

Thank you again, and with a most cordial handshake.

Marc Chagall

286. EDWARD SACKVILLE-WEST TO FRANCIS POULENC

Cooleville House, Clogheen, Co. Tipperary, Ireland, 29 January 1958

Mon cher Francis,

I hope you will forgive my writing to you in English: it is so difficult to express oneself *fully* in a foreign language, even if one knows it quite well; and Alvilde[1] tells me you read English easily. I was so sorry not to have seen you at the party after the first night of *The Carmelites*,[2] but having had Asian flu for several weeks, I had not the strength to sit out a party (I still have the flu!).

So now I write instead, to tell you how deeply moved I was by the opera. I had known the (horribly printed) vocal score for some time, but got the impression that it told one almost nothing about what the music would sound like in the opera house. And so it proved. The exquisitely delicate scoring, and the generally subdued style of the music – so appropriate to the wonderful text – makes a *cumulative* effect like that of no other opera I know (except possibly *Pelléas*), so that the last two scenes emerge as overwhelmingly touching and beautiful. I thought the one spoken scene a brilliant idea, too: it seemed to drive home, in a different way, Blanche's fear of fear (and I suppose Bernanos was thinking of St Peter, too, in this scene).

The simplicity of the means used throughout the opera is very impressive. I am certain you have never composed more finely or more profoundly, and I am not surprised to learn that the opera caused you much mental stress. One senses that you *felt* it all very deeply – and that, of course, is why the music fits the text like a glove.

I hope you were pleased with the performance. I thought the sets perfectly lovely, and how well nuns always look on the stage! I was astonished, however, by what seemed to me the excellence of the ensemble. But the hero and heroines of the occasion were surely Kubelik and Miss Sutherland.[3] Obviously, Kubelik loves the score, for he made the orchestra play like angels. I have often heard Miss Sutherland *sing* beautifully but I never knew she could act! Usually she is like a gawky schoolgirl with too much chin, but as the Prioress she had an authority and a touching dignity that were quite new. Only Jean Watson disappointed me – and even she was better on the first night than in rehearsal – less cross!

I have not seen many of the notices since I arrived here, but, to judge by the reception on the first night the opera ought to do well – I only hope well enough for us to be able to keep it in the repertoire next season.[4] I wrote Kubelik a line of congratulations and shall no doubt hear from him how the subsequent performances went. But whatever happens, from a public point of view, I am certain we were right to put on the opera at Covent Garden. It imposed itself.

With every good wish,

Yours ever
Eddy Sackville-West

P.S. Don't bother to answer this letter, but if you do, by all means write in French.

287. Francis Poulenc to Pierre Bernac

Blue Bar, Cannes, Thursday [March 1958]

Mon petit Pierre,

The acupunctor is doing me *some* good (it is true that I am only up to my third session). He is a charming man with the subtlety common to all Asiatics. He claims he will restore my equilibrium; let's hope so, but I have not reached that state yet. Anyway, I hear from all sides that he is thoroughly respectable.

I am still abominably nervous. If Chevalier [Dr Louis Chevalier] were not such an honourable man I would take him for a quack when he claims that I have come through my crisis.

However, yet again my creativity is intact. In two days I have sketched a plan and part of *La Voix*[1] which has amazed Richard [Chanlaire]. Of course, it is terrifying and ultra-sensitive. I have in mind – when 'She' recounts her attempt at poisoning herself – a slow waltz in C minor. I was afraid it might sound too much like Piaf but Richard says not. At any rate, it is certainly unusual. Parts of it have already come to me. I am quite definitely a man of the theatre. I would be incapable nowadays of writing any of the three symphonic commissions from America.[2] But I do not think this indicates that my music is unimportant (look at Verdi, Puccini).

My great big peasant is adorable. He brings me relaxation in the evenings. Richard is also very precious to me. *He is my security*. Anyway,

I am better off away from Paris, from musical – and other – milieux. I avoid reading any articles on music.

I am leaving on Monday for Rome, in theory for two weeks. Then three weeks in Cannes and, after that, Noizay. I feel I shall get back into my stride there, but I say that . . . from here.

Even being happy (and, here, how could I not be), loving is not a good thing for me.

I think of you *very often* with all that is most affectionate and most sincere in me. Write to me c/o Mimi [Contessa Pecci-Blunt], 3 Piazza Aracoeli, and tell me about everything, concerts, records, etc. I am going to hear Fournier this afternoon. I am dining with him. What do you think of Henri's book? I find the whole tone of the thing very pleasing.[3] Keep on at Adès Pradère[4] about our records. I feel far better here than in Brussels where, despite our Lambiottes (both *very sad* – she especially – about their future solitude) *everything* made me 'retrospective'!!! Apologies for this phrase 'à l'Equanil'.*

I embrace you.
Francis

288. FRANCIS POULENC TO PIERRE BERNAC

Saint Raphaël, Easter 1958

Mon petit Pierre,

A pity that we are so near and yet so far. Anyway, it did me good to hear you in such good voice, from which I deduce that this year you will not be arriving in Avignon completely worn out. *You* are now the young man just about to fly off to America, and I the old maestro having to cancel Aldeburgh.[1] It is a positive fact that the sea does me the greatest harm. I have always instinctively hated it. Nebel was right, I am a man of the mountains at heart. The only thing that calms me is an altitude for cows. I realize this when I go up to Louis'.[2] The silence, the fabulous view, calms me. I am sure the acupunctor is doing me very *profound* good. He is a man of entirely Asiatic subtlety. He agrees completely with what my instinct tells me: I must pull myself together, I was about to write *ovairement.* Believe me, contrary to how I was three years ago, I am very rational about my own case. I know that there is nothing wrong with me physically and that my only imbalance comes from my 'mind'.† [Dr] Chevalier knows perfectly well that this stems from doubts about my work. What has often been praised as my charming modesty is fundamentally nothing more

---

*Equanil is a tranquilliser and antidepressant.
†In English in the original text.

than an inferiority complex that has now taken on a pathological form. Example: at Cocteau's I meet two American reporters who don't quite catch my name and which they hear as Poulens, Poulenz. When they realize who I am, their expression changes, as if they have just been introduced to Wagner. I am so embarrassed I do not know where to put myself. It takes all my nerve to sit down at the piano on stage, or to speak in public. This became clear last winter in Brussels (Satie) and in Milan (Ravel). I know I shall pull through all this, but it is difficult, I can tell you.

My *total* absence of faith this morning at mass is not helping matters much.

Fortunately, my work is not affected. I have written a short song for Bathori, 'Une Chanson de porcelaine' (Eluard),[3] which is delightful. I have completed two improvisations (Lambiotti and Hell)[4] but mostly I can think of nothing but *La Voix humaine*. The sole protagonist is more or less myself – not that Louis is ditching me (he is an angel) but military life is taking him away from me this autumn. Perhaps it is better this way. I am far too attached to him. I tell you again and again that he is *exquisite*. In fact, what I should really be writing is *Bérénice*,[5] but my catharsis is *La Voix humaine*.

Cocteau approves of my whole plan which structures the text into 'phases'. (Phase of the dog, the lie, the overdose.) I have a lot of ideas already. Two shocking themes, among others, which '*ces messieurs*' will find quite scandalous: one full of love, the other erotic. For the responses, the rhythm came to me quite instinctively. I do not have any fears about the orchestral volume (medium). The ensemble is horrific. 'She' tells of her overdose to the rhythm of a sad, Sibelius-like waltz.

As there is much singing between the instrumental 'harping' there is no problem about understanding it all. The orchestra *pounds* away. The lie ('If you were lying out of kindness and I found out') is unbearable. The whole ensemble flouts every rule: bars doubled, even trebled, but this style, normally worth nothing, is successful here, I think.

[. . .]

I like the recording of *Les Dialogues*.[6] I do not think one loses interest. I listened to it again with Richard [Chanlaire] (an angel to me). He agrees with me. He is stunned by *La Voix*, which I find encouraging. I would like to get a move on with it at Noizay. *I want it to go on* next winter at La Piccola [Scala]. It will *keep me busy*, together with the various *Carmélites*. Essentially, I am a man of song in all its forms. If I succeed with *La Voix*, it will reinforce this situation. After all, there are no symphonies by Verdi, nor operas by Brahms.

Give Simone [Girard] a big hug from me. Thank heavens I do not have to plague the life out of her this time. I hope that I will enjoy Lisbon. The Blanche (N. Panni) of Trieste, whom I saw in Rome, is *sublime*.[7] I embrace you.

                                                                            Fr.

289. FRANCIS POULENC TO SIMONE GIRARD

Tuesday [Spring 1958]

Ma Simone,

With my faithful Richard [Chanlaire] at my side I am working on *La Voix* in my ravishing house where I am bored to tears. When will I learn to be a good boy? Simone, is it at all possible to grant me the great joy of one last concert with Pierre to perform *Le Travail* and various other songs?[1] Will you think about it? The team Duval–Poulenc loses its virginity in Bordeaux on the 15th. Denise in top form.

Think of me, love me. Forgive me. I embrace you.

Fr.

290. FRANCIS POULENC TO BENJAMIN BRITTEN

13 June [1958], Feast of St Anthony of Padua!

Mon cher Ben,

By an odd stroke of fortune, your première,[1] like that of my *Stabat* in '51, is taking place on the day of the Feast of St Anthony, my favourite saint. May he not take offence at the 'Balloon-breasts' of Thérèse-Tirésias! I think of you constantly with *wild* regret. I am much better (I am sleeping a little again) but my doctor has once more forbidden me to go near the sea. The long stay in Touraine has done me good. I finished *La Voix humaine* there, a mono-opera by Jean Cocteau.

Do not forget to send me photos. I want to see Peter in a dress. I am sure that, thanks to you, dear Ben, the music will be marvellous.

I was looking forward to this performance so much, and I want to thank you with all my heart for holding it all together and for having so kindly understood that my defection was as melancholy as it was involuntary.

I embrace you as well as Peter.

Your faithful
Francis

Kindest regards to all our friends and especially to the Harewoods.

291. FRANCIS POULENC TO PIERRE BERNAC

Tourrette-sur-Loup, 11 August [1958]

Vieux Pierre,

I have copied out *La Voix*.

It is a 'monstrous' work lasting 40 minutes but perfectly singable with the pauses. There are times when I am horrified by this intolerable child but

Richard [Chanlaire] (always difficult to please) is so enthusiastic that I take heart! This is really music composed in a state of trance. I am playing it to Cocteau today. When the time comes to let you hear it, I shall be in full command of the role! At the moment I am still stumbling over my words. Anyway, the prosody is very interesting.

I am enjoying my stay here very much. Richard is, as ever, a good guardian angel. As for Louis the builder,[1] who appears every other day, I feel with joy that he is growing more fond of me with each day. I have been twice to Menton with a music-mad Doctor from Dijon and his boy. Very boring Vivaldi concert by I Virtuosi di Roma. How right Dallapiccola is when he says: 'Vivaldi wrote the same concerto 600 times.' *Admirable* Schubert concert by the Hungarian Quartet.

I shall stay here until the 21st and will be in Noizay on the 22nd, until 22 September, when I leave for Italy (Ricordi jury) followed by a little trip for which I am going to need a few tips from you.

[. . .]

Tell me everything about America. And our record?

Very brilliant Carmelitan winter: Vienna, Naples, Palermo, Barcelona, Geneva, Ghent and perhaps Genoa.

For *La Voix*, Paris, Milan, Lisbon and Toulouse. Not bad!

I have been made a *Commandeur* of that absurd *Légion d'honneur des Belles-Lettres et Arts*!! It has brought me more congratulations than the Oxford Doctorate. How funny people are![2]

Embrace the Countess[3] *warmly* on my behalf (this letter is for both of you). *I miss you.* I embrace you. Write.

Fr.

292. Jean Cocteau to Francis Poulenc

'Santo-Sospir', St Jean Cap-Ferrat, 6 December 1958

Mon très cher Francis,

Take this letter to our Karuska ladies as they understand me even before I have uttered a word. *Voilà:*[1]

The appearance of the character must not be tragic. It must not be frivolous.

No studied elegance.

The young woman has simply put on what was to hand but she is waiting for that telephone call from her lover *and believes she will be visible to him.*

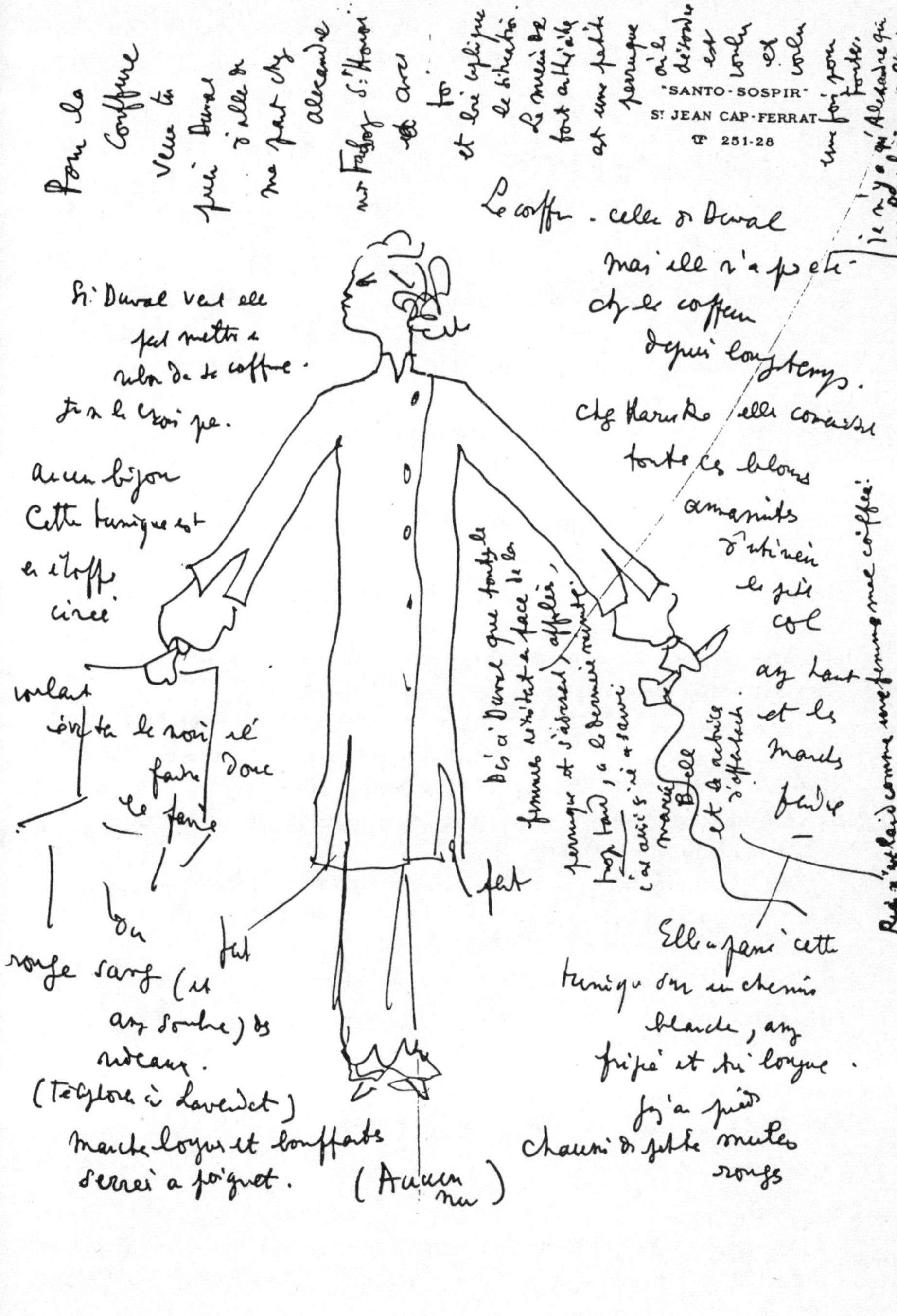

In spite of her lie about the pink dress[2] there is a natural elegance about her, that of a young woman used to looking elegant.

The tragic touch will come from a shawl, or a trench-coat, or a loden, which she will throw over her shoulders without a trace of *coquetterie* – because she is cold, 'cold within'. This is how I will show her inner coldness on stage.

Attached is a drawing of the costume.

> I embrace you.
>
> Jean

If Duval likes, she can put a ribbon in her hair, but I don't favour it.

The hairstyle – as Duval usually wears it but as if she had not been to the hairdresser for a long time.

No jewellery. The tunic must be in a shiny cloth. As we want to avoid black, it will have to be in the same, dark, blood-red of the curtains. (Phone Lavardet.) At Karuska's they know those oriental tunics with little high collars and slits in the sleeves. She has put this on over a white nightdress – long, puffed sleeves gathered in at the wrist – quite crumpled and very long, right down to her feet, which are in little red mules. (Nothing left bare.)

For the hairstyle, will you ask Duval to go with you to Alexandre's, in the rue du Faubourg St-Honoré. Tell him I sent you and explain the position to him. By far the best idea for the theatre is a small wig so that the disorder is deliberate – and is there once and for all. Alexandre is the only one who knows how to create this pastiche.

Tell Duval that all women resist the notion of a wig and then come running to him in a panic, *too late*, at the last minute. This is how he saved Marie Bell and the Offenbach actresses. Nothing is as ugly as a woman with her hair in a mess! But the effect is quite the opposite if enhanced by one of Alexandre's minuscule wigs.

Tell Alexandre that I want hair that is slightly reddish, or with red tints in it, through which she has run her hands a thousand times during the last few days.

It is essential to highlight the forehead and to leave it completely bare.

293. FRANCIS POULENC TO PAUL ROUART

[End of 1958]

Mon petit Paul,

Delightful stay in Vienna where I went to a splendid *Siegfried*, conducted by Karajan, a memorable *Wozzeck*, and impeccable *Carmélites*.

I wonder if it is not these profoundly Catholic and musical people who reach most deeply into the heart of the work.

In any case, it has been an unbelievable success: eleven performances this winter – fourteen planned for '59–'60.

Comments that have reached me about the concert have touched me greatly. I shall never forget that I am indebted to you for that moving evening which allowed me to prove to the Parisian public that – even if a large part of my being has broken down – as far as my work is concerned I am hanging on. Which is already a great deal.

Enjoy the festivities. *Above all*, be reasonable. Get some rest. I embrace you as well as Agathe.

Francis

294. FRANCIS POULENC TO ROSE DERCOURT-PLAUT

Hotel Ritz, Barcelona, 30 January [1959]

Ma chère petite Rose,

I came here for *Les Carmélites*. The performance was pathetic. Disgraceful orchestra. Duval, Scharley and Crespin remarkable but all the rest (really crude) 36th rate. Thank heavens I will have *Les Carmélites* on 12 February in Vienna with Zeefrish [Irmgard Seefried] and all the great ladies.

My *Voix humaine* is opening in Paris on 6 February and in Milan on the 18th. Duval is *superb* in an astonishing production by Cocteau. I will send you the music of this atrocious tragedy (my own). It is a musical confession!!![1]

I am less than well but am growing used to anguish and sadness. I only hope I will be able to write music again one day. For the moment I do not have much inclination to do so.

Will you be an angel and go and see Franco Colombo at Ricordi, 16 West 61st, who will give you a record on my account. Then let me know the exact number of the record.

I am absolutely broke at the moment so I need to get back into work *quickly*. I am obliged to accept commissions while having very little musical appetite. And this is what love has reduced me to. Anyway, I owe him *La Voix humaine* (which is certainly something). Do not judge me severely. Go on being fond of me. I think of you, of Fred, of New York as of an inaccessible paradise.

Fond kisses
Francis

295. Francis Poulenc to Louis Aragon

[1 February, 1959]

Mon cher Louis,

On my return from Barcelona where *Les Carmélites* has just been performed, I found your message asking for an advance notice on *La Voix humaine*.[1]

It is physically impossible for me to write a full article, as I am in Nice for twenty-four hours finalizing details of the production with Jean Cocteau. Jean, who has been ill, is thankfully much better but he must avoid the strain of travelling to Paris.

It was in Nice, at the beginning of January, that he devised the *mise en scène* for Denise Duval. In the course of this work, I was filled with admiration again for his prodigious musical insight.

In fact, though his production is specifically one for an actress, he has been constantly aware of the demands of the voice and of the music. His task was greatly facilitated by the extraordinary dramatic gifts of Denise Duval.

What we are therefore going to see is a singer performing as if she were on a *scène des boulevards* – a rare phenomenon these days.

Curiously, it is only now, after forty years of friendship, that I am collaborating with Cocteau.[2] I think I needed a great deal of experience to respect the perfect construction of *La Voix humaine* which, musically, has to be the opposite of an improvisation. Cocteau's short phrases are so logical, so human, so charged with implications that I have had to write a rigorously ordered score, full of suspense.

The music is in fact silent as soon as the sole character listens to her interlocutor. The impact of the music then suggests what she has heard.

I think I needed the experience of the spiritual and metaphysical anguish of *Les Carmélites* to avoid betraying the terribly human anguish of Jean Cocteau's superb text. I hope I have succeeded in my task.

In devoted friendship, as ever.

Francis Poulenc

296. Francis Poulenc to Brigitte Manceaux

Hotel Excelsior, Naples, Wednesday [1959]

Ma Brige,

Les Carmélites here in Naples is *sensass*. La Carteri, beautiful as Flavie, is prodigious. A sort of lily and reed Tebaldi. Marvellous tenor. Excellent orchestra. Unbelievable sunlight. It is spring!

I shall be in Nice on Saturday, in Avignon on Monday. As '59 is thankfully not '54, I intend making all my own decisions. My sole aim is to get back to work. Only one thing is out of the question: returning to Paris.

Try to see that no one pays any attention to me. It is all that part that makes me loathe the capital.

Denise is doing *La Voix* again on the 4th. She continues to revolutionize Milan.

A thousand loving kisses.

Fr.

297. PIERRE BERNAC TO FRANCIS POULENC

Thursday, 23 April [1959]

Mon petit Francis,

It is kind of you to worry about my health and I apologize for not writing sooner. I have not yet managed to arrange my day properly – I have more to do than I can cope with and am having great difficulty in finding a few minutes of rest. The only definite thing is that I do not go out in the evening any more and I go to bed at 9.30. This helps a lot and I am hoping in this way to be able to keep going. The little circulatory problem I had (which was very unpleasant) has been a good warning, or rather one more warning as I know my arteries are not in good condition. I must say, the prospect of ending up like my poor father, paralysed and aphasic, is not very heartening. But I cannot see myself giving up and retiring now – which would probably not help matters anyway; and besides, I am not financially in a position to do so. Otherwise the idea of going to live peacefully in Villeneuve with Simone [Girard], cultivating her garden and her mind, would be terribly tempting. But there is no question of this and I do not see any possibility of organizing a flow of pupils down there. Well, let's hope I can manage to keep going for a while. I am taking care of myself: injections and various medicaments. Result: I am extremely tired. However, they are making sure my blood pressure does not drop too much.

I am writing this before going to the Salle de L'Ecole Normale for a public concert broadcast. I am singing your *Banalités*, accompanied by Ambrosini. I hope it will be reasonable, but I don't know why I agreed to do it. The day before yesterday, too, I recorded *Le Travail du peintre* for radio, and I heard . . . an extraordinary performance of your Trio, for HARP, flute and bassoon. Hmm . . . Did you authorize that? If so, why? It goes on the air on the 3rd at 8.15 to 9.15 in the evening, but perhaps it is better if you do not listen!

I telephoned Kiesgen to make sure of the date of the concert, as I did not know whether we had finally settled on the 25th, 26th or 27th. It is Wednesday 27th. Yvonne [Gouverné] seems happy as she can have a lot of rehearsals. Come back in time to get involved in all that because it is imperative for this concert to be a success.[1]

Your stay in Bagnols seems to be going well. May you come away saturated and . . . disinfatuated!

I am sending you the text of the *Gloria* and its translation and am delighted that you are tackling this work. You will no doubt need time to get back into your stride.

Well, I am going to rest for a while before putting on my suit and having a quick bite. Write again soon. I embrace you.

P.

298. FRANCIS POULENC TO CHARLES MUNCH

Hotel Bristol Palace, Genoa, Italy, 23 May 1959

Dear and alas invisible friend, I am writing to you from Genoa where, after Naples and Catania, my *Carmélites* is being performed. I am supposed to be writing a new opera for La Scala but as the choice of a libretto has not yet been settled (perhaps *La Machine infernale* of Cocteau) I have a certain amount of time at my disposal to begin a symphonic work. The Koussevitzky Foundation having twice asked me for a work, I have suggested writing a *Gloria* for mixed choir, soprano solo and orchestra, 20 to 25 minutes in duration.[1] You may perhaps be able to sway the balance in my favour if there is any hesitation. You know that the pure symphonic form is not my forte whereas with the human voice – no allusion to my latest work – I am usually successful.

I still had hopes that you might conduct my *Stabat* in Boston, but alas . . . you have no doubt entirely forgotten me. Believe me, the extraordinary success of *Les Carmélites* has not made me less sensitive to certain omissions. However, I still admire you and am as fond of you as ever.

Thank you in advance for what you may be able to do for me and believe, *cher ami*, in my loyal affection.

Francis Poulenc

299. FRANCIS POULENC TO CLAUDE ROSTAND

June 1959

Claudichon joli,

Your article in *Carrefour* is enchanting and moved me from top to tail! Thank you for saying so many things so well. The greatest joy the concert gave me was the knowledge that ambiguities are gradually being dispelled and that I am coming to be accepted as I am, in totality and not in part.[1]

The performance in Vienna was also very encouraging for me. It is the one city where I have been able to judge *Les Dialogues* IN ABSOLUTE TERMS. Performed for the 9th time since February (14 performances planned for '59–'60!!) between *Siegfried* and *Wozzeck*, I realize that it can hold its own. What's more, I was given an extraordinary reception. But what counts the most is that people are going back to see it two or three times. Whereas in Italy, with the lack of permanence, one felt it was just a flash in the pan.

Clearly, the Vienna performance was almost cold in its perfection, whereas in Catania there was a lot of lusty passion in the air, not to mention under the costumes. It was far more 'me' in Sicily, but Vienna represents a post-mortem glory that is certainly reassuring.

The performance of *Wozzeck* was UNBELIEVABLE. Now there the *sperme au vin blanc* was good and truly flowing! Naturally Goltz is more Mary than Mother Mary. Gorr is far superior to her, or that monster of an Olivero.[2]

I found the city enchanting, the people too. What exquisite views around the Opera!!!!!! A far cry from that pompous, pedantic Germany. I kept thinking this while listening to Berg again. With him I do not feel in enemy country.

A charming critic with a wisp of blond hair over an egg-shaped head came to see me twice. Quite a difference from Ströbel!

I am coming home on the 16th and am counting on seeing you at Jolivet's *Vérité*.[3] I only hope Hilda [Jolivet] does not emerge naked from a well!

I would like Georgette[4] to go to *La Voix humaine* (with *Capriccio*) on the 25th. Try to go too, and see if this most secret part of myself really does still elude you. I cannot reconcile myself to the fact that you are the only one who is not moved by this work – written with the heart of a 20-year-old, alas, and the experience of a 60-year-old, double-alas. See you very soon.

With a kiss,

Fr.

300. FRANCIS POULENC TO SIMONE GIRARD

Bagnols-en-Forêt, Saturday [June 1959]

Divine, impossible to telephone on Thursday as I had to go to Cannes. I have just spent ten very peaceful days here. First of all, the roof on Louis' house is about to go up and the house itself has a great deal of style. It is a true farmhouse built for a farmer and without anything of the Côte d'Azur about it. Louis, who has a good understanding of things, is once again *le bon garçon d'Avignon*, and Francis, who also understands things – such as his age and the consequences thereof – is back in the saddle again.

I must tell you that the success of *La Voix*, of *Les Carmélites* in Vienna (I will tell you more later) and finally of the concert, has made me at peace with myself, by which I mean with Monsieur Poulenc. What memories I shall always have of 27 May![1] And if my heart was full of tears, how I revelled in Pierre's glory! There was not one person who did not salute, hat in hand, that *great* artist. I feel that he is so profoundly happy, despite his pretence at detachment, that I think this has contributed to his revival. The day before yesterday he said to me on the telephone: 'I feel better and better.'

As for me – and God knows how much care I took of every detail – that concert was of major importance in setting things straight. Not that I am intoxicated with the idea of being a *grrrrrand musicien*, but it nevertheless exasperates me to be thought of by so many people as nothing more than a *petit maître érotique*. If I once used to fondle every note (forgive me, Countess) it is a damned long time since then, and after all, *Les Litanies* and *Tel jour* do not exactly date from yesterday.

What is necessary now is to be on target with the *Gloria*. Enough pain, enough passion. One must concede that from the *Stabat* to *La Voix*, life has not been a laughing matter. I think I needed all those painful experiences (so often such a plague to certain adorable creatures in Vaucluse) to prove myself, but I have had enough now. Peace! . . . peace!

I am going back to Paris on Tuesday for *La Vérité de Jeanne*. Let's hope that this Vérité does not emerge, naked, from a well in the plump form of Hilda [Jolivet]!! After that, I shall leave for a good fortnight in Brive, where I always work so well. Then I shall spend a full week at Le Tremblay before returning to the Midi. What I have to do now is to wage a war against sleeping tablets. It is my last victory to be won.

Well, Vienna was marvellous, not the sublime fire of Catania – rather a cold but *impeccable* performance (post mortem) of a standard work, and all before a full and enthusiastic house, with not a friend among them!!!

I hope that Avignon still loves me, despite my morose mood (to put it mildly). Write to me *coquine jolie*, in Paris. Letters will be forwarded.

I embrace you warmly.

Fr.

301. LOUIS DUREY TO FRANCIS POULENC

Saint-Tropez, 20 June 1959

Bien cher Francis,

Your letter has just reached me here and it has, as you can imagine, given me very great pleasure. You say that 'the older you get, the more you like to think back on our youth'. This is the surest way of refusing to grow old; and being as I am 11 years your senior, I can assure you that the prescription is one of the best. I have the rare good fortune of not yet feeling too greatly the ravages of time; and the youthfulness I imagine I still possess sustains itself at the source of our friendship – an extraordinary friendship that will always stand as an example to those younger than ourselves. It has lasted for 40 years, dear Francis – and although that famous article by Henri Collet[1] dates from early January 1920, it merely sanctioned something that was already in existence, that had been growing during the preceding months – notably through the concerts at the Vieux-Colombier organized by our admirable Jane [Bathori].

I think it would be a good thing if we could have a reunion one day, in private, during the coming autumn, to celebrate this 40-year friendship and our indestructible ties of fellowship. Although, alas, Arthur [Honegger] has already left us, his memory is always with us, and this can only bind us together even more strongly. In any event, it would be a great joy to me if we could meet again before long.

I did think of sending you a copy of the article I wrote for *Europe* about your songs; only my usual negligence, which led me to procrastinate day after day, has prevented me from doing so. Listening to the two records, I was really very struck by their unity and by the distinctive quality of the works, which have become true classics. Since then I have also had the opportunity of speaking about your very successful Sonata for flute and your Trio.

Unfortunately, my trip to Poland did not come off. The Ministry for Foreign Affairs had led me to expect a subsidy for the trip but at the very last minute they refused it. The Concert des Six which I had prepared took place in spite of this: it consisted of the second Sonata for violin by Darius, the *Chansons françaises* by Germaine, the Apollinaire settings by Arthur, the Trio for reeds by Georges, your Sonata for flute, and my *Choeurs de Métiers*. As for the talk I was due to give, it was published in a Polish literary review. I was very disappointed but perhaps there will be another opportunity some time.

In connection with *Le Bestiaire*, you mention the rue Boissonade. I will not be staying there much longer. We have in fact been expropriated by the Welfare Board, which adjoins our property. Our house is going to be demolished and will be replaced by the morgue for the hospitals that are being built behind us. Too many memories are attached to the place for me not to be devastated by all this. Consequently, I am more than delighted with our house in St Tropez; the spot where we are is sufficiently secluded – it is two kilometres away from the town – to be free from noise and disturbance, even in mid-summer.

This year we have come here earlier than usual, right at the beginning of May, because we are looking after my daughter's two boys (aged two and four). She is working in the government services at Bagneux and cannot look after them. It is a very great strain on my dear wife. 'The art of being a grandfather' is not just a bed of roses: it brings with it plenty of worries as well.

I received the two tickets you sent me and passed them on to friends, who were delighted with them. I was very sorry indeed, due to our great distance from Paris, that we were not able to go to that birthday concert, the date of which – May 27th – coincided with my 71st! But I was entirely with you in thought.

I don't know if you have the Chant du Monde record, *Musique de Louis Durey*. If you want it, phone my friend Jean Roire, the director of the firm (WAG. 67–73), I am sure he will be very glad to send it to you.

I hope that it will soon be possible for us to see each other again. My affection for you remains as much as ever alive, immediate and necessary.

I embrace you.

Louis

302. FRANCIS POULENC TO DENISE DUVAL

19 July [1959]

Ma biche jolie,

How are you enjoying your stay in the musical Ile de Ré?[1] How many fishermen have already thrown themselves into the sea for love of you?

After your departure Paris was a furnace of hearts on fire!!! That is what happens when you play the vamp!

I have just spent ten exquisite days at my sister's. Normandy, in these dog days, is a blissful place. I am leaving tomorrow for Paris where I shall be lunching with one of my rivals, a publisher wild about stars!! We are going to work out the itinerary for a certain Duval (French I think), at any rate the one and only.[2]

On Tuesday I shall be in Bagnols where I hope to be able to work in peace. The roof is built (ouf!) and the mood is good. Write to me, at Bagnols-en-Forêt, Var.

I am awaiting replies from New York to my latest letters. I have also written to Colombo. Please start thinking seriously about the programme for the recital. We must not let this unique opportunity slip by. Bernac writes that my planned return to New York is already causing great excitement. Practise Mélisande so that you are not caught unprepared. I am relying on the dear old trainer (Jouatte) to see that my filly wins all her Derbys.[3] *Write soon.*

Francis

303. PIERRE BERNAC TO FRANCIS POULENC

Villeneuve-lès-Avignon, 3 August [1959]

Mon petit Francis,

Ouf! What joy to come to this heavenly place of rest after having travelled so far and worked so hard.[1] After only two days here I already feel quite relaxed and therefore much more tired! But I have all the time in the world to recuperate. The main thing is that I managed to get through it all. In fact, I was on far better form at the end of my tour than at the beginning. There is no doubt – and I have always been struck by this – that the USA has a very stimulating climate. And yet I assure you that the climate in New York in summer is appalling. A real steam bath. During my two weeks in Seattle this year the weather was fortunately much cooler, which I found less tiring as the major part of my work was there. Private lessons during the day and a three-hour class in the evening. Santa Barbara was fairly restful. Only two classes in the evening, which went very well. I think everyone was quite surprised at how different my classes were from those of Lehmann, who must teach rather like Croiza did, but in her own way. My classes, on the other hand, are obviously very serious and very hard work. At any rate, I was immediately invited again for next year. Lehmann was not there as she is spending her holidays in Europe this year; but all the directors of the School – and also Lehmann's brother – were very enthusiastic. Some interesting singers. But what a lot of work there is to be done. Lehmann's style with French music strikes me as terrifying!

While in Santa Barbara I took the opportunity to spend a few hours in Los Angeles in order to speak to the Dean of the University. I now have a definite proposition for next year but there seems to be an enormous amount of work for not much money. The only thing that would make it viable would be if I could combine it with Santa Barbara.[2]

On the East Coast I have been advised not to accept anything unless it is well paid, but I do not have anything definite there yet. They are trying to wangle Tanglewood for me, and I have written to Munch myself, but I shall be surprised if it works. Naturally, I would prefer to stay on the East Coast, quite different culturally from the West Coast. It is so strange arriving in Boston after that monstrous city of Los Angeles – you feel as if you are arriving in London! I stayed in Boston for only two days to give some private lessons, then I spent the weekend at Alice Esty's in Connecticut. Finally one week in New York for more private lessons – for which I charged a great deal as one has to be very careful not to underrate oneself in that strange country.

Despite its dreadful climate, New York remains very fascinating. I stayed again with dear old Edward,[3] and all our old friends were wonderful. Allen[4] has not done a thing about the book! We spent a very entertaining evening with him in Greenwich Village, which is becoming a real St-Germain-des-Près. I went with Alice Esty to see an operetta, nothing special. Unfortunately *West Side Story* had already finished.

I heard your news from the Jolivets, whom I met last night at the Avignon Festival (very bad production of *Midsummer Night's Dream*). It seems your performance in Aix was *brillantissime*! At any rate, they seem very pleased with the success of their thing. It must compensate for the bitterness over the Institute! But I am nevertheless surprised that Auric did not make it.

Drop me a line occasionally. How long are you planning to stay in Bagnols? What arrangements have you made for your stay in Noizay? Will you have Anna? In the meanwhile, work well in the excellent climate – both mental and physical – of Bagnols. I did not quite know what to say to Doulens about your arrival with Denise, so I was discretion itself.

I embrace you.

P.

304. Francis Poulenc to Pierre Bernac

Bagnols-en-Forêt, Monday [1959]

Mon petit Pierre,

I am working non-stop on the *Gloria* and it seems to be coming right. I would like it to be a single entity made up of six or seven closely related sequences – something like *La Fraîcheur et le feu*. Since there is only one text it cannot be split up ad infinitum. It is just as much of a problem work as *La Voix [humaine]*. I also want to avoid the perpetual four-part scheme – too easy a solution. Yet on the other hand it must not seem too scant either. In short, I am working and reworking each bar in every conceivable way.

I am also practising my Concerto for Menton.

I would love to see the Bergi couple.* After 15 August, why not come to dinner and sleep over? I would also like to show you Louis' house. Suzanne Peignot was very satisfied with our hotel, for one night. Discuss it with Simone. The itinerary through the mountains is magical. I shall expect you.

I embrace you, and the lady too.

Fr.

*Bernac and Simone Girard.

305. FRANCIS POULENC TO SIMONE GIRARD

19 August [1959]

Divine,

I am missing you both but I understand your reasons which are more than valid. Let Pierre rest as much as possible.

I am terribly sad today as I have just heard about the death of my dear Wanda.[1] I was hoping so much to see her again this winter. I suppose she quite literally faded away. What genius she had! And what lovely memories.

Last night the first apples appeared on the table, first fruits of the autumn that I loathe. Tante Liénard used to say: 'One must always look on the bright side of things.' I shall try.

Work is going fairly well. I have the whole plan [of the *Gloria*]. The final Amen, if I make a success of it, could be very beautiful. The tiny little English chorus is done and is touching, I think.[2]

Let me hear from you before leaving (I am here until the 31st).

Affectionate kisses to all.

Fr.

Pierre must get the *maximum* rest. Tell him to write to me.

306. FRANCIS POULENC TO PIERRE BERNAC

[Bagnols-en-Forêt], 20 August [1959]

Mon petit Pierre,

I would like to have seen you but can only approve your decision to preserve your strength.

My stay is anyway coming to an end. I shall be leaving in a week for Monte Carlo. Then back to Bagnols for the 30th, and on the 31st I shall be in Paris. My six weeks here have been well spent in a quietness that has been very beneficial to me. I feel now as if I have really done my duty. The house is ready, built by Louis *all by himself* and exactly as he conceived it. Whatever happens, thanks to his own labour, he now has a very nice asset. I fully realize that the *possibility* of this little house not being completed contributed greatly to my distress of last winter.

At my age, what I would like for myself is total freedom. I am in any case on the right track once again and slowly getting back into my stride. These two works, *Les Dialogues* and *La Voix*, that have done so much for my world renown would nevertheless be dangerous if I did not try to become the Poulenc of '37 again. I do not mean of *Les Mamelles* but of the Mass and the Concerto for organ.

How beneficial Anost used to be for me.

As I told you, I think I have decided on the plan for the *Gloria*:

> I Gloria   II Laudamus   III Domine Deus
> IV . . . unigenite Jesu Christe   V Domine Deus
> VI Sedes ad dexteram   VII Amen

The few opening bars of the Gloria will precede the Amen (long vocalizing from the soprano and chorus).

I would like No. VI to be glorious, also No. VII: 'let us return to heaven after having sung for you'. There are very lovely themes, very bare. What I cannot see at all at the moment is No. V in relation to the B minor III (slow 6/8).

The little English chorus (or rather the unison for children, with piano) is very pretty and I think very much in the spirit of the poem.

I shall wait until I am at Noizay before committing the *Elégie* to paper.[1] I am quite eager to get there – Marie-Thérèse Mabille is coming for the first two weeks, and my sister after that.

Send the photographs back to me. The one of me as a mountaineer is for you.

I embrace you.

Fr.

307. FRANCIS POULENC TO ARTHUR GOLD AND ROBERT FIZDALE

[28 September 1959]

Mes enfants,

The *Elégie* is finished.[1] Rose Plaut will bring you the music on 15 October. Do with it as you see fit.

It is an odd piece, rather 'sweet'* in style. I know you will make something of it. The *Elégie* consists solely of alternating chords. I hope the balance is good. Tell me quite frankly what you think of it. Anyway, it is very easy – too easy perhaps for serious critics, but that's too bad. To hell with them. How was Venice?

I embrace you. See you soon.

Francis

Think of Marie-Blanche when you play the *Elégie*.

*In English in the original text.

308. MAURICE GOUDEKET TO FRANCIS POULENC

9 rue de Beaujolais, 5 November 1959

Cher Francis,

A plaque is going to be put up on Colette's house, and it will be inaugurated by the minister, André Malraux.[1] An honorary committee is being formed for this purpose. I would like you and Georges Auric to be on it as representatives of music and friendship.

May I ask you for a prompt reply? There is no need for me to tell you how dearly I hope you will agree.

With regards,
Maurice Goudeket

309. FRANCIS POULENC TO PIERRE VIDAL

Tuesday [November 1959]

Cher Monsieur,

I have waited anxiously for your letter. Everything is in order for the 16th but please let me know the exact time of the meeting.[1]

Will you get hold of *Les Mamelles*, which I do not have in Paris, and the Véga record of my settings of Eluard and Apollinaire by Pierre Bernac (not the one with the selection of songs on it). I am still hoping to receive the test pressings of *La Voix humaine* in time for the meeting but I am not sure.[2] If you had *Dialogues des Carmélites* it would add diversity. I shall be back in Paris on the 13th. Ring me on Saturday morning at about 9 o'clock: Danton 52–23. In any event, I am relying on you for the records.

I am looking forward to this little treat as your programmes are first rate.

Yours sincerely
Francis Poulenc

Perhaps you could also get the *Litanies à la Vierge noire*. Erato – above all not Pathé-Marconi.

310. FRANCIS POULENC TO GENEVIÈVE SIENKIEWICZ

Monday [21 December 1959]

Ma chère Geneviève,

You are going to receive a parcel that will surprise you but, I hope, also amuse you. It contains the manuscript of my *Chabrier*[1] which you will be the *first* to read! Naturally, I shall still be making corrections to the typed copy, but I hope you will like it so far. I have written it for all music-lovers who use the series *Solfège* (you no doubt have the Schubert by Schneider) but who unfortunately consider Chabrier a minor musician.

As so many people need affirmation of their tastes, I think names like Manet, Renoir, Cézanne, Mallarmé, etc. will satisfy their *snobisme*. And the examples in the book are pertinent enough to make it worth while for experts as well.

My familiar tone will obviously incur the disapproval of many a bespectacled pedant but I don't give a damn, and Chabrier, I feel sure, would have reacted in similar fashion.

I'll be back on the 28th. I will make straight for Noizay on the 2nd to copy out the *Gloria*, completed at last.

When I played you those few bits from it, your reaction encouraged me a great deal. I badly needed this as no other work has posed so many problems for me.

Often, during my fits of self-doubt, alas more and more frequent, I ask myself if it is not sterility that causes me to compose so slowly. But since I have chosen this path, I have to stick to it. I cannot, like Milhaud, play ducks and drakes with my gift. One day I will explain to you exactly how I constructed this *Gloria*. Anyway, I think the sound quality of the ending will be very beautiful. I love the voice so much!

My stay in Milan was enchanting. La Tebaldi (in *Tosca*) was more sublime than ever. Gobbi and Di Stefano marvellous. Very beautiful performance of *Otello* with Del Monaco.[2]

Brigitte [Manceaux] writes: 'Geneviève seems to be better and better'. Hold on as long as you can. *We need you*, and I more than anyone, who am far less self-assured now than in the days when you first took me to Viñes.

See you very soon. Happy Christmas. I embrace you fondly.

Francis

311. FRANCIS POULENC TO DENISE DUVAL

Tuesday [December 1959]

Ma cocotte jolie,

I am not put out that you find my fellow-composers' music harder than your Poupoule's. Quite honestly, with us, it's as if we were making babies together. Nobody has impregnated you more than I!!! and who would have believed it?

It was very funny to see you surrounded by all your men friends . . . In fact your three brawny *gardes du corps* caused me much amusement. I, however, am your *garde du coeur*, which is a far lovelier thing to be, don't you think?*

* *garde du corps* – bodyguard; *garde du coeur* – guardian of your heart.

You know, when I heard the recording [of *La Voix humaine*], alone, at home, I was quite overwhelmed, but not tearfully, almost joyously. Having brought this beautiful, sad child into the world, all that we went through for it seems worth while. When I think back on the period of gestation of this work – which I am now convinced is a masterpiece – I do so almost with tenderness. I see again my room in Cannes, in Saint-Raphaël. Yes, it is certainly worth while to have lived through all that.

I am leaving for Bagnols-en-Forêt, Var. Write to me soon, a long letter which I'll find when I arrive, telling me all the details of the première. You are alone now; it will give you something to do.

How happy you will be to put on your red cloak once again and to weep about love. Deep down, we French understand each other so well.

Tender kisses from your Poupoule who adores you.

Fr.

312. FRANCIS POULENC TO PIERRE BERNAC

Hotel Ambassador, Chicago, Wednesday [February 1960]

Mon petit Pierre,

La Duval amazes me more and more each day. Last night, in a very formal evening dress, without any props, with no telephone, she held spellbound a hall filled to capacity, and had all the women sobbing. Her concert appearances are going marvellously well. She gets better each time and she has her audience in the palm of her hand. Even those who are indifferent are won over every time and that says it all. What she does with my songs is quite divine. How lucky I am to have you both![1] 'Air champêtre' and 'Voyage à Paris' have of course unleashed wild enthusiasm.[2]

Everyone asks me about you and sends you very best wishes. I think . . . they are going to bring out our record! Lieberson is charming, I am busy recording the Sextet for them. I am not crazy about this but it is very well paid. I am hoping to do *Aubade*.[3]

I will not be back until the 20th and I am not complaining. I quite definitely enjoy being in America. It makes me feel young again and I was badly in need of this! I hope to hear from you soon.

I embrace you.
Fr.

313. FRANCIS POULENC TO STÉPHANE AUDEL

Hotel Ambassador, Chicago, February 1960

Mon vieux Stéphane, you have no doubt heard of the triumphs of La Duval! She is fantastic, and has caused an unbelievable stir here. This trip has made me ten years younger. Which I badly, badly needed!!! *La Voix* has met with undreamed-of success.

I shall not be back until the 20th. There is no doubt about it: I love America and America loves me. I hope you are not too bad. I send you a good discharge of the right fluid and embrace you!

Francis

Affectionate regards to your wife.

314. Pierre Bernac to Francis Poulenc

Thursday, 10 March [1960]

Mon petit Francis, I think tonight is the night of your Town Hall recital and I cannot resist speaking to you about it.[1] I am convinced it will all go marvellously now that you and Denise have been 'broken in'. Thank you for all your good, kind letters. I am so happy to know that you are having such success. The USA has always been so good for you in every way. It does not surprise me in the least that Denise is becoming more and more successful in recital – she is so intelligent, such a fine musician and so gifted artistically. I am sure she can teach American singers a lot when it comes to French music! In any case, I can tell you that I missed her greatly in *L'Heure espagnole* the other evening at the Opéra. The girl who is singing now has a beautiful voice but is in no way the right woman for the role. Total mistake on the part of Dussurget. What one sees is in fact very ugly; but what one hears is good. Rosenthal is the triumphant victor of the evening. His *Daphnis* is wonderful. And the choreography is excellent. As for Chagall's décor, it may be very beautiful but it is completely foreign to the work.[2]

Apart from that, music is in rather a slump over here. When one thinks of the prodigious musical vitality of New York! Not that every concert over there is good, I know, but all the same there is excitement around. And enormous audiences. Here the halls are half empty.

Nothing major to recount. Lessons are rather dull this winter and the standard of the pupils is much lower. Nothing new about my trip to the USA. Still no reply from Los Angeles. I really doubt if it will work now. I have started to look in various other directions to try and find something else, at least for next summer, as it really does make life a little more comfortable. If the opportunity arises, put in a good word for me here and there.

Good news from the Countess,[3] who is in the thick of preparations for her next concert on the 14th. I believe the one after is on the very day you arrive in Avignon.

Please tell Denise how happy I am about her success and embrace her for me.

I embrace you,

P.

I see the weather is dreadful in New York. Here, it is just like spring.

315. FRANCIS POULENC TO BENJAMIN BRITTEN

2 April [1960]

Cher Ben,

I am coming to Aldeburgh on 11 June for your opera.[1] Can you book a seat and a room for me right now? I am so looking forward to hearing your new work.[2] I have just come back from America where I had a very pleasant visit. At the moment I am in the South of France, orchestrating my *Gloria*. Will we see you this summer in Aix? We will be doing *La Voix humaine*.

See you soon. I embrace you, and Peter, too.

Francis

316. FRANCIS POULENC TO PIERRE BERNAC

[Rocamadour], Lundi [1960]

Mon petit Pierre,

On this day of the year, I am what I would wish to be. The weather is perfect: bright and cheerful. Tomorrow I shall launch into my last eight pages[1] and the songs for children.[2] I am beginning – not without fear – to think of the *Office des Ténèbres!*[3] May the Holy Virgin grant that I carry out this ambitious task successfully. I played the *Gloria* again after leaving it for two months. Yes, it is good. I am staying until the 7th at 4 Place Krüger, Brive. Happy retreat at Bec.[4] The abbot frightens me horribly!

I embrace you,

Fr.

I am thrilled with the record!

317. FRANCIS POULENC TO DENISE DUVAL

19 July 1960

Mon Rossignol à larmes,*

I loved your joyful voice on the telephone. Like me, you are not made for solitude.

*One of Poulenc's favourite terms for Denise Duval: a nightingale who brings tears to your eyes.

They can talk of nothing but you and *La Voix* in Aix. Everything else, they say, is just an hors-d'oeuvre (sic).

On Sunday the audience will be much more amusing: the likes of Bourdet, Lopez, etc.

Be on form and keep working at your '*je devenais fol-le*' which you do so well when you concentrate. I was really happy the other night; it was wonderful.

With the two of us, you are so much me that it is as if I were split in two.

When you see your impresario, try to be a little firmer with him. I know how indulgent you feel towards him but this does not make our work any easier.

Until Sunday.

I adore you.

Fr.

318. FRANCIS POULENC TO PIERRE BERNAC

Bagnols-en-Forêt, Var, [August 1960]

Mon petit Pierre,

The seven Carême songs [*La Courte paille*] are finished. I am extremely pleased with them as they are very poetic and very whimsical.

As far as the prosody is concerned there are some lovely details. Anyway, I am longing to show them to you. Naturally, they are made to measure for the Diva:

and what's more the G is sung at full strength, almost at the end of the last song. The fast passages are very much like *Les Mamelles*. The slow ones not difficult in style.

I have made my choice now for the *Office des Ténèbres*. I am trembling with fear as it is terribly difficult to make it sound varied. At any rate, I have followed the chronological order. Will you type out for me each *répons* recto verso with the accents in red?

The weather is delightful – after *one* bad day, the sun has come out again and it is bright and cool. I hope you are not being drowned!

Write soon, and thank you.

Warmest regards to you and the Countess.[1]

Fr.

Everyone tells me that Gérard [Souzay] sang *Tel jour telle nuit* marvellously in Menton.

Claude [Rostand] wrote a fine article in *Carrefour*. I shall be back in Paris on the 25th and will be in Noizay on the 27th.

319. FRANCIS POULENC TO PIERRE BERNAC

5 September 1960

Mon Pierre,

You might say that I am *dans les ténèbres* as, for the moment, it feels as if I am entering a tunnel. It is always like this. I am not too worried. [. . .] I am passionate about this work but it also terrifies me! I have promised Rocamadour a superb bell if . . .

Brigitte liked *La Courte paille* very much. I, too, think it is very good. Eschig is printing it. I want Denise to start immediately. She knows her *Vol de nuit*[1] already, so she has the time.

She is delighted with the Debussy item. I think it suits her very well. At any rate, the Italians love this programme. She is singing *La Voix* at the Farnese[2] with Prêtre on the 9th. It is a *grandissime* evening with ambassadors, Gronchi, etc. It will be very good publicity for her, in any case. And Edinburgh, which she was dreading, has been a real *triumph*. It has stopped raining and she has discovered Cuénod, whom she never lets out of her sight, even for a moment, which is perfect.

The weather here is exquisite and I have flowers galore. I received a letter from Wallmann this morning. They are doing *Les Carmélites* in Vienna on the 6th and the 23rd. Karajan told Wallmann that 'it is now part of the repertoire' as it is 'sold out'.* It's odd. It seems that all those women adore their roles.

Where are you?

Do write. I embrace you both.

Fr.

Did I tell you that I wrote a long letter to [Jacques] Pradère? Hell has just completed his sleeve-notes, as usual excellent on the poets.[3]

320. FRANCIS POULENC TO PIERRE BERNAC

Wednesday [Autumn 1960]

Mon petit Pierre,

After four *abominable* days, I think I have found my first *répons*. It is more Mantegna than Zurbaran.[1] I would have preferred it to be otherwise

*In English in the original text.

but never mind. Either it is *superb* or too theatrical. At any rate, it is definitely 'something'.

From 'Una hora' to 'Vel': darkness. From 'Judam' to 'Judaeis': an armed crowd. From 'Quia dormitis' to the end: calmness and forgiveness. 'Judas, mercator pessimus' will also be tragic. I have taken this phrase from another *répons* – it seems right to me. But the crucial problem comes later, in the solo. I am not a misogynist but the idea of a woman's voice replacing the child's does not appeal to me at all. For the choir, it does not really matter.

Since 'Green' or 'Soir'[2] can be sung equally by a man or a woman, do you think that, if I cannot have a child's voice, I could have a white tenor, something like Cuénod?

If I do not calculate my music at the exact pitch, it might work. Though I disapprove of *Madécasses* sung by a man, because the dominant becomes the sub-dominant, I find the Mallarmé's possible,[3] and my 'Feu du soir' can work if sung by a [Leontyne] Price. What do you think of the problem? Hearing Rallès with Cuénod it occurred to me immediately. Obviously I will note in the edition that everything possible must be done to have a child's voice.

At any rate, I do not think it will resemble in any way whatever either the *Gloria* or the *Stabat*. Very full orchestration. I would have loved Holbein!!!

Duval has had an incredible press in England,[4] average for me . . . quite bad for Cocteau. Why?

Let me know what you think of the white tenor idea.

I embrace you, charming travellers.

Fr. P.

321. PIERRE BERNAC TO FRANCIS POULENC

Hôtel Mirabeau, 4 rue de Candolle, Geneva, Tuesday, 20 September [1960]

Mon petit Francis,

I found your two letters waiting when I arrived here on Friday night and since then I have been so busy adjudicating that I have not had time to reply to you until now. You must have received a few vague postcards that we sent at various stages of our trip which, on the whole, was very successful, in spite of rather poor weather: not much sun, no pretty light over the lakes, but no rain either except on the last day over Lake Maggiore where it was really catastrophic.[1] I was afraid I would not get to Geneva in time for the jury. I assure you I shall never forget our departure from Stresa, where it had been raining for twenty-four hours as I had never before seen it rain! Roads cut off in the valley; and as for the Simplon Pass, it was quite simply terrifying: in the Gondo Gorge we had to drive right through veritable waterfalls cascading down the mountainside. I think we were one of the last cars to get through. Since then, in Geneva, it has been raining practically without stopping. I don't really mind but I have three days ahead without work and I would have liked to be able to enjoy some of the country. This is quite out of the question.

The competition has been very disappointing apart from two or three individuals. Needless to say, the French are not exactly covering themselves in glory . . .

I am delighted to hear that your work is going so well now, after the inevitable 'black-out'* of the first few days. Bravo for your idea of replacing, if need be, the child's voice by an oratorio tenor's voice! Marvellous idea! It will be infinitely better than the sensuality of a female voice. And that type of tenor can easily be found. Michel Sénéchal, for example, would be possible in France. But be careful not to write a tessitura that is too low. Keep mainly above middle G and – even for a child – I would not hesitate to write a few carefully prepared Gs in the upper register.

I am longing to hear *La Courte paille* which I am sure must be very good.

Simone went back to Avignon on Sunday morning, delighted with her trip, but naturally devastated at having to leave. Fortunately she will be kept very busy now with preparations for her new season of concerts.

As for me, I shall have to remain here until the 28th and shall return to Paris on the 29th. To what? I know not. But my season this year will have to be better than last year's, which was more than mediocre in every way, and as I did not have the USA this summer . . .

I embrace you.

P.

322. Mstislav Rostropovitch to Francis Poulenc

Mstislav Rostropovitch, Conservatoire, Moscow, USSR, [1961?]

Cher Maître Monsieur Francis Poulenc!

I beg your pardon for disturbing you with this letter which my friend will deliver to you. For a long time I have been trying to play the cello well, but to tell the truth I do not know if I have succeeded. I have asked my friend to give my letter to you and also the records of the Symphony-concerto by Prokofiev and the one by Shostakovich, which have been dedicated to me.[1] I hope very much that you will listen to them if you have a free moment. I am writing to you because I am one of the great admirers of your music. In autumn, in Edinburgh, I heard your *La Voix humaine*. It is marvellous.

*In English in the original text.

In all musical literature there is no composition as admirable as the *Poème* for violin by Chausson. But this genre is just as beautiful for the cello, which is able to sing with a 'human voice'. You are the only one who can make it sing as wonderfully as Denise Duval. I beg of you on behalf of cellists the world over to offer this gift to all musicians. Tomorrow I shall be leaving for Mexico and South America. I shall spend a day in London to play with the composer Benjamin Britten, who has dedicated a work to me.[2]

I hope to hear from you. I can think of nothing but this work. If you do write this sonata of my dreams I shall, if you wish, come to Paris for the first performance, then to Moscow, anywhere you like. In Moscow you would be welcomed by all musicians.[3]

All my affectionate respects
and my love to you*
Mstislav Rostropovitch

323. FRANCIS POULENC TO PIERRE BERNAC

Sheraton Plaza Hotel, Boston, Massachusetts, Tuesday [January 1961]

Mon petit Pierre,

My first long letter is for you.[1] Phone it through to Brigitte afterwards and she will do the same for you with the next letter. The concert here promises to be *very good*. An excellent 'Monique', young, pleasant, catches on quickly and loves my Concerto.[2] As for the *Gloria*, if I had not come here, what peculiar music would have been heard! Dear, adorable, exquisite Charlie [Charles Munch] had understood precisely *nothing*.

Arriving late for the first rehearsal of the choir, I heard something so unlike me that my legs almost failed me on the staircase. *Excellent* choir but [Alfred Nash] Patterson is not the intuitive [Robert] Shaw and all those worthy Protestants were singing sharp and shrill (especially the women) as they do in London, with that 'Oh! my good Lord' quality. *All* Munch's tempi were *wrong* – all too fast, naturally. A well-intentioned lady was singing the part of Addison[3] (who had not yet arrived), with a voice like a goat and all out of tune. A pale, wan pianist tinkled the keys, and not always the right ones!! I tell you, I wanted to run a mile. My poor child was really presenting itself badly. What a burden music is!!!

I didn't say a word before the interval but then I explained everything. Mr Patterson, hearing me demonstrate, said: 'Oh! so they have to sing like Maurice Chevalier.' 'Exactly!' When we started again, I played the piano,

---

*Tous mes respects affectueux
et mon amour pour vous.*

the soloist sang no more, Munch calmed down, and the thing was *perfect*. Ouf!!!

Basically, Charlie only understands Arthur [Honegger] and Roussel. How very Strasbourgeois he is, the dear treasure! I had lunch at his place. It was divine. Everyone is adorable here, but what a dismal town – I am dying of boredom despite the radio and the TV in my room. Quick, New York!

Here is this winter's barometer of virtuosos: Richter – delirium; Samson – triumph with orchestra, recital less good; Monique – went unnoticed; continued success of Entremont, who will become Casadesus (don't tell 'his' Countess!!!). The Met. wild with excitement in anticipation of the joint débuts of Price and Corelli in *Trovatore*. I shall be there. Tebaldi – Della Casa: usual success. Enormous success of la Simionato in *L'Incoronazione di Poppea*.

I must go to my rehearsal with orchestra. Wonder what that will bring! Very much affection to you and the Queen of Hearts.

Fr.

P.S. I was not made for going on tour on my own.

324. PIERRE BERNAC TO FRANCIS POULENC

20 January 1961

Mon petit Francis,

What joy to receive your long letter this morning! As I woke up it occurred to me that today was your big day. And we were all so sad that we did not know your address and could not send you a telegram. So your letter came just at the right time. Despite your dismay on hearing the typically Protestant choir and despite the uncertainties and inconsistencies of Charlie's conducting, you seem now to have a positive impression of him, and I feel sure everything will go off well. Particularly since Addison will certainly be excellent. As for the Concerto, if you have a good 'Monique',[1] everything will surely go well. We will nevertheless be waiting eagerly to hear from you. What a terrifying thing music is! And especially for a composer, who is so dependent on his interpreters.

Yes, Boston is rather a dull town, and despite the uncertainties of my present situation, I have never regretted turning down the superb position offered to me there. I shall nevertheless be spending two or three days there next summer, before or after Chicago, as I may have a few private lessons to give. You, I suppose, are going to hot-foot it back to New York as soon as possible, so I shall address this letter there. The story of Rose [Dercourt-Plaut] and the radio is hair-raising! Enjoy your week seeing all our old friends in that fascinating city to which I, unfortunately, cannot see myself returning.

Nothing out of the ordinary to report from here. I go out a lot with Simone [Girard] who leaves again on Monday morning. We were very happy with our Cuevas evening, a really delightful show.[2] Excellent concertos played by De Samson François (Bartók and Chopin) at the Concert Colonne on Sunday; but the orchestra, which I had not heard for quite some time, has really deteriorated. We are going to Jacques' [Février's] concert tomorrow . . . Let's hope everything goes well.

I see, in connection with the latest air disaster, that there are terrible snow-storms over New York. I hope they will be gone by the time you arrive. Here, on the other hand, the weather has been exceptionally pleasant since your departure. All the same, long live temperate climates! Be careful not to slip in the snow when you are rushing around New York. *Il Trovatore* at the Met. will be fun. An American pupil told me that the performance of *Don Juan* at the Opéra the day before yesterday was, from all points of view, worse than a small-town university production in America! Oh! There was also *Dolores* by Maestro Jolivet at the Opéra-Comique. Because we had Cuevas that evening, we attended the last rehearsal the night before. As far as we could judge (since final rehearsals are nearly always disastrous) it seems to be quite successful. I was familiar with large sections of it through having once had to sing them. It is very much the 'genre espagnolade', though obviously not quite *L'Heure espagnole*! But it is quite inventive and it has a certain freshness that no doubt would be lacking from his compositions now (it dates from 17 years ago). Quite well produced from a singing point of view: a young soprano whom I did not know called Sylvie – pretty voice, good, sound intonation, acts like a schoolgirl; J. C. Benoit excellent; Giraudeau funny; Depraz did not know his part; Jansen delightful to look at but insipid. Hideous, idiotic décor by Yves Brayer, badly executed, badly lit. Wishy-washy conducting by Jésus Etcheverry. I believe the première (with *Vol de nuit*) went very well and enjoyed a fair amount of success. But what shoddy work some of these theatres produce; it is dreadful!

Simone joins me in embracing you.

P.

325. Francis Poulenc to Pierre Bernac

Boston, Thursday morning [January 1961]

Mon petit Pierre,

The rehearsal yesterday was *extraordinary*. Munch *suddenly inspired*; as for Addison, she drives you wild, she is sheer heaven, with that warm Negro purity.

Everyone was full of enthusiasm. Clearly, you know me better than I know myself. The *Gloria* is without doubt the best thing I have done. The orchestration is marvellous (the ending, among other things, is astonishing). There is not a single note to be changed in the choral writing and at least the women do not shriek their heads off on the upper As and Bs. I must confess that I have surprised myself.

It has given me a confidence *that I badly needed*. How right I was not to rush *Les Répons*. I am sure it will benefit from this. Everybody is delighted here. And I have at last shaken off the torpor of the time-change.

Rose [Dercourt-Plaut] is arriving this evening, wild with delight about this honeymoon!!!!! We are going to hear Marlene Dietrich! I am enjoying it all very much. The Consul, a great-nephew of Vincent d'Indy, is handsome and charming. His wife as well. But what a hard country! Arthur [Honegger] is hardly ever played here any more, except by Munch. It is frightening. For the moment I am still going strong, thanks to the choral works, concertos and wind compositions. Long may it last.

Phone Brigitte [Manceaux] right now, and Geneviève [Sienkiewicz].

I embrace you,

Fr.

I miss you. To quote *La Voix* [*humaine*]: 'I am not used to travelling alone any more.'

326. FRANCIS POULENC TO PIERRE BERNAC

Boston, Monday [1961]

Eh bien mon enfant, it was a triumph to beat all triumphs!

You heard that because of the snow, Friday's concert was put off until yesterday – Sunday. Saturday night's concert went ahead. Very good, very beautiful, successful, but Munch was less inspired than at the final rehearsal. Yesterday, on the other hand (all the critics were there), *sublime* performance. Charlie in a trance but controlled, the choir unbelievable, Addison *beyond belief*, so ovation after ovation. They tell me the press is excellent this morning. Marlene Dietrich was there, embraces, photos, etc.

I am *delighted*, as audiences here – quite dreadful – *give you marks*! I can already feel a favourable reaction from Bernstein. I am busy arranging something for you in Boston for this summer. The Consul, Charles de Pampelonne, is exquisite (great-nephew of d'Indy). I will tell you about him when I get back. Yes, we would soon have been at your funeral had you accepted Boston. Munch has had just about enough.

My week here promises to be entertaining with Leontyne Price, Laurence Olivier in *Becket*, visits to Horowitz, Titou, Rubinstein, etc.

I find this country interesting but frightening. You have to be really on top of things not to suffer the whims of the public and the press; even stranger than at home.

Thank you for writing at such length. I can assure you that you are not forgotten here. If you see Lesur[1] tell him about the success of the *Gloria*. I had a letter from an ecstatic Carteri.[2] So, let's take advantage of the fair weather!

I embrace you,
Fr. Poulenc

Ring Brigitte.*

327. FRANCIS POULENC TO HENRI HELL

2 March 1961

Cher Henri,

I am literally in despair over *l'Express*. Why, when it comes to music, do they write like *Marie-Claire*? It is so important that you should have a voice in Paris!

I am utterly demoralized by it all. You, who know me so well, were able to divine my present state of nerves. My doctor Chevalier was not wrong. This time it is not love that has plunged me into this state of anxiety, but solely myself. I beg of you, not a word of this to anyone, especially not to Brigitte [Manceaux]. I have seen my marvellous Chinese acupuncturist again in Cannes and I already feel better. My blood pressure is fine: 16, 16 and again 16, so it is all entirely my nerves. Not being as prolific a composer as Darius or others, each one of my compositions must make its mark, since I put everything I have into it. This is why, after the indisputable success of Boston (I will show you the reviews), Paris has caused me the greatest anguish. Thank goodness the *Gloria* was regarded as *important*. I know very well that I am not exactly in vogue but I need at least to be recognized. And this has happened. In any case, I think that in the future I will be played more often than Barraqué or Pousseur.[1] After all, my music is not all that bad, although every now and then I do ask myself why I continue composing, and for whom?

It is at such times that people like you and Richard[2] save me from going under. I lack pride . . . I think there is a lot of confusion at the moment. Please note that I am not jealous – there is a place for everyone.

Having said all this, I must return to my piano to practise *Aubade*. It will be good if you can come to the recordings of this work and of the Sinfonietta, so that you can get back into circulation.[3]

*In English in the original text.

The important thing is that these old compositions should stand the test of time. What counts is not what is played but what is played again and again! Did I tell you that 'Meylan'[4] finds your Lausanne column excellent? Believe me, it is *widely* read and it *does count*.

The weather is divine. As I told you, I shall be back in Paris on the 19th and am relying on you for lunch on the 20th. I am also booking you for Whitsun at Noizay, with Brigitte and Pierre.

Pathé-Marconi profess to be delighted with the recordings. The organ at Saint-Etienne is superb – the rehearsal without orchestra was thrilling. The balance is apparently very good. It was difficult. I will tell you what to say about Duruflé's father for your sleeve-notes.[5]

I shall be sorry to miss the Boulez on the 15th. They certainly know how to advertise! I received a letter fromStröbel ordering me to report for service (S.S. style) for that evening. I am quite honestly sorry to miss *Pli selon pli*[6] for I feel sure that it is more than worth while.

I would love to get a letter, but knowing you . . .

Kisses from your old friend,

Benjamin Godard!!![7]

328. FRANCIS POULENC TO PIERRE VIDAL

[Bagnols-en-Forêt], 15 March 1961

Cher Vidal,

Impossible on the 27th as I shall be in Charleroi that evening with Gavoty. But Monday 24th would suit me very well.[1] Can you get hold of *España*, *Fête polonaise*, the Marcelle Meyer records, *Joyeuse marche* and especially the four songs by [Camille] Maurane on Erato. My *Chabrier* has just been published by Plon. The *Gloria* and the new recording (superb) of the Concerto for organ should in theory be out by Easter.[2] Just wait till you hear the organ of St Etienne du Mont played by Duruflé – it's fantastic!

As for the *Gloria*, there is no connection whatever between the recording and the performance at the Théâtre des Champs-Elysées, particularly with regard to Carteri. Thank you for your very kind article.[3] Phone me on Monday the 20th at 9 o'clock Danton 52–23, to confirm the date.

With kindest regards,

Poulenc

329. FRANCIS POULENC TO STÉPHANE AUDEL

Ash Wednesday [19 March 1961]

Cher enfant,

I imagine you have received my letter by now, which must have crossed with yours. In it, I told you I had not been able to bring back the Poulet record because you were one step behind me all the way to Paris, etc.

Since my return from America I have had various minor health problems – my ears were affected by the Boeing, and now, two months later, I still hear a whistling from time to time. This ear trouble causes loss of balance (sic). They thought it might be blood pressure but nothing of the kind: 15½–16! I also went to see my oculist as I sometimes have spots dancing in front of my eyes. There is absolutely *nothing* wrong with me other than a slight attack of nerves which the admirable [Dr Louis] Chevalier detected on the very first day. We are familiar with this. I feel better already.

I was on edge because of the première of the *Gloria* in Paris, then there was Anna's departure, followed by a disinclination to work. Fortunately, the Midi is having a calming effect.

My *Chabrier* has come out. You will be receiving a copy. I am very pleased with it, and the response – both written and spoken – has been excellent. I have also done some recordings, including *Aubade*, and my ultra-beloved Prêtre has recorded the *Gloria* and the Concerto for organ with the hand of a master.

When will you be back? I picture you sated with sun and no doubt other things as well. I am very happy for you and I embrace you.

Francis

Everything is fine with the Manceaux family.

330. HENRI SAUGUET TO FRANCIS POULENC

Fargues, Coutras (Gironde), 19 May 1961

Cher Francis,

Your dear card adds even more to the immense pleasure you gave me by coming to Bordeaux for the first performance of my cantata.[1] Thank you with all my heart: what you have said to me and written to me gives me profound joy. I realize that we are right to continue composing our music, as you (and with what irrefutable individuality!) and I are doing. Besides, the music is not in the clothing of the composition but in its spirit. Either there is music in a work or there is not . . .

Yesterday I had a visit from the adorable Suzanne Peignot on her way to Bonneval. It was my 60th birthday. I am very sad, however. Life now is bereft of too many loved ones. The death of poor Hélène J-M[2] has deeply upset me. Thank you, dear Francis, with all my old, devoted, admiring and constant friendship.

Henri S.

331. FRANCIS POULENC TO DARIUS MILHAUD

23 May 1961

Maître aimé,

One of your most fervent admirers will give a lecture about you on 24 July in Aix-en-Provence. He is someone who knows your music very well and who really loves it. I will tell you his name later.

I am writing from Noizay where I am spending the whole of May with my dear old [Richard] Chanlaire to keep me company.

I am working on my *Répons de la semaine sainte* for Bernstein. It is not going badly as I have scrapped all that I did last autumn and begun again. I thought it would be like Zurbarán but it has turned out to be like Mantegna.[1]

In April I wrote a monologue on a text by Jean [Cocteau] (*La dame de Monte-Carlo*) for Duval and orchestra. I think it suits us all very nicely.[2] In Bordeaux I heard an exquisite, adorable, intoxicating cantata by Henri [Sauguet]. It is his garden and himself transposed into music. I was pleased about his success. The Jolivet couple were there, both haughty and gracious at the same time.

When are you leaving for Israel? Needless to say, I am the one who will be giving the lecture in Aix, in the form of a conversation with Armand [Lunel], which I hope will be an affectionate, familiar and instructive homage to you. Title: The theatrical works of Darius Milhaud. You are in for a few surprises afterwards – pleasant ones, naturally. Samuel[3] will launch into a homage to Satie.

In early June I am recording *Trois mélodies* with Pierre.

Lots of kisses to you both.

Fr.

For *Socrate*, take Danco, believe me.

332. FRANCIS POULENC TO PAUL ROUART

Saturday, 24 June 1961

Mon vieux Paul,

Long live Strasbourg, which is doing me good. What a performance of the *Gloria* – I was delighted. I have never heard it done so well.

It is really not bad at all. And the fact that Agathe and Sabine were there as well made the whole occasion quite complete.

My sister adores you, in the plural. I shall be back home on Monday evening and will come and see you immediately.

I embrace you.

Francis

333. FRANCIS POULENC TO STÉPHANE AUDEL

Noizay, Saturday [23 September 1961]

My silence is unmentionable, but I am going all out in an *attempt* to finish my *Répons des Ténèbres* by 2 October. I have copied out five of the seven but two are still partially – *very* partially – incomplete.[1]

Forgive me and come and have lunch any time from Monday 2nd on. We will catch up on everything.

Much love in haste
Francis

Have you seen Lombroso who has a great deal of affection for you?

334. FRANCIS POULENC TO ARTHUR GOLD AND ROBERT FIZDALE

Hôtel Beau-Rivage, Lausanne-Ouchy, [1 November 1961]

Mes anges,

Have you played and recorded the double concerto yet?[1] Were you applauded or booed? I want the truth. I played it last night with Jacques Février. Not as polished as my 'boys' – but then, we composers do what we can.

We recorded *l'Embarquement*[2] for radio. For a really good lift, my bad boys, don't play this dissolute idyll too fast.

I have finished the *Répons des Ténèbres*. It is VERY AUSTERE but quite beautiful, I think.

How I long for the spring to bring you back to our old Europe . . .

Let me know about the recording.

I embrace you affectionately.

Poupoule

Pay my respects to the unforgettable 'hostess' of West Central Park. I still laugh whenever I think of it.[3]

335. FRANCIS POULENC TO DENISE DUVAL

Thursday [early January 1962]

Ma chère enfant,

Please understand that everything I said to you on the telephone this morning is thoroughly sensible. I am delighted about this week's [*Paris-*] *Match*, which you ought to have had for *La Voix*. You owe all this to the good fairy, via the Milles, but keep in with Dior's which is irreplaceable for

you, especially since, at the moment, Marc Bohan – who has a lot of talent –
is giving the firm a push. This is why you must do something for Suzanne
[Peignot], because they love you at Avenue Montaigne.

Now, I beg of you, prepare your concert. There is not much to do.

I know that the theatre is your only love but you must at least allow
yourself the *possibility* of appearing in recital. Don't worry, I do not intend to
involve you in endless concert tours, you have better things to do, but Italy
must be perfect. What you have to learn is negligible. Get the notes into your
head quickly, the rest will follow quite naturally. Let's not have a recurrence
of New York now that we have all the winning cards in our hands.

As I said, you need an elegant evening gown for two concerts (Trieste
and Turin) and one for the other afternoon concerts. Listen to your old
maestro, who embraces you fondly.

Fr.

ITALIAN TOUR

Depart 3rd in evening (train) for Trieste.

Arrive Trieste about 11 a.m. on 4th.

    Evening – dinner in our honour at Favello Bamfield's.

5th – concert.

6th – depart for Milan where we spend three nights as we will be brought
    back by car after the concert on 7th in Turin.

8th – lunch in honour of Duval.

    Evening – grand gala *Don Carlos* at La Scala.

9th – depart for Florence. Retire early.

10th – concert Florence.

11th – concert Perugia (80 km from Florence).

12th – depart for Rome where we stay with the Peccis.

13th – day of rest in Rome.

14th – depart for Naples. Retire early.

15th – concert Naples.

16th – plane Naples–Paris.

As you see, except for Florence–Perugia, you always have one or two
days, sometimes even three (Rome) between concerts. Distances are short.
So the whole thing will not be very tiring.

Programme:

DEBUSSY: 'Beau soir' – 'L'Echelonnement des haies' – 'La Chevelure' –
    'Mandoline' (it exists in two keys).

POULENC: (*Court paille*) – *La Voix* (with one cut which I will show
    you).

Three RAVEL.

336. Francis Poulenc to Henri Hell

[February 1962]

Cher Henri,
    What are you up to? Nothing more in *Candide.*[1] Thank heavens. Duval
had a *triumph* yesterday in Florence. I am delighted with this tour. I was
nervous. I have orchestrated five out of the seven *Répons*. What will I write
afterwards? No doubt nothing.[2] I shall be in Rome on Tuesday, in Bagnols on
the 20th, in Paris on the 28th.
    Do not forget me.

                                                              I embrace you.
                                                                        Fr.

337. Francis Poulenc to Pierre Bernac

Monday, 26 March 1962

Mon petit Pierre,
    I have finished *Les Ténèbres*. I think it is beautiful and I do not regret
having taken all this time over it as it is very well done.
    With the *Gloria* and the *Stabat* I think I have three good religious works.
May they spare me a few days of purgatory, if I do narrowly avoid going to
hell.
    It is with melancholy that I put the final full stop to this last composition
from Bagnols as Louis has decided to look for work in Cannes. After
providing the rare, few rich of Bagnols with showers, sinks and WCs, he has
no more work. His morale, aggravated by the solitude and his accident, is
very low. So he has decided to look for work in Cannes. I can only encourage
him, particularly since next winter I shall be constantly on the move. You
know that a change has fortunately taken place inside me, as it did long ago
with Raymond, and that I now think of him as a child whom I *adore*. This
makes things so much easier.
    So Bagnols of the *Gloria* and *Les Ténèbres* joins Anost in my fondest
memories. I now feel happily free of everything and am looking to
Providence for another creative period – musically, that is. I'll write a few
notes for Cocteau's *Renaud et Armide* for Baalbek this summer.[1] This trip
and the Festival of Menton, where I will play my Sonata [for flute] with
Lardé and Debussy's with my other Pierre [Fournier], will fill my summer,
for once rather disorganized. I will have my sublime Pleyel moved to my
friend André's in Cannes, where I shall be staying from time to time next
winter. And that's that.
    One summer's evening in Nazelles, Mme Henriot (Renoir's) read my

palm and predicted . . . a daughter,[2] and work – divided into clear-cut periods. Since all this has happened (she could foresee the Mass at the time I was writing *Les Biches*) I am giving in to it.

I have brought our records here. What a lot of talent I had for this *genre*, a thing of the past for me now!

And with that, I embrace you.

Fr.

338. PIERRE BERNAC TO FRANCIS POULENC

Thursday morning [March–April 1962]

Mon petit Francis,

Yes, there is the sadness of things coming to an end, of pages being turned. As for Bagnols, one may certainly say that it has done you good. The *Gloria* and *Les Ténèbres* are far from insignificant. But as you must now change the type of music you are writing, a change of scene may not be a bad thing. You are right to trust in Providence for inspiration. This has certainly worked well for you in the past. Witness, for example, *Les Dialogues*. As for the 'transference' that has taken place in you regarding Louis, this could not be better. He will always remain a dear being, an incentive to go to the Midi which you cannot do without; and Cannes – which you have always loved – could become an excellent haven for you.

I am delighted that you will have the chance to go to Baalbek in the summer. They say it is sublime and the country must be fascinating. With a bit of the Midi as well, your summer should be very pleasant.

Saw Denise very briefly. How I regret not having been able to work quietly on *Pelléas* with her. It was clear to me how much I could have told her. Having said this, I feel sure she will be very good once she has worked on the scene. For the moment, it is too dramatic and not mysterious enough, not poetic enough. I would also have liked to take out certain rhythmic distortions and certain false accents, which would have vastly improved her interpretation from the point of view of the singing. But she is not the sort of person one can easily control. She telephoned this morning to speak to me about the problem with her child. I will try to help by asking around. It is a post that could well suit somebody perfectly.

There have not been any really exciting concerts here. The one by young [Claude-Marie] Bruel from Avignon was much better than I anticipated. He has talent and a superb honesty. I assure you his *Gaspard de la nuit* was more than creditable. He also played some modern Italian pieces: Malipiero, etc. . . . very bad. Poor copy of Messiaen.

You are fortunate to be going to Venice for a few days. At this time of year it will be delightful. Let's hope that the *Pelléas* of Messrs Dussurget, Dervaux, Crochot and Co. will not be too bad . . .

As for me, I am leaving on Palm Sunday for Avignon, where I shall spend about ten days. Simone [Girard] still seems distressingly edgy . . . Yet what a pleasant life she leads.

Let me know what you think of Venice. Bon voyage!

I embrace you.

P.

339. FRANCIS POULENC TO YVONNE GOUVERNÉ

Rocamadour, 3 July 1962

How long ago it was, the time of *Les Litanies*, yet still so warm in my heart, dear Yvonne.[1]

I have asked our Holy Mother for a beautiful record of *Figure humaine* for this winter.[2]

Exquisite stay, divine weather. Have a happy summer. I embrace you.

Francis

340. FRANCIS POULENC TO PIERRE BERNAC

Bagnols-en-Forêt, 14 July 1962

Cher enfant,

I have just had Simone [Girard] on the line whom I summoned to the 'Priory'. She tells me that you are bored, which does not surprise me. Thank heavens you have your inner resources. I myself would not have held out, particularly with my poor English. Here I am in Bagnols after an *exquisite* stay in Brive, my real holiday for the year. The heat is torrid here but fortunately there is a breeze. I am going to start work on Monday. I began quite a few things on Marthe [Bosredon's] piano. I have the elements for an oboe sonata; the first movement will be elegiac, the second scherzando and the last a sort of liturgical chant. I think that writing for wind instruments is now the right solution for me.[1]

I am going to Aix on Sunday, the 22nd. I shall stay there for three days (*Seraglio*, Berganza, *Malheur* and *Noces*). I haven't had a hint of anything yet, Mélisande[2] being either asleep or out. Jacques [Février] arrived yesterday. Of course, after the dramas of Venice I am not risking a single rehearsal, especially after having played *Les Noces* 40 times. The Menton Festival promises to be dazzling. I hope the child Bernard[3] will be on form.

As for me, I am quite ready. I shall be leaving for Baalbek on the 12th. I hope I will not be too hot.

Good news from Tourrette, where Richard is playing the indulgent uncle.[4] Write to me here.

I embrace you.

Fr.

341. PIERRE BERNAC TO FRANCIS POULENC

Union Building, University of Illinois, Urbana, Illinois, 21 July [1962]

Mon petit Francis,

Thank you for your letter of 14 July. I was very happy to hear your good news, and to know that you have settled down in Bagnols and are busy with an oboe sonata. I am sure it will be played everywhere, like your flute sonata. And you are right to compose for instruments that you like and which have always inspired you.

I have looked at the catalogue of the music library here. Almost all your songs are there except: 'A sa guitare', 'La Grenouillère', 'Priez pour paix', 'Ce doux petit visage', 'Montparnasse', 'Le pont', 'Paul et Virginie', 'C' – in fact all the separate songs. The cycles are all there. I think there are collections of individual songs now, but I am not very familiar with them. Can't you get the publishers to send them? Almost all of your piano music is there – except the Sonata for two pianos. The Sonata for flute and the one for cello are also missing. Your three lyric works are there. Oddly enough, it is your choral music that is *almost entirely* missing – except the Mass, the *Ave verum* and the *Stabat*. Something ought to be done about this – tell the publishers.

It will be very annoying if Véga go bankrupt. Once again we will lose our recordings . . . Shouldn't we perhaps buy some copies ourselves? What a pity that Véga did not let Westminster have some – there would have been a certain demand for them here.

Yes, I am fairly bored here but I keep telling myself that it is thanks to this that I am able to keep up my standard of living – and that is certainly worth while. And, besides, this is the only way of securing a constant flow of pupils as, unfortunately, the French do not come to me. The life here is rather rigid and the country ugly, dull, without resources – beyond anything you can imagine. No, I cannot see you here! The temperature has fortunately been slightly less inhuman over the last few days. I must admit that I have had terrible bouts of fatigue (not a word to Simone). Thank heavens I can have a lot of rest at night. I am leaving here on the 9th and will spend 48 hours in New York to get my affairs in order. I shall be back in Paris on the 12th, will give my two days of classes at Fontainebleau, and then we leave for Edinburgh on the 19th.

When is your concert in Menton? When will you be able to get together with Bernard [Kruysen]? Naturally, I have not heard a word from him. You will have to tell me about Aix – I see you do not have any news yet. I wonder how it is all going with those ladies and gentlemen. Gérard [Souzay] has had a rough time with *Pelléas* – but you gave him a good talking-to – and I told him I knew all about not being a prophet in one's own country . . .

Write again soon. I embrace you.

P.

Simone seems extremely edgy. It is heart-breaking.

342. HENRI SAUGUET TO FRANCIS POULENC

Hôtel Jerome, Aspen (Colorado), 23 July 1962

Cher Francis,

Since my arrival here,[1] I have heard some marvellous performances of your music: first, on 14 July, the Trio for horn, trumpet and trombone, which I had not heard for some time and which has retained an extraordinary, fresh force and fantastic individuality. Then, Jenny Tourel sang your *Fiançailles pour rire* SUBLIMELY (divinely accompanied by Johannesen, a marvellous pianist). I think you would have loved her interpretation, her stage manner, her artistry: in 'Violon' (and particularly in the last song) she did astonishing things. And finally, yesterday, your *Gloria* – absolutely heavenly – with Addison (whom I prefer to Carteri, as she brings to her performances a seraphic quality which places your work on a more spiritual level). The choir (more than 200 singers) had some miraculous moments (*p*'s and *pp*'s that took your breath away) and the orchestra, which Susskind conducted magnificently, was perfect in its precision. The work had a *very great success*, as it does everywhere – this *Gloria* of yours has really become the darling of America.

My Symphony No. 3 was in the same programme and also had a huge success. Marvellously performed, what's more. I was extremely moved by a quite unexpected and very enthusiastic reception. Immense crowd (more than 2,000 people) in that Buffalo Bill tent in which the concerts take place. I arrived here on the 13th after a few days in Connecticut and a brief stay in New York. This week they are doing *La Contrebasse* and *La Voyante* at the Opera.[2] Jenny Tourel is singing and Madeleine [Milhaud] is directing. Darius is as well as can be expected. The air here is excellent (we are more than 2,000m above sea level) and the place is grandiose.

I am leaving on the 31st for Santa Fe to hear *Mavra*, *Renard* and *Le Rossignol* conducted by Stravinsky, whom I saw in New York after a concert at the Stadium for an audience of 15,000. He has aged a little but is still his same old self. I think I shall be returning (via New York where I will spend two to four days) around 8/10 August. This trip has been thrilling. Messiaen and Yvonne Loriod are expected this week. Virgil [Thomson] was here until this morning. I feel well here, the weather is perfect. Aspen, during the summer, is one of the capital centres for music. More than 500 students, with the youth of the Far West, lend a very charming character to the town. People cannot do enough for you!

Dear Francis, we think of you with affection and admiration, and I embrace you with all my heart.

Henri S.

343. FRANCIS POULENC TO IGOR STRAVINSKY

Noizay, Indre-et-Loire, 5 August 1962

Très cher Igor,

As no one has been able to give me your precise present address,[1] I am entrusting Boosey & Hawkes with the responsibility of transmitting these birthday wishes to you which, belated though they may be, are none the less warm with affection and admiration. I spent every evening in the country this spring listening to all your recordings. I still have *exactly* the same sense of wonder as when I was twenty – even more so, if that is possible!

Very recently, in Aix, *Les Noces* plunged me back into one of the most wonderful periods of my life. Alas, I do not see you any more and this truly saddens me. However, you may be sure that you are always very much in my heart.

If I no longer send you my music it is because I simply do not think it would interest you any more.

Embrace Vera tenderly, as I embrace you, dear Igor.

Yours ever, .
Francis Poulenc

How I love *A Sermon, a Narrative and a Prayer!*[2] It is marvellous.*

*At the end of this letter is a note written in ink and signed by Stravinsky: . . . *ai répondu de Santa Fé le 12 Août/62 sur une carte de visite* (. . . replied from Santa Fe on 12 August '62 on a visiting card). See letter 347.

344. FRANCIS POULENC TO PIERRE BERNAC

6 August 1962

Cher Pierre,

My paper is as good as yours! It is all I can find in Bagnols!

You must have received my letter from Menton.

Though the 'Colloque' was superb, I do not think Debussy's songs gain anything from being sung in the open air.

I am just about to leave here. Thank God – the heat here this summer makes me long for rainy Normandy.

The two sonatas are fairly well advanced.[1] Noizay will do the rest. Same proportions as the one for flute but more incisive, given the nature of these two woodwinds.

The closer we get to your arrival, the more excited Simone becomes!

Edinburgh will take care of everything. Tell me what you think of *La Atlántida* in which there is after all $\frac{1}{3}$ Falla – all the homophonic choruses, $\frac{1}{3}$ tampering and $\frac{1}{3}$ entirely bogus (this for the complete version).[2]

I will be at Le Tremblay on the 22nd and at Noizay on the 29th. Write.

I embrace you,
Fr.

The *Gloria*, with Addison, has had a *delirious success* in Aspen. Standing ovation! Flood of letters including an adorable one from Sauguet for whom things went *very well*, especially *La Contrebasse*.

345. FRANCIS POULENC TO HENRI SAUGUET

9 August 1962

Cher Henri,

Thank you for your very dear letter. I hear through Labunski that you have had a real and profound success at Aspen and that you have of course won the hearts of everyone there.

Your trip must have been great fun – you have almost made me regret not going, although America in April for *Les Ténèbres* is quite enough to satisfy my wanderlust.[1]

I am leaving tomorrow for Baalbek with little enthusiasm as I dread the heat. *Renaud et Armide* bores me and my music is of *no* interest whatever.[2] So I'll look at the ruins. In any event, I shall be in Normandy at my sister's on the 22nd. The heat has been *torrid* here. It has put me in a foul mood and I have worked badly after an excellent start in Brive. And anyway these

Festivals bore me to death. I played in Menton, which was not what you would call stimulating, with the charming Lardé!

And with these 'Memoirs of an old Grump' I embrace you both very affectionately.

Fr.

I am dying to see Jacques' *D. Carlos*.[3]

346. DARIUS MILHAUD TO FRANCIS POULENC

Aspen, 11 August 1962

Mon cher Francis,

Your lovely letter has just arrived. But it is I who ought to have written to you because your *Gloria* was a tremendous success here. And so was your *Sonate cor-trp-trb* [for horn, trumpet and trombone] followed shortly after by *Fiançailles pour rire* in which Jenny [Tourel] surpassed herself. Adele [Addison] *angelic* in the *Gloria*. The French Festival has been a triumph. Henri, *very happy*, was perfect, extremely charming and sociable, doing all the right things. His Symphony No. 3 was given a most enthusiastic *standing* ovation. Jenny was sensational in *La Voyante*, although she nearly drove us crazy by waiting until the very last minute before learning the work. *La Contrebasse*, directed by Mady, was charming proof of what can be done with students.

The Messiaens? Difficult with the Festival but also charming. She played *Le Réveil des oiseaux* and, later, *Les Oiseaux exotiques*.[1] She also gave a recital which left everyone panting, particularly when, after Debussy, Jolivet, Messiaen, etc., she played as an encore a little Andante by Mozart, quite wonderful in its simplicity. They have now left for Canada. Henri [Sauguet] spent five days in Sante Fe at Virgil [Thomson's] invitation – very big Igor festival. Then he went on to look at the Indians and, after that, spent a few days in New York before leaving again for Coutras for the marriage of his niece – very worried about all the preparations because the wedding is taking place at his home.

That is all the news from Aspen. The temperature here this year has been delightful and I am enjoying myself enormously.

What are you going to do in Baalbek? The heat must be appalling there.

Mady sends you a hug.

Your old friend,

D.M.

347. IGOR STRAVINSKY TO FRANCIS POULENC

Santa Fe
12 August 1962

Très cher Poulenc, your letter touched me deeply.[1] I too deplore the fact that we do not see each other any more, but when you say that your music no longer interests me, I must assure you that it is not a question of YOUR music; I am losing touch with practically all contemporary music. *Mouvements, Sermon . . ., Le Déluge*[2] are the latest examples of this. ET APRÈS LE DÉLUGE . . . MOI – I who never give up hope of carrying on.

Yours very affectionately,
I. Stravinsky

348. FRANCIS POULENC TO BENJAMIN BRITTEN

[Open letter written under the title 'Hommage à Benjamin Britten' and published, in French, in *Tribute to Benjamin Britten on his 50th Birthday*, Faber & Faber, 1963.]

Cher Ben,

At fifty, there you are, glorious as a young Verdi. Nobody could be more delighted than I, for as well as having a very real affection for you, I have always been in awe of the multiplicity of your gifts.

Were I a prey to jealousy – which, thank God, I am not – I think I would have expired of it long ago! Even in the few areas in which I feel secure, I have always seen you forging ahead, as often as not triumphantly.

That is why, after listening to you accompanying Peter Pears one night in Aix-en-Provence, I declared to Pierre Bernac, whom I was then partnering in a duo: 'After hearing Ben, I will never play Schubert again.'

More recently, your marvellous *Requiem* has quite shaken that little fortress of religious music in which I am now happily thriving. But, I repeat, this gives me very great joy because of my profound admiration for you.

I also recall with emotion that concert in January 1945 when we played my Concerto for two pianos at the Albert Hall. It was my first return to England after five years of isolation.

Thanks to you, too, *Les Mamelles de Tirésias* was performed to absolute perfection at your Aldeburgh Festival. You yourself played the 'piano-orchestra' part.

In memory of all these things, allow me to regard you as *mon frère d'outre-Manche** (a great honour for me) and permit me to embrace you very affectionately.

Francis Poulenc
October '62

*'My brother across the Channel'.

349. FRANCIS POULENC TO ROSE DERCOURT-PLAUT

Gritti Palace-Hotel, Venice, 9 December 1962

Ma chère Rose,

I am delighted to know that your concert went so well. This does not surprise me as you were in good form this autumn.

I am writing from Venice where I am spending three days between adjudicating in Trieste and preparing *Les Mamelles* which will go on in Milan on 2 March. The weather is unbelievably beautiful and Venice, empty of tourists, is delectably melancholy, which is in keeping with 'my mind'.* In fact I am about to spend my last Christmas in Bagnols as my 'boy', who has sold his house, is going to become manager of a bar in Cannes. I will of course still see him but it will not be quite the same. As I adore him – not physically any more, thank heavens, but rather as if he were my child – this makes me sad. But that's life.

Unfortunately, at times like these it is certainly not my work that takes my mind off things. I know it is very wrong but my music causes me more anxiety than enjoyment. But let's discuss it nevertheless. Apart from the financial aspect, I think the programme for 10 April is well conceived.[1] At the instigation of Mr Schwartz I have agreed to a baritone – Mr Gramm[2] (Bernac says he is excellent) – who will sing *Priez pour paix*, *Le Bestiaire* and two *Chansons villageoises*. The other day I played my Sonata for clarinet. It sounds good. So does the one for oboe. My apartment has been redone. It is very cheerful. Thank heavens!

The whole family is well. The Raymonds are coming to Paris for the New Year. As Christmas is approaching I send you and Fred my fondest wishes for 1963.

Let me know what happens about our session for Radio.

I embrace you affectionately, and Fred, too.

Francis

Above all, no moralizing, please!

350. FRANCIS POULENC TO ROSE DERCOURT-PLAUT

22 January 1963

Belle dame,

I have booked for Tuesday 2 April. I shall be arriving in New York, by Air France, at about 7 o'clock in the evening. Can you reserve a room at the Wyndham for me from the 2nd to the 17th, date of my departure for Chicago.

---

*In English in the original text.

Bernac, Suzanne Peignot and Debussy's stepdaughter[1] will be arriving on
30 March. Perhaps include them for your party. Arrange everything as best
you can for the recordings (the programme is *perfect*) but not on the night of
the 5th as I have a dinner at Bobsy Goodspeed's.[2] It is horribly cold, for Paris.
I am leaving for Holland for four days. Brrr! Fortunately I shall be going to
Cannes on 4 February. Then Milan for *Les Mamelles*. A very big hug to you
both.

Francis

On Saturday 26 January 1963 Francis Poulenc gave a concert in Maastricht
in Holland, with Denise Duval. After the concert, he sent flowers to her
hotel room, with a card saying:

> *Ma Denise,*
> *Je te dois ma dernière joie.*
> *Ton pauvre Fr.*

[My Denise, to you I owe the latest (? the last) of my joys. Your poor Fr.]

Poulenc returned to Paris on the following Monday. On the Tuesday, he
telephoned Denise Duval to say that he would lunch with her the next day
but on Wednesday morning, the 30th, he called again. His voice was hoarse
and he said he felt he should not go out. At one o'clock he died of a heart
attack.

Poulenc's Correspondents

ARAGON, Louis (1897–1982). French poet, novelist, and essayist, one of the founders of the Surrealist movement and, with André Breton and Philippe Soupault, of the review *Littérature* (1919–24). In 1927 Aragon joined the Communist Party, becoming spokesman for the movement and a committed political activist. This resulted in his eventual estrangement from the Surrealists. He was later editor of the Communist weekly on arts and letters, *Les Lettres françaises*. Poulenc met Aragon during the First World War, at Adrienne Monnier's bookshop. He set only two poems by Aragon, 'C' and 'Fêtes galantes', both written during the Second World War.

AUDEL, Stéphane (*d.* 1984). A devoted friend of Poulenc, the actor Stéphane Audel has left a touching legacy in his series of fourteen interviews with Francis Poulenc broadcast by Radio Suisse-Romande in 1953, 1955 and 1962, and published in 1963 by La Palatine, Paris and Geneva, under the title *Moi et mes amis* (English translation by James Harding, *My Friends and myself*, Dobson Books, London, 1978). In his preface to this book Stéphane Audel writes:

> When he was alone at Noizay, [Poulenc] never failed to make up a hand at cards in the company of the local innkeeper, the chauffeur and the carpenter, with whom he was as much at ease as in the salons of the Princesse de Polignac or the Vicomtesse de Noailles. A guest in princely palaces and in the luxury abodes of international society, he would sometimes spend weeks on end in a monk-like room in Provence and feel entirely happy there, provided he was allowed to have a piano. [*FP-MMA* p. 13]

BAKST, Léon (1866–1924). Russian artist who, as chief stage designer for Diaghilev's Russian Ballet, changed a generation's taste in theatre design (and also in fashion and household furnishing). After settling in Paris, he created sets for the tragedies of d'Annunzio, one of which, *Le Martyre de Saint-Sébastien*, with music by Debussy, is the subject of Poulenc's letter (No. 40).

BARTÓK, Béla (1881–1945). Poulenc met the Hungarian composer Bartók in 1922, when he came to Paris to perform his second piano concerto there. Poulenc found his music powerfully original: 'Bartók has an incomparable sense of form. One has to go back to Beethoven to find so much fantasy within the rules.' (*ECR* p. 183). Poulenc included Bartók among his seven favourite composers of the twentieth century, with Debussy, Stravinsky, Satie, Falla, Ravel and Prokofiev (*ECR* p. 187).

BEAUMONT, Comtesse Etienne de. Born into a family of noble Flemish origin, Edith de Taisne married Comte Etienne de Beaumont, wealthy patron of the arts, balletomane and lavish entertainer. Their palatial eighteenth-century Paris residence in the rue Duroc was the scene of many of the most famous costume-balls in the first half of this century. The Comtesse de Beaumont was an elegant, cultivated woman who read Greek poetry and published a translation of Sappho in 1950, with illustrations by Marie Laurencin. She and her husband are said to have served as models for the Comte and Comtesse in Raymond Radiguet's novel *Le Bal du Comte d'Orgel*.

BERNAC, Pierre [Pierre Louis Bertin] (1899–1979). French baritone, teacher and author. He changed his name from Bertin to Bernac when he began his professional career because there was a well-known actor, who also sang, called Pierre Bertin. Born on 12 January 1899, five days after Poulenc, Bernac met Poulenc in 1926, formed a duo with him in 1935 that lasted for 24 years, and continued to teach and give master classes on French song, always including Poulenc's works, for a further twenty years. Over 90 of Poulenc's 145 songs were written for Bernac to sing. To Stéphane Audel, Poulenc said that the three most important encounters of his career – those that profoundly influenced his art – were with Wanda Landowska, Paul Eluard and Pierre Bernac. And to Simone Girard, he said: 'There is something so healthy about Bernac's voice, he is so vocally sound, that I can make him do anything I want. I need his voice and I do not need the voice of anyone else.' (*PB-IP*)

Poulenc dedicated to Bernac 'Rôdeuse au front de verre' (from *Cinq poèmes de Paul Eluard*), 'Figure de force brûlante et farouche' (from *Tel jour telle nuit*) and 'Tu vois le feu du soir' (from *Miroirs brûlants*).

BOSREDON, Marthe. Friend of Poulenc who lived in Brive. She was a fine amateur pianist, with a deep love of music and literature. Poulenc stayed with her during the summer of 1940, after he was demobilized. The initial sketches for his Sonata for cello and piano, and for *L'Histoire de Babar, le petit éléphant*, date from this stay in Brive. Both works are partly dedicated to Marthe Bosredon. She is also the dedicatee of the songs 'Hôtel' (from *Banalités*) and 'C'est ainsi que tu es' (from *Métamorphoses*).

BRITTEN, Benjamin (1913–76). English composer, pianist and conductor, lifelong partner of the tenor Peter Pears (1910–86), who inspired much of his vocal music. In 1947 they settled in Aldeburgh and, in the following year, founded the Aldeburgh Festival, to which Poulenc contributed in the mid-1950s. Poulenc performed his Concerto for two pianos with Britten at the Albert Hall in 1945, and again at the Royal Festival Hall in 1955. In the programme notes for a concert tribute to Poulenc in Thorpeness on 15 June 1964, Britten and Pears wrote: 'One of his most adorable qualities was that he was incapable of being anything but himself – a delightful friend and a lovable musician.'

CASA FUERTE, Yvonne de (1895–1984). Born Yvonne Giraud, she married Illan Alvarez de Toledo, Marquis de Casa Fuerte. She was a gifted violinist and classmate of Milhaud at the Paris Conservatoire. She was the founder and president of the music society La Sérénade. From 1941–55 she lived in the USA, where she continued to play the violin. Poulenc greatly valued her friendship and her opinions on music. He dedicated to her his cantata on poems by Edward James, *Sécheresses*.

CHAGALL, Marc (1887–1985). The Russian-born artist Chagall collaborated in 1946 with Paul Eluard on a volume entitled *Le Dur Désir de durer*. For this volume Eluard chose drawings by Chagall and illustrated them in poetry. The first poem, 'A Marc Chagall', was reprinted two years later in Eluard's collection on painters, *Voir*. Poulenc, intrigued by Eluard's idea of painting in poetry and wanting in turn to paint in music, chose 'A Marc Chagall', with six other poems from *Voir*, for his cycle, *Le Travail du peintre*. Chagall's letter to Poulenc (No. 285) thanks him for the manuscript of this work.

COCTEAU, Jean (1889–1963). French poet, novelist, playwright, artist, art critic, choreographer, actor, film director, and publicist – among other things – for Satie and Les Six. His role in the arts is aptly described by the bookseller Adrienne Monnier: 'Cocteau is never the first to stand in the breach, but it is always he who hoists the flag.' (*AM-RO* p. 101). For Poulenc, he was '. . . our manager of genius . . . our brilliant spokesman . . . our poetic chronicler . . . our loyal and exquisite friend.' (*ECR* p. 45; *FP-MMA* p. 52). Poulenc's association with Cocteau began about 1917 and lasted until the end of his life (he and Cocteau died in the same year). Yet Poulenc made only two early settings of poems by Cocteau, the song 'Toréador' (1918) and the set of three songs *Cocardes* (1919), then waited 40 years before setting two more texts by Cocteau, *La Voix humaine* (1958) and *La Dame de Monte-Carlo* (1961). The letters show that, in the year before his death, Poulenc began to think about writing an opera on Cocteau's play *La Machine infernale*.

COLETTE [Sidonie-Gabrielle] (1873–1954). Poulenc set only one text by the French writer Colette, *Le Portrait* (1938), a prose-poem which she gave him imprinted on a large gauze handkerchief. He felt that his music expressed 'very inadequately' his admiration for her. (*DMS* p. 45). He saw her as 'one of those rare beings for whom growing old is a constantly enriching experience'. (*HH-FP* p. 216). An unpublished, undated letter from Colette to Poulenc captures quite simply the essence of their relationship:

> Ah! quell' joi', quell' joi', quell' joi',
> J'ai Francis Poulenc chez moi!
> Je vous embrasse. A vendredi. Merci. Colette.

COLLAER, Paul (1891–1989). Belgian musicologist and pianist, former teacher of physics and chemistry, who became one of the leading promoters in Belgium of avant-garde music. In 1920, with the support of the Pro Arte Quartet, Collaer founded the *Concerts Pro Arte* which specialized in contemporary chamber music and song recitals. From 1937 to 1953 he was musical director of the Flemish service of Belgian Radio. His publications on music include a study of Stravinsky

(1930), a History of Modern Music (1961) and a comprehensive study of all Milhaud's works (1947), updated and reissued by Editions Slatkine (Geneva, Paris) in 1982, with catalogue of Milhaud's works compiled by Madeleine Milhaud and discography by Francine Bloch. Poulenc dedicated his third Nocturne for piano to Paul Collaer.

CONRAD, Doda (*b.* 1905). Bass of Polish origin, who spent many years in the USA. He is the son of the singer Marya Freund. He is well-known for his recordings of Monteverdi, Brahms and Rameau as a member of Nadia Boulanger's Ensemble Vocal. Poulenc wrote two songs as birthday celebrations, both requested by Doda Conrad: 'La Souris', for Marya Freund's 80th birthday, and 'Mazurka', from *Mouvements du coeur*, a homage to Chopin on his centenary. Poulenc's song 'Hymne' on a poem by Ronsard was written for Doda Conrad, and dedicated to him. The friendship between Marya Freund, Doda Conrad, and Francis Poulenc is best conveyed in an unpublished letter from Conrad to Poulenc, dated 1961:

> My *illustrissime* mother is moved to tears at the mere sound of your name, and your autographed effigies, under glass, have been installed with great pomp, beside those of Brahms, Schoenberg and our Francis of 1922. Je t'embrasse, Doda.

DERCOURT-PLAUT, Rose. Polish-American soprano who met Poulenc during his first tour of America in 1948–49, and thereafter came on regular visits to France to work with him. In the Fred and Rose Plaut Archives at Yale University, New Haven, are some 60 letters from Poulenc to Rose Dercourt-Plaut, written from 1951 until the month of his death, January 1963. The letters bear testimony to his great affection for the singer and her husband Fred Plaut, sound engineer who worked on Poulenc's recordings for CBS, and accomplished photographer (many of Poulenc's favourite photographs were the creations of Fred Plaut). Poulenc dedicated his song 'Nuage' (from *Deux mélodies 1956*) to Rose Dercourt-Plaut and he made one recording with her in 1957 (Turnabout [Vox] TV 4489). In a letter written in the same year, he says: 'Write to me, and above all, *work well.* When I reprimand you it is in my capacity as teacher and not as affectionate friend – "he who loves well chastises well" says the proverb. I embrace you both tenderly.'

DIAGHILEV, Serge de [Sergey Pavlovich] (1872–1929). The illustrious Russian impresario moved to Paris in 1906, introduced the Ballets Russes in 1909, and changed the development of the arts in Western Europe. Poulenc's first major work, the ballet *Les Biches* (1923), was the result of a commission from Diaghilev. Poulenc said:

> My collaboration with the Ballets Russes was an unhoped for bit of luck, a great happiness, the warmest of the memories of my youth . . . Dear Diaghilev, irreplaceable Diaghilev, you were the wonderment of my twenties, not only because you gave me your confidence and your esteem, but because I owe you my most violent aesthetic shocks. [*ECR* p. 50]

DUREY, Louis (1888–1979). French composer who came to music in his adulthood, after studying languages and accountancy and working in his father's foundry as a book-keeper. At the age of nineteen he began to go to the opera and allegedly watched every performance of *Pelléas et Mélisande* before the war. He took private lessons in composition from a teacher at the Schola Cantorum, became a member of Les Nouveaux Jeunes and was included in the group Les Six. One of his first interpreters, Jane Bathori, said of him:

> In his early days as a composer, Louis Durey produced quite a number of works, mostly songs, on poems chosen with great taste and care. But because of a shyness and a fear of displaying his works beside those of his colleagues, he retired within himself and was forgotten – at first a little and then a lot. [*BIRS* No. 15, p. 243]

Durey left Paris and went to live in St Tropez, devoting his life to Communism, and to writing works that would serve the cause, such as the cantata *La Longue marche* to words by Mao Tse Tung (1949). Poulenc dedicated his first song cycle, *Le Bestiaire* to Louis Durey (see letter 19, note 1).

DUVAL, Denise (*b*. 1923). French soprano who, after studying dramatic art and opera at the Bordeaux Conservatoire, began her career in Paris at the Folies-Bergères. Later, while preparing for her début at the Opéra-Comique in *Madame Butterfly*, she was brought to Poulenc's notice by the producer Max de Rieux. Poulenc was in search of a singer for the title role in *Les Mamelles de Tirésias*. Duval remembers that when Poulenc heard her sing, he began shouting and gesticulating, yelling: 'Oh! She is exactly the woman I need! Max, you're a genius!' (*FP-ASO* p. 103). On 3 June 1947, she made her début at the Opéra-Comique, not as Butterfly, but as Thérèse-Tirésias. She became Poulenc's favourite leading lady. For her, he wrote the leading part in *Dialogues des Carmélites* (Blanche); *La Voix humaine*; and *La Dame de Monte-Carlo* (dedicated to Duval). His last song cycle *La Courte paille* was written for her to sing to her six-year-old son and dedicated to Duval and her first husband Richard Schilling. She is also the dedicatee, with Raymond Destouches, of Poulenc's Concerto for piano. After Bernac's retirement, Poulenc accompanied Duval in concert tours in Europe and the USA. To Claude Rostand, he confessed: 'When I met Denise Duval, I was immediately struck by her luminous voice, her beauty, her elegance, and especially by that ringing laugh of hers which is so marvellous in *Les Mamelles*.' (*ECR* p. 150). To Bernac, in a letter dated 4 August, he wrote: 'For me, this girl is pure sunlight.'

ELUARD, Paul [Eugène Emile Paul Grindel] (1895–1952). French poet, founder – with Breton, Aragon and Soupault – of the Surrealist movement in poetry, later one of the most important lyric voices of the twentieth century, committed to the ideals of freedom, brotherhood and love. 'Paul Eluard was truly my spiritual brother – through him I learnt how to express the most secret part of myself and especially my vocal lyricism.' (*H à FP* p. 13)

Poulenc met Eluard in 1917 at Adrienne Monnier's bookshop, but it was not until 1935 that he felt able to set Eluard's poetry to music. Thereafter he wrote 34 songs and three choral works to poems by Eluard. His song 'Voyage à Paris' (from *Banalités*) is dedicated to Eluard. Poulenc considered his meeting with the poet as one of the most important encounters of his life:

> I immediately took to Eluard, firstly, because he was the only Surrealist who tolerated music and then because his entire poetic output is sheer musical vibration. [*ECR* p. 93]
>
> If on my tomb could be inscribed: Here lies Francis Poulenc, the musician of Apollinaire and Eluard, I would consider this to be my greatest claim to fame. [*DMS* p. 69]

ESTY, Alice (*b.* 1904). American soprano who studied with Pierre Bernac and who commissioned many contemporary composers to write works for her, including Lennox Berkeley, Darius Milhaud and Vittorio Rieti. Alice Esty is the dedicatee of Poulenc's *Le Travail du peintre*. She gave the world première of this work in Paris in 1957, with Poulenc accompanying, and the first American performance, with David Stimer, at Carnegie Recital Hall, in the following year (see note 1 to letter 276). After Poulenc's death, Alice Esty commissioned a series of songs to his memory, which she sang – again at Carnegie Recital Hall, New York – on 13 January 1964. The following composers contributed to this *Hommage à Poulenc*: Henk Badings, Lennox Berkeley, Henri Dutilleux, Frank Martin, Darius Milhaud, Vittorio Rieti, Ned Rorem, Manuel Rosenthal, Henri Sauguet, Germaine Tailleferre, Virgil Thomson, Ben Weber.

FALLA, Manuel de (1876–1946). Poulenc met the Spanish composer Manuel de Falla in 1918 at the home of Ricardo Viñes and remained in contact with him until he and his sister left Spain for the Argentine in 1939. Poulenc dedicated his Trio for piano, oboe and bassoon (1926) to Falla: 'I dedicated that little trio to Falla to show him as best I could my loving admiration.' (*FP-MMA* p. 122)

Poulenc was profoundly moved by Falla's religious fervour, his spiritual intensity, and his mysticism: 'It has often been said of Falla that he was inscrutable, yet nothing could be further from the truth. Falla was quite the opposite – he was the purest of mystics, limpid, like a piece of crystal.' (*FP-MMA* p. 118)

GIRARD, Simone (1898–1985). Friend of Pierre Bernac until his death in 1979. Simone Girard was secretary and organizer of the renowned music society in Avignon, the Société Avignonnaise de Concerts. Winifred Radford said of her:

> She was a very good pianist, not professional, but an excellent musician with unfailing musical perception and taste in her organization of the concerts and in her choice of programmes and performers. [*BIRS* No. 70–71, p. 775]

She was married to Dr Pierre Girard, who died in 1955. She first met Bernac and Poulenc when she engaged them to give a recital for her society in 1936. They returned regularly to perform in Avignon, soon becoming close friends. Poulenc wrote the following dedication to her on the score of his *Stabat Mater*: 'To the valiant, the faithful, the affectionate, the tenacious, the heroic Simone Girard, with my loving friendship and my blessings. Dom Francesco, Avignon, 11 November 1951.'

GOLD AND FIZDALE, Arthur Gold (1917–90) and Robert Fizdale (*b*. 1918). American duo pianists and authors whose partnership lasted for close on 50 years. They met Poulenc in 1948 during their first visit to Europe and performed his Concerto for two pianos in Paris the following year. When Poulenc heard this performance, he promised to write a work specially for them. This resulted in the Sonata for two pianos (1953), with dedication to Gold and Fizdale. *L'Embarquement pour Cythère* and *Elégie* were also written with them in mind. Other composers who wrote works for Gold and Fizdale include John Cage, Darius Milhaud, Luciano Berio, Germaine Tailleferre, Virgil Thomson, Vittorio Rieti, Ned Rorem and Paul Bowles. Gold and Fizdale are the authors of biographies of Misia Sert (1980) and Sarah Bernhardt (1991), and of *The Gold and Fizdale Cookbook* (1984).

GOUDEKET, Maurice (1889–1977). French writer and journalist, born in Paris of a French mother and a Dutch father. He was a classmate of Cocteau at the Lycée Condorcet. At the age of sixteen Goudeket discovered the novels of Colette. He met her some twenty years later and married her ten years after that. The marriage – Colette's third – took place in April 1935. She was 62. Goudeket was 45. He remained her companion until she died, aged 81. His memoirs on their life together, *Près de Colette*, were published by Flammarion in 1955. Goudeket's second marriage was to Sanda Dancovia, widow of the couturier Lucien Lelong.

GOUVERNÉ, Yvonne (1890–1983). French chorus master and musicologist, conductor of the French radio choir, Les Choeurs de la RTF, from 1935 until the 1960s, and of an early music choir, La Société de Musique d'Autrefois. Through her teacher, the composer and conductor, André Caplet, she met Bernac in the early twenties and became his *répététrice*. For ten years, she worked with him every day, accompanying him in most of his early concerts. When Bernac and Poulenc formed their duo, she continued to coach them. From 1935–39, she spent her summer holidays with them, working on their new repertoire. Poulenc never ceased to value her friendship and her advice. To her, he dedicated 'Nous avons fait la nuit' (final song in the cycle *Tel jour telle nuit*) and the second of his *Quatre motets pour un temps de pénitence*. In an address she gave at Rocamadour to commemorate the 10th anniversary of Poulenc's death, Yvonne Gouverné said: 'Richly gifted, Francis Poulenc was, beneath a somewhat nonchalant exterior, the most unconventional of people. We loved him because he was HE and everything about him remains irreplaceable.' (*FP-ROC* p. 9)

GREY, Madeleine (1897–1979). French soprano who devoted her career to contemporary song. She gave the first performance of Ravel's *Deux Mélodies hébraïques* with orchestral accompaniment in 1920, and of Fauré's song cycle *Mirages*. Poulenc sometimes accompanied Madeleine Grey in recital. He made a record with her in January 1938 but, on hearing the test pressings, advised her not to allow it to be released (see letters 134 and 137).

HELL, Henri (1916–91). French writer and critic, also accomplished pianist, born in Caracas, Venezuela. After studies in law and philosophy, he devoted himself to his two equal passions, literature and music, contributing critical articles in both disciplines to numerous journals and newspapers. From 1940–47 he was co-editor of the review *Fontaine*. He was later associated with the French publishing firm of Fayard. Henri Hell met Poulenc in the mid 1940s and remained a close and valued friend of the composer. It was after reading Hell's article on *Les Mamelles de Tirésias* and *Figure humaine* in the September 1947 issue of *Fontaine* (no. 61) that Poulenc urged him to write a study of his music. This resulted some ten years later in Henri Hell's *Francis Poulenc – musicien français*, published in 1958 by Plon, and in 1978, in a revised edition, by Fayard. Henri Hell is the dedicatee of Poulenc's *Improvisation* No. 14 for piano (1958).

HONEGGER, Arthur (1892–1955). Swiss composer who spent most of his life in France. He formed a firm friendship with Milhaud while studying at the Paris Conservatoire and was included in Les Six, despite his very different tastes and tendencies. Honegger found Satie uninteresting and Cocteau too iconoclastic. He admired the serious and the austere in music, revered Bach, and felt an affinity for the music of Wagner, Richard Strauss and Schoenberg. Poulenc met him in 1917 at the home of the singer Jane Bathori. He found Honegger intimidating and remote, an impression that was to persist for some years:

> Quite frankly, Arthur found my music too light and I found his too heavy! Much later, we formed a quite different opinion of each other but by then we had already gone entirely different ways. We held each other in great esteem but only developed a real liking for each other's music towards the end of Honegger's life. [*FP-MMA* p. 148]

Honegger's autobiography, *Je suis compositeur*, was published in 1951 (Editions du Conquistador). In 1962 Poulenc dedicated his Sonata for clarinet and piano to Honegger's memory.

HUGO, Jean (1894–1984). French artist, stage designer and illustrator, great-grandson of the poet Victor Hugo. A friend of Cocteau, Radiguet, Paul Morand, and the Groupe des Six, Jean Hugo designed the costumes – among other things – for *Les Mariés de la Tour Eiffel* in 1921. From 1919–29 he was married to the artist Valentine Gross (see below). Jean Hugo's letter to Poulenc (No. 277) indicates that Poulenc had asked him to design the sets for the Paris production of *Dialogues des Carmélites* in 1957, an undertaking that Hugo felt unable to accept.

HUGO, Valentine (1887–1968). Born Valentine Gross, she was a painter, designer and illustrator. In a series of celebrated drawings and sketches, she produced the most extensive pictorial documentation of the Russian Ballet in Paris, recording Nijinsky in nearly all his roles. She designed sets for the Vieux-Colombier performances of the group known as Les Nouveaux Jeunes (out of which grew Les Six). She was a close friend of Cocteau and Satie, who were witnesses at her marriage to Jean Hugo in 1919. After her divorce in 1929, she formed an association with the Surrealist poets, becoming the companion of André Breton.

She worked closely with Paul Eluard until his death, illustrating many of his collections of poetry. Poulenc dedicated to her his piano piece *Mouvements perpétuels*, and two songs: 'Il la prend dans ses bras' (from *Cinq poèmes de Paul Eluard*) and 'Une Roulotte couverte en tuiles' (from *Tel jour telle nuit*).

JACOB, Max (1876–1944). French poet, novelist and painter, born into a Jewish family in Britanny. He moved to Paris in 1901, frequenting the bohemian circles of Picasso and Apollinaire and oscillating between decadence and penitence. After seeing a vision of Christ on the wall of his room in Montmartre, he converted to Catholicism and later retired into semi-seclusion at the monastery of Saint-Benoît-sur-Loire. At the age of 68, Max Jacob was arrested by the Gestapo and taken to the concentration camp at Drancy, where he died in 1944. Poulenc met Max Jacob in 1917, introduced by the fifteen-year-old Raymond Radiguet. Poulenc felt that beneath the verbal clowning, the puns and the parodies, one of the fundamentals of Max Jacob's character was fear – fear of damnation, fear of not being liked, of displeasing Picasso, of quarrelling with Breton and Eluard, fear of his friends Reverdy and Cocteau. 'He was a great-hearted and sensitive man . . . a Venus of Bohemianism . . . who ended his life in exemplary devotion.' (*FP-MMA* pp. 94, 109, 110). Poulenc's *Chansons bretons*, *Le Bal masqué* and *Parisiana* are settings of texts by Max Jacob.

KOECHLIN, Charles (1867–1950). French composer and teacher. On the advice of Darius Milhaud, Poulenc studied harmony and counterpoint with Koechlin from 1921–1924 and remained in contact with him throughout his life. Referring to him affectionately as 'my master with the beard of a river god' Poulenc said of Koechlin:

> His knowledge was prodigious but even more marvellous was his ability to adapt to each pupil's needs. [*FP-MMA* p. 41]
> My choral music owes everything to Charles Koechlin. He understood my eminently harmonic nature. He gave me the chorales of Bach and made me harmonize them in four parts. That is how I learnt the art of writing for voices. [*FP-PG*]

LANDOWSKA, Wanda (1879–1959). Polish-born pianist and harpsichordist who initiated the revival of interest in the harpsichord and its repertoire in the twentieth century. She taught at the Schola Cantorum, the Ecole Normale de Musique, and lectured at the Sorbonne. In 1927 she founded a school for the study of early music at Saint-Leu-la-Fôret. In 1941 she moved to the USA. Among the works she inspired were Falla's Concerto for harpsichord and Poulenc's *Concert champêtre*. Poulenc met Landowska in 1923 at the home of the Princesse de Polignac:

> Meeting Landowska was an event of major importance in my career. I have for Wanda Landowska as much artistic respect as human tender-ness. I am proud to be her friend and will never be able to express how much I owe to her. It was she who gave me the key to Bach's keyboard music. It was she who taught me all I know about the French

harpsichordists. What is miraculous about her is that she makes the music of the past immediate and alive. [*ECR* pp. 74–75]

Poulenc dedicated to Landowska the *Concert champêtre* and the seventh of his *Huit chansons polonaises*.

LAURENCIN, Marie (1885–1956). French painter, natural daughter of a Frenchwoman of Creole descent. Picasso introduced her to Apollinaire in 1908. Her stormy liaison with the poet lasted until 1912, during which time she inspired much of his poetry. In 1914 she married a German artist, Baron Otto von Wätgen and fled to Spain with him during the war. She divorced him in 1921 and returned permanently to Paris. The devoted companion of her later years was Armand Lowengard, member of the Duveen family and nephew of the art collector and dealer, René Gimpel. Among her stage designs, Marie Laurencin created the décor for Poulenc's ballet *Les Biches* (1924) and for the birthday tribute to Jeanne Dubost, *L'Eventail de Jeanne* (1929). Marie Laurencin's portraits, like her theatre décor and book illustrations, are all distinctive. Albert Flament said of her: 'Marie Laurencin looks like her life and her pictures look like her. Everything is one homogeneous whole.' (*MLC*)

Poulenc dedicated his song 'L'Anguille' to her (from *Quatre poèmes de Guillaume Apollinaire*).

LEGUERNEY, Jacques (*b.* 1906). French composer known especially for his songs, mainly settings of verses by sixteenth-century French poets. Leguerney's formal training in composition – with Nadia Boulanger – lasted for less than a year. Encouraged by the advice and interest of Albert Roussel, Leguerney pursued his own style of composition, producing more than 60 songs. Many of these were commissioned and premièred by the baritone Gérard Souzay, his sister the soprano Geneviève Touraine, and the pianist Jacqueline Bonneau. Bernac and Poulenc also included songs by Leguerney in some of their recitals. Other compositions include three ballets and numerous chamber works.

LEHMANN, Maurice (1895–1974). French theatre director who began his career as an actor, first at the Comédie Française and then at the Théâtre de la Porte Saint Martin, where he played opposite Mistinguett. For more than twenty years, Lehmann was director of the Théâtre du Châtelet which he made famous for its lavish productions of *opérettes à grand spectacle*. Lehmann was appointed director of the Paris Opéra from 1945 to 1946 (assisted by Reynaldo Hahn), and from 1951 to 1955 (assisted by Emmanuel Bondeville).

LINOSSIER, Raymonde (1897–1930). Close childhood friend of Poulenc who greatly influenced his taste in reading and who introduced him to the literary world that frequented the bookshop of Adrienne Monnier, *La Maison des Amis des Livres*. Raymonde Linossier was the author of *Bibi-la-Bibiste* (1917), dedicated to Poulenc. After studies in both Law and Orientalism, she was admitted to the Paris bar when she was 24 but soon became more fascinated by Orientalism and joined the Musée Guimet where she worked from 1923 until her death, at age 33, from an intestinal obstruction. She was buried holding in her hands the manuscript of Poulenc's *Les Biches*. Her friend, the poet Léon-Paul Fargue paid homage to her in his poem 'La Violette noire'. Poulenc dedicated to her his Sonata for horn, trumpet and trombone, and 'Epitaphe' for voice and piano. He dedicated to the memory of Raymonde Linossier his song 'Ce doux petit visage', his ballet, *Les Animaux modèles*, and 'Voyage' (from *Calligrammes*).

MANCEAUX, Brigitte (1914–63). Poulenc's niece, close friend and confidante. She was the elder daughter of his sister, Jeanne, and André Manceaux. Fifteen years younger than Poulenc, Brigitte was a gifted pianist and a discriminating musician. Poulenc set much store by her opinion of his work. He dedicated to her his *Improvisation* for piano (No. 3). She died tragically at the age of 49, following an operation, three months after the death of Poulenc. She is buried in the same tomb as Poulenc in the cemetery of Père Lachaise in Paris.

MILHAUD, Darius (1892–1974). French composer, conductor, pianist and teacher. He was a member of the group known as Les Six. He wrote more than 400 works of all genres and was professor of composition at the Paris Conservatoire and in the USA. His 'Olympian wisdom and Buddha-like serenity' were legendary. (Claude Rostand, *ECR* pp. iv–v). In 1917 he went to Rio de Janeiro as secretary to the poet Paul Claudel, then ambassador for France. 'Milhaud's presence among us dates effectively from his return from Brazil,' Poulenc said.

> When he came back from Brazil, I was totally smitten, an emotion as valid in friendship as in love. How appealing he was, this hearty Mediterranean, dressed in pale grey, with his rhinoceros-skin cane and his strawberry-pink and lemon-yellow ties. How entertaining he was, with his stories of the tropics, and how delightful it was to hear him playing – with that adorably nonchalant touch – his 'albums de voyage', *Saudades do Brazil* and *Le Boeuf sur le toit*. What a vital source of music and what a magnificent character! [*ECR* pp. 43–44; *FP-MMA* p. 52]

Some 30 years later, to celebrate Milhaud's return to France from the USA after the war, Poulenc wrote, and dedicated to Milhaud, *Les Mamelles de Tirésias*. Milhaud's memoirs were reissued in 1987 under the title *Ma vie heureuse* (Belfond, Paris).

MONNIER, Adrienne (1892–1955). French writer who, from 1915–51, owned the Paris bookshop *La Maison des Amis des Livres* at 7 rue de l'Odéon. She was the close friend of the American Sylvia Beach (1887–1962), owner of the English bookshop *Shakespeare and Company*, located opposite Adrienne Monnier's. Both these bookshops were celebrated meeting-places for avant-garde writers and are vividly recalled in Monnier's *Rue de l'Odéon*, reissued by Albin Michel, Paris, in 1989. Poulenc first went to Monnier's bookshop in October 1917. Monnier describes her impressions of him in a tribute to their mutual friend Raymonde Linossier:

> Francis Poulenc came to the bookshop, alone, a few days after the first visit of Raymonde. He was carrying in his arms an enormous pot of flowers, destined for some relative in the area, and he had put on his best

air of a baby elephant whose nose has not yet been pulled.*[AM-GAZ
p. 65]

At Monnier's bookshop, Poulenc heard Apollinaire read his own poetry, and first met Paul Eluard. And he saw Satie playing his *Socrate* there, with Suzanne Balguerie singing all the parts. Poulenc and Adrienne Monnier remained firm friends until her suicide in 1955. Suffering from Ménière's Disease, a disorder of the inner ear that left her with unremitting tinnitus, she took an overdose of sleeping tablets. See Poulenc's postscript to letter 265.

MUNCH, Charles (1891–1968). Alsatian conductor and violinist, born in Strasbourg. He succeeded Koussevitzky as music director of the Boston Symphony Orchestra from 1949–62. With this orchestra he accompanied Poulenc in the first performance of his Concerto for piano and orchestra in January 1950, and also gave the first performance of Poulenc's *Gloria* in January 1961. In the same year Munch recorded Poulenc's Concerto for organ with the Boston Symphony Orchestra and Berj Zamkochian (RCA Victor LM 2567). In 1967, the year before his death, Munch formed the Orchestre de Paris with the conductor Serge Baudo.

PECCI-BLUNT, Contessa Mimi [Anna Laetitia]. Anna Laetitia Pecci, known as Mimi, was the great-niece of Pope Leo XIII. She was married to an American, Cecil Blunt (originally Blumenthal). Their residence in Rome, which included a private theatre, played a significant role in Italian musical life. In 1933 Contessa Pecci-Blunt founded a music society together with the composers Vittorio Rieti and Mario Labroca. The concerts organized by this society took place in spring, at the home of the Conte and Contessa Pecci-Blunt, and were known as the Concerti di Primavera. The society was closely associated with La Sérénade in Paris and had as its objective the introduction of contemporary foreign – and particularly French – musicians to Rome. Contessa Pecci-Blunt also organized lecture-recitals, known as the Sabati di Primavera.

PEIGNOT, Suzanne (*b.* 1895). French soprano and lifelong friend of Poulenc, who described her as 'the matchless interpreter of all my early mélodies for female voice'. (*ECR* p. 86). Accompanied by Poulenc, she gave the first performances of *Le Bestiaire* in 1919; *Poèmes de Ronsard* in 1925; *Trois Poèmes de Louise Lalanne* in 1931; *Quatre Poèmes de Guillaume Apollinaire* in 1931; and 'Berceuse' and 'Souric et Mouric' from *Cinq Poèmes de Max Jacob* in 1932. She is the dedicatee of 'Air champêtre' from *Airs chantés*; 'Attributs' from *Poèmes de Ronsard*; 'La Petite servante' from *Cinq poèmes de Max Jacob*, and 'Il vole' from *Fiançailles pour rire*. In 1930 she recorded *Airs chantés* with Poulenc at the piano. In an article written for the journal *Adam* in February 1964, Suzanne Peignot said:

> For me, Francis was even more than a brother; he was an incomparable friend and the guiding light throughout my career . . . His judgements about music were always illuminating and right. Working with him was a thrilling and richly instructive experience.

*Reference to Kipling's 'The Elephant's Child', from *Just So Stories* (1902).

POLIGNAC, Comtesse Jean de (1898?–1958), known as Marie-Blanche. Woman of renowned beauty and intellect, patron of the arts, accomplished pianist and singer (she made acclaimed recordings of madrigals by Monteverdi as a member of Nadia Boulanger's Ensemble Vocal). Born Marguerite di Pietro, she was the daughter of the couturière Jeanne Lanvin. Her first marriage was to René Jacquemaire, grandson of the French statesman Georges Clemenceau. Her second marriage was to Comte Jean de Polignac, nephew of Prince Edmond de Polignac. At their Paris residence in the rue Barbet-de-Jouy, they held regular Sunday *soirées musicales* at which many contemporary compositions were performed for the first time, including almost all the songs Poulenc wrote for his concerts with Pierre Bernac. Marie-Blanche was a classmate of Poulenc's friend, Raymonde Linossier. He met her in 1918, when the violinist Hélène Jourdan-Morhange took him to the home of Jean de Polignac. Marie-Blanche became a cherished friend of Poulenc and a respected musical adviser. She gave the first performance of Poulenc's *Trois poèmes de Louise de Vilmorin* in 1938 at the Salle Gaveau. She is the dedicatee of some fourteen songs, two piano pieces, and the chamber cantata *Un Soir de neige*.

POLIGNAC, Princesse Edmond de (1865–1943). Born Winnaretta Singer, she was the elder daughter of the American sewing-machine magnate, Isaac Merritt Singer and his French wife, Isabelle Eugénie Boyer. Winnaretta grew up in Paris and London. Her first marriage was to Prince Louis de Scey Montbéliard, her second, to Prince Edmond de Polignac (1834–1901), 31 years her senior, a composer and lover of art and ballet. The Princesse de Polignac was a gifted painter, pianist and organist. She became one of the greatest patrons of the arts in France. Among those who benefited from her friendship and her patronage were Diaghilev, Fauré, Chabrier, Ravel, Stravinsky, Satie, Falla and Poulenc. Poulenc's Concerto for two pianos and his Concerto for organ were both commissioned by her and dedicated to her. The patronage of the Princesse de Polignac is continued by the Fondation Singer-Polignac, created and endowed by her in 1928 to give support to French nationals for outstanding projects in the arts and sciences.

RADIGUET, Maurice. Father of Raymond Radiguet, who was the eldest of his seven children (see below). Maurice Radiguet was an artist who made a modest living as a cartoonist for various newspapers in Paris.

RADIGUET, Raymond (1903–23). French poet and novelist. He entered literary and intellectual circles in Paris at the age of fifteen, working as a journalist and contributing articles and poems to avant-garde reviews. He became the protégé and passion of Jean Cocteau. He died of typhoid at the age of twenty. His first novel, *Le Diable au corps*, tells of a boy of sixteen who seduces the wife of a soldier fighting on the front. It was written when Radiguet was seventeen and, in the words of a contemporary critic, it 'exploded into the sky of Paris like a last cannon blast after the armistice'. (*RADIG* p. 40). His second novel, *Le Bal du Comte d'Orgel*, published posthumously, was said to have had as its models the Comte and Comtesse de Beaumont. Poulenc composed the music for his comédie-bouffe *Le Gendarme incompris*, written in collaboration with Cocteau in 1921. In 1946 Poulenc set one of Radiguet's poems, 'Paul et Virginie', and in the same year dedicated his song 'Le Pont' (Apollinaire) to his memory.

ROSTAND, Claude (1912–70). French music critic, writer and radio producer who completed a degree in law before studying harmony, counterpoint and composition. He contributed articles to most of the major newspapers and music journals in France, and to several in the USA. His many publications include studies of Fauré, R. Strauss, Bartók, Brahms and Messiaen. His radio interviews with Milhaud and with Poulenc were published by Julliard in 1952 and 1954 respectively. Claude Rostand's friendship with Poulenc dated from the 1930s and he is the originator of the much-quoted characterization of Poulenc as both *moine et voyou* ('monk and riffraff'). He marvelled at the ease with which Poulenc was able 'to reconcile the tradition of Versailles with that of Belleville', and how naturally he might have been 'a member of Louis XIV's chapel while also the most authentic of the boys from the *bals musette*'. (*CR-FP*). Poulenc dedicated to Claude Rostand his 'Chanson d'Orkenise' (from *Banalités*).

ROSTROPOVITCH, Mstislav (*b.* 1927). Renowned Soviet cellist, pianist, conductor and teacher, married to the soprano Galina Vishnevskaya. He left the USSR in 1974 and did not return to perform there until 1990. In 1977, after the death of Benjamin Britten, he became artistic director of the Aldeburgh Festival. Friendship with Rostropovitch had inspired Britten to write a sonata for cello, the Cello Symphony and three unaccompanied suites for cello. Other composers who have written works for Rostropovitch include Khachaturian, Miaskovsky, Prokofiev, Shostakovitch, Schnittke and, in France, Jolivet, Dutilleux, Sauguet and Jean Wiéner. Despite Rostropovitch's letter of appeal (No. 322) Poulenc contributed only one work to the cello repertoire, a sonata for cello and piano, completed in 1948 for Pierre Fournier.

ROUART, Paul (1906–72). Friend of Poulenc and publisher of many of his works, including *Figure humaine*, printed unofficially and in secret during the German occupation and flown to England for a BBC broadcast in January 1945 (see letter 161, note 3). Paul Rouart was a member of the eminent family that founded the music publishing firm of Rouart in 1905. When Jacques Lerolle (nephew of the composer Chausson) joined the company in 1908, the firm became known as Rouart-Lerolle. In the early 1940s it was bought out by Francis Salabert and its publications incorporated into Salabert's catalogue.

ROUART-VALÉRY, Agathe (*b.* 1906). Friend of Poulenc, daughter of the poet Paul Valéry (1871–1945) and wife of Paul Rouart (see above).

SACKVILLE-WEST, Edward Charles (1901–65). He became the fifth Lord Sackville in 1962, three years before his death. He was brought up at Knole, the historic family estate in Kent that was the setting for Virginia Woolf's novel, *Orlando*, inspired by her love for Edward's cousin, Vita Sackville-West.

Educated at Eton and Oxford, Edward was the author of five novels, a biography of Thomas De Quincey, a play for radio, *The Rescue*, with music by Benjamin Britten and, in collaboration with his cousin Vita Sackville-West, the translator of Rilke's poetry. He was a producer of programmes on literature and music for the BBC and contributed numerous critical articles on music to the *New Statesman*. He was co-author with Desmond Shawe-Taylor of *The Record Guide* and *The Record Year* in the 1950s. Formerly a Trustee of the Royal Opera House, Covent Garden, Edward Sackville-West was, at the time of his letter to Poulenc, on the sub-committee of the Opera which advised on additions to the repertory.

SATIE, Erik (1866–1925). Eccentric French composer, mentor first of Les Six and later of L'Ecole d'Arcueil. One of his disciples, Germaine Tailleferre, described him in her memoirs:

> Satie wore a pince-nez and a blond beard in a point. He could never speak without holding his hand over his words, which at first were vague, then suddenly staccato, so that one heard: 'Bonjou . . . ma bonne dame, alors, alors, ma bonne dadame.' He lived in hiding; no one ever penetrated his little room in Arcueil and when he was asked his address, he replied: 'I live in a cupboard.' [*MGT* p. 28]

Poulenc's friendship with Satie lasted for eight years, from 1916–1924. He dedicated his *Rapsodie nègre* to Satie in 1917. Their relations soured during the 1924 season of the Russian Ballet in Monte Carlo. Satie died, unforgiving, in the following year. (A detailed account of this feud is given in note 1 to letter 77.) Poulenc never failed to acknowledge his debt to Satie, saying in 1954: 'His influence on my music was immediate and profound . . . Even today, I still ask myself "What would Satie have thought of this?" . . . He was a wizard who was able to divine the essence of my personality.' (*ECR* pp. 47–48)

SAUGUET, Henri [Henri-Pierre Poupard] (1901–89). French composer, student of Koechlin, disciple of Satie and founder-member of the Ecole d'Arcueil. His works include opera, ballet, song, orchestral and chamber music, and film and stage music. He was born in Bordeaux and moved to Paris in 1922 at Milhaud's invitation. He was introduced to Milhaud's friends as 'the charming young man from Bordeaux who speaks in the past historic tense'. Poulenc asked him to dinner on his second day in Paris and remained a lifelong friend. He admired the 'authenticity and sincerity' of Sauguet's music, its unpretentiousness, its 'poetic sensibility.' (*ECR* pp. 194–195). He dedicated his song 'Le Disparu' to Sauguet in 1947. The singer Jane Bathori said of him: 'Sauguet is above all a lyrical composer. He sings, and his song is abundant and clear . . . He is not ashamed of having a heart and of showing it . . . Sauguet is a true friend.' (*BIRS* No. 15, p. 244)

Sauguet was also an ardent cat-lover and contributed a delightful interview to the book *Chat huppé* (Editions Pierre Horay, Paris, 1986). His memoirs, *La Musique, ma vie*, with preface by Raphaël Cluzel, were published in 1990 by Librairie Séguier.

SCHAEFFNER, André (1895–1980). French musicologist whose wide-ranging interests included the study of ethnology, theology and archaeology. In 1929 he founded the department of ethnomusicology in the Musée de l'Homme in Paris and was its director until 1965. Concurrently, he worked on the catalogue of the Paris Conservatoire Library, worked at the Centre for Scientific Research, acted as artistic secretary of the Paris Symphony Orchestra and the Pléiade Concerts, specialized in the study of European and non-European instruments and conducted six scientific excursions in central and western Africa, edited the third French edition of Riemann's Musik-Lexicon, wrote studies of Debussy and Stravinsky and contributed articles to numerous reviews. From 1948–61, André Schaeffner was vice-president, then president, of the Société Française de Musicologie. Poulenc's song 'Le Mendiant' (from *Chansons villageoises*) is dedicated to André Schaeffner.

SIENKIEWICZ, Geneviève. Madame Sienkiewicz was a friend of Ricard Viñes and also of Poulenc's mother. It was through her that Poulenc first met Ricardo Viñes and began to study the piano with him at the age of fifteen. Geneviève Sienkiewicz was a great lover of music and the arts, and held a salon every Sunday in her apartment in the rue Chaptal (an apartment which the composer Xenakis took over after her death). Poulenc's *Thème varié* for piano, written in 1951, is dedicated to Geneviève Sienkiewicz.

STRAVINSKY, Igor Fyodorovich (1882–1971). The Russian composer came to Paris in 1910 for the production of his ballet *L'Oiseau de feu* by Diaghilev's Russian Ballet. In that year, Poulenc, aged eleven, heard his music for the first time. At fifteen he took part in the battle raging over *Le Sacre du printemps*:

> The shock of those strange, dissonant harmonies was beyond anything I had ever dreamed of . . . The SOUND of Stravinsky's music was something so new to me that I often ask myself: 'if Stravinsky had not existed, would I ever have written any music?' [FP-MMA pp. 188–190]

At seventeen he met Stravinsky by chance at his music publisher's in Paris. When he was eighteen his *Rapsodie nègre* made a strong impression on Stravinsky. A friendship developed between the two composers that continued throughout Poulenc's life. Although his letters reveal an estrangement from some of Stravinsky's works in the 1950s, Poulenc was able to say in 1962, the year before his death: 'I consider myself a son of Stravinsky, the kind of son he would no doubt disown, but nevertheless his spiritual son.' (FP-MMA p. 188)

La Fraîcheur et le feu (1950) is dedicated to Stravinsky.

VIDAL, Pierre (b. 1932). Musicologist and critic for *Journal musical français*, *Harmonie, Compact*; producer for Radio France. From 1955 to 1967 he organized the meetings of the Club des Trois Centres (see letter 309, note 1) at which Poulenc spoke on three occasions:

> Poulenc was an anxious man who did not like to subject himself to the question-and-answer games widely practised by some of his colleagues. He preferred to speak alone, with a plan in mind, while pretending to improvise. It was hard to judge whether it was the composer or the

audience who enjoyed themselves the most. Whatever the case, this witty man, bubbling over with conviviality, took unconcealed delight in the experience, and was so captivating that he could have held the hall spellbound well beyond the time imposed. [Pierre Vidal, sleeve-notes: *FP-CAS*]

VILMORIN, Louise de (1902–69). French writer and poet, born into a family of renowned scientists and horticulturalists, author of three collections of poetry and several novels, including *Madame de* (1951) and *La Lettre dans un taxi* (1958). In the early 1920s she was engaged briefly to the writer Saint-Exupéry. In the late 1920s she married an American twice her age, Henry Leigh Hunt, descendant of the English poet James Henry Leigh Hunt, a friend of Byron. Her second marriage, in 1937, was to Count Paul Pálffy of Slovakia. In later years she was the companion of André Malraux. Poulenc first came into contact with her through Marie-Blanche de Polignac, in about 1936. The sound of her name and the beauty of her face evoked for him the seventeenth century, and in her poetry he found 'a kind of sensitive audacity, a wantonness, an avidity, which extended into song all I had expressed, when very young, in *Les Biches*, with Marie Laurencin'. (*PB-FP* p. 131). Delighted with this 'material for truly feminine songs', Poulenc made settings of her poems under the titles *Trois poèmes* (1937), *Fiançailles pour rire* (1939) and *Métamorphoses* (1943).

VIÑES, Ricardo (1870–1943). Spanish pianist who, in the words of the poet Léon-Paul Fargue, 'transformed the piano into an express-bar of delights'. (*REF* p. 192). The first interpreter of many works by Debussy, Falla, Ravel and Poulenc, he was the dedicatee of Debussy's *Poissons d'or*, Falla's *Nights in the Gardens of Spain*, Ravel's *Oiseaux tristes* and Poulenc's Suite in C and *Trois pièces* (Pastorale, Toccata, Hymne). Poulenc was introduced to Viñes by a family friend, Geneviève Sienkiewicz, and he studied the piano with him from 1914–17:

> That meeting was of fundamental importance to me. *I owe him everything.* [*ECR* p. 29]
> First it was agreed that I would have a half-hour lesson each week, but this soon became an hour, then two, and, imperceptibly, I began to spend my life with this Hidalgo with the face of a kindly inquisitor. [*FP-MMMA* p. 522]

Through Viñes, Poulenc met, among others, Auric, Cocteau, Falla, Satie, Landowska and, a fellow pupil, the pianist Marcelle Meyer.

VIÑES SOTO, Elvira. Niece of Ricardo Viñes (see above). As an enduring tribute to Viñes' greatness she planned to reissue recordings he had made in 1930. Poulenc's letter to her, written in 1949 (No. 197) offers encouragement and advice on her project.

WIÉNER, Jean (1896–1982). French pianist known above all for providing the music in the famous Parisian night-club of the 1920s, Le Boeuf sur le Toit, and for his legendary two-piano duo with the Belgian Clément Doucet (1894–1950), with whom, between 1926 and 1939, he gave more than 2,000 concerts in France and abroad. Wiéner was also a composer of many genres, including some 350 film scores, and the founder in 1921 of the Concerts Wiéner, a series specializing in contemporary music. His memoirs, *Allegro appassionato*, were published in 1978 by Belfond, Paris.

Notes

Letter 1

1. Simone Tilliard. Pianist and friend of Poulenc's. She collaborated in many of his early concerts and is the dedicatee of his Sonata for piano 4 hands (1918) and the song 'L'Espionne' from *Calligrammes* (1948).

2. At the time of this letter, Milhaud was twenty-three and Poulenc sixteen. They had met shortly before at the country home of mutual friends, where they had played tennis together. (*MVH* p. 82). Poulenc refers to Milhaud's letter some 40 years later in his radio interviews with Claude Rostand:

> A rather pompous note Milhaud sent me, in reply to my request for an autograph, made me fear he would be a bit of a know-all, whereas in fact he was the most genial of friends. [*ECR* p. 44]

Letter 2

1. Poulenc met Satie in 1916, at the home of the Spanish pianist, Ricardo Viñes, with whom he was studying at the time (see under Poulenc's Correspondents). Recalling that meeting in his radio interviews with Claude Rostand, Poulenc said:

> At first, Satie was wary of me, for he thought I was nothing but a 'Daddy's boy' . . . but when he saw my enthusiasm for *Parade*, he adopted me completely. [*ECR* p. 46]

Satie's ballet *Parade*, with libretto by Cocteau, décor by Picasso and choreography by Massine, was first performed by Diaghilev's Russian Ballet on 18 May 1917.

2. Poulenc's father, Emile, died on 15 July 1917. His mother, born Jenny Royer, had died two years earlier. After his father's death, the eighteen-year-old Poulenc went to stay with his sister Jeanne. Thirteen years his senior, she was married to the distinguished notary André Manceaux. They lived in an apartment, first at 76 then at 83 rue de Monceau, where Poulenc occupied a bachelor flat in the courtyard of the building, above what had once been the stables and coach-house.

Letter 3

1. The home of Poulenc's maternal grandparents was in Nogent, on the banks of the Marne, about ten miles to the east of Paris. His great-grandfather had been a horticulturalist there during the First Empire. Until the age of 25 Poulenc spent most of his holidays in Nogent and, in his interviews and writings, speaks nostalgically of its river-boats, café-concerts, open-air dance halls, its smell of

fried potatoes and its sound of piano accordions. Nogent was the inspiration for much of his music (see particularly letter 334, note 2). To Claude Rostand Poulenc said: 'What you sometimes refer to as my "bad boy" side developed quite naturally in Nogent . . . For me it was paradise . . . It was there that I first heard the songs of Christiné and Scotto which became my folklore.' (*ECR* pp. 17–18). Henri-Marius Christiné (1867–1941) and Vincent Scotto (1876–1952) were prolific composers of popular *chansons* of the period.

LETTER 4

1. Paul Vidal (1863–1931). French conductor and composer, mainly of ballets and operettas. He taught classes in solfège, piano accompaniment and composition at the Paris Conservatoire. At the time of Poulenc's letter, he was also musical director of the Opéra-Comique (from 1914–1919).

2. The *Rapsodie nègre* was Poulenc's first work to be performed (see letter 6). Written for piano, string quartet, flute, clarinet and baritone voice, it has five movements. The central movement is a vocal intermezzo for which Poulenc chose a text from a collection of pseudo-African poetry, *Les Poésies de Makoko Kangourou*, beginning as follows:

> Honoloulou, poti lama!
> Honoloulou, Honoloulou,
> Kati moko, mosi bolou
> Ratakou sira, polama!

Poulenc dedicated the work to Erik Satie.

3. In his radio conversations with Stéphane Audel (*FP-MMA* pp. 173–177) Poulenc says that he first met the composer Maurice Ravel (1875–1937) in March 1917, a meeting arranged by Ricardo Viñes. This is questionable in view of the dates of the above letter and of letter 6. Poulenc recalls that the meeting did not go according to plan: he had wanted to play Ravel's *Sonatine* and parts of *Le Tombeau de Couperin* but the older composer stopped him after three minutes. Ravel cast a cursory glance over Poulenc's compositions and proceeded to praise the music of Mendelssohn and Saint-Saëns while belittling that of Schumann, Chabrier and the later works of Debussy. Poulenc left, feeling deeply disappointed. He continued to feel estranged from Ravel until he saw his opera *L'Enfant et les sortilèges* in Monte Carlo in 1925.

4. André Gédalge (1856–1926). French composer, professor of fugue and counterpoint at the Paris Conservatoire. Among his pupils were Ravel, Schmitt, Milhaud and Honegger.

5. Schola Cantorum. Music School founded in Paris in 1894 by Vincent d'Indy, Charles Bordes and Alexandre Guilmant, committed to furthering the ideas of the composer César Franck (1822–90).

LETTER 6

1. In the autumn of 1917 Poulenc was drafted into the army and had to forgo any plans of formal study at this stage.

2. Jane Bathori [Jeanne-Marie Berthier] (1877–1970). French singer renowned for her pioneering efforts in bringing before the public works by contemporary

composers. She gave the first performance of many songs by composers including Debussy, Ravel, Roussel, Milhaud and Poulenc (his 'Vocalise' in 1927 and *Airs chantés* in 1928). It was said of her in 1919: 'Who has not heard Jane Bathori sing has not penetrated French song.' (Georges Jean-Aubry: *BIRS* No. 4, p. 102). Poulenc dedicated to Jane Bathori 'A son page' (from *Poèmes de Ronsard*), 'Air vif' (from *Airs chantés*), and 'Une Chanson de porcelaine', written in homage to her on her 80th birthday. During the First World War, Jane Bathori became director of the Théâtre du Vieux-Colombier in the absence of its founder, the writer, actor and producer, Jacques Copeau (1879–1949). She organized the concert on 11 December 1917 at which Poulenc's *Rapsodie nègre* was first performed.

LETTER 7

1. From January to July 1918, Poulenc was stationed in Vincennes. He then served with an anti-aircraft division in the Vosges. In October of the same year he was sent to Saint-Martin-sur-le-Pré, near Châlons-sur-Marne. In December, he joined the anti-aircraft division at Pont-sur-Seine. July 1919 saw him assigned to the Ministry of Aviation in Paris, in a secretarial post. He remained there until October 1921, when he was demobilized. (*HH-FP* pp. 35–36). At the time of his letter to Valentine Gross, Poulenc was confined to the guardhouse for overstaying his leave in Paris, a frequent failing of his (see letter 10).

2. Jean de Brunhoff (1899–1937). Artist and illustrator, creator of the children's stories about an elephant, *Babar*. In the 1940s, Poulenc set to music the first of the series, *Histoire de Babar, le petit éléphant*. See letter 183, note 2. Jean de Brunhoff's brother, Michel, also a friend of Poulenc's, was editor of *Jardin des modes* and later of *Vogue* magazine in Paris.

3. Comte Etienne de Beaumont (1883–1956). Great host, patron and ballet lover who financed, among other things, Satie's *Parade* and Cocteau's *Le Boeuf sur le toit*. He was the originator in 1924 of the *Soirées de Paris*, a season of ballet and theatre productions at the Cigale Theatre in Montmartre, for which he commissioned such works as Satie's *Mercure* and Milhaud's *Salade*. See also Comtesse Etienne de Beaumont, in Poulenc's Correspondents.

4. Express letters in Paris were transmitted by pneumatic tube and were known familiarly as *pneus*. Most of Satie's letters to Poulenc were sent in this form.

LETTER 8

1. Valentine Gross married Jean Hugo in 1919. See Poulenc's Correspondents.

2. Jean Cocteau was staying in Le Piqueÿ, a small fishing village in the bay of Arcachon, on the Atlantic coast of France.

LETTER 9

1. The tram terminus at Place de la Madeleine was the nearest stop to Cocteau's apartment at 10 rue d'Anjou, which he shared with his mother.

2. Cocteau refers to a party in the garden of Comte Etienne de Beaumont's Paris residence, which had one entrance in the rue Duroc and another in the rue Masseran. The party caused a great stir as it was allegedly the first in Paris to

feature American jazz, played on this occasion by Black American soldiers. Poulenc's *Rapsodie nègre* was also performed at the party.

3. This marked the first artistic collaboration between Poulenc and Cocteau. Poulenc wrote *Jongleurs*, and a percussion prelude to precede it, for a proposed 'Homage to Music-Hall' at the Théâtre du Vieux-Colombier, devised by Cocteau and Pierre Bertin (see letter 11, note 3). This project did not materialize. Three years later a number by Poulenc entitled *Le Jongleur* was included in a programme performed by the dancer Caryathis (see letter 27, note 1). It is not clear whether this was the same *Jongleurs*. Neither this work nor the percussion prelude appears to have survived. Poulenc's song 'Toréador' on words by Cocteau was written for this same 'Homage to Music-Hall' (see letters 11 and 12).

4. Juliette Meerovitch (1896–1920). Pianist, pupil of Cortot and first-prize-winner at the Paris Conservatoire at the age of fourteen. Poulenc's piano suite *Napoli*, completed in 1925, is dedicated to her memory.

Letter 10

1. During the First World War, Comte Etienne de Beaumont organized an ambulance service under the auspices of the French Red Cross. Among those who joined these 'Auxiliary Convoys' was Jean Cocteau, in 1916.

2. Eugenia Errazuriz. Chilean heiress who spent much of her time in Argentina and in France. When Picasso married Olga Koklova on 12 July 1918 (with Cocteau, Max Jacob and Apollinaire as witnesses), Madame Errazuriz invited the couple to spend the summer in her villa in Biarritz.

3. The cubist painter André Lhote (1885–1962) and his wife.

4. In 1918 Poulenc dedicated his Sonata for two clarinets to Edouard Souberbielle (1899–1986), pianist, organist and composer.

Letter 11

1. Bobino. Popular music hall at 20 rue de la Gaîté, in the Montparnasse area of Paris.

2. Cocteau sets his Spanish drama in Venice.

3. Pierre Bertin (1895–1984). French actor, singer and playwright, married to the pianist Marcelle Meyer (see letter 44, note 2). He was associated with the Théâtre de l'Odéon, the Comédie Française and the Compagnie Jean-Louis Barrault. In 1917 he organized talks and literary evenings at the Théâtre du Vieux-Colombier and, with Jane Bathori, was responsible for the concert at which Poulenc's *Rapsodie nègre* was first performed. Poulenc dedicated his setting of 'Toréador' to Pierre Bertin. It was intended that Bertin should sing the song in Cocteau's 'Homage to Music-Hall'. See letter 9, note 3.

Letter 12

1. Walther Straram (1876–1933). Violinist and conductor, founder of the Walther Straram Orchestra in 1923 and of the Concerts Walther Straram. Pierre Bernac studied singing with Straram from 1925–1933.

LETTER 13

1. There is no sonata for piano, violin and cello among Poulenc's published works.

2. Poulenc revised the Sonata for piano 4 hands, or 2 pianos 4 hands, in 1939. He revised the Sonata for two clarinets (1918) in 1945.

3. The violinist Hélène Jourdan-Morhange recalls playing a sonata for piano and violin by Poulenc during the 1917–18 season of concerts organized by Félix Delgrange, cellist, conductor and promoter of concerts of avant-garde music. 'Poulenc did not have time to complete the piano part. We played only the first two movements which were extremely beautiful. Poulenc never in fact published this sonata which he dedicated to me.' (*MAM* p. 74). Poulenc also destroyed a second violin sonata, written in 1924 for Jelly d'Arányi (1895–1966), Hungarian-born violinist and dedicatee of Ravel's *Tzigane*. Poulenc's published works include only one sonata for violin and piano, written in 1942–43, for Ginette Neveu (1919–49). See letter 160, note 4.

4. It was this epidemic of Spanish influenza that also claimed the life of the poet Guillaume Apollinaire (1880–1918), and four months later, of his Polish mother, Olga de Kostrowitzky (*APOL* pp. 271–276). Born in Rome but educated in France, Apollinaire was a key figure in the literary and artistic avant-garde of Paris, his writings greatly influencing the development of Cubism in art and Surrealism in poetry. He was the inventor of the word 'Surréalisme', which he used first in his programme notes to Satie's ballet *Parade* in 1917 and again a few weeks later in the subtitle to his burlesque play *Les Mamelles de Tirésias – drame surréaliste*. Poulenc encountered Apollinaire only briefly but felt a deep affinity for his poetry (see also letter 32 and note 1). Between 1919 and 1954, he composed thirty-three songs to poems by Apollinaire and, in 1944, wrote his first opera, *Les Mamelles de Tirésias*, on Apollinaire's play of that name.

5. Annette Chalupt was the wife of the poet René Chalupt (1885–1957). His works were set to music by Satie, Milhaud, Roussel and Schmitt.

6. Léon-Paul Fargue (1876–1947). Poet and novelist who wrote at length about Paris. He was a friend of Ravel and of Satie (who set two poems of his, 'Les Ludions' and 'La Statue de bronze') and of the bookseller Adrienne Monnier. Poulenc saw Fargue as the 'presiding spirit' of Monnier's bookshop, *La Maison des Amis des Livres* (*FP-MMA* p. 131). See also letter 38, note 5.

LETTER 14

1. 'Le Panama', 'J'ai tué' and 'Profond aujourd'hui' are poems by Blaise Cendrars (1887–1961), French-speaking poet, essayist, novelist, art critic and musicologist, born of a Scottish mother and a Swiss father. Cendrars was an adventurer whose largely autobiographical writings exalt a life of action and danger. An ardent defender of new forms in art, music and literature, he was associated with the concerts of Les Nouveaux Jeunes and Les Six from about 1916 onwards.

2. The entire poetic output of Arthur Rimbaud (1854–91) was written between his fifteenth and twentieth years and ranks among the highest in French literature.

3. Léonce Rosenberg. Pioneering art dealer whose Paris gallery, *L'Effort moderne*, was the venue for regular poetry-readings, often combined with performances of contemporary music. See letter 19.

LETTER 15

1. Poulenc refers to the concerts that became known under the name of Lyre et Palette and that took place regularly from 1917 to 1920 in the rue Huyghens. These events were subsidised by Blaise Cendrars, Pierre Bertin and Félix Delgrange, who also directed them. They combined music with poetry-readings and art exhibitions.

2. Viñes did in fact give the first performance of Poulenc's *Mouvements perpétuels* at the Lyre et Palette concert on 9 February 1919.

3. *La Soirée de Viroflay*. Piano piece by Roland-Manuel (1891–1966), later destroyed by the composer.

4. In 1918 Poulenc wrote three *Pastorales* for Ricardo Viñes. They remained unpublished, except for the first. This, in a revised form, appeared in a triptych for piano published by Heugel in 1928: *Pastorale*, *Toccata* and *Hymne*.

LETTER 17

1. Otto Marius Kling (1866–1924). Director of the English firm of music publishers, J. and W. Chester, from 1915 until his death in 1924.

2. Georges Jean-Aubry (1882–1949). French writer on music and promoter of new works. From 1919 he was editor in London of the journal *The Chesterian*. He was also active in organizing concerts of contemporary music in France and in England. His books include *La Musique française d'aujourd'hui* and *La Musique et les nations*.

3. Madame Edwards, or 'Misia', born Marie Sophie Olga Zenaïde Godebska (1872–1950). She was married first to Thadée Natanson, one of the founders of *La Revue blanche*, then to Alfred Edwards, prominent figure in artistic and social circles in Paris, and finally to the Catalan painter of murals, Jose-Maria Sert. Misia was a great patron of the arts whose salons were frequented by many renowned poets, musicians and artists of the time. She was painted by Toulouse-Lautrec, Vuillard and Bonnard, was said to be Diaghilev's closest woman-friend and claimed to have discovered Coco Chanel. Poulenc dedicated his ballet *Les Biches* to her, and the second of his eight Polish songs, 'Le Départ'.

4. The French Cubist painter, Georges Braque (1882–1963), was commissioned by Diaghilev to create the décor for Auric's ballet *Les Fâcheux*. He is one of the seven artists included in Poulenc's song cycle on painters, *Le Travail du peintre*. See letter 262.

5. Léonide Massine (1895–1979). Russian dancer and choreographer of more than 50 ballets. He joined Diaghilev's Russian Ballet in 1914. His career as a choreographer began in the following year.

LETTER 19

1. *Le Bestiaire* is Poulenc's first song cycle, written during April and May of

1919 at Pont-sur-Seine, where he was stationed. The work consists of settings of six poems taken from Apollinaire's first volume of poetry, *Le Bestiaire, ou Cortège d'Orphée*, a series of quatrains portraying a procession of animals following Orpheus and his lyre, each poem illustrated with a woodcut by Raoul Dufy. First published in 1911, the book was reprinted in 1918. Adrienne Monnier sent a copy to Poulenc at Pont-sur-Seine. Poulenc set twelve of the 30 poems but, on the advice of Georges Auric, he discarded all but six. The work is scored for voice and flute, clarinet, bassoon and string quartet, or for voice and piano. The first performance was given by Suzanne Peignot accompanied by Poulenc, in 1919, at the home of a Madame Vignon, in the Avenue de la Tour-Maubourg, Paris. Unbeknown to Poulenc, Louis Durey had already set the complete *Bestiaire*. When Poulenc discovered this, he dedicated his work to Durey.

LETTER 20

1. In his second group of songs, *Cocardes*, Poulenc set three poems by Cocteau, 'Miel de Narbonne', 'Bonne d'enfant' and 'Enfant de troupe'. The poet Raymond Radiguet, describing Cocteau at this time, has aptly captured the atmosphere of *Cocardes*:

> Unwittingly, Cocteau invented a new kind of melancholy: the melan-
> choly of travelling funfairs and of fireworks just as they fade. [From
> 'Lettre à l'intention de Jacques Doucet', 1920, in *RAD*]

Poulenc's setting was scored for voice and violin, trumpet, trombone and percussion, or voice and piano, and was dedicated to Georges Auric. It was first performed by the Russian tenor Alexander Koubitzky at the Comédie des Champs-Elysées on 21 February 1920, as part of a 'spectacle-concert' devised by Cocteau for the première of Milhaud's *Le Boeuf sur le toit*. See letter 23.

2. Speaking in 1947 on his songs and the poets who had inspired them, Poulenc said: 'I have always needed contemporary poets, as – to be quite honest – I only feel musically at ease with poets I have known'. (*FP-MMLP* p. 508)

3. *Cocardes* was published in 1920, not by Chester, but by Editions de la Sirène (founded by Cocteau and Cendrars in 1918, and for which the emblem was a siren in the form of a sea horse, drawn by Jean Hugo).

4. See letter 7, note 2.

5. In August 1919, Cocteau and Durey went together to Ahusky, a remote Basque village in the Pyrenees, known for its mineral spring, and accessible only by foot or on muleback. In a letter to Radiguet, Cocteau wrote: 'After a four-hour walk, very steep, in cloudy heat, we reached the farm . . . Not a tree, not a patch of shade. The shepherds sing Poulenc . . .' (*COCT* p. 250)

6. See note 1 above.

7. This presumably became *Album des Six*, published by Demets in 1920. It consisted of *Prélude* by Auric, *Romances sans paroles* by Durey, *Sarabande* by Honegger, *Mazurka* by Milhaud, *Valse* by Poulenc and *Pastorale* by Tailleferre.

LETTER 21

1. It was through Stravinsky's prompting that the publisher Chester in London first issued Poulenc's music.

2. Poulenc had recently heard Stravinsky playing his *Piano Rag Music* at the home of Valentine and Jean Hugo. Poulenc had first encountered Stravinsky by chance in 1916, at a music publisher's in Paris: '. . . when I saw him coming through the door, I thought it was God Himself arriving!' (*FP-MMA* p. 190). Poulenc had with him the four-hand arrangement of *Petrushka* which he asked Stravinsky to sign for him. This was his first contact with *le grand Igor*.

LETTER 23

1. Milhaud and Cocteau were in London to attend rehearsals of their show *Le Boeuf sur le toit* which opened at the Coliseum on 12 July 1920. It was advertised in *The Times* of that date as follows:

> For two weeks only: Hugo Rumbold presents his company in Jean Cocteau's *Le Boeuf sur le toit* as *The Nothing-Doing-Bar*. Invented and produced by Jean Cocteau; music by Darius Milhaud; scenery and masks by Dufy; costumes by Fauconnet. THE ENTIRE PRODUCTION DIRECT FROM THE COMÉDIE DES CHAMPS-ELYSEES.

Included in the London programme were turns by Gertrude Lawrence, Ruth Draper, and the Swiss clown Grock.

Le Boeuf sur le toit had its origins in a score written by Milhaud on his return from Rio, based on a popular samba he had heard there, *O Boi no telhado*. Cocteau devised a farce around this music, which he set in a North American bar during Prohibition. Financed by Comte Etienne de Beaumont, the show was first performed on 21 February 1920, at the Comédie des Champs-Elysées (see letter 20, note 1).

2. Milhaud refers to a large fan that plays an important part in the action of the farce: when it is switched on by the barman of the *Nothing-Doing-Bar*, its blades decapitate a policeman, who is later inexplicably resuscitated.

3. Milhaud exaggerates slightly: the hall seats 2,700.

4. The young dancing pupils at the Paris Opéra were called *les Rats*.

5. Under the heading: 'A Sad French Farce at the Coliseum', the notice in *The Times* of 13 July 1920 included the following paragraph:

> *The Nothing-Doing-Bar*, a pantomime farce invented by M. Jean Cocteau and described as a skit on Pussyfoot America, is about as exhilarating as Professor Leacock would have us believe a banquet becomes under Prohibition regulations. It is a 'farce' without a giggle, much less a laugh, a harlequinade with the tempo marked *adagio* instead of *presto*. A taste for humour of the kind which M. Cocteau offers might be cultivated, but a Coliseum audience could make nothing of it.

6. Albert Roussel (1869–1937). French composer and teacher, originally a naval officer. His compositions include the opera *Padmâvati*, orchestral, piano and chamber works, and about 35 songs. Among his students were Satie, Martinů and Varèse.

LETTER 24

1. The Sociedad Nacional de Música, founded by Falla, Adolfo Salazar and Miguel Salvador (who became its president), held its concerts in the main lounge of the Ritz Hotel in Madrid.

2. *Le Tricorne* is Falla's ballet *El Sombrero de tres picos*, with choreography by Massine, and sets and costumes by Picasso, first performed by the Russian Ballet at the Alhambra Theatre, London, on 22 July 1919, with Ernest Ansermet conducting. The work was published by Chester in 1921.

LETTER 25

1. *Les Fâcheux*. Ballet by Georges Auric with costumes and sets by Braque and choreography by Nijinska, commissioned by Diaghilev for his 1924 Monte Carlo season.

Georges Auric (1899–1983) studied at the Paris Conservatoire and the Schola Cantorum and was one of the group termed Les Six. He was a prolific composer of most genres but is best known for his ballets and his many film scores. Auric also wrote music criticism and was director of the Paris Opéra and Opéra-Comique from 1962–68. Poulenc met Auric in 1917 at the home of Ricardo Viñes. He said of this meeting: '[Auric] immediately became what he has never ceased to be for me since: my true spiritual brother.' (*FP-MMA* p. 48). (See also letter 165, note 1.) Poulenc dedicated to Auric *Cocardes* (1919), his fifth *Improvisation* for piano (1932), 'Dans le jardin d'Anna', from *Deux poèmes de Guillaume Apollinaire* (1938), and his Sinfonietta (1947).

2. By his use of the letters SIC, Cocteau refers not only to the Latin categorical affirmative *sic*, but also to the magazine *Sic*, edited by the poet, playwright and essayist Pierre Albert-Birot (1876–1967) who chose the title because the initials stood for the words *sons, idées, couleurs* (sounds, ideas, colours).

3. *La Noce*, or *La Noce Massacrée*, was soon to become *Les Mariés de la Tour Eiffel*. This tragi-comedy set in a restaurant on the Eiffel Tower one 14th of July had a libretto by Cocteau and music by Les Six (bar Louis Durey). The work was the first and last collective enterprise of the group. It was produced by Rolf de Maré for the Swedish Ballet Company, with choreography by Jean Börlin, décor by Irène Lagut and costumes by Jean Hugo. The orchestra was conducted by Inghelbrecht. It opened at the Théâtre des Champs-Elysées on 18 June 1921 and caused an historic *scandale*. Forty-five years later a recording of the work was made (Adès 15501; 14007) with Darius Milhaud conducting. In his sleeve notes, Milhaud said: 'I am grateful to Lucien Adès for allowing me to conduct this work which, to me, epitomizes the joyous, optimistic, brilliant era of the 1920s.'

4. In 1921 Cocteau completed *Vocabulaire*, a collection of poems which he dedicated to Auric, Durey, Honegger, Milhaud, Poulenc and Germaine Tailleferre, the group dubbed Les Six by the critic Henri Collet in 1920 (see letter 301, note 1).

LETTER 26

1. Poulenc was in Rome with Darius Milhaud in March 1921. This is confirmed by the following postcard to Ricardo Viñes (Music Department of the Bibliothèque Nationale):

Rome, 26.3.21

A thousand regards from Roma where I am with Darius Milhaud.
Everyone here speaks about you, so great was the impression you made. I
shall soon be back in Paris and will, of course, tear over to your place to
play you my new things. Affectionately, Poulenc

2. In 1910 Debussy set three fragments of a long poem by the seventeenth-
century poet Tristan L'Hermite, *Le Promenoir des deux amants*.

3. Although Poulenc admired Radiguet's poetry, he set only one of his poems,
'Paul et Virginie', and this in 1946, after unsuccessful attempts in the early 1920s.
He was extremely attached to this short song, 'made of a little music, of much
tenderness and of silence'. (*DMS* p. 91)

Paul et Virginie is also the title of a libretto by Radiguet and Cocteau for a
comic opera. See letter 29, note 1.

LETTER 27

1. Satie refers to a performance in June 1921 at the Théâtre du Colisée of
his suite *La Belle excentrique*, written for the dancer Caryathis (1889–1971).
Born Elisabeth Toulemon, she was for ten years the companion of the actor
and stage director, Charles Dullin (1885–1949), and later the wife of the writer
Marcel Jouhandeau (1888–1979). Her dance programme included *La Danse
d'aujourd'hui* by Auric and Ravel's *Rapsodie espagnole*. There was also an item
by Poulenc called *Le Jongleur*, 'an extremely difficult number in which . . .
[Caryathis] both juggled and danced intricate steps wearing an elaborate but
hampering costume designed by Goncharova'. (*SAT* p. 191)

LETTER 28

1. *La Danse de la baigneuse de Trouville*, a waltz by Poulenc composed for *Les
Mariés de la Tour Eiffel*.

2. *Le Discours du général*, a polka for two cornets which preceded *La Danse de
la baigneuse*.

3. *Esquisse d'un fanfare* written as the overture to Act V of Cocteau's
adaptation of *Roméo et Juliette*.

4. *Le Gendarme incompris*. One-act farce by Radiguet and Cocteau, with
music by Poulenc. The words spoken by the gendarme are borrowed from a
prose-poem by Mallarmé, *L'Ecclésiastique*, which – to the delight of the authors
– neither the public nor the critics recognized. In a letter to Paul Collaer dated 6
December 1920, Poulenc wrote of his part in this farce:

> I am working at the moment on a little score for a one-act play by
> Cocteau and Radiguet: *Le Gendarme incompris*, which I think will be
> performed in Paris at the end of January. There will be an overture, two
> songs, two duets and a finale with a little dance. My chamber orchestra
> will consist of a double bass, a cello, a violin, a clarinet, a trumpet and a
> trombone. There are three characters: a gendarme; Monsieur Médor, a
> police inspector; and the marquise de Montonson. It's hilarious. [Quoted

by Paul Collaer in: *Lettres, arts et sciences humaines*, June–July 1974, pp. 2–3.]

Billed as a *critique bouffe*, the work was performed in May 1921 at the Théâtre Michel in the rue des Mathurins, Paris, in a programme directed by Pierre Bertin which included Satie's *Le Piège de Méduse*, Max Jacob's *La Femme fatale*, Milhaud's *Caramel mou*, and a two-act play by Radiguet, with music by Auric, about a family called *Les Pélican*.

The text of *Le Gendarme incompris* was published in *Cahiers Cocteau*, No. 2, Gallimard, 1971. Poulenc's score, thought to be destroyed, was discovered in the 1970s through the research efforts of the Canadian conductor and musicologist, Daniel Swift (*b.* 1950). Swift's authorized edition of the score is to be published by Editions Salabert. A piano version, in Poulenc's hand, with orchestral indications, is in the Bibliothèque Nationale in Paris.

5. Ernest Ansermet (1883–1969) had been the conductor for Diaghilev's Russian Ballet since 1915 and was a close associate of Stravinsky.

6. Vincent d'Indy (1851–1931). French composer, conductor and teacher, author of studies on Franck, Beethoven and Wagner. A pupil and disciple of Franck, he was one of the founders of the Schola Cantorum (see letter 4, note 5).

7. *Renard*, 'a burlesque in song and dance', adapted by Stravinsky from his readings of the fables of Afanasiev (1826–71). The work was commissioned in 1915 by the Princesse Edmond de Polignac. It is performed as a puppet play or as a ballet.

8. There does not appear to be any evidence of a 1921 string quartet by Poulenc ever having been completed. In 1945 Poulenc wrote a quartet, but later destroyed it. See letter 175, note 6.

9. See letter 35.

10. Written in 1921 and published by Chester in 1923, Poulenc's *Promenades* is a work in ten sections for piano, each section describing a different means of transport. It is dedicated to Arthur Rubinstein. Poulenc revised the score in 1952.

LETTER 29

1. In 1920 Cocteau and Radiguet had the idea of writing a comic opera based on the eighteenth-century idyll by Bernardin de Saint-Pierre *Paul et Virginie*. Satie was approached to provide the music, and a libretto was read to him towards the end of 1920. Although Cocteau announced in the fourth and final issue of his broadsheet *Le Coq* that *Paul et Virginie* would be 'Satie's next work and his farewell to composing', Satie never completed this work and it is doubtful whether he ever began it. After his death, only the libretto was found, with the dialogue written in Cocteau's hand and the arias in Radiguet's. Cocteau then asked Poulenc to write the music. He in turn passed it on to Sauguet. The opera was never written. This saga is chronicled in letters 38, 43, 82, 91, 92, 113, 114.

2. The composer, organist and conductor Gabriel Pierné (1863–1937) was principal conductor of the Colonne Orchestra from 1910–1934 and was responsible for bringing before the public many new works by fellow composers.

3. An important influence on Poulenc's early life was his uncle and godfather,

Marcel Royer (his mother's brother). Generally known as 'Papoum', Marcel Royer owed this nickname to Poulenc who, as a child, could not pronounce the word for godfather, *parrain*. To Poulenc, he was the epitome of the old-time, cultured Parisian, a lover of the theatre who never missed a play at the Théâtre de l'Odéon, a painter who painted only for himself, in the style of Toulouse-Lautrec, a worldly raconteur whose tales of night-life and boulevard-life were a source of constant fascination. Pierre Bernac saw Papoum as belonging to a lost race, that of the 'man-about-town':

> He was smitten with the theatre, haunted the wings and struck up friendships with celebrated actors and singers. Whenever he came to see his sister their conversation fascinated Francis who, pretending to play under the table with his mechanical railway, did not miss a word. [*PB-FP* pp. 21–22]

There is a snapshot in one of the Poulenc family albums of Uncle Papoum: he is short and dapper, and sports a boater in the style of Maurice Chevalier. Poulenc's song 'C' (from *Deux poèmes de Louis Aragon*, 1943) is dedicated to Papoum.

LETTER 30

1. In the summer of 1921, Cocteau and Radiguet left Paris for the Auvergne, in the company of Pierre Bertin and his wife, Marcelle Meyer. They were joined by Georges Auric. The group then moved on to Le Piquey, in the Gironde.

2. See letter 28, note 8.

3. Poulenc's orchestral arrangement of his music for *Le Gendarme incompris* (see letter 28, note 4) was performed on 11 July 1921, conducted by Ernest Ansermet, during the season of the Russian Ballet at the Prince's Theatre, London. It was also performed on 15 December 1921, at a Concert Wiéner in Paris.

4. The painter Irène Lagut (1893–?) was a regular supporter of the Groupe des Six. She designed the décor for *Les Mariés de la Tour Eiffel* (and also for the original production of Apollinaire's play *Les Mamelles de Tirésias* in 1917). Raymond Radiguet wrote a poem about her, entitled 'Dictée'. She is said to have been particularly attached to the young poet, to Cocteau's consternation. (*COCT* pp. 249–51)

5. Lucien Daudet (1879–1946) was the son of the novelist Alphonse Daudet (1840–97). He was an elegant and amusing man-about-town, a writer and a friend, among others, of Proust, Cocteau, Max Jacob and the ex-Empress Eugénie, whose letters he published under the title: *A l'Ombre de l'Impératrice Eugénie*. Poulenc dedicated his song 'Paul et Virginie' to Lucien Daudet in 1946.

LETTER 31

1. Les Terrasses was the home of the mother of André Manceaux, Poulenc's brother-in-law.

2. Charles Koechlin accepted Poulenc as a private student and continued to teach him until 1924. They remained in contact until the end of Koechlin's life. Poulenc always valued Koechlin's opinion – see Poulenc's Correspondents and letter 159.

LETTER 32

1. In a lecture he gave in 1947 entitled 'Mes mélodies et leurs poètes', Poulenc said of his settings of Apollinaire's poetry:

> The most important thing was that I heard the sound of his voice. I think this is essential if a musician does not want to betray a poet. The tone of Apollinaire's voice, like that of his poetry, was both melancholy and joyous. And now and then, there was a hint of irony in his words . . . [*FP-MMLP* p. 509]

LETTER 33

1. This ballet was to become *Les Biches* (see letter 45, note 1, and letter 48, note 1). Diaghilev refers here to Germaine Bongard, to whom the original idea of the ballet is attributed:

> In about [1921] Germaine Bongard devised a ballet with cantata, for which Poulenc was to provide the music and Marie Laurencin the costumes . . . This project did not materialize, but Poulenc and Laurencin eventually collaborated on the ballet *Les Biches* (1924). [*MODE* p. 210]

Germaine Bongard (1885–1971), born Poiret, was a sister of the couturier Paul Poiret (1879–1944). Herself a couturière of distinction, she counted among her clientèle many of Paris's artistic and musical elite. During the First World War her salon in the rue de Penthièvre became the venue for art exhibitions organized for the benefit of painters at the front, and of *soirées musicales*, including, in 1917, a concert of works by Satie, for the Red Cross. Germaine Bongard had two sisters equally renowned in the world of fashion, the dress designer Nicole Groult (1887–1967) and the jeweller Jeanne Boivin (1871–1959).

2. *Les Biches* was not completed until 1923 and was first performed by Diaghilev's Russian Ballet on 6 January 1924, at the Théâtre de Monte-Carlo. The conductor was Edouard Flament, the choreography was by Nijinska, the décor and costumes by Marie Laurencin. The costumes were executed in the atelier of Vera de Bosset Sudeikina, later the second wife of Stravinsky.

3. Bronislava Nijinska (1891–1972), sister of Vaslav Nijinsky (1888–1950), first danced with Diaghilev's Russian Ballet during the 1909 Paris season. In 1921 she was engaged by Diaghilev both as dancer and choreographer. From 1921–25 she was the sole choreographer for the company. Her ballet creations during this period included Stravinsky's *Renard* and *Les Noces*, Auric's *Les Fâcheux*, Milhaud's *Le Train bleu* and Poulenc's *Les Biches*. Later, she had a long and eminent career as choreographer and teacher both in Europe and the USA.

LETTER 34

1. Although they had corresponded in 1921, Poulenc and Bartók did not meet until 1922 when Bartók came to Paris for the first performance of his second piano concerto. Poulenc invited him to lunch, with Erik Satie and Georges Auric:

> I remember a strange luncheon at my home, on 8 April 1922, during which Bartók and Satie met for the first and last time. The date is particularly fixed in my mind as they both dedicated certain works to me on that day.

Like two birds with different songs, Bartók and Satie observed each other,
mistrusted each other, and maintained an overwhelming silence that
Auric and I tried in vain to break. For me, this has remained an
extraordinary and very symbolic memory. [*ECR* p. 47]

2. Alfredo Casella (1883–1947). Italian composer, conductor, pianist, teacher
and concert organizer, active in promoting new music. Talking of Casella's great
gifts as a pianist, Poulenc said that his own writing for piano had been influenced
by Casella's technique:

I was spellbound by the way this marvellous musician played the piano.
With what casual precision did his long fingers wander over the keys! What
perfect Staccato and what ingenuity in distributing parts between the two
hands! Without him, I would probably never have written the beginning of
my Concerto for two pianos in the way I did. [*ECR* p. 34]

3. Karol Szymanowski (1882–1937). Polish composer, one of the founders
in 1901 of the Young Poland movement, aimed at bringing Polish music to
international notice.

4. Bartók's ballet *The Wooden Prince* was written in 1914–16. His only opera,
Duke Bluebeard's Castle, was written in 1911.

5. The Waldbauer String Quartet was founded in 1909/10 by Imre Waldbauer
(1892–1952). It was the first ensemble to bring the quartets of Bartók and Kodály
before the public.

LETTER 35

1. In 1921 Poulenc asked Max Jacob to write a group of poems which he set to
music, dedicated to Darius Milhaud, and later destroyed. (*FP-MMA* p. 104)

LETTER 37

1. Max Jacob alludes to the prelude by Debussy entitled *Le Vent dans la plaine*.

2. A reference to René Maran (1887–1960) who, in the previous year 1921,
became the first black writer to win the Prix Goncourt with his novel *Batouala*.
Max Jacob indulges in a complicated pun here, as the word 'nègre' in French is also
a ghostwriter.

LETTER 38

1. Marie Laurencin was suffering from severe peritonitis following the removal
of her appendix in April 1922. (*ML* p. 206)

2. Cocteau and Radiguet were spending the summer of 1922 in Le Lavandou and
the nearby village of Pramousquier, on the Mediterranean coast.

3. The writer André Gide (1869–1951) was one of the founders in 1909 of the
monthly literary review, *La Nouvelle revue française*. He waged a consistently
hostile campaign against Cocteau.

4. See letter 29, note 1.

5. The poet Léon-Paul Fargue is reputed to have spent a large part of his life
sitting with his back to the murals which his father (the ceramic artist Fargue)
had created in one of the literary cafés of St-Germain-des-Prés.

6. Cocteau refers to the writers Jean de Tinan (1874–1898) and Paul-Jean Toulet (1867–1920).

7. Radiguet had rewritten the ending of his first novel *Le Diable au corps*. Auric was typing the manuscript for him.

LETTER 40

1. In 1911 Debussy, assisted by André Caplet, wrote the incidental music for *Le Martyre de Saint-Sébastien* by Gabriel d'Annunzio. The work was a synthesis of vocal and orchestral music, speech, dance and mime, with choreography by Michel Fokine and décor by Léon Bakst. The Russian dancer Ida Rubinstein played the title role. First performed at the Théâtre du Châtelet in 1911, the five-hour production was not a success. Later, attempts were made to revive the work in a modified form. It is to the June 1922 revival at the Paris Opéra that Poulenc refers in this letter.

LETTER 41

1. Suzanne Süe (born Bernouard) was the sister of the publisher François Bernouard and the wife of the architect Louis Süe, one of the founders of the Compagnie des Arts Français.

2. Marie Laurencin was recovering from peritonitis. See letter 38, note 1.

3. Marie Laurencin refers to her décor for Poulenc's ballet *Les Biches*.

4. Blanche was Marie Laurencin's maid.

LETTER 43

1. Raymond Radiguet's second novel, *Le Bal du Comte d'Orgel*.

2. *Chandelles romaines*. Unpublished ballet by Auric, written in 1918.

3. Cocteau refers to the incidental music for *La Femme silencieuse* (after Jonson), which Auric completed in 1925.

4. The drawing shows Stravinsky and Nijinsky at the piano during rehearsals for *Le Sacre du printemps* (*The Rite of Spring*). Stravinsky's ballet – evoking pagan rituals in ancient Russia – was composed for Diaghilev in 1911–13, with sets by Roerich and choreography by Nijinsky. The first performance of the work, at the Théâtre des Champs-Elysées on 29 May 1913, caused a celebrated riot.

LETTER 44

1. *The Song of the Nightingale* is a symphonic poem by Stravinsky, also used as a ballet score, derived from the second and third acts of his opera *The Nightingale*.

2. Poulenc's piano pieces, *Cinq Impromptus*, were composed in 1920–21 (revised in 1939) and dedicated to the pianist Marcelle Meyer (1897–1958). Poulenc also dedicated to her the third of his *Feuillets d'album pour piano* in 1933. Marcelle Meyer was a pupil of Viñes and Cortot and met Poulenc through Viñes. She was closely associated with Les Nouveaux Jeunes and Les Six and was married to Pierre Bertin (see letter 11, note 3).

3. See letter 45.

LETTER 45

1. Poulenc's ballet music *Les Biches* comprises an overture and eight dance movements. Three of these movements originally incorporated texts and tunes from traditional seventeenth-century French songs, set for offstage chorus, and entitled: 'Chanson dansée', 'Jeu', and 'Petite chanson dansée.' In 1947 Poulenc reworked his score so that the chorus could be used or not as required.

2. In 1922 Poulenc and Milhaud went to Austria with the singer Marya Freund (1876–1966). Polish by birth but resident in France, Freund was renowned as a singer of Lieder and also of many contemporary works. She had recently given the first performance in France of Schoenberg's *Pierrot lunaire* with Milhaud conducting. During their visit to Austria they repeated this performance in a double programme, contrasting their interpretation of the work with that of Schoenberg and the German singer Erika Wagner. While in Vienna, they met Mahler's widow, Alma, who introduced them to Schoenberg, Berg and Webern.

3. *Mavra*. Comic opera in one act by Stravinsky, on a libretto by Boris Kochno after Pushkin's poem 'The Little House of Kolomna'. Poulenc's article on *Mavra* appeared in the June–July issue of *Les Feuilles libres*, following the first performance of the work in Paris on 3 June 1922.

4. The critic Boris de Schloezer (1881–1969) published an article in the July 1922 issue of *La Nouvelle revue française* (no. 106, pp. 120–25) entitled 'Les Ballets Russes', containing such statements as '*Mavra* is Stravinsky's first failure . . . a sort of musical joke that is not sufficiently amusing . . . the subject is too thin, and the Italo-Russian and black-American styles do not mix.'

5. Richard Hammond (1896–1980) became one of Stravinsky's closest friends. At the time of this letter he was on the board of the Franco-American Music Society, connected with the Composers' Music Corporation in New York.

LETTER 46

1. Léo Latil was the son of the Milhauds' family doctor in Aix-en-Provence. He was a young poet of profoundly Catholic faith and a close friend of Milhaud. He was killed in action in 1915. He left his diary to Milhaud, extracts of which Milhaud used in the second movement of his Third String Quartet with Voice (1916) – written in memory of Léo Latil – and in a work for voice and piano, *Poème* (1921). Milhaud also set four of his poems under the title *Quatre poèmes de Léo Latil* (1914).

2. Les Saintes-Maries-de-la-Mer is a village in the Camargue, on the Mediterranean coast of France, known for its relics of St Marie-Jacobé and St Marie-Salomé who landed there in a small barque with their black servant Sarah after fleeing from the persecutions in Judaea about the year AD 40. In May and October, gypsy pilgrims come to honour Sarah, their patron saint. Milhaud was haunted by this village, which inspired, among other works, his chamber opera *Les Malheurs d'Orphée*, written for the Princesse Edmond de Polignac in 1924.

3. L'Enclos was the Milhaud family's home in Aix-en-Provence.

4. Fourques, near Lunel in the South of France, was the home of Jean Hugo. It became a celebrated meeting place for many of the artists and writers of the time.

5. Maggy Hugo. Sister of Jean Hugo.

6. Paul Morand (1889–1976), writer and diplomat. His diary, *Journal d'un attaché d'ambassade* (Gallimard, Paris, 1963), paints a fascinating picture of artistic circles in Paris in the first part of the twentieth century.

7. Chicherin (1872–1936) succeeded Trotsky as the Soviet Union's commissar for foreign affairs in 1918. He wrote a book on Mozart, which was published in Leipzig in 1975.

The 'Dimitri–Chanel marriage'. Reference to Chanel's liaison with the Grand-Duke Dimitri Pavlovitch, cousin of the last Tsar.

Saül. Play by André Gide written in 1897–99.

For Germaine Tailleferre, see note 9 below.

8. Comte Louis Gautier-Vignal, known in Milhaud's circle as 'a charming decadent who wrote a little'.

9. The French composer Germaine Tailleferre (1892–1983) was born in the same year as Honegger and Milhaud, and was a classmate of the latter at the Paris Conservatoire where, between 1913 and 1915, she won first prize for harmony, counterpoint and piano accompaniment. She was later included in the group Les Six. Poulenc met her in 1917 and remained in contact with her throughout his life (he called her Bidulette). Reminiscing about her to Claude Rostand in 1954, Poulenc said:

> How lovely she was in 1917, our Germaine, with her satchel full of all the first prizes from the Conservatoire! How sweet and gifted she was! She still is, but I somewhat regret that, through an excess of modesty, she was never able to exploit all the possibilities in herself as could, for example, someone like Marie Laurencin, who knew how to extract the most from her feminine genius. Be that as it may, she has made a most charming and precious contribution to music, and one that always delights me. [*ECR* p. 42]

10. There are further references to *Marches militaires* in letters written in 1924 and 1925 (see Nos. 79, 93 and 95). The composition is also mentioned in an undated postcard to André Schaeffner and in a letter to Stravinsky, written in the autumn of 1923, in which Poulenc says:

> I am working on some military marches for orchestra which are very complicated to do, at least as far as the construction is concerned. I think I may keep to a kind of 'Harlequin' of marches, welded together in such a way that each one gives the impression of developing out of the other.

However, no composition of this title, or fitting this description, appears among Poulenc's published works. The only marches by Poulenc are *Deux marches et un intermède*, dedicated to Antoinette d'Harcourt and written for the World Exhibition in 1937, as a musical accompaniment to a supper given on 24 June by Duke François d'Harcourt 'in honour of the writer Harold Nicolson and several other English intellectuals. . . . The guests partook of their pineapple dessert to the sounds of Poulenc's *Marche 1889*, their cheese to the strains of his *Intermède champêtre*, while his *Marche 1937* brought the supper to its close.' (*HH-FP* p. 144)

11. See under Paul Collaer in Poulenc's Correspondents.

12. The French writer and diplomat Henri Hoppenot (1891–1977) was secretary to the French Legation in Brazil while Milhaud and Claudel were there, from 1917–19. He wrote the libretti for Milhaud's three *Opéras-minute* (1927). In 1945 Hoppenot was appointed French Ambassador in Berne.

LETTER 48

1. To Claude Rostand, Poulenc describes how he came to name the ballet:
   One July evening I was returning from the Bastille in an open carriage with Valentine Hugo. I was trying to find an animal title, something like *Les Sylphides*, and suddenly I yelled: 'Why not *Les Biches*', thus playing on the animal nature of certain of Marie Laurencin's women and also on the double meaning of the word *biche* in the French language. [*ECR* pp. 54–55]

(The primary meaning of *biche* is *doe*. It is also used as a term of endearment, *my dear*, *my darling*. It was formerly used to mean a kept woman.)

2. The final form of the ballet was as follows: *I – Ouverture. II – Rondeau. III – Chanson dansée. IV – Adagietto. V – Jeu. VI – Rag-Mazurka. VII – Andantino. VIII – Petite chanson dansée. IX – Final.* Nos. III, V and VIII were scored for offstage chorus. See letter 45, note 1.

3. Boris Kochno (1904–90). As a young Russian poet, he became Diaghilev's secretary at the age of seventeen. He wrote the libretto for Stravinsky's *Mavra* and provided the poetic argument for many ballets, including Prokofiev's *Prodigal Son*. He later became artistic director for a series of major ballet companies in France and America and commissioned works by such composers as Milhaud, Sauguet and Kurt Weill.

LETTER 51

1. Poulenc's Sonata for clarinet and bassoon (dedicated to Audrey Parr), and his Sonata for horn, trumpet and trombone (dedicated to Raymonde Linossier), were completed in the autumn of 1922 (revised 1945). Jean Wiéner wanted the two sonatas for a Satie–Poulenc Festival he was organizing on 2 November 1922, as part of his celebrated series, the Concerts Wiéner. Poulenc, however, declined on two counts in a letter to Wiéner written in September 1922. He said:
   In the first place, November 2nd is *All Souls' Day*! In the second place, as I have already tried to explain to you, my Sonatas (both for clarinet and bassoon, and for horn, trumpet and trombone) are *very difficult*. Especially the latter, where the balance between the instruments is *fearful*. I need to be present at the first readings, which I hope will take place around 24 October. So the Sonatas could be ready towards the end of November. I swear to you, *mon petit Jean*, that this is not affectation on my part. I am sure you will understand how important these two first performances are for me. I have been working like a slave, and from the

point of view of technique I do not have anything as polished as these
latest productions. I think I am entering my great period, of which *Les
Biches* will undoubtedly be No. 1. But I must not sacrifice works on a
smaller scale which show a parallel development – in fact quite the
contrary.

Poulenc's letter evidently had the desired effect, as Jean Wiéner delayed the
Satie–Poulenc concert until 4 January 1923, when both Poulenc's sonatas – for
clarinet and bassoon, and for horn, trumpet and trombone – were given their
first performance in the same programme as Satie's *La Belle excentrique* and
Socrate, the latter sung by Suzanne Balguerie, with orchestra conducted by
André Caplet. (*AA* p. 52)

LETTER 52

1. Stravinsky refers to a concert of his works given on 26 December 1922 at the
Théâtre des Champs-Elysées, conducted by Ernest Ansermet.

LETTER 53

1. Poulenc refers to the concert version of Falla's *El Amor brujo*, a ballet with
songs in one act. It was not until 22 May 1925 that the first stage performance
was given in Paris, at the Trianon-Lyrique, with Falla conducting. Chester
published the score in 1921.

2. Falla's *Fantasía Baetica*, a 25-page bravura piece for piano solo, written in
1919 for Arthur Rubinstein and first performed by him in New York in 1920. The
work was published by Chester in 1922.

3. This was to be Poulenc's Trio for piano, oboe and bassoon, written and
published in 1926.

LETTER 54

1. *El Retablo de Maese Pedro* (Master Peter's Puppet Show), puppet opera for
voices and orchestra with libretto by Falla based on an episode from Cervantes'
Don Quixote. This work was commissioned by the Princesse de Polignac in 1919.
The first concert performance, to which Falla refers in this letter, was given on
23 March 1923 by the Orquesta Bética de Cámara for the Sociedad Sevillana de
Conciertos, with Falla conducting. On 25 June 1923, the first private puppet
performance took place at the home of the Princesse de Polignac in Paris. The
harpsichord part was played by Wanda Landowska. Ricardo Viñes helped
to manipulate the puppets. (It was during the rehearsals for this performance
that Viñes introduced Poulenc to Landowska.) The conductor was Vladimir
Golschmann (1893–1972). Of Russian parentage, he was closely associated with
the group Les Six and its precursors. In 1919 he founded the Concerts
Golschmann devoted mainly to avant-garde music. From 1920–24 he was
conductor for Diaghilev's Russian Ballet and from 1931–56 of the St Louis
Symphony Orchestra.

LETTER 55

1. Emile Poulenc (father of Francis) and his two brothers Gaston Joseph and

Camille were the founders of the chemical company Poulenc Frères which, after
the 1914–18 war, merged with Usines du Rhône to become Rhône-Poulenc,
manufacturers of chemical and pharmaceutical products and artificial textile
fibres. Poulenc was instrumental in obtaining a position for Raymond Radiguet's
brother Paul in the chemical plant.

LETTER 56

1. Auric was typing Radiguet's second novel, *Le Bal du Comte d'Orgel*. Earlier
in July 1923, Radiguet wrote to his father: 'I await Auric like the Messiah. He has
a typewriter!' (*RAD* p. 88)

2. During the summer of 1923, which he was spending with Raymond
Radiguet at Le Piqueÿ, in the Bay of Arcachon, Cocteau wrote *Le Pauvre
matelot*, a drama in three acts about a sailor fatally caught in a trap he himself
has set. Faced with Auric's lack of enthusiasm for his scenario, Cocteau
approached Darius Milhaud, who found the story appealing and who composed
the music for it in 13 days in the summer of 1926.

LETTER 57

1. For his 1924 Monte Carlo season, Diaghilev planned to produce three comic
operas by Gounod and one by Chabrier, replacing the spoken passages between
arias with music. For these recitatives, which he wanted written in the same
style as the opera, Diaghilev commissioned the following composers:

Satie – *Le Médecin malgré lui* (Gounod)
Poulenc – *La Colombe* (Gounod)
Auric – *Philémon et Baucis* (Gounod)
Milhaud – *L'Education manquée* (Chabrier)

According to Auric, when Gounod's heirs heard his recitatives for *Philémon et
Baucis*, they refused permission for them to be performed, but willingly accepted
those of Satie and Poulenc. Chabrier presented no problems as he had no heirs.
(*QJL* pp. 28–29)

LETTER 60

1. There is no quintet for strings and clarinet among Poulenc's published
works.

LETTER 61

1. *Thomas l'Imposteur* was one of Cocteau's first two novels, written during
the summer of 1922 while he was at Pramousquier with Radiguet, and published
in 1923.

2. On the reverse of Cocteau's postcard to Poulenc is a picture of a voluptuous
young woman on a swing. Written across it, in Cocteau's hand, are the words:
'Misia, by Renoir'.

3. Cocteau and Radiguet were spending the summer in a fisherman's shack at
Le Piqueÿ.

LETTER 62

1. Satie refers to the Gounod recitatives that he and Poulenc were writing for Diaghilev. See letter 57, note 1.

LETTER 63

1. Max Reger (1873–1916). German composer, conductor, and professor of counterpoint at the Leipzig Conservatoire.

2. Robert Lyon (1884–1965). Director of the music publishing and piano manufacturing firm, Pleyel & Cie.

3. Les Rochers. Stravinsky's residence in Biarritz.

4. By 'the Danes', Poulenc refers to the music publishing firm in Copenhagen, Wilhelm Hansen.

5. In 1923 Poulenc took rooms in the house La Lézardière, in Nazelles, Touraine, belonging to Mme Virginie Liénard (1845–1935), a friend of the family and a widow. Her husband Paul (they were known as 'Paul et Virginie') was killed in the 1870 war, shortly after they were married. Virginie Liénard was a woman of great culture. She had heard Wagner conduct *Lohengrin* in Brussels, had been present at one of Liszt's last concerts in Italy and, at 89, was devoted to the music of Stravinsky. Poulenc was deeply attached to her and always addressed her as 'Tante Liénard'. He lived in her house in Nazelles for some five or six years until he bought Le Grand Coteau in the neighbouring village of Noizay. He also made frequent use of an apartment she owned in Cannes. His piano pieces *Les Soirées de Nazelles* (1936) are dedicated 'to the memory of Tante Liénard'.

LETTER 65

1. *Chanson à boire*, for unaccompanied male choir, was Poulenc's first choral piece. It was written under the guidance of Charles Koechlin in 1922 for the Harvard Glee Club. For this work, Poulenc chose an anonymous seventeenth-century text from the same anthology of poems that he later used for his *Chansons Gaillardes*.

Poulenc did not conduct the work in Spain, despite Falla's urgings. Soon after he had despatched his boisterous drinking song to Harvard, prohibition laws came into effect, making it impossible for the song to be performed. He then forgot about the work, until in 1950, in Holland, he heard it sung by the male Choir of The Hague, in the same programme as his *Prières de Saint François d'Assise*. Poulenc attached great importance to the *Chanson à boire*, feeling that it contained the germs of all his later choral techniques. (*ECR* p. 97)

2. No *Fantaisie espagnole* appears among Poulenc's published works. Falla probably refers to the *Caprice espagnol* which Poulenc mentions in letter 53 and which he says he has scrapped.

LETTER 66

1. Stravinsky's ballet cantata, *Les Noces*, is a series of choreographic scenes based on Russian peasant themes and customs, scored for soprano, mezzo-soprano, tenor and bass soloists, chorus, four pianos and percussion ensemble. It

was first performed in Paris in 1923 by Diaghilev's Russian Ballet. In the opening season, Poulenc played one of the four piano parts, with Georges Auric, Marcelle Meyer, and Hélène Léon. (Poulenc did not take part in the actual première due to an attack of jaundice; he was replaced by Edouard Flament, who conducted the première of *Les Biches* in Monte Carlo in 1924.) In 1962 Poulenc told Stéphane Audel that he had played in *Les Noces* on more than 40 occasions. (*FP-MMA* p. 191)

LETTER 68

1. Poulenc was orchestrating his ballet *Les Biches*.

2. Poulenc often refers to the 'intuitive genius' of Nijinska who choreographed *Les Biches* and who seemed 'to feel instinctively' the subtle allusions and suggestive ambiguities in the ballet. (*ECR* pp. 53–54)

3. Roger Désormière (1898–1963), known as 'Déso'. Conductor and composer who, with Henri Sauguet, Maxime Jacob and Henri Cliquet-Pleyel formed the Ecole d'Arcueil under the aegis of the Maître d'Arcueil, Erik Satie. Désormière conducted premières of Poulenc's *Pastourelle*, from *L'Eventail de Jeanne* (1927), the Concerto for organ with Maurice Duruflé (1939), the ballet *Les Animaux modèles* (1942), and the Sinfonietta (1948). Poulenc considered his 1952 recording of *Les Biches* (Decca LXT 2720) to be the best there was: 'No one will ever conduct this work as perfectly as Désormière. His recording captures the whole flavour of *Les Biches* in all its cynical freshness.' (*ECR* p. 52)

LETTER 69

1. *La Création du Monde*, ballet in one act by Milhaud, to a libretto by Blaise Cendrars and with décor by Fernand Légar, composed in 1923 for the Swedish Ballet Company.

2. *Pierrot lunaire*, work for female voice and chamber orchestra by Schoenberg, composed in 1912. See also letter 45, note 2.

LETTER 70

1. Raymond Radiguet died of typhoid fever in the early hours of 12 December 1923, aged twenty. Cocteau recounts that on 9 December, in his delirium, Radiguet had said to him: 'In three days I am to be executed by God's firing squad . . . The order has been given. I heard the order . . .' (Preface by Cocteau to Radiguet's *Le Bal du Comte d'Orgel*, Grasset, 1924, p. 8.)

LETTER 71

1. Radiguet's funeral was arranged by Coco Chanel. The church and coffin were covered in white flowers, as was the hearse, drawn by two large white horses, which carried the coffin to the cemetery of Père Lachaise. Cocteau, too ill with grief, did not attend the funeral. (*COCT* pp. 314–317)

LETTER 72

1. See letter 57, note 1.

2. *La Brebis égarée*, Milhaud's first opera, with a text by Francis Jammes (1868–1938), was written in 1910–14 and first performed at the Opéra-Comique in Paris in December 1923, conducted by Albert Wolff (1884–1970). Wolff had been conductor at the Opéra-Comique since 1911. He was director of music there from 1921–24 and director from 1945–46. Wolff was also associated with the Concerts Lamoureux and the Concerts Pasdeloup. From the late 1940s he was conductor at the Paris Opéra where he conducted many first performances, including Poulenc's *Les Mamelles de Tirésias* in 1947.

Albert Carré (1852–1938) was director of the Opéra-Comique from 1898–1913 and, with Emile and Vincent Isola, from 1919–25. Carré, shocked at the audience's violent response to *La Brebis égarée*, placed on each seat a copy of the sarcastic reviews that had greeted the first performance of Debussy's *Pelléas et Mélisande* together with the warning: 'Be careful!'

LETTER 73

1. *Le Bal du Comte d'Orgel* was published after Radiguet's death, in 1924, by Bernard Grasset, with a preface by Cocteau.
2. See letter 55, note 1.

LETTER 74

1. In an unpublished letter to Poulenc written in March 1923, Marie Laurencin expresses a similar sentiment:

> I am so disgusted with my work, and I say this without the slightest affectation. Everyone else's style of painting seems so much more suitable than mine for décor and the dance.

LETTER 75

1. Poulenc's Sonata for clarinet and bassoon (1922) and his Sonata for horn, trumpet and trombone (1922) were published by Chester in 1924.
2. *Les Biches* was published by Heugel in 1924.
3. Satie's cheerful mood did not last. See letter 77, note 1.
4. Edouard-Léon-Théodore Mesens (1903–71). Belgian composer, poet and painter, a founder of the surrealist movement in Belgium. He settled in London in 1937. In 1938 he became director of the London Gallery and editor of the London Bulletin. His articles and exhibitions aimed at forging links between the English, French and Belgian Surrealists. He translated French surrealist poetry into English, including, with Roland Penrose, Paul Eluard's *Poésie et Vérité 42*.

LETTER 76

1. The ballet *Les Biches* is set in a white salon in which the only piece of furniture is a vast couch in what Poulenc referred to as 'Laurencin blue'.

LETTER 77

1. Satie plays on the words *Sieur* (Sire) and *Scieur* (slang for 'a great bore').

L.L. was the writer, musicologist and critic, Louis Laloy (1874–1943). A close friend of Debussy, he had been a severe critic of the music of Satie and Les Six. During the 1924 Monte Carlo season, however, he warmed towards Auric, Poulenc and Cocteau, and wrote enthusiastic articles about *Les Biches* and *Les Fâcheux*. Satie, who despised Laloy, saw the growing friendship between his disciples and Laloy as a personal betrayal. After flinging abuse at Auric and Poulenc, he is said to have left Monte Carlo in a rage, standing in the corridor of the train during the entire journey back to Paris. (*COCT* pp. 321–322)

Matters deteriorated when Poulenc and Auric bought a child's rattle, in the shape of a bearded head closely resembling Satie's, and sent it to him in Arcueil. Satie reacted angrily to this prank. (*HH-FP* pp. 75–76)

He became estranged from the two younger composers following two further events. The first occurred in June 1924. Poulenc, in an association he later regretted, joined a group of Surrealists in a protest against the ballet *Mercure* for which Satie had written the music.

The second occurred in November 1924. In an article entitled 'Adieu, Satie', Auric published a severe criticism of Satie's music for Picabia's ballet *Relâche*. Reconciliation was now impossible.

Both Poulenc and Auric regretted their part in this feud and never failed to acknowledge Satie's influence on their lives. In his memoirs, published in 1979, Auric wrote: 'At this stage of my life, I believe I was undoubtedly wrong . . . to quarrel with this great elder to whom I still owe so much. He literally *adopted* me and our conversations remain as present and as topical as ever.' (*QJL* p. 32). And Poulenc, in his interviews with Claude Rostand in 1954, said: 'Satie's influence on me was considerable, both spiritually and musically . . . His music remains one of the treasures I hold most dear in all of music.' (*ECR* p. 46)

LETTER 79
1. Vera Nemchinova danced the role of the Girl in Blue in Poulenc's ballet *Les Biches*.

2. In *Paris-Journal* of 15 February 1924, in an article entitled:

THE RUSSIAN BALLET AT MONTE CARLO
by Erik Satie
(Travel Notes)

Satie described *Les Biches*, *Les Fâcheux* and the Gounod operas as 'Gloriously oversweet', 'syrups of all kinds', 'musical lemonade' and 'lollipop music'.

3. See letter 46, note 10.

LETTER 80
1. On Poulenc's score of Stravinsky's Concertino, the following inscription appears:

For Francis Poulenc, this score, which I promised him, but which he bought for 15 francs!!! His friend who likes his music very much, I. Stravinsky. Café de la Paix, 16 February 1924.

LETTER 82

1. Cocteau had joined Georges Auric in a villa in Villefranche-sur-mer, called 'Le Calme'. He was trying to recover from the effects of his grief over Radiguet's death and his experiments with opium to assuage that grief.

2. Cocteau considered himself free from any obligations to Satie and free to offer *Paul et Virginie* (see letter 29, note 1) to Poulenc, in view of Satie's openly expressed antipathy towards them since the Monte Carlo season in January 1924.

LETTER 83

1. Poulenc had made copies of the photographs of Radiguet in his possession. He sent these to Cocteau and to Radiguet's father. See letters 84 and 87.

2. In this letter, as in all his letters since 1921, Cocteau addressed Poulenc by the familiar form *tu*. His use here of the collective plural *vos oeuvres* implies that it was not only Poulenc's works that kept him going, but the works of all those in the group.

LETTER 85

1. Poulenc did not complete his Trio for piano, oboe and bassoon until 1926. He dedicated the work to Manuel de Falla. It was first performed on 2 May 1926 at a concert of works by Auric and Poulenc, in the Salle des Agriculteurs.

2. According to a postcard from Poulenc to A. Schaeffner (Bibliothèque Gustav Mahler) this concerto was the composition *Marches militaires*.

LETTER 88

1. For Poulenc's meeting with Wanda Landowska, see under Poulenc's Correspondents and also letter 54, note 1.

2. Landowska's mother, Eve, had just died.

LETTER 89

1. Satie died on 1 July 1925, after six months of a degenerating illness diagnosed as cirrhosis of the liver combined with pleurisy. He died in the Hôpital Saint-Joseph in Paris, in a private room secured for him by Comte Etienne de Beaumont who had endowed a ward there. Refusing to see either Auric or Poulenc, Satie remained intransigent to the end, saying to Milhaud: 'They have said goodbye to me already, and now that I am ill I prefer to hold them to it. One must stick to one's guns to the last.' (*MVH* p. 145)

LETTER 90

1. Satie's predilection for umbrellas is well-documented. In his interviews with Stéphane Audel, Poulenc comments:

Winter and summer alike, Satie never appeared without the bowler hat
that he respected, or the umbrella that he worshipped. When he died and
people were at last able to enter his room at Arcueil – where, during his
lifetime, no one had ever dared venture – a hundred or so umbrellas were
discovered . . . some still in their wrapping paper. [*FP-MMA* p. 85]

2. Eugénie was Satie's stepmother.

3. These and various other initials were used as a secret code between Poulenc
and Raymonde Linossier, and dated from their childhood. It is said that no one
was ever able to decipher this code.

LETTER 91

1. Satie's brother Conrad did not know the address of their sister, who had
married and lived somewhere in Buenos Aires. According to French law, Satie's
belongings therefore had to have seals placed on them until a public sale of his
property could be held. Milhaud describes in his memoirs how he and his wife
Madeleine, the conductor Roger Désormière, the pianist Jean Wiéner and the
young composer Robert Caby, together with Conrad Satie, evolved a plan to
acquire among themselves everything personal that had belonged to the
composer. Désormière was given the task of standing next to the auctioneer and
of bidding for anything of interest to the group. In this way, Comte Etienne de
Beaumont acquired a portrait of Satie playing the organ by Antoine de la
Rochefoucauld; Braque bought a portrait by Desboutins, as well as Satie's old
piano; and Milhaud himself came away with walking-sticks, drawings, rough
drafts and sketches, and a large painting of Satie by Zuloaga. Prior to the sale,
Milhaud had also been entrusted with all Satie's personal papers, letters and
manuscripts. (*MVH* pp. 146–147)

2. See letter 29, note 1.

LETTER 92

1. Milhaud married his cousin Madeleine Milhaud in May 1925. They were to
spend their honeymoon in Palestine, but Milhaud fell ill in Beirut and they
returned to France via Egypt.

Madeleine Milhaud was born in Paris in 1902. She studied the piano with
Marguerite Long and dramatic art with Charles Dullin. Although much of her
married life was devoted to nursing Milhaud through the prolonged arthritic
attacks from which he suffered, she had an active career in teaching and
producing French plays with students, first during the summer sessions at Mills
College, California (where the Milhauds spent the years 1940–47) and later at
Aspen, Colorado, where she returned every summer from 1950–70. She wrote,
or adapted, libretti for three of Milhaud's operas and, in 1982, compiled a
comprehensive catalogue of Milhaud's works, published by Editions Slatkine,
Geneva–Paris.

LETTER 93

1. See letter 46, note 10.

2. Poulenc's suite for piano (originally called *Caprice italien* and renamed *Napoli*) was inspired by a trip to Italy with Milhaud in 1921 (see letter 26, note 1). Poulenc did not complete the work until 1925. It consists of three parts: (1) Barcarolle (2) Nocturne (3) Caprice italien. Marcelle Meyer performed the first two movements at a concert on 17 March 1924, and gave the first performance of the complete work at the Auric–Poulenc concert on 2 May 1926, in the Salle des Agriculteurs. In later years, Poulenc rejected this work entirely. Reviewing his piano compositions in his interviews with Claude Rostand in 1954, he said:

> . . . I can tolerate *Mouvements perpétuels*, my old Suite in C major, and *Trois pièces* (the former Pastorales). I am very fond of my two sets of *Improvisations*, an *Intermezzo* in A flat and certain of the *Nocturnes*. I condemn outright *Napoli* and the *Soirées de Nazelles*. As for the rest, I don't care one way or the other. [*ECR* p. 35]

3. During the summer of 1925, Cocteau completed *Orphée*, his play about Orpheus and the birth of poems. He also illustrated new editions of his novels *Le Grand Ecart* and *Thomas l'Imposteur*, and wrote *Lettre à Jacques Maritain*, a document in celebration of an artist's disintoxication and his return to the sacraments.

LETTER 94

1. *Esther de Carpentras*, *opéra-bouffe* in two acts, Milhaud's setting of a comedy by his friend Armand Lunel (see below) based on old family stories interwoven with an eighteenth-century play in the Hebraic-Provençal dialect.

2. Milhaud refers to his four-hand arrangement of Satie's music for the film *Entr'acte* by René Clair, shown during the interval of Picabia's ballet *Relâche*.

3. Armand Lunel (1892–1977), writer and teacher of philosophy, was a lifelong friend of Milhaud. They were born in the same year, attended the same school, and began collaborating at the age of eighteen. Several of Milhaud's songs are settings of poems by Lunel. He also wrote the libretti for various operas by Milhaud, including *Les Malheurs d'Orphée* (1924) and *David* (1952), written for the 1954 Festival of Israel.

LETTER 95

1. The family of the writer Alphonse Daudet owned a turreted residence near Amboise, in Touraine, known as Le Château de la Roche.

2. Madeleine Le Chevrel (1881–1954). Society hostess who entertained 'le Tout-Paris' at her mansion in the rue de Ranelagh during the 1920s and '30s.

3. The Baron and Baroness Adolf de Meyer. The Baroness, born Olga Alberta di Caracciolo, was a godchild of Edward VII and an intimate of the Princesse Edmond de Polignac before the First World War.

4. *Les Matelots*. Ballet by Auric with choreography by Massine, commissioned by Diaghilev for his 1925 season.

LETTER 96

1. Max Jacob's collection of poetry *Les Pénitents en maillot rose* was

written in 1925. Five 'Poèmes burlesques' from this collection are dedicated to Poulenc.

2. The flirtatious back-chat and wordplay known as *marivaudage* derives from the comedies of Marivaux (1688–1763).

3. Russell Greeley, a wealthy American, and his friend Comte François de Gouy d'Arcy were flamboyant drinkers and men about town, members of the Radiguet–Cocteau–Auric set.

LETTER 97

1. Claire Croiza (1882–1946). French mezzo-soprano, born Claire Connolly, of an American–Irish father and an Italian mother. She sang in opera and in recital and was closely associated with composers including Fauré, Saint-Saëns, Duparc, Debussy, Roussel, Bréville and Honegger. Poulenc thought highly of Croiza's interpretation of *Le Bestiaire*, and accompanied her in a recording of this work in 1928 (Columbia D 15041). He dedicated to her 'Je n'ai plus que les os' from *Poèmes de Ronsard* (1925).

2. Baroness d'Erlanger lived in the former town-house of Lord Byron, in Piccadilly.

3. Vittorio Rieti (*b.* 1898). Italian composer who studied both music and economics in Milan, graduating as a Doctor of Economics in 1917. In the early 1920s he was associated with Massarani (1898–1975) and Labroca (1896–1973) in a group calling itself I Tre, in imitation of Les Six. From 1925–40, Rieti divided his time between Rome and Paris and, from 1931–40, was on the selection committee of the chamber music society, La Sérénade, in Paris. In 1940, he moved permanently to the USA.

4. Alice Nikitina (1909–78), Russian dancer who joined Diaghilev's Russian Ballet in 1923. Lydia Sokolova [Hilda Munnings] (1896–1974). British dancer, the first English ballerina to join Diaghilev's company (in 1913).

5. After its success at the 1924 Monte Carlo season, Diaghilev took *Les Biches* to the London Coliseum, where it was performed in 1925 and 1926.

LETTER 98

1. Falla's Concerto for harpsichord (or pianoforte) was completed in 1926 and dedicated to Wanda Landowska.

2. The Russian-born conductor, composer and double bass virtuoso, Serge Koussevitzky (1874–1951) was, from 1924–49, conductor of the Boston Symphony Orchestra, for whom he commissioned many new works. He was the creator of the Serge Koussevitzky Music Foundation, formed as a memorial to his first wife Natalia who died in 1942. The aim of the Foundation was to commission and have performed new works by composers of all nationalities. From 1949 the Library of Congress, Washington DC, was made the repository of all scores commissioned by the Foundation. Poulenc's *Gloria* was the result of a commission from this Foundation. See also letter 298, note 1.

3. At the time of this letter, the conductor Leopold Stokowski (1882–1977) was director of the Philadelphia Orchestra, a post he held from 1912–36.

4. Landowska did not perform Falla's Concerto in Paris in the spring of 1927, as planned. There were differences of opinion between herself and Falla which led to Falla himself playing the solo part at the Paris première. (*FP-MMA* pp. 126–127)

5. When Poulenc heard Landowska's performance of Falla's *El Retablo de Maese Pedro* in 1923 at the home of the Princesse de Polignac, he promised her that he would write a concerto for her. But it was not until 1926, when he visited her at her home in Saint-Leu-la-Forêt (see below), that he found the inspiration for this composition: 'I decided to compose a rustic concerto reminiscent of the forest of Saint-Leu, where Rousseau and Diderot once strolled and where Couperin, like Landowska, once lived.' (*FP-MMA* p. 57)

His first concerto, the *Concert champêtre* for harpsichord and orchestra, was completed in 1928 and dedicated to Landowska.

6. In 1925 Landowska built a house at Saint-Leu-la-Forêt, to the north of Paris, at the edge of the forest of Montmorency. Filled with her collection of musical instruments, books and scores, it looked out over a classical French garden with recital room at one end, in which she gave celebrated Sunday afternoon concerts. It was here that she founded her *Ecole de musique ancienne*.

LETTER 99

1. Stravinsky's oratorio *Oedipus Rex* had its première on 30 May 1927 at the Théâtre Sarah-Bernhardt in Paris, with Stravinsky conducting. The libretto, based on the tragedy of Sophocles, was a Latin translation of a text by Cocteau.

LETTER 100

1. Suzanne Peignot is puzzled by Poulenc's remark that she had a relative who was a pianist.

2. Falla was unable to accompany Suzanne Peignot in his *Seven Spanish Folksongs* which she sang at the home of a Madame Juge, a friend of the Poulenc family.

LETTER 101

1. It was not until the following year, on 3 May 1929, that Landowska gave the first public performance of Poulenc's *Concert champêtre* in the Salle Pleyel, Paris, with the Paris Symphony Orchestra conducted by Pierre Monteux. A few days before this event, Landowska performed the concerto for a private audience at her home in Saint-Leu-la-Forêt, with Poulenc playing the orchestral part at the piano. (*HH-FP* p. 91)

LETTER 103

1. Poulenc refers to the two volumes of Koechlin's *Traité de l'harmonie* written between 1923 and 1926 and published by Eschig in 1927 and 1928.

2. See letter 105, note 1.

3. In 1928 Poulenc bought Le Grand Coteau on the outskirts of the village of Noizay, near Amboise, in Touraine. The house, built in the sixteenth century and extended in the eighteenth, stands on a gentle slope surrounded by vineyards. It

leads on to a formal terrace, designed for Poulenc by his brother-in-law, André Manceaux. To the left of the house is a grove of linden trees. In the music room, Poulenc installed his grand piano, his upright piano, and his work table, where he always sat with his back to the windows and the view. Poulenc bought Le Grand Coteau because he needed a place where he could work in solitude, away from the distractions of Paris. In 1964, the year after Poulenc's death, the road that leads to Le Grand Coteau was officially named Le Chemin Francis Poulenc.

4. Poulenc had lent Charles Koechlin 2,000 francs early in 1926. (Unpublished letter in the collection of Madeleine Li-Koechlin.)

LETTER 104

1. Landowska gave the first performance of Poulenc's *Concert champêtre* on 3 May 1929.

2. As Landowska had no children, it is thought that she refers here to two of her devoted followers, one of whom would have been Denise Restout, editor of *Landowska on music* (London, 1965).

LETTER 105

1. Poulenc's *Aubade* for female dancer, piano and eighteen instruments, was the result of a commission by the Vicomte and Vicomtesse de Noailles (see letter 129, note 5) for a costume ball given at their Paris residence in the Place des Etats-Unis on 18 June 1929. Poulenc composed a 'choreographic concerto' simultaneously highlighting a female dancer and a pianist. As with all his ballets, Poulenc wrote the scenario himself, basing it on the myth of Diana, condemned to eternal chastity. For the first performance at the home of the Noailles, Nijinska devised the choreography, in accordance with Poulenc's concept of Diana's melancholy isolation. The first public performance, however, on 21 January 1930 at the Théâtre des Champs-Elysées, was choreographed by Georges Balanchine, who changed the scenario to incorporate the myth of Diana and Actaeon. Poulenc strongly disapproved of this version. He felt that the intrusion of the male presence betrayed his music by shattering the essentially feminine solitude he had sought to evoke. (*ECR* pp. 79–81)

2. Sauguet's opera *La Chartreuse de Parme*, with libretto by Armand Lunel after Stendhal, was not completed until 1936 and was first performed at the Paris Opéra in 1939.

3. The two works mentioned by Sauguet are *Le Plumet du colonel* (1924), his *opéra-bouffe militaire* in one act, for which he also wrote the libretto, and his settings of verses by Schiller, *Quatre poèmes de Schiller* (1928).

LETTER 106

1. When Falla received the score of Poulenc's Trio he wrote to Poulenc:
    I was overjoyed to receive the Trio – MY TRIO! – so eagerly awaited. I like it so much that, at the very first opportunity, we will perform it in Seville (keeping the piano part for myself, of course) . . . Many thanks, dear friend, for the joy your music brings me, and for dedicating your Trio to

me, of which I am nobly proud. (Unpublished letter dated 12 January 1927.)

2. Falla refers to the recording of Poulenc's Trio published in 1929, (French) Columbia D 14213/4, with Poulenc (piano), M. Lamorlette (oboe) and G. Dhérin (bassoon).

LETTER 107

1. Poulenc's painter friend was Richard Chanlaire. Poulenc met him in the mid-1920s and they remained friends throughout Poulenc's life. Richard Chanlaire had a studio-flat on the Quai des Grands-Augustins in Paris and a boutique in Tourrette-sur-Loup in the South of France, where he exhibited his pictures, hand-painted scarves and screens. He died in the early 1970s.

2. The Orquesta Bética de Cámara of Seville was founded at Falla's instigation by the Sevillan cellist, Segismundo Romero, and the choirmaster of Seville Cathedral, Eduardo Torres. The orchestra was regularly conducted by Ernesto Halffter, Falla's pupil.

LETTER 108

1. The main body of this letter is in typescript. The ending is in manuscript. The letter was typed by the composer's sister, María del Carmen de Falla, who devoted her life to keeping house for him and caring for him through his many illnesses. Falla suffered from attacks of iritis, haemorrhages, high fevers, and severe weight loss, but the exact nature and cause of his illnesses remains obscure.

LETTER 109

1. In this broadcast of Poulenc's *Concert champêtre*, relayed from the Queen's Hall, Landowska was accompanied by the BBC Symphony Orchestra conducted by Ernest Ansermet.

2. The Spanish composer and conductor Bartolomeo Pérez Casas (1873–1956) founded the Philharmonic Orchestra of Madrid in 1915.

3. The Spanish cellist Pablo Casals (1876–1973) founded the Orquesta Pau Casals in Barcelona in 1919.

LETTER 111

1. *Il y a* is a collection of works by Apollinaire published in 1925, containing 41 poems written between 1895 and 1917, and articles on literature and painting. Most of the poems by Apollinaire which Poulenc set to music were taken from this volume, with the exception of *Le Bestiaire* and *Calligrammes*.

2. Poulenc set *Trois poèmes de Louise Lalanne* in 1931. The first poem 'Le Présent' and the third, 'Hier', are by Marie Laurencin. The central poem, 'Chanson', is by Apollinaire. Poulenc dedicated the work to the Comtesse Jean de Polignac. It was first performed by Suzanne Peignot with Poulenc accompanying, on 1 June 1931 at a Poulenc Festival. See letter 112.

3. Apollinaire was for a time secretary of the literary review *Les Marges*. Beginning early in 1909 and continuing for over a year, he wrote a column on women authors, under the pseudonym of Louise Lalanne. In addition to articles on women writers, he reviewed the works of his 'sister-poets' and also contributed several poems of his own. To end the hoax it was announced that Mlle Lalanne had been abducted by an army officer.

LETTER 112

1. It was Suzanne Peignot, not Gilbert Moryn, who gave the first performance of *Quatre poèmes de Guillaume Apollinaire* at this concert.

2. Poulenc's Sextet was not performed at this concert as it was not completed until 1932. The first performance was given in December 1933 at a concert of La Sérénade. In 1939, Poulenc revised the entire work. This revised version was first performed in December 1940 at the Salle Chopin, by members of the Association Musicale Contemporaine.

3. The 'famous concert' had taken place on 2 May 1926. Poulenc and Auric hired the Salle des Agriculteurs (no longer in existence) to present an evening entirely of their own compositions, and found that they had to turn away more than 200 people. At this concert, Poulenc's Trio was first performed, and Pierre Bernac sang for the first time accompanied by Poulenc, in his *Chansons gaillardes*. (For the formation of the Bernac–Poulenc duo, see letter 123, note 1.)

LETTER 113

1. See letter 29, note 1.

LETTER 114

1. See letter 29, note 1. It is not clear whether Sauguet ever began work on *Paul et Virginie*, but no operetta of this name appears among his published compositions.

2. The German composer and music theorist Paul Hindemith (1895–1963) formulated a harmonic system based on the revision and enlargement of traditional tonality. He was an opponent of Schoenberg's twelve-tone serialism. His compositions include the opera *Mathis der Maler* (1934–35) and the piano work *Ludus tonalis* (1942), a cycle of studies in counterpoint and tonal organization. Poulenc, asked by Claude Rostand in 1954 whether he admired Hindemith's sense of form, replied:

> The form is not what I admire most in Hindemith – I find it often too academic. What I admire most is his lyricism, both heavy and lively, like quicksilver, in works such as his ballet *Les Quatre tempéraments*. Or, on the other hand, the wonderfully static quality of his *Nobilissima visione*. [*ECR* p. 183]

LETTER 115

1. Poulenc's article: 'A propos de la *Symphonie de Psaumes* d'Igor Stravinsky'

appeared on page 249 of the February 1931 issue of *Le Mois*. It concluded with the words: 'I salute you, Johann Sebastian Stravinsky!'

LETTER 117

1. 'L'Anguille' is the first of the four poems by Apollinaire that Poulenc set to music in 1931, under the title *Quatre poèmes de Guillaume Apollinaire*.

2. The second of the *Quatre poèmes*, entitled 'Carte postale', begins:

L'Ombre de la très douce est évoquée ici
(The shadow of the sweet one is evoked here).

3. Colette refers to the third poem, 'Avant le Cinéma, which contains the following lines:

Si nous étions des Artistes	If we were Artists
Nous ne dirions pas le cinéma	we would not say the cinema
Nous dirions le ciné	we would say the ciné
Mais si nous étions de vieux professeurs de province	but if we were old professors from the provinces
Nous ne dirions ni ciné ni cinéma	we would say neither ciné nor cinema
Mais cinématographe	but cinematograph
	[translation: Winifred Radford]

4. '1904' is the last of the *Quatre poèmes de Guillaume Apollinaire*.
5. 'As Hebe who served the gods' and not 'whom the gods served'.

LETTER 118

1. 'Souric et Mouric' is the fifth song in Poulenc's *Cinq poèmes de Max Jacob* for voice and piano, composed in 1931. The poems are from Max Jacob's collection *Chants Bretons*, written under the pseudonym of Morven le Gaëlique, inspired by his Breton heritage. (In the literary edition 'Souric et Mouric' is called 'Chanson'.) Poulenc says of this work: 'It was composed at Nogent where I was spending two months in 1931 in the house of my childhood, quite empty but full of memories. I cannot play this song without thinking of my dog, Mickey, lying under the piano.' (*DMS* p. 31)

2. *Le Bal masqué*, a secular cantata for baritone and chamber orchestra, was commissioned by the Vicomte and Vicomtesse de Noailles, for a 'spectacle concert' to be performed in the Théâtre d'Hyères on 20 April 1932. As well as Poulenc, the following people contributed to this production: Buñuel, Giacometti, Markevitch, Bérard, Auric, Nabokov and Sauguet.

Poulenc's cantata has six movements, two of which are purely instrumental. The vocal sections are settings of poems from Max Jacob's collection, *Le Laboratoire central* (1921). Poulenc was especially fond of *Le Bal masqué*, feeling that in it he had managed to glorify the particular atmosphere of Parisian suburbia that was so dear to him: '*Le Bal masqué* is for me a sort of Nogent carnival, with the portraits of a few monsters I remember from my childhood, on the banks of the Marne.' (*ECR* p. 142)

In the first performance at the Théâtre d'Hyères, the orchestra was conducted by Roger Désormière and the baritone solo was sung, 'with marvellous truculence', by Gilbert Moryn. (*Ibid.*)

LETTER 119

1. See letter 108, note 1.

LETTER 120

1. Poulenc refers to 'Souric et Mouric', from *Cinq poèmes de Max Jacob*.

2. Pierre de Ronsard (1524–85), the most eminent and prolific poet of the French Renaissance, was renowned for his court poetry, his love sonnets, and his celebration of his native countryside – the Loire Valley. Poulenc's house in Noizay, Le Grand Coteau, dates from the era of Ronsard. Poulenc set six of Ronsard's poems, five in 1924–25, under the title *Poèmes de Ronsard* and the sixth in 1935, 'A sa Guitare', written specially for the singer Yvonne Printemps (1894–1977) in her role as Marguerite de Valois in the play *La Reine Margot* by Edouard Bourdet (1887–1945).

LETTER 121

1. For the Pro Arte Concerts, see under Paul Collaer in Poulenc's Correspondents.

2. The concerts given by the Philharmonic Society of Brussels were directed by Henry Le Boeuf.

3. Henry Prunières (1886–1942). Writer on music and founder in 1920 of *La Revue musicale*.

4. Poulenc's Concerto in D minor for two pianos was commissioned by the Princesse Edmond de Polignac and dedicated to her. The work was composed in 1932 and first performed on 5 September of that year at the ISCM Festival in Venice, with the orchestra of La Scala, Milan, conducted by Désiré Defauw (see below) and with Poulenc and Jacques Février as soloists. Poulenc had known Février (1900–79) since childhood and had a great respect for his musicianship. He wrote his concerto for two pianos with a view to performing it with Février. Février recorded a number of Poulenc's works for piano and was artistic director of a set of the complete chamber works (VSM 2C 165–12519/22) in which he also took part. He is the dedicatee of Poulenc's sixth *Improvisation* (1932).

5. Désiré Defauw (1885–1960). Belgian conductor and violinist, prominent as a performer of contemporary music. He became conductor of the Brussels Royal Conservatoire Orchestra and, from 1926–40, director of the Brussels Conservatoire. From 1943–49 he was conductor of the Chicago Symphony Orchestra.

LETTER 122

1. Poulenc was working on the first version of his Sextet in 1932. This seems to suggest that his letter to Marie-Blanche de Polignac was written in the winter of 1932–33, rather than in 1936, the date given to the letter in *Correspondance*. See also notes 2 and 3 below.

2. The 'concerto of this summer' is his Concerto for two pianos (see letter 121, note 4).

3. Poulenc's main pianistic output was concentrated in the years 1932–34: *Nocturne* (No. 1); *Valse-Improvisation sur le nom de Bach*; *Improvisations* (Nos. 1–10); *Feuillets d'album*; *Villageoises* (6 'petites pièces enfantines'); *Presto*; *Deux Intermezzi*; *Humoresque*; *Badinage*.

4. 'Le grand Georges' was Georges Salles, as opposed to 'le gros Georges', Georges Auric. Georges Salles was curator at the Louvre and later Director of National Museums in France. His many writings include the book *Le Regard*, much-lauded by Adrienne Monnier. During the early 1930s, whenever Poulenc was in Paris, he stayed in the home of Georges Salles. Poulenc's Sextet (1932–39) and his work for mixed choir *a cappella Exultate Deo* (1941) are dedicated to Georges Salles.

5. Marie-Blanche de Polignac's aunt by marriage, the Princesse Edmond de Polignac, had commissioned the Concerto for two pianos. Poulenc presumably refers here to the Paris première of the work, the world première having taken place in Venice on 5 September 1932.

LETTER 123

1. This is the first communication from Pierre Bernac to Poulenc. It is quoted by Poulenc in his conversations with Claude Rostand (*ECR* p. 89).

The background to this note is outlined by Bernac in the fourth of ten interviews with Gérard Michel for French radio *France Culture* (20 November 1970–15 January 1971). He recalls that after giving the first performance of *Chansons Gaillardes* in 1926 (see letter 112, note 3) he and Poulenc lost contact until June 1934, when they met at a *matinée musicale* in the home of a mutual friend, Madame Mante-Rostand, sister of the playwright Edmond Rostand. Bernac said:

> She was an excellent musician who played the piano very well . . . and that day she was accompanying me in songs by Debussy. Poulenc was among the guests. When the music came to an end he told me, while eating his *petits fours*, that he, too, would like to accompany me in songs by Debussy and, of course, in his own songs. I answered that this would be a great pleasure for me but would have to be discussed again later in the autumn as I was leaving in a few days for Salzburg to work on my Lieder repertoire with my dear old master, Reinhold von Wahrlich.
>
> In Salzburg that summer, a certain American woman had rented a superb house overlooking the Mirabell Gardens. She was very rich and quite mad – when you visited her you invariably found her in bed, with a toy rifle aimed in your direction. This woman had the excellent idea of organizing a private Debussy evening, and she asked me to sing. I knew that Poulenc was due to arrive in Salzburg to review the Festival for *Le Figaro*, so I left a note at his hotel asking him to accompany me. . . .
>
> That Debussy evening was to have far-reaching consequences for us both. And what a strange evening it was! First of all, there was an orchestral concert at the Mozarteum, conducted by a young man for whom a great future was predicted: Herbert von Karajan. Then, the audience went into the Mirabell Gardens where, in that verdant theatre,

Serge Lifar and the Vienna Opera Ballet danced *L'Après-midi d'un faune*. After the ballet, the audience crossed the Mirabell Gardens, scaled a very high wall with the help of a wooden staircase specially commissioned for the occasion by the American lady, and landed in the garden of her house!

There, beneath an enormous tree, was a piano. And it was there that, on the stroke of midnight, Francis Poulenc and I gave a concert that was to be the first of a very long series. For such was the success of that concert and of our musical affinity that we decided to form a duo dedicated to bringing to the vocal repertoire a similar attention to perfection and ensemble that is sometimes found in certain instrumental duos.*

Bernac and Poulenc gave their first recital on 3 April 1935 in the Salle de l'Ecole Normale de Musique in Paris. Their last recital took place on 27 May 1959 at the Salle Gaveau. In the intervening 24 years Poulenc wrote over 90 songs for Bernac to sing at their concerts.

LETTER 124

1. Poulenc's *Poèmes de Ronsard* (see letter 120, note 2) were first performed by Suzanne Peignot accompanied by Poulenc at the Salle des Agriculteurs on 10 March 1925. At the time of this letter to Suzanne Peignot, Poulenc was preparing an orchestral version of the work. The first song, 'Attributs', is dedicated to Suzanne Peignot.

2. These hopes of a Promenade Concert did not materialize, although Suzanne Peignot remembers giving recitals in London in 1937 and in 1945 with Poulenc, Auric and the pianist Monique Haas.

3. Poulenc refers to the activities of the organization Le Triton, which gave twice-monthly concerts of chamber music and song by contemporary musicians. It was founded by Pierre Octave-Ferroud (1900–36) (see also letter 130, note 1). The composer and critic Florent Schmitt (1870–1958) was a member of the Comité d'honneur of Le Triton, together with such composers as Bartók, Casella, Falla, Schoenberg and Stravinsky.

4. Marya Modrakowska (1896–1965), Polish singer with whom Poulenc toured North Africa in 1933 and for whom he arranged eight Polish folksongs, *Huit chansons polonaises*. The eighth song in the set is dedicated to Modrakowska.

5. The German soprano Lotte Lehmann (1888–1976), who was known to use a score when giving solo recitals.

6. Suzanne Peignot's second husband, Henri Laubeuf.

LETTER 126

1. Poulenc's beloved 'Tante Liénard' (Mme Paul Liénard) died on 11 May 1935, aged 90.

*Bernac used this interview in a slightly varied form as part of the introduction to his book *Francis Poulenc – the man and his songs*, trans. Winifred Radford, Gollancz, London, 1977 (*Francis Poulenc et ses mélodies*, Buchet/Chastel, Paris, 1978).

2. In September 1932, Falla and Poulenc – also Arthur Rubinstein – were among the guests of the Princesse Edmond de Polignac in her Venice home, the Palazzo Polignac on the Grand Canal. Poulenc was in Venice for the first performance of his Concerto for two pianos (see letter 121, note 4). This was the last time that Poulenc saw Falla. In his conversations with Stéphane Audel, he recalls an evening walk with Falla to a small Venetian church with a magnificent organ. As the two composers entered the church, the organist was playing something by Frescobaldi. Falla sank to his knees, plunged in prayer: 'My final picture of him is that of a man, or rather a Zurbarán monk, deep in prayer in a church in Venice.' That night, Falla left Venice to return to Spain and in 1939, moved to the Argentine, where he died in 1946. (*FP-MMA* pp. 115–119)

3. *Don Quichotte à Dulcinée* is Ravel's last composition, written in 1932. The three songs on texts by Paul Morand were intended for a film directed by Pabst with Chaliapin as Don Quixote. In the event, they were not used, music by Ibert being substituted for Ravel's. Although scored for voice and orchestra, Ravel provided his own arrangement of the accompaniment for piano. Poulenc recalls that while rehearsing this cycle with the singer Madeleine Grey for one of her recitals, they had performed it to Ravel himself to hear his opinion. (*FP-MMA* pp. 185–186). It is perhaps to this 'distinguished guidance' that Falla refers in his letter.

LETTER 127

1. The date given to this letter in *Correspondance* is 1939. However, Eluard was no longer living in the rue Legendre in 1939. He left there in October 1938 and, until he was called up in September 1939, he and his wife Nusch lived in 'La Maison grise' at Le Pecq. 1936 seems a likelier date as Eluard was in Spain with Picasso during January and February of that year and the poem included in his letter to Poulenc was written at this time.

2. According to Louis Parrot (*PE-LP* p. 43) this poem was written one night on the table of a café in Madrid where the Spanish poet Lorca and his friends used to meet. It was published in 1936 as part I of five poems entitled 'Intimes' in the collection *Les Yeux fertiles*. Although Poulenc did not set this particular poem, he chose part IV ('Figure de force brûlante et farouche') and part V ('Je n'ai envie que de t'aimer') from 'Intimes' for his song cycle *Tel jour telle nuit*.

LETTER 128

1. From these three collections of poetry by Eluard, Poulenc was to choose the last poem in *Facile*: 'Nous avons fait la nuit' as the final section of his song cycle *Tel jour telle nuit* (1938).

2. In March–April 1936, at Noizay, Poulenc composed *Sept chansons* for mixed choir *a cappella*. Five of the seven poems set in this work are by Eluard, Nos. 2–5 from *La Vie immédiate* (1932), and No. 7 from *Répétitions* (1922). Nos. 1 and 6 that complete *Sept chansons* are by Apollinaire. The work is dedicated to André and Suzanne Latarjet (sister of Raymonde Linossier), and to the Chanteurs de Lyon, who gave the first performance on 21 May 1937 at a concert of La Sérénade.

LETTER 129

1. Poulenc's Concerto for organ, string orchestra and timpani, was commissioned by the Princesse Edmond de Polignac and dedicated to her. Although the score gives the date of this concerto as 'April–August 1938', the above letter and letter 130 show that Poulenc was already working on this concerto as early as 1936. There is a further indication of the time he spent writing this concerto in his statement to Claude Rostand: 'It was I who suggested writing an organ concerto . . . and the Princesse de Polignac even allowed me to put off the delivery date for a year, knowing how slowly I work.' (*ECR* p. 164). The concerto was first performed on 21 June 1939 at the Salle Gaveau by Maurice Duruflé and the Paris Symphony Orchestra conducted by Roger Désormière.

2. The 15th *arrondissement* in Paris includes the rue de Vaugirard.

3. In 1936 Poulenc took a small *chambre de bonne* at 5 rue de Médicis, overlooking the Luxembourg gardens, in the same building occupied by his uncle Papoum. It was not until after his uncle's death in November 1945, that Poulenc moved into a full apartment at the same address (see letter 192, note 4). He maintained this apartment as his Paris home until the end of his life. A plaque at the entrance door commemorates Poulenc's presence there. At the nearby corner of the rue de Vaugirard and the rue de Tournon there is a further homage to the musician, the Square Francis Poulenc.

4. Kerbastic, also familiarly known as Kekker, had been the Britanny home of the Polignac family for generations. It was the favourite residence of Marie-Blanche de Polignac and a meeting-place for many of her friends during the summer. Both she and Comte Jean de Polignac chose to be buried near it, on a hill overlooking the river Laïta.

5. For Misia, see letter 17, note 3.

Marie-Laure, Vicomtesse de Noailles, was the daughter of a wealthy American banker named Bischoffsheim and, on her mother's side, a descendant of the Marquis de Sade. In 1923, at the age of 21, Marie-Laure married the Vicomte Charles de Noailles. In their residence in Paris, their château near Fontainebleau and their home in Hyères, they held some of the most dazzling salons and parties of the era. The Noailles were lavish supporters of the arts, commissioning such films as *L'Age d'or* by Buñuel and Dali, and *Le Sang d'un poète*, by Cocteau. Poulenc's *Aubade* and *Le Bal masqué* were written for them and dedicated to them. To Marie-Laure, Poulenc also dedicated his seventh *Improvisation* for piano, the song 'Peut-il se reposer' (from *Cinq poèmes de Paul Eluard*), and 'Je nommerai ton front' (from *Miroirs brûlants*).

LETTER 130

1. The worst of the year 1936 was yet to come: it was during his stay in Uzerche that summer that Poulenc learned of the death of his friend, the composer Pierre-Octave Ferroud, who was killed in a car accident at Debrecen, in eastern Hungary, on 17 August 1936. Poulenc says that the shock of this event, which brought home to him the frailty of the human condition,

awakened in him a religious fervour that had its roots in the devout Catholicism of his father's family. (*ECR* pp. 107–109 and *FR-ROC*). His first religious work dates from this time, the summer of 1936. See letter 339, note 1.

2. Poulenc puns on the name Yvonne Gouverné: Yvonne the Governess and Pierre the Governed. Towards the end of the summer, Poulenc and Bernac would meet to work on the repertoire for the forthcoming season of concerts. Yvonne Gouverné would join them to coach and advise them.

3. Titillon was Marie-Blanche de Polignac's dog, immortalized in a painting by Edouard Vuillard (1868–1940) showing the countess seated on a bed with the dog on her lap. (Musée d'Orsay)

4. Poulenc presumably refers to Poonie, Marie-Blanche de Polignac's Persian cat.

5. Léon Blum (1872–1950). French writer and statesman, the first Socialist (and the first Jewish) premier of France, presiding over the Popular Front coalition government in 1936–37.

6. Colonel de La Roque (1885–1946). French politician who, after his retirement, formed the ex-servicemen's para-military organization, the *Croix de Feu* which developed into a right-wing political party, the Parti Social Français.

7. Emile Loubet (1838–1929). French statesman, President of the French Republic from 1899–1906. He contributed to the controversial break between the French government and the Vatican (1905) and to improved relations with Great Britain by signing the Entente Cordial in 1904. He was also responsible for setting Dreyfus free.

8. Georges Clemenceau (1841–1929). French statesman known as 'The Tiger', dominant figure in the French Third Republic and premier from 1917–20. He was a champion of radical causes such as Zola's campaign for Dreyfus, was a major contributor to the Allied victory in the First World War and an architect of the post-war Treaty of Versailles. His grandson René Jacquemaire was the first husband of Marie-Blanche de Polignac.

9. The playwright Edouard Bourdet was appointed director of the Comédie Française in 1936. He owed this appointment to Jean Zay (1904–1944), Minister of Education in France from 1936–39. Zay was responsible for many enlightened scholastic reforms. During the Second World War he joined the Resistance movement, was arrested on the orders of the Vichy government and executed.

10. The Popular Front Government celebrated its accession to power in 1936 by a gala theatrical performance of Romain Rolland's 1902 drama, *Le Quatorze Juillet*. The composers commissioned to write the music for this patriotic pageant were Koechlin, Roussel, Honegger, Ibert, Auric, Milhaud and Daniel Lazarus.

11. The second of Poulenc's *Deux Intermezzi* for piano (1934) was dedicated to Marie-Blanche de Polignac.

LETTER 131

1. Verrières-le-Buisson was the estate of the Vilmorin family. The house, dating from 1680, was built by Louis XIV for Mlle de la Vallière. The Vilmorins, scientists and horticulturalists for generations, had purchased it

towards the end of the eighteenth century and had added to it over the years.

2. Louise de Vilmorin's three poems, 'Le Garçon de Liège', 'Au-delà' and 'Aux Officiers de la Garde blanche' were set to music by Poulenc at the end of the following year, 1937, under the title *Trois poèmes de Louise de Vilmorin*. They were first performed by Marie-Blanche de Polignac – to whom they were dedicated – on 28 November 1938 at the Salle Gaveau, with Poulenc accompanying.

3. Louise de Vilmorin met Jean Hugo in 1935, while travelling to the South of France with Georges and Nora Auric. Jean Hugo told her that as a child he had collected words, that his parents had rewarded him for being well-behaved by giving him a word. Louise de Vilmorin ascribed her own awareness of words to this meeting with Jean Hugo. (*LV* p. 99)

LETTER 132

1. Poulenc had written a song cycle on nine poems by Eluard, the first eight from Eluard's *Les Yeux fertiles* (1936) and the last, 'Nous avons fait la nuit . . .', from *Facile* (1935). Feeling that *Les Yeux fertiles* (Fertile eyes) was too visual for song settings, Poulenc asked Eluard to suggest other titles. He chose Eluard's second suggestion, *Tel jour telle nuit* (As the day, so is the night).

LETTER 133

1. Nadia Boulanger (1887–1979), French conductor, composer, organist, pianist and teacher, the first woman to conduct an entire programme for the Royal Philharmonic Society in London (in 1937) and the first woman conductor of the Boston Symphony Orchestra, New York Philharmonic, and Philadelphia Orchestra (in 1938). She was also the founder and conductor of a vocal ensemble renowned particularly for its performances of Monteverdi. Among the singers who performed with this ensemble were Hugues Cuénod, Paul Derenne, Doda Conrad and Marie-Blanche de Polignac. In 1936, at the home of the Princesse Edmond de Polignac, Poulenc had been present at several performances of Monteverdi Motets given by Nadia Boulanger's Ensemble Vocal. The performances inspired in him a deep appreciation of what he called 'these polyphonic marvels', and greatly affected his later choral writing. (*ECR* p. 98). Nadia Boulanger's influence as a teacher was extensive. See letter 233, note 1.

2. The poet Blaise Cendrars, in his capacity as concert organizer, was going to Brazil and hoped to arrange a recital there for Suzanne Peignot, but this did not eventuate.

3. Charles Panzera (1896–1976). Swiss baritone and teacher renowned for his interpretation of the *mélodie*. He formed a celebrated duo with his wife, the pianist Madeleine Baillot.

4. Suzanne Peignot says that she took Poulenc's advice and joined Nadia Boulanger's vocal ensemble.

LETTER 134

1. In *Correspondance*, this letter is dated 1935. However, according to the

postmarks on the envelopes clearly accompanying Poulenc's letters to Madeleine Grey (in the Music Department of the Bibliothèque Nationale), this letter and letter 137 are respectively dated December 1937 and June 1938.

2. A footnote in *Correspondance*, p. 94, suggests that Poulenc was due to make a recording with Madeleine Grey for the publisher Enoch. It would appear that the recording was made, but destroyed on Poulenc's advice (see letter 137).

LETTER 136

1. Poulenc's *Sept Chansons* on poems by Eluard and Apollinaire. See letter 128, note 2.

2. Poulenc's 'symphony' is his cantata for mixed choir and orchestra, *Sécheresses*. See letter 138.

3. Poulenc composed his Mass in G in the summer of 1937, in Anost, near Autun in the Morvan, where he was spending a month with Bernac and Yvonne Gouverné, working on the repertoire for the forthcoming season of concerts. Dedicated to the memory of his father, the Mass is Poulenc's first liturgical work.

LETTER 138

1. The date given in *Correspondance* is 1940. This conflicts with the fact that the Concerto for organ, which Poulenc was working on when he wrote the letter, was completed in 1938 and first performed on 21 June 1939.

2. Poulenc's cantata for mixed choir and orchestra, *Sécheresses*, on poems by Edward James (see below) was first performed at a Concert Colonne in May 1938, by the Chanteurs de Lyon. This performance was one of Poulenc's most memorable failures. He described the events to Claude Rostand:

> Everything seemed to conspire against me. The singers from Lyons were grossly overtaxed, having given the first performance that very morning of my Mass, in the Dominican Chapel of the rue du Faubourg Saint-Honoré. In addition, there was only one rehearsal on the Saturday morning with the conductor Paul Paray who, held up in Sweden due to plane trouble, arrived in Paris 48 hours late. In spite of his skill and his immense good will the performance was a disaster and the reception was glacial. I can still see myself coming out of that concert, saying to Auric: '*Sécheresses* will never be performed again. It is a total failure, I am going to destroy it,' and Auric, with his usual perspicacity, replying 'You can quite easily destroy your *Poèmes de Ronsard* or your *Soirées de Nazelles*, but on no account this!' [*ECR* pp. 100–101]

The work was successfully revived, not the following year, as Poulenc would have liked, but on 16 February 1941, by the Chorale Yvonne Gouverné, at a concert of the Société des Concerts du Conservatoire, conducted by Charles Munch.

3. Poulenc revised the work again in 1951.

4. Edward James (1907–84). Minor English poet and wealthy collector of surrealist art. In the 1940s he moved first to California and then to Xilitla, a remote mountain village in the Mexican jungle. There he constructed a series of surreal follies, all of which remained unfinished at the time of his death. He left

most of his vast fortune to West Dean College, a craft centre which he founded after the Second World War in what had been his family's principal house, West Dean Park, in West Sussex.

5. It was not Charles Munch but Roger Désormière who conducted the first performance of Poulenc's Concerto for organ, on 21 June 1939.

LETTER 139

1. This letter was probably written in 1938 (not 1936, as suggested in *Correspondance*) as Poulenc mentions his completed Concerto for organ (1938) and, in the final paragraph, urges Marie-Blanche de Polignac to work on the Vilmorin settings 'for the coming season'. She gave the first performance of *Trois poèmes de Louise de Vilmorin* in November 1938.

2. The Hon. Anthony Chaplin and his wife Alvilde, born Bridges. She was a close friend of the Princesse Edmond de Polignac, particularly during the last years of the Princesse's life. She later married the English historian and man of letters, James Lees-Milne.

3. See 1 above.

LETTER 140

1. Poulenc had asked Eluard to find a title for his two songs 'Tu vois le feu du soir' and 'Je nommerai ton front' – settings of Eluard's poems 'Nous sommes' and 'Vertueux solitaire' that first appeared in the review *Mesures* (15 July 1938) and later in the collection *Chanson complète* (1939). See letter 141.

2. At the end of September 1938 Paul and Nusch Eluard rented 'la Maison grise' in Le Pecq, near Saint-Germain-en-Laye, an outlying suburb to the west of Paris. They remained there until September 1939 when Eluard, a lieutenant in the reserve army, was called up.

LETTER 141

1. Poulenc accepted Eluard's suggestion of *Miroirs brûlants* (Burning mirrors) as a title for his set of two songs 'Tu vois le feu du soir' and 'Je nommerai ton front'.

2. Line 21 of the poem 'Tu vois le feu du soir' ends with the words 'leur miroir ancien' (their ancient mirror).

3. 'Gold and Cold Water.' Eluard used this title for a poem that appeared in his 1939 collection, *Chanson complète*.

4. Lines 7–8 of 'Tu vois le feu du soir' contain the words 'mélancolie dorée' (golden melancholy).

5. *Vivre d'amour et d'eau fraîche* – (to live on love and fresh air).

LETTER 142

1. The dress rehearsal for Sauguet's opera *La Chartreuse de Parme* which had its première at the Paris Opéra in March 1939.

2. The décor for *La Chartreuse de Parme* was created by Sauguet's great friend, the artist and stage designer Jacques Dupont (1908–76).

3. Sauguet's 1938 setting for voice and piano of the poem 'Le Chat' by Baudelaire, from *Six mélodies sur des poèmes symbolistes*.

LETTER 143

1. The two songs Poulenc mentions, 'Garçon de Liège' (from *Trois poèmes de Louise de Vilmorin*) and 'La Grenouillère' were both dedicated to Marie-Blanche de Polignac. 'La Grenouillère' was published by Deiss in 1939.

LETTER 144

1. An edition of Louise de Vilmorin's poetry was published by Gallimard in 1939 under the title *Fiançailles pour rire*. Under the same title, Poulenc set six poems from this collection towards the end of 1939. *Fiançailles pour rire* was first performed on 21 May 1942 by Geneviève Touraine, accompanied by Poulenc. In 1945, Winifred Radford gave the first performance of this work in England, accompanied by Gerald Moore.

2. In 1937 Louise de Vilmorin married Count Paul Pálffy of Slovakia and went to live in his castle, the Château de Pudmerice, in the foothills of the Carpathian Mountains.

LETTER 145

1. See letter 140, note 2.

LETTER 146

1. For his first operatic work, Poulenc chose as his libretto a play by Apollinaire, written in 1903, with a Prologue and a final scene added in 1916, *Les Mamelles de Tirésias*. Poulenc had attended the première in 1917 but it was not until the late 1930s that he had the idea of setting it as an *opéra-bouffe*. His letter to Sauguet confirms that although the date of composition is given on the score as 'May–October 1944', Poulenc had begun working on it as early as 1939.

Apollinaire's burlesque takes place in the exotic setting of Zanzibar. A young woman, Thérèse, dissatisfied with her role as mother and housewife, determines to rid herself of her womanhood. She opens her blouse and her breasts float away – in the shape of two balloons. With a cigarette-lighter, she bursts the balloons and promptly begins to sprout a beard. Then, as Tirésias she is free to pursue a career, and it is her husband who must assume the role of child-bearer. He obliges by producing some 40,000 babies a day. Eventually Thérèse returns to him and, while they dance an amorous waltz, the chorus spells out the message of the play: 'Frenchmen, make babies!'

The 'slight modifications' that Poulenc refers to were made with the approval of Apollinaire's widow. In addition to minor cuts in the play, Poulenc changed the action from 1917 to 1912 'because 1912 is the heroic era of Apollinaire', and substituted Monte Carlo for the exoticism of Zanzibar 'because Monte Carlo, which I adore, and where Apollinaire spent the first fifteen years of his life, is quite tropical enough for the Parisian that I am'. (*ECR* p. 148). Dedicated to Darius Milhaud in celebration of his return to France from the USA after the war, *Les Mamelles de Tirésias* opened at the Opéra-Comique on 3 June 1947, in a production by Max de Rieux, with décor by Romain Erté. The conductor was Albert Wolff. The role of Thérèse/Tirésias was sung by Denise Duval.

LETTER 147

1. Princesse Henri de Polignac was the sister of Jean de Polignac and the mother of Prince Louis de Polignac.

LETTER 148

1. The Princesse de Polignac recalls the two concertos (for two pianos, and for organ) that she had commissioned Poulenc to write.

2. Audrey Colville died on active service in England on 7 May 1940. She was at that time married to her third husband, Colonel Norman Colville, and was assistant county director for the Cornwall Branch of the British Red Cross. Born Audrey Gunzbourg in France, she was of German, Polish and Brazilian lineage. During the First World War, married to her second husband Raymond Parr, Secretary to the British Legation, she had been in Rio at the same time as Milhaud and Claudel and they had become firm friends. She designed, among other things, the décor and costumes for Milhaud's ballet, with scenario by Claudel, *L'Homme et son désir*. In Milhaud's words, she was 'a delightful friend of dazzling beauty and irrepressible high spirits' (*MVH* p. 66). Claudel was fascinated by her. He 'fluttered round her like a great moth around a whirling flame' (*CPC* p. 18). Poulenc's friendship with her dated from the beginning of the 1920s. In 1922, he dedicated his Sonata for clarinet and bassoon to her. In 1939 he stayed at her home in London, having taken ill during a concert tour. From 24 Hyde Park Gardens, he wrote to the Marquise Elisabetta de Piccolellis, cancelling his forthcoming concerts in Italy:

> I have the most dreadful 'flu, caught in that glacial Ireland where the ailment is rampant at present. Bernac, who had been resisting, succumbed with a temperature of 104° this morning . . . I am staying, thank God, at Audrey Parr's, an angel to me. [*Correspondance* pp. 108–109]

Poulenc's song 'Hyde Park' (1945) is dedicated 'To the memory of Audrey Norman Colville'.

LETTER 149

1. On 3 September 1939 Eluard, under his original name of Grindel, and with the rank of lieutenant, was called up for service and given the post of quartermaster at Mignères-Gondreville, Loiret, where he remained until his demobilization on 25 June 1940.

2. Eluard suffered from tuberculosis and his health was always precarious. In a letter to his first wife, Gala, dated 27 September 1939 from Mignères, he wrote: 'Although I am doing my best in a post which is not unpleasant, since it prevents one from thinking for twelve hours a day, I feel – on certain mornings and

evenings – quite tired and depressed. I am coughing a lot [. . .] Will I hold out?'
(*PE-LàG* p. 299)

3. Eluard's second wife, Nusch, was born Maria Benz, the daughter of itinerant circus performers from Alsace. She met Eluard when she was 23, in December 1929, a few months after Gala had left Eluard for the Catalan painter, Salvador Dali. Eluard married Nusch in August 1934. From then until her death at 40 from a cerebral haemorrhage in November 1946, she remained his constant companion, inspiring much of his greatest love poetry. She was also the inspiration for celebrated portraits by Picasso and Magritte, and photographs by Man Ray and Dora Maar. Poulenc's 'Le Front comme un drapeau perdu' (from *Tel jour telle nuit*) is dedicated to Nusch Eluard. After her death, Poulenc set and dedicated to her memory a poem from Eluard's collection *La Vie immédiate* entitled 'Peu de vertu' (Small virtue). Instead of using that title, Poulenc chose the last two words of the poem, '. . . mais mourir' (. . . but to die), as the name of his song.

LETTER 150
1. 'Pont-aux-Dames' is a retirement home for actors.
2. Poulenc's favourite saint was Saint Anthony of Padua. See letter 163, note 2.

LETTER 151
1. Poulenc refers to a letter he wrote to Adrienne Monnier during the First World War, dated 28 December 1918, on paper headed Villenauxe-la-Grande (Aube), in which he said:

And this evening at your bookshop, Mademoiselle, someone will be at the piano, another reading Fargue's poetry, you will all be among friends, in the warmth of sympathetic surroundings. How ill it makes me to think of all these joys whilst I am here, shivering in a hovel without doors! This time it is the absolute limit. Never have I been so miserable. I am stuck here in this hole where there is not even a piano. Yesterday – I'll admit this to you because you are a very good friend – I cried like a baby when I thought of Paris and all my friends; I cannot see an end to all this and that is what makes me despair [. . .] Colette David, to whom I am usually quite indifferent, appears almost desirable when I think of her now, as I do of the furniture in your shop.

2. 'Ce doux petit visage' for voice and piano was written in April 1939 at Noizay and published by Rouart-Lerolle in 1941. It is a setting of part VII of Eluard's poem 'Passionnément' from his volume *Cours Naturel* (1938). Poulenc expressed a great liking for this song: 'I have tried here to transfuse into music all the tenderness of Eluard's poem. I think I have succeeded.' (*DMS* p. 51)

LETTER 152
1. La Tour de Masse is a farm owned by relatives of Francis Poulenc, centering on a fifteenth-century tower, in the hills of Aveyron, near Espalion (birthplace of Poulenc's father). Built in 1453 as a wine farm by the monks of a neighbouring Cistercian monastery, the Tour de Masse was bought by Poulenc's grandfather,

Etienne Poulenc, in 1864. It passed from him to his son Camille, uncle of Francis, and is now owned by Pierre Poulenc, son of Camille and cousin of Francis.

2. In Greek mythology Philemon and Baucis offered hospitality to Zeus and Hermes when all others turned them away, and were immortalized as symbols of conjugal love.

3. Poulenc's second ballet, *Les Animaux modèles*, based on six fables by La Fontaine. See letter 154.

LETTER 154

1. Poulenc completed his ballet *Les Animaux modèles* in September 1941. He based this work on six fables by La Fontaine, choosing only those fables with human characters, or replacing animals with their human counterparts – the cricket becoming a faded ballerina, the ant, an old maid from the provinces, the amorous lion, a rake who dances the Javanaise. Poulenc set the ballet in the time of Louis XIV, which he felt was the most 'specifically French' of all historical eras. To reinforce these nationalistic undertones, he introduced into the seventh scene (The Two Roosters) the theme of the old song *Non, non, vous n'aurez pas notre Alsace-Lorraine*. (*ECR* p. 58)

The title *Les Animaux modèles* was one of five suggested by Paul Eluard (see letters 155 and 156). The ballet was first performed at the Paris Opéra on 8 August 1942, with choreography by Serge Lifar, sets and costumes by Maurice Brianchon, and orchestra conducted by Roger Désormière.

2. Marcelle Dullin. Wife of the actor and stage director Charles Dullin.

3. Rose Adler (1890–1959). Bookbinder and picture framer. Among the people she worked for was Jacques Doucet (1853–1929), eminent couturier and collector of art, books and manuscripts. After his death she was active in The Friends of Jacques Doucet, a group that devoted itself to safeguarding Doucet's collection, and through whose efforts the Bibliothèque Jacques Doucet came into being, housed in the Bibliothèque Saint-Geneviève, Place du Panthéon, Paris.

4. Poulenc's niece and godchild, Rosine Seringe, daughter of Jeanne and André Manceaux and sister of Brigitte Manceaux.

5. Louis Jouvet (1887–1951). French actor, director and producer, one of the most influential figures in twentieth-century theatre. From 1924 to 1934 he was director of the Théâtre des Champs-Elysées and from 1934 until his death in 1951, director of the Athénée. Louis Jouvet also had a distinguished career in films.

6. Poulenc's house at Noizay was left intact during the war. The 'looting' he refers to may have taken place in the village of Noizay.

7. Daniel, son of Madeleine and Darius Milhaud, born in Paris in February 1930.

LETTER 155

1. This letter and the following one are dated 1944 in *Correspondance*. 1941 seems more likely as Poulenc's ballet *Les Animaux modèles* (whose title is the subject of these letters) was completed in 1941 and performed in 1942 under that title.

2. Marcel Herrand (1897–1953). French actor who made his début in Apollinaire's play *Les Mamelles de Tirésias* in 1917. In 1921 he took part in Cocteau's *Les Mariés de la Tour Eiffel*. In 1929, with Jean Marchat, he founded the theatre company known as Le Rideau de Paris.

LETTER 157

1. Sauguet played the role of Madame Pernelle in Molière's *Tartuffe* staged by the company of Marcel Herrand and Jean Marchat, Le Rideau de Paris.

LETTER 158

1. Eluard dedicated to Poulenc the poem 'Les Excellents Moments' in *Le Livre ouvert, II* (1942). See below. He wrote a second poem to Poulenc, entitled *A Francis Poulenc* – see letters 178, 179, 208 and 209.

> *LES EXCELLENTS MOMENTS*
> *à Francis Poulenc*
>
> De velours et d'orange la maison sensée
> D'argent détruit de cuir de planches
> La maison accueillante
>
> Quatre murs pleins de grâce et gravés à l'aiguille
> Ouvrant leurs yeux visionnaires
> Sous le front du plafond
>
> Plantes et fleurs toutes à l'heure et gorgées d'air
> De sève et de graines ardentes
> La seule route de la force
> Passe par notre repos
>
> Sous la mousse du ciel notre toit nous accorde
> Des mots légers des rires d'ambre
> Et le chant d'un grand feu rêveur
> Mûrit entre nos paupières.

[Of velvet and orange the sound house
of beaten silver leather and timber
the welcoming house

Four gracious walls engraved in needle-point
opening eyes filled with visions
beneath the ceiling's brow

Plants and flowers on the hour draughts of air
of sap and ardent seeds
the very road to strength
goes via our repose

Under the froth of sky our house grants us
light-hearted words amber laughter
and the song of a great dreaming fire
ripens within our eyes.]

LETTER 159

1. Three scenes in Poulenc's ballet *Les Animaux modèles* are marked by a particular gravity and serenity: scene 6, between Death and the Woodcutter, based on the fable 'La Mort et le Bûcheron'; the opening scene 1, in which the peasants set out for the fields at dawn; the final scene 8, in which they return for the midday meal.

2. When *Les Animaux modèles* opened at the Paris Opéra on 8 August 1942, the programme included Ravel's *Boléro* and a suite of dances with music by Chopin, orchestrated by the conductor and composer André Messager (1853–1929). Messager was especially known for his many operettas and his ballet *Les Deux Pigeons*. He conducted the first performance of Debussy's *Pelléas et Mélisande* in 1902 and the first Paris performance of Poulenc's *Les Biches* on 26 May 1924, at the Théâtre des Champs-Elysées. Poulenc felt a deep admiration for Messager, whom he called 'that master of French operetta' (*FP-MMA* p. 54) and of whom he said: 'To write successful operettas one needs special skills, like those of the great Messager – yes, Messager was a great musician.' (*ECR* p. 151)

LETTER 160

1. Jean Françaix (*b*. 1912). French composer and pianist, pupil of Nadia Boulanger. He recorded Poulenc's Sextet in 1952 (see letter 235, note 5) and wrote an orchestral version of Poulenc's *Histoire de Babar* (see letter 183, note 2) published by Chester in 1962.

2. Jean Hubeau (*b*. 1917). French pianist and composer, appointed director of the Conservatoire of Versailles in 1942 and professor of chamber music at the Paris Conservatoire in 1957.

3. Marcel Delannoy (1898–1962). French composer who turned from painting to composition, encouraged by Honegger. He wrote operas, ballets, an oratorio, orchestral works and songs.

4. Poulenc's Sonata for piano and violin was first sketched in 1940, reworked in 1942 and completed at Easter 1943. Written for the violinist Ginette Neveu and dedicated to the memory of the Spanish poet Federico Garcia Lorca (1898–1936), it was given its first performance by Ginette Neveu and Poulenc on 21 June 1943 at a Concert de la Pléiade. Poulenc revised it in 1949 but was never satisfied with it:

> Despite some delectable violinistic details due entirely to Ginette Neveu who helped me a great deal with the instrumentation, this sonata is clearly a failure ... mainly because of its artificial pathos ... and also because, quite frankly, I do not like the violin in the singular! [*ECR* pp. 119–120]

5. Of his settings of six 'folk poems' by Maurice Fombeure (*b*. 1906), *Chansons villageoises*, Poulenc said: 'The texts by Fombeure evoke for me the Morvan where I have spent such wonderful summers! It is through nostalgia for the surroundings of Autun that I have composed this collection.' (*DMS* p. 71)

Conceived as a vocal showpiece for 'a heavy Verdi baritone', it was first performed by Roger Bourdin with Poulenc accompanying on 28 June 1943. The fourth song, 'Le Mendiant', is dedicated to André Schaeffner.

6. Stravinsky's *Pribaoutki* (Song Games) is a setting of four Russian traditional texts, scored for male voice and nine instruments.

7. See letter 180, note 4.

8. Pierre Souvtchinsky (1892–1985). Russian-born man of letters and musicologist, close friend of Stravinsky. He organized concerts of contemporary music in his native Leningrad and in Moscow, and established a succession of journals on philosophy, music and the arts. From 1922 he lived in Paris, where he became a leading figure in French musicological circles.

LETTER 161

1. Georgette Chadourne. Photographer and friend of Poulenc.

2. Poulenc met Raymond Destouches in the early 1930s, not long after moving into Le Grand Coteau at Noizay. Destouches was a driver of taxis and ambulances, and he soon became Poulenc's driver and an intimate friend, the relationship developing later into something more paternal on Poulenc's side. Destouches was devoted to Poulenc and this devotion persisted throughout his life and throughout his marriage to Céline. It is summed up in a letter from Poulenc to Bernac dated 20 August 1952 (Bibliothèque Nationale), in which Poulenc says: 'The Raymonds are adorable, delighted with their house, and Raymond himself very touching. The first thing he did after moving their bed into the bedroom was to place a picture of me on his bedside table!'

In 1940 Poulenc dedicated his piano piece, *Mélancolie*, to Raymond Destouches, and Destouches shares with Denise Duval the dedication of the Concerto for piano, written in 1949. He died on Christmas Day, 1988.

3. Poulenc's secular cantata, *Figure humaine*, is in eight movements for double mixed choir *a cappella*, on texts by Eluard. He describes the genesis of the work in an interview with Claude Rostand:

> During the Occupation, a few privileged beings, of whom I was one, would receive with the morning mail wonderful typed poems bearing pseudonyms that disguised but did not conceal the authorship of Paul Eluard. It was in this manner that I received most of the poems contained in *Poésie et vérité 42* . . . After a pilgrimage to Rocamadour, I had the idea of composing a clandestine work which could be prepared and printed in secret and then performed on the long-awaited day of liberation. With great enthusiasm, I began *Figure humaine* and completed it by the end of the summer . . . I composed the work for unaccompanied choir because I wanted this act of faith to be performed without instrumental aid, by the sole means of the human voice . . .
> My friend and publisher Paul Rouart agreed to print the cantata sub rosa and in this way we were able to send the music to London where, before the end of the war, in January 1945, in a broadcast conducted by Leslie Woodgate, the BBC Choir gave the first performance of this work.

With the help of the English Ambassador in Paris, Duff Cooper, Poulenc was flown to London on a military plane and was able to attend the final rehearsals of the work. It was sung in English, in a translation by Rollo Myers. (*ECR* pp. 103–105)

4. On my exercise books / On my desk and the trees / On the sand and on the snow / I write your name. / On all the pages read / On all the blank pages / Stone blood paper or ash / I write your name [. . .] And through the power of a word / I begin my life again / I am born to know you / To name you / Liberty.

5. The artist and stage designer Christian Bérard (1902–49) was known as Bébé.

6. Papoue was the nickname of the soprano Geneviève Touraine, sister of the baritone Gérard Souzay (see letter 200, note 4). Their original family name was Tisserand. Geneviève Touraine is the dedicatee of Poulenc's 'L'Enfant muet' from *Trois Chansons de F. Garcia Lorca* (1947).

7. The Sonata for violin and piano was published by Eschig in 1944.

8. The first drafts of Poulenc's Sonata for cello and piano date from 1940, the same period as his ballet *Les Animaux modèles*. He did not complete the work, however, until 1948, for his recital tour in Italy with the cellist Pierre Fournier (1906–85). The work is dedicated to Fournier and to Marthe Bosredon.

9. See letter 162.

LETTER 162

1. As a title for Poulenc's secular cantata (eventually *Figure humaine*) Eluard suggests a line from the last verse of the poem 'Liberté'. See letter 161.

2. The title chosen by Eluard for the edition of his wartime poems was *Poésie et vérité 42*, ironically borrowed from Goethe's *Dichtung und Wahrheit* (1811–14).

3. Denyse Parrot was the wife of the writer Louis Parrot (1906–48), author, among other things, of a study on Eluard for the series *Poètes d'aujourd'hui*, published by Seghers.

LETTER 163

1. This letter was probably written in the summer of 1943 rather than 1958, as suggested in *Correspondance*. Poulenc refers to Marthe Bosredon's 'latest song', which is presumably 'C'est ainsi que tu es', since he dedicated only that and the earlier 'Hôtel' to her. 'C'est ainsi que tu es' (from *Métamorphoses*) was written in the summer of 1943 and published in 1944. Also, Marie-Blanche de Polignac, of whom he speaks in the present tense, died on 14 February 1958.

2. St Anthony of Padua, Poulenc's favourite saint, was the most celebrated of the followers of St Francis of Assisi. Depicted in art with a book, a heart, a flame, a lily, or the child Jesus, he is known as a miracle worker and is invoked for the return of lost property. Poulenc was to honour the memory of St Anthony in 1959 in his *Laudes de saint Antoine de Padoue* for unaccompanied male choir.

LETTER 164

1. Mme La Rochette was an aged *cocotte* from Amboise whom Poulenc had

befriended and to whom he gave the title of Comtesse de la Rochette because of her delusions of grandeur. See postscript to letter 165.

2. In a letter dated 6 June (1944) Bernac wrote:

I have been thinking about your characters in *Les Mamelles*. In fact it is quite simple. The role of the woman is typically a lyric soprano, like *Manon* – with a good middle register but able to give you a dazzling high D. Look at the score again. You will find frequent vocal flights as high as C and upper D in, for example, Act III Scene 1. The policeman is very much a baritone, or rather, a comic bass. Don't make the tessitura too high. You could have a few Es and even Fs if you have to, here and there, in passing, the normal tessitura not exceeding the D. This will give you a very good contrast with the husband who should in fact be more of a light baritone-second tenor. The type of comic tenor known as a 'Trial', usually to be found in every operatic company. Tessitura not too high – but you can give him some Gs – G sharp (A). It is in fact the same tessitura you would use for me – more or less.

3. *Manon*. Opera in five acts by Massenet (1842–1912), first performed at the Opéra-Comique in 1884, based on Abbé Prévost's novel *Manon Lescaut* (1731).

4. 'Fêtes galantes'. Second of *Deux poèmes de Louis Aragon* for voice and piano, set by Poulenc in 1943. It relies entirely on word-play and word-pictures. The first song in the set is 'C'.

5. *L'Heure espagnole*. Comic opera by Ravel in one act, written in 1911.

6. Poulenc completed both the Apollinaire settings, 'Montparnasse' and 'Hyde Park', in January 1945, and he and Bernac first performed them on 27 April 1945, at the Poulenc Festival. See note 11 below.

7. Marie-Thérèse Mabille. Photographer and artist who lived in Tours, and a friend of Poulenc.

8. 'Une foule enfin réunie'. Last line of the seven poems by Eluard that form the collection *Sur les pentes inférieures*. These poems were the first that Eluard wrote under the German occupation of France. They were republished in *Poésie et Vérité 42*. The first six of these poems were chosen by Poulenc for *Figure humaine*.

9. Messiaen's *Trois petites Liturgies de la présence divine* is for women's chorus and orchestra, and was written in 1944.

10. See letter 165, note 2.

11. In *Correspondance*, Suzanne Peignot's name appears here, but in the original letter (Bibliothèque Nationale), Poulenc writes the name of the French soprano, Suzanne Balguerie (1888–1973). A letter to the Marquise de Casa Fuerte dated 30 July 1945 confirms that it was Balguerie and not Peignot who took part in this Festival:

This spring, on 27 April, I gave the first Poulenc Festival, a song recital with Balguerie and Bernac. The programme was as follows – *Banalités*; *Fiançailles pour rire*; *Tel jour telle nuit*; *Cinq poèmes de Max Jacob*; 'Montparnasse'; 'Hyde Park'; 'Le Jardin d'Anna'; 'Allons plus vite'; 'C'; 'Fêtes galantes'. The programme looked beautiful, with a guitar by Picasso on the cover. Full house at Gaveau. All my colleagues were there.

I was ill with nerves, before and after the concert, despite its success. I am doing it again this winter in Brussels.

12. Autun, renowned for its Romanesque architecture, was one of Poulenc's favourite towns in the Morvan region of France.

LETTER 165

1. Poulenc often remarked that Georges Auric was his 'true spiritual brother'. In 1954, asked by Claude Rostand how he had met the friends who were to become the Groupe des Six, Poulenc replied:

With rare logic, the one I met first is the one who has since become my true spiritual brother: I refer to Georges Auric. We are exactly the same age – I am barely a month older than he is – yet intellectually, I have always felt the younger. The precociousness of Auric, in all spheres, was such that at fourteen his compositions were being performed at the Société Nationale de Musique. At fifteen he was discussing sociology with Léon Blum and theology with Maritain. And at seventeen, Apollinaire read him *Les Mamelles de Tirésias* to hear his opinion of it . . . As soon as I met Auric, I was fascinated by the extent of his culture, and I have never parted with him since. [*ECR* pp. 38–39]

2. Messiaen studied composition with Paul Dukas (1865–1935) and the organ with Marcel Dupré (1886–1971). Both taught at the Paris Conservatoire, where Dupré, a celebrated organist, was director from 1954–56.

LETTER 166

1. Charles was married to Poulenc's cook, Anna, and fulfilled the role of general manservant, valet and butler in Poulenc's household.

LETTER 167

1. Poulenc was always at pains to explain that Touraine was his chosen setting, but that he had no roots whatever there: 'There is absolutely nothing in me of the Tourangeau, neither by blood nor by culture . . . *Poulenc le Tourangeau* is a facile slogan, but as false as false can be!' (*ECR* p. 11)

LETTER 169

1. 'The Gabriel buildings' were designed by Jacques-Ange Gabriel (1698–1782), member of a celebrated family of architects, principal architect to Louis XV, and director of the Academy of Architecture from 1742. Among his best-known works are the Ecole Militaire in Paris (1752) and the Place Louis XV, now Place de la Concorde (1755).

LETTER 170

1. *La Gageure imprévue* (1942), comic opera in one act by Sauguet, on a libretto by Pierre Bertin after Sedaine. It was first performed at the Opéra-Comique in Paris in 1944, in a production by Pierre Bertin, with décor by Jacques Dupont, conducted by Roger Désormière.

2. *Les Mirages*, ballet by Cassandre and Lifar, with music by Sauguet, written in 1943 and first performed at the Paris Opéra in 1947 with décor by Cassandre, choreography by Lifar, conducted by Louis Fourestier.

LETTER 171

1. Emile Vuillermoz (1878–1960). French musicologist and critic, one of the founders in 1910 of the Société Musicale Indépendante and editor of *SIM Revue musicale* from 1911. His many writings include biographies of Debussy and Fauré.

2. 'Conceal the art by art itself' was a maxim of the composer Jean-Philippe Rameau (1683–1764).

3. Mademoiselle de la Vallière (1644–1710). Maid of Honour to Henrietta Anne of England and for a while favourite of Louis XIV. In 1674 she withdrew to the convent of Carmel where she remained until her death.

LETTER 172

1. The Russian dancer and choreographer, Serge Lifar (1905–86), was ballet master of the Paris Opéra Ballet from 1930 but was dismissed after the Second World War for entertaining German occupying troops. He was reinstated at the Opéra in 1947, where he remained until his retirement as a dancer in 1956.

2. Louis de Vocht (1887–1977). Belgian conductor and composer. He founded the Chorale Sainte-Cécile (Caecilia Choir) in 1916 and was its conductor until 1967. He was also conductor of the Concerts Classiques and Nouveaux Concerts in Antwerp. He played a leading part in introducing into Belgium new works by contemporary composers.

3. Of his 1945 Albert Hall appearance with Benjamin Britten, Poulenc said:
During my stay in London, dear Benjamin Britten agreed very kindly to play my Concerto for two pianos with me at the Albert Hall. You can imagine my joy, after four years under the occupation, at being once more in England, which had provided me – through Stravinsky – with my first publisher, Chester, and with my most loyal audience in Europe. [*ECR* p. 104]

4. Comte Jean de Polignac suffered recurring attacks from the effects of gas during the First World War. In 1942, he entered a Paris clinic for further treatment and died there in October 1943.

LETTER 173

1. Milhaud, with his wife Madeleine and son Daniel, spent the years 1940–47 in America, teaching at Mills College, California.

2. Milhaud suffered from severe arthritis, which often obliged him to spend long periods in bed and in a wheelchair.

3. Raymond Deiss was a friend of Milhaud's and publisher of some of his music. He used his publishing business to print subversive pamphlets for the Resistance movement, was captured during the occupation, imprisoned and later executed. After the war, his publishing business was salvaged by Francis Salabert (see letter 190, note 6).

4. Daniel Milhaud (*b.* 1930) did, in fact, become a painter, studying with Corrado Cagli (*b.* 1910) and Oskar Kokoschka (1886–1980).

5. Alexandre Tansman (1897–1986). Polish-born composer and pianist who lived in Paris from 1919. He spent the years 1941–46 in the USA where he toured extensively as a concert pianist and composed, among other things, many film scores. He was a friend of Stravinsky, on whom he wrote a book, published in 1948. His wife was the pianist Colette Cras.

6. Pierre Monteux (1875–1964). French-born violinist and conductor. From 1911–14 he conducted for Diaghilev's Russian Ballet. He formed the Paris Symphony Orchestra in 1929 and, from 1936–52 was conductor of the San Francisco Symphony Orchestra, introducing many works by contemporary French composers to American audiences. In 1961, aged 86, he became chief conductor of the London Symphony Orchestra.

LETTER 174

1. See letter 173, note 3.

2. Fabio, son of Vittorio and Elsie Rieti.

3. Jean, son of the Marquis and Marquise de Casa Fuerte.

4. Milhaud's project to write songs specially for Bernac and Poulenc did not materialize.

LETTER 175

1. In his radio interviews with Gérard Michel for *France Culture* (20 November 1970–15 January 1971) Bernac remembered this first visit to London after the liberation of Paris: 'You can imagine how great our joy was at being able to leave France. When we came onto the platform at the Wigmore Hall the entire audience stood up and my emotion was such that, instead of beginning to sing, I began to weep.'

2. Rollo (Hugh) Myers (1892–1984). English music critic and writer. He met Poulenc in Monte Carlo in 1924, where he was reporting on *Les Biches* for the *Daily Telegraph*. His books include studies of Debussy, Ravel, Satie and Chabrier, and a translation of Cocteau's *Le Coq et l'Arlequin*.

3. Jacques Rouché (1862–1957) was director of the Paris Opéra from 1915–45.

4. Poulenc confirmed these views on Messiaen in a letter to the Marquise de Casa Fuerte, dated 30 July 1945:

I am sure you know that the great rising star in musical Paris is Messiaen. He has disciples, priestesses, etc. In fact, a veritable cult. What is being written about his music is unimaginable, but the music itself is distinctly beautiful. His disciples booed the latest Stravinsky. This occasioned a furious response from me in *Le Figaro* following an article in which Jolivet claimed that *true* French music (no doubt his own) owed *nothing* at all to Stravinsky.

Poulenc's article entitled 'Vive Stravinsky!' included the following:

Unbelievable as this may seem, I find myself, in 1945, having to put pen to paper in order to defend Igor Stravinsky, for there is at the present moment – just as there was in the most glorious days of *Le Sacre du*

Printemps – a 'scandale Stravinsky'! Except that those who vilify him today no longer belong as they once did to the musical right, but to a quasi-left comprising a few youths – and, worse still, a few pseudo-youths – who all owe the light veneer of modernism overlaying their works to nothing other than the Stravinsky innovations of 1913, which he himself has long since left behind.

5. Henri Sauguet's ballet *Les Forains*, with sets by Christian Bérard (Bébé), choreography by Roland Petit, and conducted by André Cluytens, was first performed at the Théâtre des Champs-Elysées in Paris in 1945.

6. Poulenc destroyed this attempt at a string quartet in 1947:

This quartet is the embarrassment of my life. Joseph Calvet was kind enough to play through three movements for me one morning in '47. I still blush at the thought. From the very first bars I kept saying to myself: 'That part would be better on the oboe; here it needs a horn, there a clarinet.' . . . I could not get out of Calvet's place fast enough, and it was with the wildest joy that I threw the entire manuscript into the sewer of the Place Pereire! [*ECR* p. 125]

On Auric's advice, Poulenc salvaged three themes from this work and used them in his Sinfonietta for orchestra (1947), dedicating it to Auric.

Joseph Calvet, (1897–1984), French violinist and professor of ensemble at the Paris Conservatoire, founded the Calvet Quartet which played from 1919–40.

LETTER 176

1. Koechlin refers to the Poulenc Festival at the Salle Gaveau on 27 April 1945. See letters 164 and 177.

LETTER 178

1. The date 1944 is given to this text in *Correspondance*, but an unpublished letter from Poulenc to Eluard (Harry Ransom Humanities Research Center, University of Texas, Austin) confirms that the year was 1945.

2. Roger Wild (1894–1987) was a Swiss-born painter who lived in Paris, a familiar figure in the studios of Montparnasse and a friend of Modigliani and Max Jacob. He designed the stage sets for Honegger's ballet *L'Appel de la montagne*. He also edited several journals about music, ballet and bull-fighting. Eluard's poem on Poulenc was written in response to a request from Roger Wild for a text to be included in *De la musique encore et toujours* (1946). The second section of the poem, beginning 'Francis je ne m'écoutais pas . . .' was also published in *Les Lettres françaises* (7 February 1963).

3. Poulenc had sent Eluard a cheque for two thousand francs as payment for the four poems he had set in his chamber cantata *Un Soir de neige*: (i) 'De grandes cuillers de neige' (ii) 'La bonne neige' (iii) 'Bois meurtri' (iv) 'La nuit le froid la solitude'. The first poem is from Eluard's collection *Dignes de vivre* (1944), the other three from *Poésie et vérité, 1942*. Poulenc takes the first line of each poem as his title. Written between 24–26 December 1944, *Un Soir de neige* is

scored for six mixed voices, or choir *a cappella*. It is dedicated to Marie-Blanche de Polignac.

LETTER 179
1. See letter 178, note 2.
2. See letters 208 and 209.

LETTER 180
1. In *Correspondance* this letter is placed in the last quarter of 1944, but the postscript confirms that the letter was written in 1945.
2. Maurice Cuvelier. Belgian lawyer born in 1899, founder and director-general of the Philharmonic Society of Brussels.
3. Since 1936, Poulenc had gone on regular visits to Rocamadour in the summer.
4. Both André Schaeffner and Claude Rostand were thinking of writing books on Poulenc. It was, however, Henri Hell who carried this idea to a successful conclusion, in his study *Francis Poulenc – musicien francais*, first published by Plon in 1958 and updated, in a new edition by Fayard, in 1978.

LETTER 181
1. The Antwerp Chorale is presumably the Caecilia Choir. See letter 172, note 2.
2. See letter 175, note 6.
3. André Jolivet (1905–74). French composer and conductor, co-founder (with Messiaen, Daniel Lesur and Yves Baudrier) of La Jeune France in 1936, music director of the Comédie Française from 1943–59, professor of composition at the Paris Conservatoire from 1965–70.
4. Pierre Capdevielle (1906–69). French composer, in charge of chamber music broadcasting for French Radio from 1944 and founder, in 1952, of the French Radio Chamber Orchestra.
5. See letter 173, note 3.
6. Claude Delvincourt (1888–1954). French composer, director of the Paris Conservatoire from 1941 until his death in a car accident in Italy.
7. Jacques Jaujard was Director General of the Arts Department of the French Ministry of Education.

LETTER 182
1. The writer and diplomat Louis Roché was born in 1903. He was attached to the French Embassy in London during the 1930s and '40s. In 1952 he was appointed French Ambassador in Canberra. Louis Roché's book of poetry, *Si proche et lointaine*, was published by Gallimard in 1946. Roché had previously written only under pseudonyms. In Poulenc's copy of *Si proche et lointaine*, Roché wrote the following dedication:

> To Francis Poulenc, who encouraged me not to keep my poems such a secret and to give up pseudonyms, this little book, as a testimony of all the old affection of his friend and admirer, Louis Roché.

LETTER 183

1. When *Les Mamelles de Tirésias* was finally produced at the Opéra-Comique in June 1947, it was not Christian Bérard but Romain Erté who designed the décor and costumes. See letter 192.

2. While staying with Marthe Bosredon in Brive-la-Gaillarde after his demobilization in 1940, Poulenc received a visit from some of his cousins. The little daughter of one of these cousins, hearing him improvising, went up to him, saying: 'Oh, Uncle Francis, what you're playing is so boring! Why don't you play this?' And she placed in front of him her copy of Jean de Brunhoff's book, *Histoire de Babar, le petit éléphant*. Poulenc began to improvise for her, noting down the ideas that appealed to her. It was not until five years later, however, prompted by the same cousin who asked 'Et *Babar*?', that Poulenc took up the work again and finally completed it. His music illustrates and elaborates upon Jean de Brunhoff's text, spoken by a narrator. (From notes by Winifred Radford for the record sleeve of *Pierre Bernac – PB1*, published in 1980 by The Friends of Pierre Bernac, England. The record includes a performance of *Babar*, broadcast on the BBC on 27 November 1977, with Bernac as the narrator and Graham Johnson playing the piano part.)

3. Charles Kiesgen, Concert Agents.

LETTER 184

1. Sauguet's comic opera *La Gageure imprévue* was later published by Editions Max Eschig, and his ballet, *Les Forains*, by Editions Salabert.

2. 'Eighteen glances at the tail of a young elephant'. (It may be pure coincidence that Messiaen's work for piano *Vingt regards sur l'Enfant Jésus* was composed in 1944.)

3. Renaud de Jouvenel, stepson of the writer Colette, whose second husband was Henry de Jouvenel.

LETTER 185

1. Poulenc wrote the incidental music for the play by Armand Salacrou (*b.* 1899), *Le Soldat et la sorcière* (1945).

2. Poulenc did not compose his Concerto for piano and orchestra until 1949.

LETTER 186

1. Poulenc's uncle Papoum, Marcel Royer (see letter 29, note 3), died in November 1945.

LETTER 187

1. See letter 175, note 4.

2. The two film-scores to which Poulenc refers are *La Duchesse de Langeais* (1942), directed by Jacques de Baroncelli, and *Le Voyageur sans bagages* (1944), written and directed by Jean Anouilh (also a stage-work – see below).

Between 1940–45, Poulenc composed the following incidental music for the stage:

Léocadia (1940), play by Jean Anouilh. (Poulenc's celebrated 'valse chantée', *Les Chemins de l'amour*, dedicated to Yvonne Printemps, comes from his incidental music for this play.)

La Fille du jardinier (1941), play by Exbrayat.

Le Voyageur sans bagages (1944), play by Jean Anouilh.

La Nuit de Saint-Jean (1944), play by James Barrie.

Le Soldat et la sorcière (1945), play by Armand Salacrou.

LETTER 189

1. 'Paul et Virginie', for voice and piano, composed in August 1946, is Poulenc's only setting of Radiguet (see letter 26, note 3). Published in Radiguet's collection *Les Joues en feu* (1920), the poem plays with the names and notions of Bernardin de Saint-Pierre's eighteenth-century idyll about two children who grow up on the Island of Mauritius. Poulenc was especially fond of this poem: 'These few lines of Radiguet have always had a magical savour for me.' (*DMS* p. 89)

LETTER 190

1. Madeleine Milhaud read the part of the narrator in Stravinsky's *Perséphone*, a melodrama in three acts, on a libretto by André Gide, for narrator, tenor, chorus, children's chorus, and orchestra, first performed in Paris in 1934.

2. In 1946 Milhaud wrote the music for the film *The Private Affairs of Bel Ami*, directed by Albert Lewin and based on the story *Bel-Ami* by Guy de Maupassant. Milhaud spent five weeks in Hollywood in November 1946 working on the score, conducting and synchronizing the music with the film.

3. Milhaud's six *Symphonies pour orchestre de chambre* were written between 1917 and 1923.

4. François Valéry was the son of the poet Paul Valéry.

5. Philippe Heugel and his brother François both played an active part in the music publishing firm, Heugel, which belonged to their father.

6. The music publisher Francis Salabert was killed in an aeroplane crash while flying to attend one of Milhaud's concerts in the USA.

7. *Alissa*, Milhaud's suite for soprano and piano based on Gide's novel *La Porte étroite*, was written in 1913, revised in 1931, and published by Heugel. In his memoirs, Milhaud describes Gide's response to this work when he first heard it:

> I do not think that Gide liked *Alissa* very much. After hearing it, he said to me in his sing-song voice: 'Thank you for having made me feel how beautiful my prose is!' thereby shifting the emphasis of appreciation very subtly away from the music and on to his prose! [*MVH* p. 43]

Gide does not comment on this in his *Journal*, but notes in his entry for 28 September 1915: 'Darius Milhaud came yesterday . . . to play me a symphonic poem he has written on my translation of verses by Tagore. All I could hear was a lot of noise.' (*AG-J* p. 508)

Milhaud's *Alissa* was first performed by Jane Bathori, with Milhaud accompanying, at Adrienne Monnier's bookshop *La Maison des Amis des Livres* in 1920. Bathori also gave the first performance of the revised version, at the

Sorbonne in Paris, in 1932. Milhaud notes that for twenty years, Bathori was its sole and frequent performer.

8. Hervé Dugardin was the director of the Paris branch of the Italian music publishing firm, Ricordi.

9. The Berkshire Music Center (now the Tanglewood Music Center) was founded in 1940 by Serge Koussevitzky as an institution where young musicians could study with the famous. The Center was financed during the Second World War by the Koussevitzky Music Foundation (see letter 98, note 2).

LETTER 191

1. The accelerando occurs at the point when Thérèse, after relinquishing her femininity by bursting her balloon-breasts with a cigarette-lighter, catches sight of herself in a mirror and sees that she is sprouting a beard. See letter 146, note 1.

LETTER 192

1. The décor and costumes for Poulenc's *Mamelles de Tirésias* were created by the Russian-born fashion illustrator and costume designer, Erté (Romain de Tirtoff) (1892–1990), who brought to the production his experience of the Folies-Bergère, where he had worked from 1919–30.

2. Poulenc compares Denise Duval to the soprano Fanny Heldy (1888–1973), who made her Paris début in 1917 as Violetta at the Opéra-Comique, and continued to sing there for more than two decades, impressing audiences with her striking beauty and personality.

3. Milhaud returned to France from the USA in September 1947, three months after the première of *Les Mamelles de Tirésias*.

4. In 1947 Poulenc moved from his *chambre de bonne* at 5 rue de Médicis into an apartment at the same address. This was not, however, his late uncle Papoum's apartment, which had passed by mutual agreement to Poulenc's sister, Jeanne Manceaux, and her family.

5. Poulenc's Sinfonietta, in four movements, was composed in 1947. It was his only symphonic work. Three of its themes were from the quartet which he had destroyed earlier in the same year (see letter 175, note 6). The Sinfonietta was first performed on 24 October 1948 by the Philharmonia Orchestra, conducted by Roger Désormière, in a BBC broadcast.

6. In 1947, Madeleine Milhaud was made *Chevalier de la Légion d'Honneur* for her contribution as teacher of French Dramatic Art in the USA. Darius Milhaud was made *Officier* (promoted on 12 July 1965 to *Grand Officier*) *de la Légion d'Honneur*.

LETTER 193

1. In November 1948, Poulenc and Bernac undertook a six-week concert tour of the USA. This was followed by two subsequent tours, in January–March 1950 (during which Poulenc and Bernac made their first American recordings), and in January–March 1952.

2. Poulenc wrote his song cycle *Calligrammes* on seven poems from Apollinaire's collection of the same name, published in 1918. The book is subtitled: *Poems of Peace and War (1913–16)*. Poulenc began this composition in May 1948 at Noizay and completed it in August 1948 at his sister's Normandy home, Le Tremblay. The work was first performed by Bernac and Poulenc on 20 November 1948, in New York.

3. The other five dedicatees are Pierre Lelong, Jacqueline Apollinaire, Emmanuel Faÿ, Jeanne [Manceaux], and Jacques Soulé.

4. See letter 161, note 8.

5. *Les Contes d'Hoffmann*, opera by Jacques Offenbach (1819–80). *Le Carrosse du Saint-Sacrément*, opera by Lord Berners (1883–1950).

6. At the time of this letter, the American conductor and composer Leonard Bernstein (1918–90) was already internationally known, having made his highly successful début five years earlier (1943), substituting for Bruno Walter at a New York Philharmonic concert.

LETTER 194

1. 'Hymne' for voice and piano on a poem by Jean Racine (1639–99). This work was dedicated to Doda Conrad, who gave the first performance of it, accompanied by David Garvey, in New York in 1949.

2. Poulenc played the piano version of his *Concert champêtre* with the New York Philharmonic conducted by the Greek-born conductor Dimitri Mitropoulos (1896–1960). He was conductor of the Minneapolis Symphony Orchestra from 1937 and of the New York Philharmonic from 1950 to 1958.

3. Poulenc refers to the 1948 recording by Arthur Whittemore and Jack Lowe, with the RCA Victor Symphony Orchestra, conducted by Dimitri Mitropoulos (RCA Victor 120366/8 DM 1235).

LETTER 197

1. The recordings which Viñes' niece, Elvira Viñes Soto, was planning to reissue, were first published in 1930 by French Columbia and La Voix de son Maître.

The following works mentioned by Poulenc in his letter are among the recordings reissued by Pathé-Marconi in the series Références in 1983 (1731791 PM 322):

Debussy: *Poissons d'or* (dedicated to Viñes); *La Soirée dans Grenade*
Borodin: Scherzo in A flat
Albeniz: *Torre bermeja*
Scarlatti: Sonata in D, K.29
Gluck (arranged Brahms): *Gavotte d'Iphigénie en Aulide (Acte 2)*.

LETTER 198

1. In 1949 Heugel published a suite for voice and piano, commissioned by the bass Doda Conrad as a homage to Chopin on the centenary of his death. Under the title *Mouvements du coeur*, the work consists of seven movements, by six different composers, to words by Louise de Vilmorin:

Prelude	Sauguet
Mazurka	Poulenc
Valse	Auric
Scherzo impromptu	Françaix
Etude	Preger
Ballade nocturne	Milhaud
Polonaise	Sauguet

Doda Conrad, accompanied by David Garvey, gave the first performance of the work in New York in 1949.

2. *Le Grand Meaulnes*, written in 1913, was the only work of the French writer Alain-Fournier (1886–1914). The ball of which Poulenc speaks is a key-scene in the novel, filled with a dream-like unreality and nostalgia.

3. 'C'est ainsi que tu es' is the second of three poems by Louise de Vilmorin which Poulenc set to music in 1943 under the title *Métamorphoses*. The first and third songs in the set are 'Reine des Mouettes' and 'Paganini'. 'C'est ainsi que tu es' is dedicated to Marthe Bosredon (see letter 163), 'Reine des Mouettes' to Marie-Blanche de Polignac, and 'Paganini' to Jeanne Ritcher. Bernac and Poulenc gave the first performance of this work on 8 December 1943 in Paris.

4. See note 1 above.

LETTER 199

1. Poulenc's Concerto for piano and orchestra, commissioned by the Boston Symphony Orchestra was first performed on 6 January 1950 in Boston – during Poulenc's second tour of the USA – with the composer as soloist and the Boston Symphony Orchestra, conducted by Charles Munch.

2. *Bolivar*, opera in three acts by Milhaud on a libretto by Jules Supervielle (1884–1960), adapted by Madeleine Milhaud. The work was first performed at the Paris Opéra on 12 May 1950, with André Cluytens conducting. The sets by Fernand Léger were widely considered to be his greatest achievement in the art of stage design.

3. Georges Hirsch (1895–1974) was director of the Paris Opéra from 1946–51 and from 1956–59.

4. The Belgian-born conductor André Cluytens (1905–67) was at this time musical director of the Opéra-Comique. In 1949 he succeeded Charles Munch as conductor of the Paris Conservatoire Orchestra.

5. Roger Désormière had fallen out with Georges Hirsch.

6. Poulenc presumably refers to the first performance in France, as he and Fournier had given the world première of his Sonata for cello and piano in Italy in 1948. See letter 161, note 8.

7. Sauguet had been named *Officier de la Légion d'Honneur*, promoted in 1987 to *Commandeur de la Légion d'Honneur*.

8. Milhaud's 'tour de force' was his Opus 291, composed at Mills College, California, between November 1948 and January 1949. It consists of two String Quartets, his 14th and 15th, which can be played as two separate works or, combined together, as an Octet.

LETTER 200

1. Royaumont. Cultural centre in the Oise valley built on the remains of a thirteenth-century monastery. Bernac had given a concert there, including songs by Ernest Chausson (1855–99).

2. In a letter to Bernac, dated 'Tuesday' (Bibliothèque Nationale), Poulenc said of his Concerto for piano:

> The best definition of the Concerto is that it is *well raked*, like my terrace.
> The orchestration is carefully polished and very varied, the piano part brilliant – a good match for me. In any case, even if it is not a triumph, it will not be a failure, as it is sound work.

(The terrace of Poulenc's house at Noizay, Le Grand Coteau, is made of well raked gravel.)

3. Solesmes. Benedictine monastery founded in the eleventh century and rebuilt in the nineteenth. It is renowned for its sixteenth- and seventeenth-century sculptures and as a leading centre for the study and performance of Gregorian chant. It was a favourite place of retreat for Bernac.

4. Poulenc seems to have revised this opinion of Souzay in later years as, in 1956, he included Souzay's interpretations of 'Priez pour paix' and 'Le Portrait' among the best performances of his songs (see *DMS* p. 107). Gérard Souzay (Gérard Michel Tisserand) (*b.* 1918) was a pupil of Pierre Bernac and Claire Croiza, among others. He has had a distinguished career both in opera and in recital and his many recordings include works by Poulenc. Poulenc dedicated to him 'Chanson de l'oranger' from *Trois Chansons de F. Garcia Lorca* (1947).

LETTER 201

1. The conductor Charles Munch. See Poulenc's Correspondents.

2. The first recording of Poulenc's Concerto for organ was published in America in 1951, with Edwards Power Biggs (organ), Roman Szule (percussion) and the Columbia Symphony Orchestra conducted by Richard Burgin (Columbia album MM 951). A recording by Charles Munch and the Boston Symphony Orchestra, Berj Zamkochian (organ) and Everett Firth (percussion), was issued in 1961 (RCA Victor LM 2567).

LETTER 202

1. Since 1936, Bernac and Poulenc had been giving regular concerts in Avignon, for the Société Avignonnaise de Concerts, presided over by Simone Girard (see Poulenc's Correspondents).

2. Dr Pierre Girard was the husband of Simone Girard.

LETTER 203

1. Nicolas de Grigny (1672–1703). French composer and organist (at Rheims cathedral from 1696 until his death), whose organ compositions are renowned for their mastery of counterpoint. Bach made a copy of his *Livre d'orgue* (1699).

LETTER 204

1. *Mouvements du coeur* (see letter 198, note 1) was first recorded in America

by Doda Conrad, accompanied by David Garvey and issued in 1950 (Robert E. Blake 2).

2. Igor II was the Russian composer and conductor, Igor Markevitch (1912–83), as opposed to Igor Stravinsky (Igor I).

3. Sauguet's 'concerto for voice' was *Le Cornette* (1951), a ballade for bass or baritone and orchestra on a poem by Rilke, first performed in Belgium in 1951 with Doda Conrad as soloist and orchestra conducted by Franz André.

4. This recording (Columbia ML 4399) includes the following works by Poulenc: *Mouvements perpétuels, Nocturne No. 5 and Suite française.*

5. There does not appear to be a recording of *Aubade* conducted by Leonard Bernstein.

6. In a letter to Yvonne de Casa Fuerte dated Monday 20 February (1950), Poulenc again expresses his admiration for the Piano Sonata written in 1949 by the American composer Samuel Barber (1910–1981): 'Have I told you how much I love the Sonata by Barber? He is undoubtedly *the best* American.' This view is repeated to Milhaud, in the postscript to letter 206.

7. Gian Carlo Menotti's opera *The Consul* (see also Poulenc's postscript to letter 206) was produced on Broadway in 1950 and won a Pulitzer Prize.

8. The first performance in America of *Figure humaine* took place on 17 February 1950 at Carnegie Hall. The conductor was Hugh Ross. Born in England in 1898, Ross worked mainly in Canada and the USA from 1921. He was conductor of the Schola Cantorum (New York) from 1927.

LETTER 205

1. Although the date 1948 is given in *Correspondance*, 1950 is more probable as *Figure humaine* was first performed in New York in that year, during Poulenc's second tour of the USA.

2. In a letter to Yvonne de Casa Fuerte, dated Monday 20 February (three days after the American première of *Figure humaine* at Carnegie Hall), Poulenc writes:

> Nothing could have pleased me more than to hear from your divine lips about the success of *Figure humaine* [. . .] I am so happy that you like it because I *know* it to be beautiful and profound. And, besides, who among my contemporaries would have composed such a work using only human voices, without drums or trumpets? Right? I hope there were fellow composers in the hall!

3. *Orpheus.* Ballet in three scenes by Stravinsky, choreographed by Balanchine, first performed in New York in 1948.

4. *Apollon musagète.* Ballet in two scenes by Stravinsky, scored for strings, first performed in Washington DC in 1928, choreographed by Bolm, and later by Balanchine for the Paris performances.

LETTER 206

1. Alfred Frankenstein (1906–81). American critic and writer on music and art. From 1935 to 1975 he was music critic of the *San Francisco Chronicle*.

2. See letter 204, note 8.

3. See letter 201, note 2.

4. Goddard Lieberson (1911–77). British-born American composer, critic and novelist. He became president of the American Columbia record company and launched a wide-ranging recording programme, including American musicals, poets reading their own works, and contemporary music. The advent of the long-playing record was largely due to him. He was the husband of the singer and ballerina Vera Zorina (*b*. 1917).

LETTER 207

1. 'Belle et ressemblante', on a poem by Eluard, is the fifth of the seven songs in *Sept chansons*. 'Toi ma patiente ma patience ma parente', also by Eluard, is the fourth section of *Figure humaine*.

2. The 'two treasures' are the children of Yvonne de Casa Fuerte, Jean and Flavie Alvarez de Toledo.

3. Poulenc expresses a similar paternal sentiment towards Denise Duval and Raymond Destouches in letter 217, to Henri Sauguet.

LETTER 208

1. Lucien Scheler (*b*. 1902). Man of letters, specialist bookseller, and friend of Eluard. Among the many works he has edited and prefaced is the first edition of the complete works of Eluard, published by Gallimard in the series Bibliothèque de la Pléiade (1968).

2. Eluard had moved to 52 avenue de Gravelle, Charenton-le-Pont, six miles out of Paris, to the south of the Bois de Vincennes.

3. See letter 209 for Eluard's reply to Poulenc.

4. Poulenc refers to Eluard's third wife, Dominique Lemor. Eluard met her at the Congress for World Peace in Mexico in September 1949, three years after the sudden death from a cerebral haemorrhage of his second wife, Nusch. Dominique shared the last three years of the poet's life. They were officially married in 1951, the year before Eluard died.

5. See letters 178 and 209.

LETTER 209

1. From April to July 1950, Poulenc worked on his setting of Eluard's poem 'Vue donne vie' from the collection *Le Livre ouvert I* (1940). Conceived as one *mélodie* in seven sections, exactly as the poem is printed, the work is known under Eluard's suggested title, *La Fraîcheur et le feu*. It was first performed by Bernac and Poulenc on 1 November 1950 in Birmingham, England. It is dedicated to Stravinsky.

2. The poem 'A Francis Poulenc' (letter 178) does not appear in any of Eluard's volumes of poetry. It is included in *Paul Eluard – oeuvres complètes*, Vol II (Editions Gallimard, 1968), in the section entitled 'Poèmes retrouvés'. The poem 'Les Excellents moments', dedicated to Francis Poulenc (see letter 158, note 1), appears in *Le Livre ouvert II* (Editions Gallimard, 1947).

LETTER 210

1. In a talk he gave at the Club des Trois Centres, Paris, on 10 January 1962, Poulenc described the genesis of his *Suite française*. In 1935, he and Auric were asked by Edouard Bourdet to compose the incidental music for Bourdet's play *La Reine Margot*. Auric wrote the material for Act I, Poulenc for Act II. The title role of Marguerite de Valois was played by Yvonne Printemps, and it was for her that Poulenc composed his song 'A sa guitare', on a text by Ronsard. Unsure of how to approach the incidental music to this play, Poulenc discussed the problem with Nadia Boulanger, who suggested that he make arrangements of sixteenth-century dances from the collection by Claude Gervaise, *Le Livre de danceries*. Using this as his source material, Poulenc composed a suite of seven movements, scored for nine wind instruments, percussion and harpsichord. At the request of the publisher Durand, a piano version of the score came out in 1935, but it was not until 1948 that Durand published the full score. (*FP-CAS*)

LETTER 213

1. Wanting to write a religious work to the memory of his friend, the painter and stage designer Christian Bérard, who died in 1949, Poulenc first thought of composing a Requiem, then found the idea too pretentious and turned instead to the more human tenderness expressed in the thirteenth-century text of the *Stabat Mater*.

Poulenc composed the work – for soprano, mixed choir and orchestra – in two months, during the summer of 1950, at Noizay. In an earlier letter to Bernac dated 19 August 1950 (Bibliothèque Nationale), he wrote:

> The *Stabat* is going at such a rate that there can only be a Rocamadour miracle behind it. Out of the twelve sections, three are already done, two almost done, and one sketched in rough – and all this in ten days! I feel as if I were back in the time of the Mass at Anost.

Poulenc completed the entire work in early October 1950. It was first performed on 13 June 1951 at the Strasbourg Festival by Geneviève Moizan, the Choeurs de Saint-Guillaume and the Strasbourg Municipal Orchestra, conducted by Fritz Münch.

LETTER 214

1. Marietti was director of the music publishers, Eschig.

2. See letter 204.

3. Between 1913 and 1922, working in close collaboration with the poet Paul Claudel, Milhaud composed the music to accompany Claudel's translation of *The Oresteian Trilogy* by Aeschylus. *Les Choéphores*, the central section of the trilogy, was composed in 1915 and was Milhaud's first completely polytonal work. It is scored for soprano, baritone, narrator, mixed choir and orchestra.

4. See letter 199, note 2. Despite the negative reaction of the critics, *Bolivar* continued to play to enthusiastic audiences for two seasons at the Paris Opéra.

LETTER 215

1. The European première of Poulenc's Concerto for piano and orchestra took place in July 1950 at the Aix-en-Provence Festival.

2. *Jeanne d'Arc au bûcher.* Dramatic oratorio by Honegger to a text by Claudel, composed in 1934–35.

3. Bartók's Viola Concerto was left in the form of unfinished sketches and was completed by the Hungarian composer Tibor Serly (1901–78).

4. *Le Coq.* Publication founded in 1920 by Cocteau and the seventeen-year-old Raymond Radiguet, with contributions from various of their followers. Four numbers only were produced, May, June, July–August–September, and November, 1920. Numbers three and four were called *Le Coq Parisien.*

5. In November 1928 in Antwerp, Louis de Vocht (see letter 172, note 2) conducted the first performance of the finale of Milhaud's opera *Les Euménides.*

6. Roland-Manuel (Roland Alexis Manuel Lévy) (1891–1966). French musicologist, composer and critic, professor at the Schola Cantorum and honorary professor at the Paris Conservatoire. His many writings include four books on Ravel, of whom he was a close friend.

7. Milhaud's ballet *La Création du Monde* (1923) was inspired by Black American jazz. Poulenc expressed his views on jazz in a talk he gave on 7 March 1935, entitled 'Mes maîtres et mes amis': 'I do not like [jazz], and I particularly do not want to hear about its influence on contemporary music. I do not mind listening to jazz while I'm in the bath, but I find it quite frankly odious to hear it in the concert hall.' (*FP-MMMA* p. 524)

8. The Swiss critic Robert Aloys Mooser (1876–1969) was known for his dismissive remarks about Poulenc.

9. Poulenc's Mass was recorded by the Robert Shaw Chorale in 1950 (Victor album DM 1409; RCA Victor LM 1088). It was one of Poulenc's most prized recordings. (*ECR* p. 156)

LETTER 216

1. Bernac was never appointed to the Conservatoire in Paris, but he had a distinguished teaching career that included classes at the Ecole Normale de Musique in Paris and at the Académie Maurice Ravel in St-Jean-de-Luz. He also gave regular master classes in the USA and in England.

2. The following year, in September 1952, Poulenc again confided his thoughts about Bernac to Simone Girard:

> In the deepest part of myself I am horribly saddened to see that we are entering the autumn of our association. We must at all costs avoid the winter. I am pushing Pierre to do the classics with [Robert] Casadesus and an all-Schumann recital with him this winter at the Salle Gaveau. With a bit of foresight, Pierre can and must retire gloriously from the platform. His Schumann recording* is a triumph in every way and will surely cause a great stir in Paris.

3. After Bernac's retirement from the concert platform in 1959, Poulenc did in fact form another duo, with the soprano Denise Duval.

LETTER 217

1. Georges Poupet, a man known for his great culture, was literary adviser to

*Dichterliebe. See letter 229, note 6.

the publishers Plon. He was also responsible for choosing the speakers for the lecture-recitals known as the Sabati di Primavera, organized by the Contessa Pecci-Blunt in Rome.

2. Poulenc wrote the music for *Le Voyage en Amérique* (1951), a film directed by Henri Lavorelle. *L'Embarquement pour Cythère*, Poulenc's 'valse-musette' for two pianos, is taken from this film (see letter 334, note 2). The dedication is as follows: 'To Henri Lavorelle, this evocation of the banks of the Marne, so dear to my childhood. Very affectionately, Francis Poulenc. October 1951.'

Cythera, symbol of idyllic love, was for Poulenc the cherished Nogent of his youth. (*ECR* pp. 176–177)

LETTER 218

1. Rene Leibowitz (1913–72). French composer of Polish birth, also conductor, teacher, and theoretician. After studying with Webern and Schoenberg in the early 1930s, Leibowitz taught serial technique to Boulez and others in the 1940s. His own compositions were all written in the twelve-note style.

Poulenc's *Thème varié*, a theme and eleven variations for piano, was completed in 1951. The coda of the final variation presents the theme in reverse and is Poulenc's mocking allusion to the twelve-tone system.

2. Sauguet had a country home, La Maison des Chants, et Fargues, in Coutras (Gironde).

LETTER 219

1. Sauguet composed the incidental music for five plays directed by Louis Jouvet: *Ondine* by Giraudoux (1939); *Les Perses* by Aeschylus (1940); *La Folle de Chaillot* by Giraudoux (1945); *Don Juan* by Molière (1947); *Tartuffe* by Molière (1950).

LETTER 220

1. Stravinsky's opera *The Rake's Progress*, on a text by W. H. Auden and Chester Kallman, had its première at la Fenice in Venice in 1951.

LETTER 221

1. Poulenc composed his *Quatre motets pour le temps de Noël*, for mixed chorus *a cappella*, between November 1951 and May 1952. He dedicated the second motet, 'Quem vidistis pastores dicite', to Simone Girard. The other three motets were dedicated respectively to Félix de Nobel, Madeleine Bataille and Marcel Couraud.

2. 'Vinea mea electa' was the second of Poulenc's earlier, more sombre *Quatre motets pour un temps de pénitence*, for mixed chorus *a cappella*, written in 1938–39.

3. Vincent Laugier, a friend of Simone Girard, was the owner of a printing business in Avignon and the conductor of a choir there.

4. The Girards lived in the rue de la Croix, Avignon.

5. The 'Mistral', an express train between Paris and Marseilles, was named after the famous wind that blows in the South of France.

6. In the late 1940s, Poulenc met Lucien Roubert, a young man from Toulon who at that time was living in Marseilles. Their relationship was a complicated one and was largely responsible for Poulenc's emotional breakdown in the mid-1950s. The painful course of this relationship emerges clearly from Poulenc's letters, particularly those to Simone Girard, Rose Dercourt-Plaut, and Pierre Bernac.

LETTER 222

1. See letter 221, note 6.

LETTER 223

1. *Le Cornette*, Sauguet's ballade for bass (or baritone) and orchestra, is a setting of a poem by Rilke. In *Visions infernales*, Sauguet set poems by Max Jacob. 'Régates mystérieuses' is the fourth of the six songs that make up this cycle.

LETTER 224

1. *La Main de César* (1951) was the latest play by the actor and playwright, André Roussin (1911–87).

LETTER 225

1. Contrexéville, near Vittel, in the Vosges mountains, is famous for its thermal springs.

2. The Romanian conductor and composer Sergiu Celibidache (*b.* 1912) began his career by studying music, advanced mathematics, and formalistic philosophy in Berlin. In 1945 he became conductor of the Berlin Philharmonic while Furtwängler was being cleared and, at the time of Poulenc's letter, was completing a five-year period as Furtwängler's assistant. He later went on to direct the Swedish Radio Symphony Orchestra and the Stuttgart Radio Orchestra. His compositions include a Requiem, four symphonies and a piano concerto.

3. The Florentine music festival, the Maggio Musicale Fiorentino, was conceived in 1933 by G. M. Gatti, who directed it until 1937. At the time of Poulenc's letter, the festival was enjoying a period of great success, which had begun under the direction of Mario Labroca (1937–44) and had continued under Francesco Siciliani (1950–56). It presented the Italian première of such works as Stravinsky's *Oedipus rex* (1937), the world première of Dallapiccola's *Volo di notte* (1940) and Prokofiev's *War and Peace* (1953). The Orchestra del Maggio Musicale has continued to attract guest and permanent conductors of international renown.

4. When Marie-Blanche de Polignac's mother, the couturière Jeanne Lanvin, died in 1946, Prince Louis de Polignac took charge of the Lanvin collection.

LETTER 226

1. The interior designer Emilio Terry was redecorating the library of the

Polignac's Paris residence, at 16 rue Barbet de Jouy. It was said of him that he invented the *style Louis XVII*.

LETTER 227

1. In April 1952, at Carnegie Hall, Robert Shaw conducted the Collegiate Chorale, the Robert Shaw Chorale and the RCA Victor Symphony Orchestra in the American première of Poulenc's *Stabat Mater*. On 12 January 1953, the New York Music Critics' Circle named the *Stabat Mater* the best choral composition of 1952.

2. In 1952, while at the wheel of his car during a trip to Italy, the conductor Roger Désormière suffered a stroke that left him partially paralysed. A moving account of the last eleven years of Désormière's life is given by his friend, the pianist Jean Wiéner, in his autobiography (*AA* pp. 181–182):

> For eleven years, until the day he died, he suffered a martyrdom that does not bear thinking on. Entirely conscious, he was unable to pronounce a single word other than *Non*. I would often visit him but I found it extremely difficult to understand what he was trying to tell me by his gestures, and what I replied never corresponded to what he wanted to hear. Then he would grow impatient. Then he would cry, and that was atrocious. Often he would get up from his armchair, would go to a cupboard and, with his walking stick, would point to a drawer. When I opened it, still with his stick, he would point to a pile of manuscripts, then to exactly the one he wanted. He had retained the absolute precision that had always been his hallmark before his misfortune . . . He would spend his evenings watching television, from the first to the last picture, and he cut himself off from everyone bar five or six close friends, one of whom, Henri Sauguet, behaved towards him like a sort of saint.

3. The American composers, Virgil Thomson (1896–1989) and Arthur Berger (*b*. 1912) were both music critics for the *New York Herald Tribune*.

4. See letter 221, note 1.

LETTER 229

1. The Hotel Beau-Rivage in Ouchy, Lausanne, overlooking the Lake of Geneva, was a favourite retreat for Poulenc during the winter. In a letter to Simone Girard dated 8 January 1953 he says of his stay in Switzerland:

> . . . I am leading the most unbelievably ordered life here. I wake at six – because I go to bed at nine-thirty – and read in bed until seven. Breakfast (sublime tea and jam) at seven-thirty. From eight to nine-thirty I prepare my twenty interviews with Rostand. At nine-thirty, off for a walk in the gardens. From ten to one-o'clock, music. One-o'clock, lunch. Two to three, walk by the lake. Three to six, music. Six to seven-thirty, stroll in Lausanne. Eight, light dinner. Nine-thirty, bed. As you can see, it is *ultra-raisonnable*. If I did not have work to do I would be bored to death a million times every hour. How can anyone come to Switzerland for pleasure?

2. In 1953 Swiss Radio broadcast a series of six conversations between Poulenc

and Stéphane Audel. A further eight were broadcast in 1955 and 1962. Four final interviews were scheduled for 30 January 1963, the day when Poulenc died. Later in 1963, these interviews were published by La Palatine, Geneva and Paris, with a preface by Stéphane Audel, under the title *Moi et mes amis*. An English translation by James Harding, *My Friends and Myself*, was published by Dobson Books, London, in 1978.

3. Horowitz's recording of Poulenc's *Pastourelle* and *Toccata* was made in 1932 and published in 1935 (HMV DB 2247).

4. Between October 1953 and April 1954 French Radio broadcast a series of eighteen interviews with Poulenc, by Claude Rostand. These were published by Julliard, Paris, in 1954, under the title *Entretiens avec Claude Rostand*. A similar series of interviews with Darius Milhaud – to mark his 60th birthday – had been broadcast and published by Julliard in 1952.

5. Heinrich Ströbel (1898–1970). German music critic, editor of *Melos*, director of the music division of Baden-Baden Radio and chairman of the International Society of Contemporary Music. Ströbel moved to France in 1939.

6. In February 1952, Bernac and Robert Casadesus made a recording of Schumann's *Dichterliebe* for CBS. In a letter to Bernac dated 2 September (Bibliothèque Nationale) Poulenc wrote of this recording:

> Some good news first: the divine Rose [Dercourt-Plaut] and the exquisite Fred [Plaut] came by last night. Your record with Robert has had a *prodigious* success, a *sensational* press and a magnificent reception from the public. It is said to be 'an incomparable recording', 'the best recording of the *Dichterliebe* ever made', etc. etc. Columbia is absolutely delighted.

LETTER 230

1. Poulenc refers to his 1953 concert tour of Italy with Pierre Fournier.

2. In a following letter to Simone Girard, dated Rome, 28 March 1953, Poulenc wrote: 'The Fournier tour is going very well in every way. It is idiotic of me to make comparisons. Fournier is first-rate and just as scrupulous as Pierre I. And his rather difficult nature is very *appealing*. We get on *perfectly*.'

In April of the same year, Poulenc again wrote to Simone Girard: '*Triumph* with Fournier in Rome. Obliged to accept two weeks next March.'

LETTER 231

1. This letter is written on consecutive postcards.

2. Nicolas Nabokov (1903–78), Russian-born composer, teacher and organizer of international music festivals. He emigrated to the USA in 1933, but from the 1950s lived mainly in Paris.

3. Suzanne and André, a married couple, were part of Poulenc's domestic staff at Le Grand Coteau. After Poulenc's death, Suzanne drowned herself in a pond at the edge of the vineyards. It is said she was suffering from depression due to fear that Le Grand Coteau would be sold. Her husband André, who tended the grounds of Le Grand Coteau, continued to live in a small outhouse on the premises until his death in the mid-1980s.

4. In 1953, Poulenc was asked by the Italian music publishers, Ricordi, to write a ballet for La Scala. The life of Saint Margaret of Cortona was suggested as a subject, but Poulenc was ill at ease with the idea of the thirteenth-century saint who, to atone for a youth of sin, spent her life serving the Franciscan Fathers of Cortona in prayer and chastisement of the flesh.

In March of 1953, while in Milan during his concert tour with Pierre Fournier, Poulenc discussed his doubts about the ballet with Guido Valcarenghi, director of Ricordi. Poulenc intimated that an operatic work would be more to his liking, and preferably one on a mystical subject. Valcarenghi suggested the play by Georges Bernanos (1888–1948), *Dialogues des Carmélites*.

The work was written during the last months of Bernanos's life, while he was ill with cancer. Originally intended as the dialogue for a film, the text was based on a novella by Gertrud von Le Fort (1876–1971), *Die Letzte am Schafott*. Bernanos's version, however, was rejected by the producers of the film. It lay among his papers until after his death, when it was found by his friend and executor, Albert Béguin, who had it produced as a play in Zurich in 1951.

The play is set in France at the time of the Revolution and centres around the historic martyrdom of sixteen Carmelite nuns of Compiègne, guillotined on 17 July 1794. The main protagonist is a fictitious character, daughter of a Marquis, Blanche de la Force, who chooses to enter the Carmelite order as Sister Blanche of the Agony of Christ. Blanche is the incarnation of fear, and through her and her struggles to transcend her fear, Bernanos meditates on the Agony of Christ, on death, and on the idea of the transference of grace. In the final, ecstatic moments of the play, Blanche, through this very transference of grace, is able to accept the vow of martyrdom taken by her sisters, and to go calmly to her death on the scaffold.

In *L'Opéra de Paris* (no. 14, 1957) and in his interviews with Claude Rostand (*ECR* pp. 211–212), Poulenc describes how he reacted to Valcarenghi's suggestion that he set *Dialogues des Carmélites*:

Naturally, I knew the play by Bernanos – I had read it, and re-read it, and even seen it twice – but I had no idea of its *verbal rhythm*, a major consideration for me. I made up my mind to examine the work later, on my return to Paris. But the following day, right in the middle of the window of a bookshop in Rome, there was *Les Dialogues*, which seemed to be just waiting for me. . . . In spite of myself, I felt I was somehow being drawn into this great adventure, which was to haunt me for the next three years. I bought the book and decided to re-read it. I sat down at a café in the Piazza Navona. It was ten o'clock in the morning . . . At two o'clock in the afternoon I sent a telegram to Monsieur Valcarenghi: 'Agreed, with enthusiasm.' I can still see myself at that café in the Piazza Navona . . devouring Bernanos's drama and saying to myself after each scene: 'But obviously, it was made for me, made for me!'

LETTER 232

1. Poulenc was staying at La Bastide du Roy, Marie-Blanche de Polignac's home in Antibes.

LETTER 233

1. Nadia Boulanger (see letter 133, note 1) was appointed director of the American Conservatory in Fontainebleau in 1950. She had been a member of staff there since 1921 and had taught many distinguished composers, including Elliot Carter, Aaron Copland, Roy Harris, Virgil Thomson and Lennox Berkeley. From 1946, Nadia Boulanger also taught an accompaniment class at the Paris Conservatoire.

LETTER 234

1. Mother Marie of the Incarnation, sub-Prioress of the Carmelite Convent.

2. In September 1953, *Les Mamelles de Tirésias* was recorded at the Théâtre des Champs-Elysées. Denise Duval sang the role of Thérèse/Tirésias, and Jean Giraudeau that of the husband. The orchestra and chorus of the Opéra-Comique was conducted by André Cluytens. The recording was made by French Columbia (FCX 230). See also letter 241 and note 5.

3. Stéphane Audel was married to the actress Cariel, a member of Louis Jouvet's company.

LETTER 235

1. Poulenc composed the role of Blanche de la Force with Denise Duval in mind.

2. Initially, Poulenc divided the opera into two acts, the first consisting of seven scenes, the second of eight. His letters relating to the composition of the opera refer to this plan. He later divided the opera into three acts of four scenes each, with interludes.

3. There does not appear to be a commercial recording of the *Stabat Mater* by Robert Shaw. Poulenc, however, ended his interviews with Claude Rostand in 1954 by playing an extract of a recording of the *Stabat Mater* 'by the Robert Shaw Chorale and the New York Philharmonic Orchestra'. (*ECR* p. 214). This could have been the recording to which Doda Conrad refers in letter 228, made during Shaw's performance of the work at Carnegie Hall in April 1952 (see letter 227, note 1). The first commercial recording of the work appears to have been made in 1955 by the Alauda Choir, soloist Jacqueline Brumaire, with the Colonne Orchestra, conducted by Louis Frémaux (Véga C 35 A 1).

4. *Sécheresses* was recorded in 1953 by the Chorale Elisabeth Brasseur, with the Paris Conservatoire Orchestra conducted by Georges Tzipine, and issued in 1954 in *Album: Le Groupe des Six* – (French) Columbia FCX 264/5.

5. Poulenc's Sextet was recorded in 1952 with Jean Françaix (piano) and members of the French Radio National Orchestra and issued in 1953 (Pathé DTX 135).

6. Suzanne Danco (*b.* 1911). Belgian soprano renowned particularly for her interpretations of the music of Debussy, Berlioz and Ravel.

LETTER 236

1. See letter 216, note 1.

2. The French violinist Jacques Thibaud (1880–1953) died on 1 September in a plane crash while travelling to French Indochina. Four years earlier, the 30-year-old violinist Ginette Neveu (1919–49) was killed in a similar crash in the Azores.

LETTER 237

1. In the final version of the opera, the female roles are distributed as follows: Blanche – soprano; First Prioress – contralto; Second Prioress – soprano; Mother Marie – lyric soprano; Sister Constance – light soprano; Mother Jeanne – contralto; Sister Mathilde – mezzo.

2. On 1 September 1953, Poulenc was made *Officier de la Légion d'Honneur*. His decoration was delivered by the wife of the Minister of the Interior, Dacier. For further honours see letter 291.

LETTER 238

1. The Sonata for two pianos, written for Arthur Gold and Robert Fizdale. See letter 268.

2. Poulenc held Robert Shaw in very high regard. There are frequent references to this throughout his correspondence and in his interviews with Claude Rostand. A protégé of Toscanini and Szell, Shaw (*b*. 1916) founded and directed the celebrated Robert Shaw Chorale, was conductor and director of the Atlanta Symphony Orchestra from 1967–88, and founder and director of the Atlanta Symphony Orchestra Chorus from 1970–88. In August 1988 Shaw assumed the lifetime position of Music Director Emeritus and Conductor Laureate of the Atlanta Symphony.

3. Jay Harrison, music critic of the *New York Herald Tribune*.

LETTER 239

1. Verdi's opera *Aida* was first performed in Cairo on 24 December 1871. The Italian première took place at La Scala, Milan, on 8 February 1872.

2. Poulenc refers to the death of the conductor and composer Louis Beydts (1895–1953), musical director of the Opéra-Comique in Paris from 1950–53.

LETTER 240

1. The extract which follows this letter in *Correspondance* (p. 215) is incorrectly placed. It is not addressed to Yvonne Gouverné, but forms the last paragraph of a letter to Pierre Bernac, now in the Frederick R. Koch Foundation Collection, on deposit in the Pierpont Morgan Library, New York. See letter 242.

LETTER 241

1. Poulenc was again spending a working winter in Switzerland, at the Hôtel Beau-Rivage, Lausanne. See letter 229, note 1.

2. The music for the film *Moulin Rouge* (1953) was composed by Georges Auric. The film was directed by John Huston and was based on a novel about the life of Toulouse-Lautrec by Pierre la Mure.

3. Stravinsky's *Cantata*, composed in 1952, consists of settings of anonymous

fifteenth- and sixteenth-century English texts under the title 'A Lyke-Wake Dirge'.

4. The American composer and writer Ned Rorem (*b*. 1923) was living in Paris at the time. He spent the years 1951–57 there, under the patronage of the Vicomtesse Marie-Laure de Noailles.

5. In a letter to Bernac written in December 1953 (Frederick R. Koch Foundation Collection, Pierpont Morgan Library) Poulenc says of *Les Mamelles*: 'I am insanely fond of this work. It is one of the rare things I have written where I would not change one single ♪.'

With regard to the recording of this work, he wrote to Simone Girard, on 4 December 1953:

> I shall try to bring you some light relief with the record of *Les Mamelles*, so sensational, so marvellous, so astonishing that I wept with emotion when I heard it!!! Pierre, who heard it too, was absolutely amazed. Cluytens is incredible and all the singers are perfect.

6. *Gaultier Garguille* is a symphonic poem written in 1953 by the French composer Emmanuel Bondeville (1898–1987), director of the Opéra-Comique from 1949 and of the Opéra from 1952.

7. Henri Hell completed his book on Poulenc four years later. See under Poulenc's Correspondents.

8. Book publishers.

LETTER 242

1. Act I of *Dialogues des Carmélites* ends with the death of the Prioress, Madame de Croissy.

2. Poulenc frequently stresses that at the heart of Bernanos's play is the concept of the transference of grace:

> If it is a play about fear, it is also – and above all, in my opinion – a play about grace and the transference of grace. That is why my Carmelites go to the scaffold with an extraordinary calm and faith. For are not faith and calm at the heart of all mystical experience? [*ECR* pp. 213–214]

3. In March 1954 Poulenc accompanied Bernac in a concert tour of North Africa. See letters 246 and 247.

LETTER 243

1. *Les Gazettes d'Adrienne Monnier (1925–1945)* published in 1953 by Julliard, Paris.

2. Page 63 carries an article by Adrienne Monnier on Raymonde Linossier, written shortly after the latter's death in 1930 and first published in *Les Nouvelles littéraires* (1930).

3. Adrienne Monnier's article on Poulenc's ballet *Les Animaux modèles* is entitled 'A l'Opéra avec Francis Poulenc'. It appears in the section of her book headed 'Les Gazettes du *Figaro Littéraire* (1942)'.

LETTER 244

1. Darius Milhaud and Paul Hindemith were renowned for their prolific and rapid output.

2. *Les Caprices de Marianne*, opera in two acts by Henri Sauguet, libretto by Jean-Pierre Grédy, adapted from the play by Alfred de Musset.

LETTER 246

1. In 1954, at the home of Comte Etienne de Beaumont, Poulenc accompanied Doda Conrad's mother, the Polish singer Marya Freund (then aged 78) in a performance of *Socrate*, Satie's 'drame symphonique' written in 1918. Marya Freund had given the first performance of this work with orchestra, conducted by Félix Delgrange, in 1920.

LETTER 248

1. This letter was written in the year before Honegger's death. He had suffered a severe heart-attack in 1947 and was in very poor health. He was staying in Basle with his devoted friends, the Paul Sachers (see below).

Poulenc spoke at length about this letter in his interviews with Stéphane Audel (*FP-MMA* p. 153):

> It is one of the last letters I received from Arthur . . . an extraordinary letter, although somewhat too eulogistic with regard to me. It defines very precisely the nature of my relationship with Arthur at the time of his death. There was a great tenderness – tenderness is the right word for it – and it was really only during the last three years of his life that we truly came to understand each other, and were able to speak freely about everything.

2. Paul Sacher (*b.* 1906). Swiss conductor, founder of the Basle Chamber Orchestra and Choir, and renowned patron of contemporary composers. He commissioned or gave the first performance of a significant number of twentieth-century compositions, often acquiring the manuscripts as well. To safeguard his personal collection of letters, books and scores, he founded the Paul Sacher Foundation in Basle in 1974.

LETTER 250

1. Charlotte, from Massenet's opera *Werther* (1892), based on Goethe's novel *Die Leiden des jungen Werthers* (*The Sorrows of Young Werther*, 1774).

2. The neurologist and psychiatrist, Doctor Delmas-Marsalet, who was attending Poulenc at the time.

3. Throughout their long association, Poulenc and Bernac always addressed each other using the formal 'you', *vous*, rather than the familiar *tu*.

4. At a time when Poulenc was already debilitated from severe depression caused by complications in his relationship with Lucien Roubert and doubts about his own state of health, he suddenly found himself faced with a legal problem concerning the performing rights to the text of his opera. The rights to any stage production based on the novel by Gertrud von Le Fort, *Die Letzte am Schafott*, had been acquired by Emmet Lavery (*b.* 1902), an American playwright, who had written his own stage version of the work, in English, under the title *The Last on the Scaffold*. Lavery then exercised his rights by prohibiting the

production of Bernanos's play – also based on the novel by Gertrud von Le Fort – unless specifically authorized by himself. Bernanos's heirs would willingly have granted the rights to Poulenc for an opera, but could not do so without the permission of Lavery, with whom they were on very bad terms. A long legal battle ensued, which caused Poulenc deep emotional strain. Finally, permission was granted, but with the proviso that Poulenc should add to all his programmes, publicity posters, and printed libretto, the phrase: 'Adapted as an opera by permission of Emmet Lavery'. (From an account of the problem given by Ricordi's director in Paris, Hervé Dugardin, in *Correspondance*, pp. 225–226.)

5. Father Carré, one of Poulenc's spiritual advisers, compared Poulenc to the main character in the opera by Massenet, *Le Jongleur de Notre Dame* (1902). Based on a story by Anatole France (1844–1924), *L'Etui de nacre*, it tells of the tumbler Jean who, mocked and derided by the crowds, enters a monastery to devote his life and his skill to the Virgin Mary. In the final scenes of the opera, accused of blasphemy by the monks, Jean dances himself to death in front of the statue of the Virgin, whose arm is miraculously extended to bless him as he dies.

6. Ligugé is a benedictine abbey where the first French monastery was founded in 361 by Saint Martin.

7. In a letter to Bernac dated 1958, Poulenc uses a similar image to describe his house, Le Grand Coteau, at Noizay: 'To tell the truth, Noizay is the wife I would never divorce, while cuckolding her all the time!' (Pierpont Morgan Library)

As Poulenc grew older, his feelings changed towards Paris and Touraine. Whereas in 1940 he had stated in a letter to Bernac (No. 152): 'I would readily sacrifice all of Noizay for Paris', on 28 April 1959, he wrote to Doctor Louis Chevalier:

> What I simply cannot understand is this sudden phobia about Paris, where I was born and where I lived so happily. Nothing interests me there any more (except the theatre). The society I used to frequent bores me to death and never have I felt so alone as in the rue de Médicis, despite the ravishing view. Fortunately, I am growing attached to Noizay as the lesser of the two evils.

LETTER 251

1. See letter 250.

2. *The First Legion; A Drama of the Society of Jesus* was written in 1934 by the American playwright, Emmet Lavery (see letter 250, note 4). His plays include *Murder in the Nunnery* (1944) and *Brief Music* (1940). He worked as a script writer in Hollywood in the 1930s.

LETTER 253

1. In the opening sentence of his memoirs (*MVH* p. 9) Milhaud describes himself as 'a Frenchman from Provence and, by religion, a Jew'. On his father's side, he was a descendant of the Jews who had settled in the county of Venaissin

in the Middle Ages, under the protection of the Popes. On his mother's side, he came from a long line of Sephardim from Italy. Milhaud felt that his Jewish heritage could not be separated from his French heritage, and that both were integral parts of his being.

LETTER 255

1. Poulenc was writing from the train, the 'Mistral' (see letter 221, note 5), and refers to his 'railway scrawl'.

2. Poulenc and Bernac were due to go on a concert tour of Germany. See letters 256 and 257.

LETTER 256

1. It is unclear whether or not this is a complete letter. No signature or initial appears at the end of the page, but no following page has so far been found.

Poulenc went on tour to Germany with Bernac but soon had to return to France, where he entered a clinic. See letters 257 and 263.

LETTER 258

1. Vincent Laugier (see letter 221, note 3) and Father Rigaud were friends of the Girards. Antoinette was the Girards' housekeeper.

2. On 2 February 1955 Poulenc and Bernac gave a concert at the Salle Gaveau to celebrate the twentieth anniversary of their professional association.

LETTER 259

1. See letter 260.

LETTER 260

1. On Sunday 16 January 1955 Poulenc and Britten performed Poulenc's Concerto for two pianos at the Royal Festival Hall. The Liverpool Philharmonic Orchestra was conducted by John Pritchard.

2. See letter 273 and note 1.

LETTER 261

1. *Plus 'noire'* – 'more dense with notes'.

2. Lucien Roubert was at this stage seriously ill with tuberculosis and had turned once again to Poulenc for support.

LETTER 262

1. In 1954, Alice Esty and her accompanist David Stimer made some private recordings in a studio in New York, including songs by Poulenc. Stimer sent one of these recordings to Poulenc and it is to this that Poulenc refers.

2. Poulenc's Sonata for two pianos, written for Arthur Gold and Robert Fizdale. See letter 268.

3. Poulenc shared with Eluard a deep love of the visual arts. 'Since my earliest childhood', he said, 'I have been passionately fond of painting. I owe to it just as many profound joys as to music.' (*FP-MMA* p. 74). The seven poems that Poulenc chose for his song cycle *Le Travail du peintre* are from Eluard's book *Voir* (Editions des Trois Collines, Geneva, Paris, 1948). The book comprises over 40 poems on painters – several from previously published collections – illustrated with reproductions of works by the artists concerned. (*PE* vol II, pp. 1085–89). The title, *Le Travail du peintre*, is that of the first poem in the collection, dedicated to Picasso. The poem is in seven parts; Poulenc set part I only as his opening song, 'Pablo Picasso'. There follow songs on Marc Chagall, Georges Braque, Juan Gris, Paul Klee, Joan Miró and Jacques Villon. Poulenc had wanted to end the cycle 'in joy and sunshine' with a song on Matisse but Eluard did not share his enthusiasm for that painter. The cycle ends 'lyrically and gravely' with Villon. (*DMS* p. 101)

In a letter to Bernac written in 1953 (Frederick R. Koch Foundation Collection, Pierpont Morgan Library), Poulenc wrote:

> More than ever am I determined to write *Le Travail du peintre*. I shall dedicate the whole cycle to you in letters of gold and I would like to give the first performance of it in a concert celebrating the twentieth anniversary of our association. I myself will underwrite the financial risk.

These plans did not materialize, as Poulenc did not complete the cycle until August 1956, eighteen months after the twentieth anniversary concert.

4. Alice Esty remembers that it was during one of her visits to Paris to study with Pierre Bernac that Bernac asked her if she would be interested in commissioning a cycle of Poulenc songs. 'He explained that Poulenc had started a cycle based on poems from Eluard's collection *Voir*, and that he had stopped, or was somehow blocked, and needed something or somebody to get him back to work on the songs.' (Letter from Alice Esty to the translator, 25 March 1989.)

Alice Esty agreed to commission the work and received a progress report from Bernac in a letter dated 3 September [1955] – written in English.

> . . . Poulenc is now extremely well and he has been working the whole summer on his Opera. It is nearly finished! So I am afraid he was too plunged into this work to have been able to start thinking to your songs. But he is now back to his country house in Touraine (where we must go and see him when you are there) and I would not be surprised if he started working on them . . .

Poulenc finally completed the work in August 1956, while staying at the home of his sister Jeanne in Normandy, the Château du Tremblay. See letter 275 to Bernac and letter 276 to Alice Esty.

LETTER 263

1. It was not until 1956 that Poulenc finally composed the song 'Nuage' for Rose Dercourt-Plaut, on a poem by Laurence de Beylié (1893–1968). It is grouped with a song dedicated to Marya Freund, 'La Souris', and published under the title *Deux Mélodies 1956*. On Rose Plaut's copy of the music, Poulenc wrote the

following dedication: 'For my dear Rose, this little song and much tenderness, Fr. Poulenc, '57.'

2. *Parisiana*, for voice and piano, settings of two poems by Max Jacob, dedicated to the memory of Pierre Colle and Paul Chadourne, and 'Rosemonde', for voice and piano, on a poem by Apollinaire, dedicated to the Comtesse Pastré, were completed in 1954 and first performed by Bernac and Poulenc at a concert in Amsterdam on 12 October 1954.

3. All Fred Plaut's photographs relating to Poulenc (see under Rose Dercourt-Plaut in Poulenc's Correspondents) are housed in the Fred and Rose Plaut Archives in the Music Library at Yale University, USA.

LETTER 264

1. See letter 263, note 1.

LETTER 265

1. *On ne meurt pas chacun pour soi, mais les uns pour les autres, ou même les uns à la place des autres*. With these key-words, Bernanos introduces the spiritual concept at the heart of his play, that of the transference of grace. In Poulenc's opera, the words are sung by Sister Constance at the end of the Interlude following Act II, scene 1.

2. In the final scene of *Dialogues des Carmélites*, Blanche goes to the scaffold, singing these last four lines of the *Veni Creator*.

3. See under Adrienne Monnier in Poulenc's Correspondents.

LETTER 266

1. In the French folksong: *C'est la mère Michel qui a perdu son chat*, old mother Michel's cat is sold as rabbit.

2. In the sanctuary of Rocamadour is a small museum of sacred art, the Musée-Trésor Francis Poulenc, named in homage to the composer and inaugurated on 4 May 1969. Among the treasures housed there are a ciborium and a chalice donated by Poulenc, signed on the base by the composer and dated respectively 1938 and 1957.

LETTER 267

1. See letter 268.

2. Poulenc refers to the end of *Dialogues des Carmélites* and the drafting of his song cycle *Le Travail du peintre*.

3. The recordings by Véga were published in 1958 in two volumes (C 35 A 33/34) under the title *Choix de mélodies 1919–1954*.

LETTER 268

1. Poulenc's Sonata for two pianos was written for, and dedicated to, Arthur Gold and Robert Fizdale. The work was begun in Marseilles in 1952 and completed at Noizay in the spring of 1953. It was first performed by Gold and Fizdale in a BBC broadcast on 2 November 1953.

2. The recording by Gold and Fizdale of Poulenc's Sonata for two pianos was first published in 1955 – (US) Columbia ML 5068.

LETTER 269

1. Simone Girard's husband, Doctor Pierre Girard, died in March 1955.
2. Lucien Roubert died in Toulon on 21 October 1955, after his long fight against tuberculosis.
3. Poulenc frequently referred to Raymond Destouches as his *vieux fox à poils durs*.
4. In a letter to Simone Girard written three years earlier, in September 1952, Poulenc explained the complications of what he called his 'sentimental and emotional life':

> I am loved *too much* in Toulon, which frightens me, as I am not totally free. Although with Raymond there has been what is referred to nowadays as a transference of feeling on my part to something far more paternal, I cannot, after twenty years, cause him any pain, and he will always have first place in my life.

LETTER 271

1. The world première of Poulenc's opera *Dialogues des Carmélites* took place at La Scala, Milan, on 26 January 1957. The first performance in France, at the Paris Opéra, was on 21 June 1957.
2. With Marcelle Meyer, Poulenc recorded *Trois Valses romantiques* by Chabrier (Discophiles français 151/2, 1955, reissued in 1982 in the series Références, La Voix de son Maître C 151 73.125/6). See also letter 275.
3. The recording of Satie's piano music to which Poulenc refers (Boîte à musique LD 023) was made in November 1955 and published in 1957. See letter 275.
4. Poulenc's views on the music of Pierre Boulez and Anton Webern are further expressed in the interview with Claude Rostand and the letter to Fred Goldbeck quoted in letter 283, note 6.

LETTER 272

1. See letter 273 and note 1.
2. Poulenc had a predilection for American shirts, underwear and socks, which he often asked Rose Dercourt-Plaut to buy for him. In a letter to her dated 23 June 1961, he wrote: 'If the socks exist in white, I would like to have two or three pairs. I have bought some shoes in white suede! An old maestro's folly!'

LETTER 273

1. On the 24 June 1956, at the ninth Aldeburgh Festival, Poulenc gave a talk in French with musical illustrations entitled: *Propos à Bâtons Rompus sur la Musique*, in which he defined his own position in relation to the various currents of contemporary music. On the evening of the same date, Poulenc performed his *Aubade* with the Aldeburgh Festival Orchestra conducted by Paul Sacher.

2. Vincent Laugier (see letter 221, note 3) and William Rochette, treasurer of the Société Avignonnaise de Concerts.

3. The Italian translation of *Dialogues des Carmélites* was by F. Testi.

4. The Odessa-born stage and film set designer, Georges Wakhevitch. His décor for the world première of *Dialogues des Carmélites* in Milan in January 1957 was also used for the British première at Covent Garden in January of the following year.

LETTER 274

1. *Peter Grimes*, opera in three acts by Britten based on George Crabbe's poem *The Borough*, first performed in 1945.

2. *The Turn of the Screw*, opera in prologue and two acts by Britten based on a story by Henry James, first performed in 1954.

3. The song by Henry Purcell that moved Poulenc to tears is 'What a sad fate is mine':

LETTER 275

1. The only commercial recording by Bernac and Poulenc of *Le Travail du peintre* is Véga C 30 A 293, published in 1960.

2. See letter 271, note 3.

3. See letter 271, note 2.

4. 'Lots of butter in the sauce'. A favourite image of Poulenc's, to describe the use of the pedals. He attached great importance to pedalling, 'that essential factor in modern music'. He had learnt about pedalling from Viñes, who could play 'with clarity in a wash of pedals'. (*FP-MMA* p. 43). He admired Gieseking, who used the pedals 'with both economy and profusion'. In his own music, he stressed that the use of pedals was of 'cardinal importance'. He wrote: '. . . my work calls for the almost constant use of the pedals [to] soften the *severity* of certain of my broken chords or of my arpeggios.' (*DMS* pp. 53–55)

5. Although Poulenc wrote the part of Blanche with Denise Duval in mind, it was not until the French production of the opera, in June 1957, that Duval sang in this role. In the world première in Italy, Virginia Zeani took the part of Blanche.

6. *Dialogues des Carmélites* at La Scala was produced by the Viennese-born Margarita Wallmann. Her collaboration with Poulenc was a close one. She assisted him with the division of Bernanos's text, produced the world première in Milan in 1957, the British première in 1958 and subsequent performances in North and South America.

7. The French première, at the Paris Opéra, was produced by Maurice Jacquemont. The décor was by Suzanne Lalique.

8. The Claude of this letter is mentioned in one other communication, letter 283 to Bernac, dated 12 July 1957.

9. Suzanne Danco does not appear to have made any recordings of songs by Poulenc.

LETTER 276

1. In accordance with the terms of the commission (see letter 262), *Le Travail du peintre* was dedicated to Alice Esty and, after working on the cycle with Poulenc and Bernac, she gave the first performance of the work on 1 April 1957 at the Ecole Normale de Musique, in Paris, accompanied by Poulenc. (David Stimer accompanied Alice Esty in the other works included in this concert – by Ford, Rosseter, Purcell, Debussy, Paul Bowles.)

In a letter to Poulenc dated 'Sunday', Bernac discusses the arrangements for this concert with Poulenc:

> Several things to tell you. First of all, the Ecole Normale would be possible on Monday, 1st April, for the Esty concert. I think this would suit you. She is to give me her reply tomorrow morning – she feels it is too soon, but in my opinion she will be ready. In any case, she prefers to do the Debussy songs with her own pianist, with whom she feels more at ease, and I have the idea that he is more or less insisting on this.

Alice Esty also gave the first performance in America of *Le Travail du peintre*, accompanied by David Stimer, on 21 February 1958, at Carnegie Recital Hall.

The first performance in England was given by Bernac and Poulenc on 5 September 1957, at the Edinburgh Festival. This performance has often been cited – including by Poulenc himself – as the world première of *Le Travail du peintre*.

LETTER 278

1. In the world première of *Dialogues des Carmélites* in Milan, the role of Blanche de la Force was sung by Virginia Zeani, the First Prioress by Gianna Pederzini, the Second Prioress by Leila Gencer, Mother Marie by Gigliola Frazzoni, and Sister Constance by Eugénia Ratti. The orchestra was conducted by Nino Sanzogno.

2. Verdi's *Otello* was first performed at La Scala on 5 February 1887, when the composer was 74.

LETTER 281

1. The cast of the Paris première of *Dialogues des Carmélites* was as follows: Blanche de la Force – Denise Duval; First Prioress – Denise Scharley; Second Prioress – Régine Crespin; Mother Marie – Rita Gorr; Sister Constance – Liliane Berton; the Marquis de la Force – Xavier Depraz; the Chevalier de la Force – Paul Finel. The orchestra was conducted by Pierre Dervaux.

2. The name of the career sergeant, 'Louis', appears frequently in Poulenc's letters from 1957 to 1963. Once again, Poulenc writes frankly of this young man's role in the last six years of his life.

3. Poulenc's Sonata for flute and piano, a commission from the Elizabeth Sprague Coolidge Foundation, was completed between December 1956 and March 1957, in Cannes. In accordance with the terms of the commission, it was dedicated to the memory of Elizabeth Sprague Coolidge. It was first performed at the Strasbourg Festival on 18 June 1957 by Jean-Pierre Rampal and Poulenc.

4. 'Dernier poème', Poulenc's setting of a poem said to have been written by Robert Desnos to his wife Youki, from the concentration camp of Terezin, Czechoslovakia, where, after being interned for activities in the French Resistance movement, he died of typhus on 8 June 1945, shortly after the liberation of the camp by US troops. The poem is a shortened version of an earlier piece, written in 1926, 'Poèmes à la mystérieuse', from the collection *Corps et biens* (1930). Poulenc's setting, 'Dernier poème', dates from December 1956 and is dedicated to Youki Desnos.

LETTER 283

1. The German première of *Dialogues des Carmélites* took place on 14 July 1957 at the Cologne Opera, in a production by E. Bormann, conducted by W. von der Nahmer. The cast was as follows: Blanche – K. Moller-Siepermann; First Prioress – L. Benningsen; Second Prioress – W. Wegner; Mother Marie – N. Hinschgrondahl; Constance – R. Bartos.

2. Gabrielle Dorziat. French actress for whom Cocteau wrote one of the leading roles in *Les Parents terribles*.

3. *On ne badine pas avec l'amour*. Play by Alfred de Musset written in 1834.

4. Paul Colin (1892–1985). French artist, stage set designer, and celebrated poster-painter.

5. See letter 275 and note 8.

6. In the bowdlerized version of this letter that appears in *Correspondance*, Poulenc's 'dodécaca' has been changed to 'dodécaphonisme'. The original letter (Frederick R. Koch Foundation Collection, Pierpont Morgan Library) reveals that Poulenc wrote clearly 'dodécaca', a favourite term of his. From Le Tremblay in 1953, for example, he said in a letter to Simone Girard: 'Come and applaud *Aubade* because in the midst of all that dodécaca I will look like a real old fuddy-duddy.'

In his seventeenth interview with Claude Rostand, Poulenc expounded at length his views on twelve-tone music (*ECR* pp. 198–202). His exposition included the following thoughts:

> For the young generation of 1940, the twelve-tone system was an unknown planet. It is quite natural that they should have wanted to explore it. Although I consider serialism to be closer to the Germanic temperament than our own, I frankly applaud the research efforts of a musician as highly intelligent as Pierre Boulez, and one as naturally gifted as Martinet. What I like in their music is that it develops in parallel with the other arts. So Boulez, in *Le Soleil des eaux*, reveals his affinity

with René Char, just as Auric and I have expressed ours with Paul Eluard. The essential thing is not to be a serialist through fear of missing the boat, because then you are bound to fall prey to stereotype and academicism. [*ECR* pp. 199–200]

Some five years later, in a letter to the music critic Fred Goldbeck written around 1959 (Bibliothèque Musicale Gustav Mahler, Paris) Poulenc described his recent meeting in Vienna with the Austrian composer Anton Heiller (1923–79):

In the home of a friend, I met Anton Heiller, about whom I knew precisely nothing. Without any fuss he sat down at the piano with his wife and both proceeded to play in the most masterly manner a *Toccata* for two pianos which was a revelation to me, just as in 1921, in that same Vienna, Bartók's *Allegro barbaro* had been when I heard it played by Steuermann at the home of Mahler's widow. The *Toccata* is without doubt the work of a very genuine musician . . . Everything about it is first rate: the pianistic writing, the sense of harmony, the construction. Perhaps Heiller will take up in Vienna the torch that has fallen from the dead hands of the marvellous Webern and the great Berg. I say this with regard to quality because, whether the outdated dodecaphonists in Paris like it or not, serial music in their hands – as in the hands of young Austrians at the moment – is nothing but a very, very distant memory. It seems that Bartók showed them the way to freedom (and also Hindemith), but that many of them have unfortunately followed the letter rather than the spirit of his teaching . . . I eagerly await the new works of Heiller, and I salute him today as, in 1937, I happily recognized in Dallapiccola the best of the young Italian musicians.

LETTER 284

1. *Les Mamelles de Tirésias* was to be performed at the 1958 Aldeburgh Festival, with the orchestral score transcribed for two pianos and performed by Poulenc and Britten. In the event, Poulenc was unable to be present. See letters 288, note 1; 290; 348.

LETTER 285

1. 'Marc Chagall' was the second of the seven poems by Eluard that Poulenc had chosen for his song cycle *Le Travail du peintre* (see letter 262).

LETTER 286

1. See letter 139, note 2.

2. At the time of this letter, Edward Sackville-West was on the advisory committee of the Royal Opera House, Covent Garden (see under Poulenc's Correspondents).

The Carmelites was first performed in England at Covent Garden on 16 January 1958. It was sung in English in a translation by Joseph Machlis. The production by Margarita Wallmann, with sets and costumes by Georges Wakhevitch, was the same as that of the world première at La Scala, Milan, in

January 1957. The role of Blanche de la Force was sung by Elsie Morrison; the First Prioress by Jean Watson; the Second Prioress by Joan Sutherland, Mother Marie by Sylvia Fisher, Sister Constance by Jeanette Sinclair. The conductor was Rafaël Kubelik, who had been musical director of Covent Garden since 1955.

3. As the Second Prioress, Joan Sutherland was appearing in one of her relatively early roles at Covent Garden. She had made her operatic debut at the Sydney Conservatory in 1951 and her Covent Garden debut in *The Magic Flute* in 1952.

4. After its initial season in January–February 1958, *The Carmelites* was performed at Covent Garden in 1959, 1963, 1977, 1978, 1980 and 1983.

LETTER 287

1. From February to June 1958 Poulenc composed his final operatic work, a one-act 'tragédie-lyrique' for soprano and small orchestra, on a text by Cocteau, *La Voix humaine*. The Paris director of Ricordi, Hervé Dugardin, suggested to Poulenc that he set Cocteau's monodrama, first performed to great acclaim by the Belgian actress Berthe Bovy (1887–1977) at the Comédie Française in 1930. The 40-minute monologue, spoken into a telephone, is the farewell of a heartbroken woman to her lover who has left her for someone else. Dugardin wanted Poulenc to write the work for Maria Callas, but Poulenc could envisage only Denise Duval as 'Elle'. In an interview with Alain Duault published in *L'Avant-Scène Opéra*, May 1983 (p. 134), Denise Duval said of this work:

> La Voix humaine was an astonishing experience for me. I watched Francis Poulenc write it for me, page by page, bar by bar, with his flesh, but also with my wounded heart, for we were both at that time going through an emotional crisis; we wept together, and *La Voix humaine* was like a chronicle of our torment. [See letters 288 and 294, note 1.]

Published by Ricordi in 1959, *La Voix humaine* was dedicated to Hervé Dugardin and his wife Daisy. It was first performed at the Opéra-Comique in Paris on 6 February 1959, produced and designed by Jean Cocteau, with Denise Duval in the solo role. The orchestra was conducted by Georges Prêtre.

2. See letter 298, note 1.

3. See under Henri Hell in Poulenc's Correspondents.

4. Lucien Adès, head of Véga records, and Jacques Pradère, record producer associated with Véga.

LETTER 288

1. Poulenc was due to go to England for the Aldeburgh Festival production of *Les Mamelles de Tirésias* on 13 June 1958. He was to have played, with Benjamin Britten, his two-piano transcription of the orchestral score, but was obliged to cancel this appearance owing to his nervous state and his intense phobia about the sea. Britten and Pears referred to this in the programme notes of a tribute to Poulenc given at Thorpeness on 15 June 1964:

To the average Englishman Francis Poulenc's music may have appeared that of the typical French composer: witty, daring, sentimental, naughty. In fact Francis was very easily depressed, shockable, unsure, and liable to panic. No one who saw it will ever forget his agony in a boat on Thorpeness Meare, and it was really his horror of the sea which finally stopped him from coming back to Aldeburgh in 1958 to play in *Tirésias*.
[Aldeburgh Festival Programme Book 1964]

The 1958 Aldeburgh production of *Les Mamelles de Tirésias* was directed by John Cranko and conducted by Charles Mackerras. The part of Thérèse/Tirésias was sung by Jennifer Vyvyan. Peter Pears was the husband. The piano parts were played by Viola Tunnard and Benjamin Britten.

2. Louis was at this time building a house at Bagnols-en-Fôret, Var, in the hills east of Draguignan.

3. 'Une Chanson de porcelaine' was the last of Poulenc's Eluard settings. It was composed for the 80th birthday of the singer Jane Bathori.

4. The 13th and 14th *Improvisations*, dedicated respectively to Mme Auguste Lambiotte and to Henri Hell. Poulenc was to complete the 15th and final *Improvisation* in 1959. The first ten had been written between 1932 and 1934, and the 11th and 12th in 1941.

5. *Bérénice*, play by Racine. Written in 1670, it has as its subject the struggle of Titus to part from Bérénice, whom he loves but whom he must renounce for political reasons, and the sufferings of Bérénice on learning of Titus' decision. The resolution of the play lies in their final acceptance of separation.

6. Poulenc refers to the recording made in December 1957 and January 1958, with the original cast of the 1957 Paris Opéra production of *Dialogues des Carmélites*, conducted by Pierre Dervaux.

7. *Dialogues des Carmélites* was produced in Lisbon in 1958 by Margarita Wallmann and conducted by Oliviero de Fabritiis. The Italian soprano Nicoletta Panni sang the role of Blanche. She had made her operatic début as Blanche in 1957, in Trieste.

Letter 289
1. Simone Girard arranged for this concert to take place in Avignon on 9 March 1959. It was Bernac's last concert for the Société Avignonnaise de Concerts. He took his leave of the concert platform two months later. See letter 300 and note 1.

Letter 290
1. Poulenc refers to the British première of *Les Mamelles de Tirésias* at the 1958 Aldeburgh Festival. See letters 284; 288, note 1; 348.

Letter 291
1. Poulenc alludes to the house that Louis was building in Bagnols-en-Forêt, a project he completed in August 1959 (see letter 306). There are several references to this house in Poulenc's letters from 1958 until December 1962.

2. On 25 June 1958, Poulenc was awarded an Honorary Doctorate by Oxford University.

3. Poulenc and Bernac referred affectionately to Simone Girard as 'the Countess of Avignon'.

LETTER 292

1. This letter contains Cocteau's instructions for the costume to be worn by the character 'Elle' in *La Voix humaine*.

2. The distraught woman, still in her nightdress, lies to her lover, telling him that she has just returned from a lunch date with a friend: 'I'm wearing my pink dress – and my black hat – I still have it on . . . '

LETTER 294

1. In a letter to Rose Dercourt-Plaut dated 20 April 1958, describing the sole character in *La Voix humaine*, Poulenc wrote: '*Elle est moi*, just as Flaubert said: "*Bovary, c'est moi*".'

LETTER 295

1. This letter appeared in *Les Lettres françaises*, No. 759, 5–11 February 1959. Louis Aragon was at that time editor of the review and had asked Poulenc for an article to publish in advance of the première of *La Voix humaine* on 6 February 1959.

2. Poulenc had not set a text by Cocteau since 'Toréador' (1918) and *Cocardes* (1919). After *La Voix humaine* he set one further text by Cocteau, *La Dame de Monte-Carlo* (1961). See letter 331, note 2. He also composed the incidental music for Cocteau's play *Renaud et Armide* in 1962. See letter 337, note 1, and letter 345.

LETTER 297

1. Poulenc's 60th birthday concert took place on 27 May 1959. It was also Bernac's last appearance on the concert platform. See letter 300 and note 1.

LETTER 298

1. At a talk he gave at the Club des Trois Centres in January 1962, Poulenc described the origins of the commission of the *Gloria* by the Serge Koussevitzky Music Foundation in 1959:

> First, they asked me for a symphony. I told them I was not made for symphonies. Then they asked me for a concerto – an organ concerto. I told them I had already written one and I didn't want to write another. Finally, they said: 'All right, then do what you like!' [*FP-CAS*]

Poulenc worked on the *Gloria* from May to December 1959:

> When I wrote this piece, I had in mind those frescoes by Gozzoli where the angels stick out their tongues. And also some serious Benedictine monks I had once seen revelling in a game of football. [*FP-CAS*]

In accordance with the terms of the commission, the work was dedicated to the memory of Serge and Nathalie Koussevitzky, and the manuscript was delivered to the Library of Congress for inclusion in the Serge Koussevitzky Music Collection. The work was first performed on 20 January 1961 in Boston. See letters 323, 325, 326.

LETTER 299

1. Poulenc's 60th birthday concert. See letter 300 and note 1.

2. The three sopranos mentioned here are the German Christel Goltz (*b*. 1912), the Belgian Rita Gorr (*b*. 1926) and the Italian Magda Olivero (*b*. 1912).

3. *La Vérité de Jeanne*. Oratorio by Jolivet composed in 1956. It is scored for six solo voices, narrator, chorus and orchestra. The text is based on the 1456 case for the rehabilitation of Joan of Arc. The work was first performed at the 500th anniversary of this event, in Domrémy, Joan of Arc's birthplace.

4. Georgette Rostand, wife of Claude Rostand.

LETTER 300

1. On 27 May 1959, to celebrate Poulenc's 60th birthday, a concert of his works was given at the Salle Gaveau. The artists participating were Pierre Bernac, Jean-Pierre Rampal, Pierre Pierlot, Maurice Allard, and the French Radio Choir directed by Yvonne Gouverné. The programme was as follows: Trio for piano, oboe and bassoon; *Sept Chansons*, for mixed choir *a cappella*; Sonata for flute and piano; the song cycle *Le Travail du peintre*; and *Figure humaine* for double mixed choir *a cappella*.

It was an historic event for it also marked Pierre Bernac's last concert appearance. He had taken the decision to retire from the platform when he turned 60 (he was born in the same year as Poulenc, five days after the composer). Poulenc wrote of this event:

> Yesterday evening I appeared on the platform for the last time with Bernac. He sang better than ever . . . The public accorded a TRIUMPH to this exemplary artist. My fingers trembled a little in beginning *Le Travail du peintre*. Then I gained control of myself. The end of such a fraternal association is very sad . . . [*DMS* p. 109]

On Bernac's copy of the programme for this concert (in the collection of Hervé Bonnasse) Poulenc wrote the following inscription: 'For my Pierre, in memory of the most moving and the best of *all* our concerts. *Bien tendrement, Francis.*'

LETTER 301

1. On 16 January 1920, the critic Henri Collet published an article in *Comoedia* entitled 'Un livre de Rimsky et un livre de Cocteau – les cinq Russes, les six Français et Erik Satie'. In this article, he compared Cocteau's treatise *Le Coq et l'Arlequin* with Rimsky-Korsakov's writings on music, and drew a parallel between the group of five late-nineteenth-century Russian composers (Rimsky-Korsakov, Mussorgsky, Borodin, Balakirev, and César Cui) and six

young French composers (Poulenc, Milhaud, Auric, Honegger, Tailleferre and Durey) included in a group of musicians, artists and writers known as Les Nouveaux Jeunes, who drew much of their inspiration from the music of Satie and the writings of Cocteau. The following week, on 23 January 1920, a second article appeared by Henri Collet, entitled 'Les Six français'.

In his interviews with Claude Rostand, Poulenc had this to say about the title 'Les Six':

> Everyone knows this endlessly repeated story. There were six of us who would often meet – by courtesy of Jane Bathori at the Vieux-Colombier and of Félix Delgrange at Lyre et Palette. Henri Collet, the critic for *Comoedia*, baptised us Les Six, after the Russian Five. The slogan was facile, but being young, we were greedy for publicity and accepted a label which in fact meant very little. The diversity of our music, of our tastes and distastes, precluded any common aesthetic. What could be more different than the music of Honegger and Auric? Milhaud admired Magnard, I did not; neither of us liked Florent Schmitt whom Honegger respected; Arthur, on the other hand, had a deep-seated scorn for Satie, whom Auric, Milhaud and I adored. [*ECR* pp. 44–45]

LETTER 302

1. The Ile de Ré is an island in the Atlantic off the coast of France, near La Rochelle. *Ré* is also the musical note D.

2. Poulenc was planning a tour of America in 1960 with Denise Duval.

3. Denise Duval was being coached by Georges Jouatte, a renowned tenor at the Paris Opéra and Professor of singing at the Paris Conservatoire.

LETTER 303

1. Pierre Bernac had been teaching and giving master classes in the USA.

2. Bernac did not return to the USA in the summer of the following year. See letter 314.

3. Edward Beck was a close friend of Bernac.

4. The American critic, Allen Hughes (*b.* 1921) who, in the words of Keith Daniel, 'has provided some of the most intimate, affectionate portraits of Poulenc'. (*KD-FP* p. 55). See particularly his two articles after Poulenc's death: 'Francis Poulenc', in *Musical America*, 83, No. 2 (February 1963) and 'Poulenc's Music Reflected Man', in *The New York Times*, 2 February 1963.

LETTER 305

1. Wanda Landowska died on 16 August 1959.

2. Poulenc's setting of the song 'Fancy' ('Tell me, where is fancy bred, Or in the heart or in the head?') from Shakespeare's *Merchant of Venice*, Act III Scene 2.

In a letter to Bernac dated 4 August 1959 (Bibliothèque Nationale) Poulenc writes:

Marion Harewood has asked me, so sweetly, to participate in a little
collection of choruses for children, with Ben, Kodály, etc. . . . that I
cannot refuse, but please guide me regarding accents and the exact
meaning of the text, which I get the gist of. 'Where is' must be sung on
two notes, mustn't it? Of course I will show you the thing before I send it.
Would this be possible, for example?

Poulenc dedicated his 'Fancy' to Miles and Flora, the two child characters in
Benjamin Britten's opera, *The Turn of the Screw*. The song is scored for voice and
piano, as is Benjamin Britten's setting of the same text. Kodály's version is for
solo voice, or small chorus. All three settings appeared first in *Classical Songs for
Children*, edited by Marion Harewood and Ronald Duncan (Anthony Blond,
1962) and later in *The Penguin Book of Accompanied Songs*, edited by Marion
Harewood and Ronald Duncan (Penguin Books, 1973).

LETTER 306

1. Poulenc's *Elégie* for two pianos. See letter 307 and note 1.

LETTER 307

1. Poulenc wrote his *Elégie* for two pianos for the American duo pianists,
Arthur Gold and Robert Fizdale. The work was composed during the summer of
1959, in Bagnols-en-Fôret and at Noizay. Poulenc dedicated the work to the
memory of Marie-Blanche de Polignac who died on 14 February 1958. In a letter

to Simone Girard, dated Tuesday '59, Poulenc says: 'I am composing a little elegy for two pianos in memory of M.B. for "les boys".'

The *Elégie*, published by Max Eschig in 1960, is preceded by the following note – in French, English, German and Spanish:

This Elegy should be played as if you were improvising, a cigar in your mouth and a glass of cognac on the piano. The syncopated notes (a sort of vibration of the preceding chord) should hardly be touched. On the whole you can never use too much pedal.

LETTER 308

1. The writer André Malraux (1901–76) was France's minister of cultural affairs from 1958 to 1969.

LETTER 309

1. From 1955 to 1967, Pierre Vidal organized meetings of the Club des Trois Centres in Paris (known from 1974 as the Groupe des Sept). This society invited composers and performers to introduce new recordings of their works and to discuss them with a public audience. Poulenc was first asked to speak at the Club des Trois Centres on 16 November 1959, to mark the release of *La Voix humaine* (Ricordi 30 CA 001), with Denise Duval and the Opéra-Comique Orchestra under Georges Prêtre. Poulenc returned to the Club des Trois Centres in 1960 to give a talk on Mussorgsky; in 1961 to introduce his book on Chabrier; and in 1962 to speak on works including his *Gloria* and his *Motets pour un temps de pénitence*.

2. Pierre Vidal confirms that the composer did receive the test pressings of *La Voix humaine* in time for the meeting and that he listened, intensely moved, to the recording:

We received the test pressing two hours before the meeting began so that we shared Poulenc's first impressions of that recording. Oblivious of his surroundings and totally absorbed, he followed the work bar by bar and word for word, his lips moving with every note of the score and his face expressing growing satisfaction. [*FP-PV*]

LETTER 310

1. Emmanuel Chabrier (1841–94) was the first composer to influence Poulenc's style. At the age of fifteen, Poulenc heard a recording of Chabrier's *Idylle* for piano, played by Edouard Risler (1873–1929). Describing the experience, he told Hélène Jourdan-Morhange: 'A harmonic universe suddenly opened up before me, and my music never forgot that first kiss of love.' (*MAM* p. 130). In his conversations with Stéphane Audel, Poulenc said: 'Ah! Chabrier, I love him as one loves a father! An indulgent father, always light-hearted, his pockets full of tasty titbits. Chabrier's music is an inexhaustible treasure-trove. *I simply could not do without it!*' (*FP-MMA* p. 67). This lifelong passion culminated in Poulenc's book *Emmanuel Chabrier*, published in 1961 by La Palatine, Paris.

2. In an undated letter to Bernac written from Milan (Frederick R. Koch Foundation Collection, Pierpont Morgan Library), Poulenc said of these performances:

> *La Tosca* was something so unbelievable that I did not have the strength to weep! The Tebaldi–di Stefano–Gobbi trio is unsurpassable. And the two men had such a desire to make La Renata shine that it was very moving. What a put-down for La Callas! Naturally, the crowd was delirious, but in a touching way, hands over hearts. What Tebaldi did in the middle and low register, *ppppp*, is indescribable . . . and all with such simplicity. Same atmosphere back-stage. Sumptuous décor and superb mise en scène by Wallmann. Last night, *Otello* with del Monaco more on form than ever, with incredible *pppp*'s in the upper register, and what an actor!! Gobbi fantastic.

LETTER 312

1. In February 1960, Poulenc returned to America to accompany Denise Duval in a series of concert performances, including *La Voix humaine* and scenes from *Les Mamelles de Tirésias* and *Dialogues des Carmélites*. In a letter to Bernac dated 7 February 1960 from New York (Bibliothèque Nationale), Poulenc wrote: 'It seems very strange to me to be going out on to the platform without you. I realize perfectly well that Duval is the only one who can give me back the taste for this kind of performance. She is succeeding beyond all my hopes.'

2. 'Air champêtre' is the second of Poulenc's four *Airs chantés*, written in 1927–28 on poems by Jean Moréas. 'Voyage à Paris' is the fourth song in the set *Banalités*, written in 1940 on poems by Apollinaire.

3. During his 1960 trip to the USA Poulenc recorded his Sextet with the Philadelphia Wind Ensemble – (US) Columbia ML 5613. In his letter from New York (see note 1 above), he wrote: 'The Sextet is being played EVERYWHERE. Wind instruments are the great vogue here. Fashion is a funny thing – a wind quintet can fill the Town Hall. Not to mention two pianos! "Les boys" are finally earning real money!'

With regard to *Aubade*, Poulenc made a recording in France with the Paris Conservatoire Orchestra, conducted by Georges Prêtre, issued in 1961 (Véga C 30 A 303).

LETTER 314

1. On 10 March 1960, Denise Duval gave her first recital in New York, at Town Hall, accompanied by Poulenc. In a letter written on that day to Simone Girard, Poulenc said:

> Tonight is the great night: our New York recital. We have already been 'broken in' in Chicago and Detroit, but Town Hall is not at all the same thing. [. . .] Need I say that every time I go on to the platform here, the baritone is constantly in my mind. Only someone like Denise could have made me take up this kind of work again; and, besides, it is quite

another repertoire. What gives me pleasure is that, wherever I go, everyone asks me for news of Pierre.

2. In the March 1960 performances of Ravel's *L'Heure espagnole* at the Paris Opéra, the role of the woman was sung by Jane Berbié. Also included in the programme was Ravel's *Daphnis et Chloé*, with choreography by Georges Skibine and décor by Marc Chagall. The conductor was Manuel Rosenthal.

3. See letter 291, note 3.

LETTER 315

1. Britten's opera *A Midsummer Night's Dream* was first performed on 11 June 1960, at the fifteenth Aldeburgh Festival.

2. Poulenc did not in fact go to Aldeburgh that year. In a letter to Britten dated Thursday (Britten–Pears Foundation, Aldeburgh) Poulenc says:

> I am heartbroken at missing the première of *Midsummer* but fate has willed that I be deprived of this joy by *obliging* me to be in Brussels on that very evening for the Belgian première of *La Voix humaine* [. . .] I embrace both you and Peter, and wish you luck the French way – *merde, merde, merde.*

> Francis

LETTER 316

1. Poulenc was orchestrating his *Gloria*.

2. *La Courte Paille* for voice and piano, settings of seven short poems by the Belgian poet Maurice Carême. Poulenc wrote the work for Denise Duval to sing to her young son. He dedicated it to Duval and to her first husband, Richard Schilling. It was completed in July–August 1960 and was Poulenc's last song cycle. See also letter 318.

3. In a letter (Bibliothèque Nationale) to Pierre Bernac dated 7 February 1960 from New York Poulenc wrote:

> The New York Philharmonic wants to commission . . . a choral work! I have more or less decided to write an *Office du Vendredi saint* for children's choir (rather than female voices), male choir and orchestra, with *perhaps* a baritone solo. Bernstein and his Committee think the idea is sublime. I only hope the music *comes* to me.

This was to be Poulenc's final choral work, *Sept Répons des Ténèbres*, settings of seven Latin meditative texts for the three holy days preceding Easter. It was eventually scored for boy soprano, mixed male choir (children's and men's voices), and full orchestra. It was commissioned by the New York Philharmonic, whose music director was Leonard Bernstein, for the opening concert of the Lincoln Center on 23 September 1962. Poulenc, however, did not complete the work in time for this concert. It was first performed on 11 April 1963 (after Poulenc's death) at the Avery Fisher Hall, by the New York Philharmonic under Thomas Schippers. The first performance in Europe took place on 10 December 1963, at the Théâtre des Champs-Elysées in Paris. Georges Prêtre conducted the French Radio National Orchestra, with the Philip Debat boys' choir and Dominique Doublier as soloist.

4. 'Bec' is the eleventh-century Benedictine monastery, Bec-Hellouin, in Normandy.

LETTER 318
    1. See letter 291, note 3.

LETTER 319
    1. *Vol de nuit*, opera by the Italian composer Luigi Dallapiccola (1904–75).
    2. On 9 September 1960, Denise Duval sang *La Voix humaine* at the Palais Farnese, the French Embassy in Rome.
    3. Henri Hell wrote the sleeve notes for the recordings made in 1958 and 1960 of songs by Poulenc, performed by Bernac and Poulenc (Véga C 35 A 33/34; C 30 A 293).

LETTER 320
    1. Always intensely aware of the visual arts, Poulenc felt that his religious music could be related in pictorial terms to the paintings of the Italian Andrea Mantegna (1431–1506) and the Spaniard Francisco de Zurbarán (1598–1664):
    Mantegna and Zurbarán correspond very closely to my religious ideal –
    the one with his mystical realism; the other with his ascetic purity that
    still permits him at times, without a qualm, to dress his women saints as
    ladies of fashion. [*FP–MMA* p. 74]
    2. 'Green' (poem by Paul Verlaine) and 'Soir' (poem by Albert Samain) are both set to music by Fauré. 'Green' is also set by Debussy.
    3. *Chansons Madécasses* and *Trois poèmes de Stéphane Mallarmé* are by Ravel.
    4. Denise Duval sang *La Voix humaine* at the Edinburgh Festival in 1960.

LETTER 321
    1. Bernac's companion on this trip was Simone Girard, with whom he spent most of his summers. There is a touching tribute to Simone Girard from the English singer, teacher and translator, Winifred Radford (*b.* 1901), Bernac's friend of more than 30 years. Speaking on Bernac at the British Institute of Recorded Sound on 9 May 1978, Winifred Radford said:
    Simone Girard became one of Bernac's closest friends, eventually to be
    someone of very great importance in his life. For many years they spent
    their summers together, travelling to various countries. She also joined
    him sometimes in the USA during his tours, and shared his visits to some
    great friends in California. Bernac's friends owe a debt of profound
    gratitude to Simone Girard for her faithful solicitude and care of him
    during the last few years when he has suffered some serious illnesses.
    [*BIRS*, 70–71, p. 775]

LETTER 322
    1. Sinfonia Concerto for Cello and Orchestra op 125 (1950–52) by Prokofiev

and Cello Concerto No. 1 (1959) by Shostakovitch, both dedicated to Rostropovitch.

2. Rostropovitch's friendship inspired Britten to write a Sonata for cello in 1961, the Cello Symphony in 1963 and three unaccompanied suites for cello (1964, 1967 and 1971).

3. Poulenc does not appear to have written for Rostropovitch. His only published work for cello is the Sonata of 1948, composed for Pierre Fournier. To Claude Rostand, he confessed that he was never at ease writing for strings, preferring wind instruments, which he found closer to the human voice: 'Nothing is further from the human breath than the stroke of a bow.' (*ECR* p. 126)

LETTER 323

1. Poulenc was in Boston for the first performance of his *Gloria* on 20 January 1961, with Adele Addison as soloist and the Boston Symphony Orchestra under Charles Munch.

2. In a letter dated 5 September 1960 to Leonard Burkat (*b.* 1919) who was at that time artistic administrator of the Boston Symphony Orchestra, Poulenc wrote:

> Without hesitation, I suggest my Concerto for two pianos for this concert. In the first place, because it is very well known in America. In the second place, because it provides a good contrast to the *Gloria*. I would like to play it with a young American pianist, someone with a touch like Turini or Frager. [Leonard Burkat Collection, Yale University]

In the event, it was the French pianist Evelyne Crochet (*b.* 1934) who played the second piano part. A student of Yvonne Lefebure, Edwin Fischer and Rudolf Serkin, she had won the Tchaikovsky Competition in 1958. In referring to her as 'an excellent *Monique*' it is thought that Poulenc was likening her either to Monique de la Bruchollerie, or to Monique Haas.

3. Poulenc was very taken with the performance of the American soprano Adele Addison (*b.* 1925) in the *Gloria*. He said he found her voice heavenly: 'C'est le *Gloria* chez les anges!' (*FP-CAS*. See also letter 325.)

LETTER 324

1. See letter 323, note 2.

2. Bernac refers to a show by the Grand Ballet du Marquis de Cuevas, a company formed and funded by Georges de Piedrablanca de Guana, Marquis de Cuevas (1885–1961). First known as the Grand Ballet de Monté-Carlo (1946), it became the Grand Ballet du Marquis de Cuevas in 1950. The company disbanded in 1962, after the death of the Marquis.

LETTER 326

1. Daniel Lesur (*b.* 1908). French composer, organist, and teacher of counterpoint, founder-member with Messiaen, Jolivet and Baudrier of the group La Jeune France (1936). At the time of this letter, he was director of the Schola

Cantorum, a post he filled from 1957–64. He also enjoyed a long association with French Radio.

2. In his talk at the Club des Trois Centres on 10 January 1962, Poulenc said of Rosanna Carteri: 'I wrote the part for soprano solo in the *Gloria* thinking of Mme Carteri – the Italian soprano who sang Blanche so incomparably in the Naples and Catania productions of *Les Carmélites*.' (*FP-CAS*)

Rosanna Carteri sang in the first European performance of the *Gloria*, which took place on 14 February 1961 in Paris, with the French Radio Choir directed by Yvonne Gouverné and the French Radio National Orchestra conducted by Georges Prêtre. The following day, the work was recorded under Poulenc's personal supervision – (French) Columbia FCX 882. Whereas Poulenc felt that the Paris première left much to be desired, he rated the recording very highly (see letter 328).

LETTER 327

1. Jean Barraqué (1928–1973). French composer of large-scale works using serial methods. A pupil of Messiaen.

Henri Pousseur (*b*. 1929). Belgian composer and theorist, associated with Boulez, Stockhausen and Berio, co-founder of the *Studio de musique électronique* in Brussels.

2. Henri Hell's great friend, Richard Negrou.

3. Poulenc's *Aubade* and his Sinfonietta were recorded by the Paris Conservatoire Orchestra conducted by Georges Prêtre (Véga C 30 A 303, 1961).

4. The Swiss musicologist, Pierre Meylan, editor of *La Revue musicale de Suisse romande*.

5. Henri Hell wrote the sleeve-notes for the recording of Poulenc's Concerto for organ with Maurice Duruflé and the French Radio National Orchestra under Georges Prêtre, recorded in the church of St Etienne du Mont in February 1961 – (French) Columbia FCX 882.

6. *Pli selon pli* by Pierre Boulez, for soprano and large orchestra, in five movements, subtitled *Portrait de Mallarmé* and first performed in 1960.

7. Benjamin Godard (1849–95). French composer known for his vast output, compositional facility and lack of self-criticism.

LETTER 328

1. Poulenc was to address a meeting of the Club des Trois Centres on the occasion of the publication by Plon of his book *Emmanuel Chabrier*.

2. The recording of the *Gloria* (see letter 326, note 2) was coupled with the Concerto for organ (see letter 327, note 5).

3. Poulenc thanks Pierre Vidal for a critique of the concert that appeared in *Journal musical français*.

LETTER 330

1. *Plus loin que la nuit et le jour*, Sauguet's cantata for tenor and unaccompanied choir, on a poem by Louis Emié (*b*. 1900).

2. The violinist Hélène Jourdan-Morhange (1892–1961). Speaking about her in his interviews with Claude Rostand, Poulenc said:

May I here salute Hélène Jourdan-Morhange, whose value as a critic is well known to everyone, but who was also, in the old days, the only truly adventurous violinist. It was to her that Ravel and Schmitt dedicated their sonatas. It was she who, with Maurice Maréchal, gave the first performance of Ravel's Sonata for violin and cello. And it was she who, with her women's quartet, gave the first performance of my *Rapsodie nègre* in 1917. With the late Meerovitch, with Bathori, Marcelle Meyer, Andrée Vaurabourg, Suzanne Peignot, Félix Delgrange and Pierre Bertin, she was the confident and courageous interpreter of the Groupe des Six at its very beginnings. [*ECR* p. 205]

Hélène Jourdan-Morhange is the author of *Ravel et nous* (1945); *Mes amis musiciens* (1955) and, with Vlado Perlemuter, *Ravel d'après Ravel* (1957).

LETTER 331

1. See letter 320, note 1.

2. Poulenc composed *La Dame de Monte-Carlo*, a 'monologue lyrique' for soprano and orchestra, in April 1961, in Monte Carlo. Cocteau had written the text some twenty years earlier for the cabaret singer and actress Marianne Oswald (1903–85). It tells of an ageing floozy, poor and alone, who tries her luck at the gaming tables of Monte Carlo and ends up by throwing herself into the sea. Poulenc was entranced by the text which he said brought back to him the years 1923–25, when he lived, 'in the imperial shadow of Diaghilev', in Monte Carlo, 'the Venice of my twenties!' (*DMS* p. 110). Poulenc wrote this work for Denise Duval and dedicated it to her. She performed it in November 1961 in Monte Carlo, and in December 1961 at the Théâtre des Champs-Elysées in Paris, with the French Radio National Orchestra conducted by Georges Prêtre.

3. The critic Claude Samuel.

LETTER 333

1. Poulenc reported the completion of *Sept Répons des Ténèbres* in a letter to Gold and Fizdale, postmarked 1 November 1961 (see letter 334). In February 1962, he wrote to Henri Hell that he had orchestrated five of the seven 'Répons' (see letter 336). On 26 March 1962, he again reported that the work was finished, in a letter to Bernac (see letter 337). According to the score, however, the composition was not completed until October 1962 and Poulenc corrected the proofs for the publisher in January 1963 (see letter 336, note 2).

LETTER 334

1. The recording by Gold and Fizdale of Poulenc's Concerto for two pianos, with the New York Philharmonic conducted by Leonard Bernstein, (US) Columbia ML 5792, was issued in 1962.

2. *L'Embarquement pour Cythère* was written in July 1951 at the request of Gold and Fizdale who had asked for a 'brilliant piece' to play at the end of a concert they were due to give at Town Hall, New York, in 1952. Poulenc produced the valse-musette, *L'Embarquement pour Cythère*, which he took from his two-piano incidental music for the film *Le Voyage en Amérique* (see letter 217, note 2). Inspired by the open-air cafés with dancing on the banks of the Marne near his grandparents' house at Nogent, the piece was considered by Poulenc to be his most 'Dufy-like' work. Poulenc felt a great affinity for the paintings of Raoul Dufy (1877–1953), whose celebrated picture *Boatmen on the banks of the Marne* was for Poulenc the visual counterpart of his Nogent music. (*DMS* p. 109). In a letter to Gold and Fizdale dated Paris, August 1951, Poulenc said of *L'Embarquement pour Cythère*: 'I don't think you should include it in your programme, but rather keep it as a *bombe-surprise* for an encore at your Town Hall recital. I have no doubt that you will play this waltz with a great deal of elegance.'

3. Regarding the 'unforgettable hostess' of Central Park West, Robert Fizdale writes (in a letter to the translator, 12 April 1988):

> We had taken Poulenc and Bernac to a performance by The Little Players, a puppet theatre on Central Park West, the creation of Frank Peschka and Bill Murdock. . . . Mr Peschka manipulated the puppets and acted and sang their parts, while Mr Murdock took care of the stage machinery. In the program we took Poulenc to, he saw and heard Peschka (as Mlle Garance, an ageing Viennese diva) sing Poulenc's song 'Hôtel' to perfection. He was overwhelmed by the performance and spoke of it often.

LETTER 336

1. Henri Hell was at the time music critic for the weekly journal *Candide*.

2. *Sept Répons des Ténèbres* was in fact Poulenc's last choral work. In his preface to the book *Moi et mes amis*, Stéphane Audel recalls being with the composer at Noizay while he was correcting the proofs of this work in early January 1963. When the proofs were ready to be sent to the publisher, Poulenc asked Audel to take them to the post for him, saying, as he handed him the parcel: 'This will be my last religious work' (*FP-MMA* p. 16).

LETTER 337

1. *Renaud et Armide*. Verse-play by Cocteau for which Poulenc wrote the incidental music, performed at the Festival of Baalbek in August 1962. Poulenc was never happy with the music – see letter 345.

2. Poulenc fathered a daughter, Marie-Ange, born on 13 September 1946. Her mother, a cousin of Suzette Chanlaire (wife of Richard Chanlaire's brother, René) had known Poulenc since 1925, when she was eighteen. She is the dedicatee, Freddy, of 'Une ruine, coquille vide' from *Tel jour telle nuit* (1936–37) and of 'Dans l'herbe' from *Fiançailles pour rire* (1939).

LETTER 339

1. This postcard was the last written communication that Yvonne Gouverné

received from Poulenc. In an address she gave at Rocamadour on 8 July 1973 to mark the tenth anniversary of Poulenc's death, Yvonne Gouverné related in detail the events to which Poulenc alludes in the card:

I shall always remember Francis Poulenc getting off the train at Uzerche, where Pierre Bernac and I had gone to meet him, in that famous month of August 1936. 'Ferroud has just been killed in a horrific car accident somewhere near Salzburg,' he said as soon as he saw us.*

We had spent the previous two summers in Salzburg where we came into daily contact with Pierre-Octave Ferroud – an extremely intelligent musician whose intense musical activities we had often shared. He had founded a chamber music society, Le Triton, for which we gave frequent first performances. Poulenc was deeply affected by his death.

The region of Uzerche where we were staying stirred in Francis a sense of his close affinity with Aveyron, birthplace of his father. It was a region conducive to spiritual revelations. Poulenc wanted to go to Rocamadour, an ancient place of pilgrimage which, thirty years ago, did not attract the crowds one finds there today. We all three entered a silent chapel in which stood the statue of the Black Virgin. Outwardly, nothing happened, yet from that moment everything in the spiritual life of Poulenc changed. He bought a little picture with the text of the Litanies to the Black Virgin, and as soon as we were back in Uzerche he began to write that very pure work for female choir and organ, *Les Litanies à la Vierge Noire*. [*FP-ROC* pp.16 and 21]

When he had completed the work, Poulenc sent the draft to Yvonne Gouverné in one of his letters of 1937, with the following postscript: 'I have put aside for you this draft of *Les Litanies* – do with it what you will . . .'. (*Correspondance* p. 265)

2. No commercial recording of *Figure humaine* was made during Poulenc's lifetime.

LETTER 340

1. The Sonata for oboe and piano was Poulenc's final work. It was dedicated to the memory of Serge Prokofiev and given its first performance, after Poulenc's death, by Pierre Pierlot and Jacques Février on 8 June 1963 at the Festival of Strasbourg.

2. Poulenc refers to Denise Duval who, in 1962, sang at Glyndebourne, in the first French opera to be produced there, Debussy's *Pelléas et Mélisande*.

3. The Dutch baritone, Bernard Kruysen, who had studied with Bernac.

4. Richard Chanlaire was 'playing the indulgent uncle' to Marie-Ange. See letter 337, note 2.

LETTER 342

1. In the summer of 1962, Norman Singer, director of the Aspen Music Festival

*See letter 130, note 1.

in Colorado, organized a Festival of French Music to celebrate Milhaud's 70th birthday. Milhaud was guest of honour, and Messiaen and Sauguet were invited, representing 'the two opposite poles of French music'. (*MVH* p. 272). Messiaen's wife, Yvonne Loriod, also took an active part in the Festival. See letter 346 and note 1.

2. *La Contrebasse*. Sauguet's comic opera in two acts, with libretto by Henri Troyat after a story by Tchekov, first performed in Paris in 1930, at the Théâtre de la Madeleine.

La Voyante. Cantata for female voice and eleven instruments, with music and words by Sauguet, first performed in 1932 in Hyères.

LETTER 343

1. This letter was sent by Boosey & Hawkes to Stravinsky at the Fonda Hotel, Santa Fe, New Mexico.

2. Stravinsky's choral work, *A Sermon, a Narrative and a Prayer*, was written in 1961.

LETTER 344

1. Poulenc was working on his two wind sonatas, for clarinet and for oboe.

2. Manuel de Falla's unfinished 'cantata scenica', *La Atlántida*, was found among his papers after his death in 1946. The work was completed by his pupil, the Spanish composer Ernesto Halffter (*b.* 1905). The first concert performance of this version was given in Barcelona on 24 November 1961 and the first stage performance took place at La Scala, Milan, on 16 April 1962. The score was published in the same year by Ricordi.

In a letter to Simone Girard, dated 22 June 1962, Poulenc says of this work:

Alas, *Atlántida* is not what Gavoty says it is. Why does that lot always want the final work of a composer to be a 'crowning point' (example: the anaemic quartet of Fauré). You know what a Falla-ist I am and how well I know his music. I can tell when there is a mere ⅓ of it drowned in a clever Halffter sauce. And besides, the whole thing smacks far too often of Honegger!

LETTER 345

1. Poulenc was due to attend the first performance of his *Sept Répons des Ténèbres* in New York, on 11 April 1963. See letter 316, note 3.

2. See letter 337, note 1.

3. Jacques Dupont was preparing the models of the sets and costumes for Verdi's *Don Carlos* at the Paris Opéra.

LETTER 346

1. *Réveil des oiseaux* for piano and orchestra (1953) and *Oiseaux exotiques* for piano, wind and percussion (1953–56) were among the first compositions in which Messiaen made use of his great interest in birdsong. At the 1962 Aspen Festival, the solo piano part in both compositions was played by Yvonne Loriod

(*b*. 1924), the composer's wife and a former student of his. Since 1943 she had been the first interpreter of all his works with piano.

LETTER 347

1. See letter 343.

2. The works referred to are Stravinsky's *Movements* for piano and orchestra (1959), his choral work *A Sermon, a Narrative and a Prayer* (1961), and *The Flood* – 'a musical play' – (1962).

LETTER 349

1. The concert on 10 April 1963 to which Poulenc refers was part of the series: 'Composer's Showcase' at Carnegie Hall, directed by Charles Schwartz. After Poulenc's sudden death on 30 January 1963, the concert was given in his memory, with the participation of: Benny Goodman and Leonard Bernstein (who gave the world première of Poulenc's Sonata for clarinet and piano, written for Benny Goodman and dedicated to the memory of Honegger); Arthur Gold and Robert Fizdale; Jenny Tourel; Simon Sargon; Abraham Kaplan and the Collegiate Chorale.

2. Poulenc probably means the American bass, Donald Gramm (1927–83).

LETTER 350

1. Debussy's stepdaughter, 'Dolly' Bardac (Mme Gaston de Tinan), was the daughter of Debussy's second wife, Emma, and her first husband Sigismond Bardac. Fauré's suite for piano duet, *Dolly*, was inspired by and dedicated to her. Poulenc was apparently very fond of her and often consulted her when he performed works by Debussy.

2. Bobsy Goodspeed was born Elizabeth Barret Fuller (1893–1980). Married to Barney Goodspeed from 1916 until his death in 1947, she lived in Chicago. A renowned art collector, she was President of the Arts Club of Chicago from 1931. She was also a frequent hostess to visiting ballet companies and to other representatives of the performing arts. Her film documents of distinguished figures in the arts, taken during her many trips to Paris in the 1930s, are housed in the Film Library of the Museum of Modern Art, New York. In 1950 she married Gilbert Chapman, Chairman of the Yale and Towne Lock Company, and moved to New York.

Chronology

Dates refer to the completion of composition unless otherwise stated. Names in brackets following vocal works refer to the author of the text.

1899   Francis Poulenc born 7 January, Paris. Father, Emile Poulenc (b. 1855, Aveyron) a director of the pharmaceutical firm, Poulenc Frères – later Rhône-Poulenc; mother, Jenny Royer (b. 1865, Paris) amateur pianist.

1904   Begins piano lessons with mother.

1907   Begins formal piano lessons. Is fascinated by Debussy's *Danses sacrées et profanes*.

1909   Can recite the whole of Mallarmé's *Apparition* by heart.

1910   Discovers, and is deeply affected by, Schubert's *Die Winterreise*.

1914   Meets Ricardo Viñes; studies the piano with him until 1917. Experiences the 'shock' of Stravinsky's *Sacre du printemps*.

1915   Meets Darius Milhaud.
        7 June: death of Poulenc's mother.

1916   Through Viñes, meets Auric and Satie. Composes first work, *Préludes* for piano (unpublished, later destroyed).

1917   Spring: composes *Rapsodie nègre* ('Makoko Kangourou', baritone voice and seven instruments).
        18 May: Satie's *Parade*.
        24 June: Apollinaire's *Les Mamelles de Tirésias*.
        15 July: death of Poulenc's father. With Raymonde Linossier, frequents bookshop of Adrienne Monnier, where he hears Apollinaire reading own poetry and meets the Surrealist poets Aragon, Breton, Eluard. Also meets Cocteau, Radiguet, Max Jacob, Jane Bathori, Honegger, Durey, Tailleferre.
        11 December: *Rapsodie nègre* performed at Théâtre du Vieux-Colombier. Provokes interest, particularly from Stravinsky and Diaghilev.

1918   January: drafted into army.
        Through Viñes, meets Manuel de Falla.
        Trois pastorales (piano). 'Toréador' (Cocteau, voice and piano). Sonata for two clarinets. Sonata (piano 4 hands). *Mouvements perpétuels* (piano).

1919   Milhaud returns from Brazil.
        Le Bestiaire (Apollinaire, voice and seven instruments or piano). *Cocardes* (Cocteau, voice and five instruments or piano). *Valse* (piano).

1920   January: Poulenc, Auric, Milhaud, Honegger, Durey, Tailleferre grouped together as 'Les Six' in article by critic Henri Collet.
        Suite in C (piano). Impromptus (piano).

1921   Visits Italy with Milhaud in March. Meets Casella, Malipiero, Labroca Rieti. Studies composition with Charles Koechlin until 1924.
        Le Gendarme incompris (Cocteau–Radiguet, comédie-bouffe). 'La Baigneuse

de Trouville' and 'Le Discours du général' from *Les Mariés de la Tour Eiffel* (collective work). *Promenades* (piano). *Esquisse d'un fanfare* (overture for Act V of Cocteau's *Roméo et Juliette*).

1922   Meets Bartók, Sauguet.
Visits Vienna and Salzburg with Milhaud and Marya Freund. Meets Schoenberg, Berg, Webern.
Chanson à boire (male choir *a cappella*). Sonata for clarinet and bassoon; Sonata for horn, trumpet and trombone.

1923   Meets Wanda Landowska.
Death of Raymond Radiguet.
Completes *Les Biches* (ballet). Recitatives for Gounod's opera *La Colombe*.

1924   6 January: première of *Les Biches* in Monte Carlo by Russian Ballet.

1925   Death of Satie.
5 Poèmes de Ronsard (voice and piano). *Napoli* (piano).

1926   *Chansons gaillardes* (anonymous, C17, voice and piano). Trio (piano, oboe and bassoon).

1927   *Pastourelle* (piano, from *L'Eventail de Jeanne*, collective work). *Vocalise* (voice and piano). *Airs chantés* (Jean Moréas, voice and piano).

1928   Buys house Le Grand Coteau at Noizay, in Touraine.
2 Novelettes (piano). *3 Pièces* (piano). *Concert champêtre* (harpsichord and orchestra).

1929   *Pièce brève sur le nom d'Albert Roussel* (piano). Begins eight *Nocturnes* (piano), completed 1938. *Aubade* (choreographic concerto for piano and 18 instruments).

1930   Death of Raymonde Linossier.
Epitaphe (Malherbe, voice and piano).

1931   *3 Poèmes de Louise Lalanne* (Apollinaire and Marie Laurencin, voice and piano). *4 Poèmes de Guillaume Apollinaire* (voice and piano). *5 Poèmes de Max Jacob* (voice and piano).

1932   *Le Bal masqué* (Max Jacob, cantata for baritone and chamber orchestra). Concerto in D minor (for 2 pianos). *Valse-Improvisation sur le nom de Bach* (piano). *Improvisations* (Nos. 1–6) (piano).

1933   *Feuillets d'album* (piano). *Villageoises* (piano). *Improvisation* (No. 7) (piano). *Intermezzo* (incidental music for play by Giraudoux).

1934   *8 Chansons polonaises* (voice and piano). *Presto* (piano). *2 Intermezzi* (piano). *Humoresque* (piano). *Badinage* (piano). *4 Chansons pour enfants* (Jaboune [Jean Nohain], voice and piano). *Villanelle* (pipe and piano). *Improvisations* (Nos. 8, 9, 10) (piano).

1935   3 April: first recital in Paris of Bernac–Poulenc duo. First settings of poems by Paul Eluard.
11 May: death of Tante Liénard.
5 Poèmes de Paul Eluard (voice and piano). *La Belle au bois dormant* (film score). *La Reine Margot* (incidental music, with Auric, for play by Edouard Bourdet). 'A sa guitare' (Ronsard, voice and piano, from *La Reine Margot*). *Suite française* (after Claude Gervaise; chamber orchestra or piano).

1936   August: death of composer Pierre-Octave Ferroud. First visit to Rocamadour.
Sept chansons (Apollinaire, Eluard, mixed choir *a cappella*). *Litanies à la Vierge Noire* (female or children's choir and organ). *Petites voix* (Madeleine Ley, choir *a cappella*). *Les Soirées de Nazelles* (piano).

1937   *Tel jour telle nuit* (Eluard, voice and piano). *Bourrée, Au Pavillon* d'Auvergne (piano). *2 Marches et un intermède* (chamber orchestra). Mass in G (mixed choir *a cappella*). *Sécheresses* (Edward James, mixed choir and orchestra). *3 Poèmes de Louise de Vilmorin* (voice and piano).

1938   'Le Portrait' (Colette, voice and piano). Concerto in G minor (organ, string orchestra and timpani). *2 Poèmes de Guillaume Apollinaire*. 'Priez pour paix' (Charles d'Orléans, voice and piano). 'La Grenouillère' (Apollinaire, voice and piano). *Miroirs brûlants* (Eluard, voice and piano).

1939   *4 Motets pour un temps de pénitence* (mixed choir *a cappella*). 'Ce doux petit visage' (Eluard, voice and piano). *Fiançailles pour rire* (Vilmorin, voice and piano). 'Bleuet' (Apollinaire, voice and piano). Sextet (piano, flute, oboe, clarinet, bassoon and horn). *Deux préludes posthumes et une gnossienne* (orchestration of piano pieces by Satie).

1940   Spring: drafted into anti-aircraft division, Cahors. Summer: demobilised in Brive-la-Gaillarde.
        Mélancolie (piano). *Banalités* (Apollinaire, voice and piano). *Léocadia* (incidental music for play by Anouilh). 'Les Chemins de l'amour' (from *Léocadia*, voice and piano). *Colloque* (soprano and baritone voices and piano). *Les Biches* (orchestral suite).

1941   *Exultate Deo* (mixed choir *a cappella*). *Salve Regina* (mixed choir *a cappella*). *Les Animaux modèles* (ballet). *La Fille du jardinier* (incidental music for play by Exbrayat). *Improvisations* (Nos. 11 and 12) (piano).

1942   8 August, première of *Les Animaux modèles* at Paris Opéra.
        La Duchesse de Langeais (film score). *Chansons villageoises* (Maurice Fombeure, voice and piano or orchestra). *Les Animaux modèles* (orchestral suite).

1943   Death of Ricardo Viñes.
        Intermezzo in A♭ (piano). Sonata for violin and piano. *Figure humaine* (Eluard, double mixed choir *a cappella*). *Métamorphoses* (Vilmorin, voice and piano). *2 Poèmes de Louis Aragon* (voice and piano).

1944   Deportation and death of Max Jacob.
        Le Voyageur sans bagages (incidental music for play and film score by Anouilh). *La Nuit de Saint-Jean* (incidental music for play by James Barrie). *Les Mamelles de Tirésias* (Apollinaire, opéra-bouffe). *Un Soir de neige* (Eluard, chamber cantata for six mixed voices or chorus *a cappella*).

1945   January: first performance of *Figure humaine*, BBC broadcast, London, BBC choir directed by Leslie Woodgate.
        November: death of Oncle Papoum. Death of Bartók, Desnos.
        'Montparnasse' (Apollinaire, voice and piano). 'Hyde Park' (Apollinaire, voice and piano). *Le Soldat et la sorcière* (incidental music for play by Salacrou). *L'Histoire de Babar, le petit éléphant* (Jean de Brunhoff, piano and narrator).

1946   13 September: birth of daughter, Marie-Ange.
        Death of Manuel de Falla.
        Chansons françaises (traditional song texts, mixed choir *a cappella*). *2 Mélodies* (Apollinaire, voice and piano). 'Paul et Virginie' (Radiguet, voice and piano).

1947   3 June: première of *Les Mamelles de Tirésias* at Opéra-Comique, with Denise Duval.
        'Le Disparu' (Desnos, voice and piano). 'Main dominée par le coeur' (Eluard, voice and piano). *3 Chansons de F. Garcia Lorca* (voice and piano).

'. . . mais mourir' (Eluard, voice and piano). *L'Invitation au château* (incidental music for play by Anouilh). *Amphytrion* (incidental music for play by Molière). Sinfonietta (orchestra).

1948 November–December, first tour of USA with Bernac.
Calligrammes (Apollinaire, voice and piano). *4 Petites prières de Saint François d'Assise* (male choir *a cappella*). Sonata for cello and piano.

1949 'Hymne' (Racine, voice and piano). 'Mazurka' (Vilmorin, voice and piano, from *Mouvements du Coeur*, collective homage to Chopin). Concerto for piano and orchestra.

1950 January–March, second tour of USA with Bernac.
Death of Charles Koechlin.
La Fraîcheur et le feu (Eluard, voice and piano). *Stabat Mater* (soprano, mixed choir and orchestra).

1951 *Le Voyage en Amérique* (film score). *L'Embarquement pour Cythère* (2 pianos, valse-musette taken from *Le Voyage en Amérique*). *Thème varié* (piano).

1952 January–March, third tour of USA with Bernac.
Death of Paul Eluard.
4 Motets pour le temps de Noël (mixed choir *a cappella*). *Matelote provençale* (orchestra, part of collective work *La Guirlande de Campra*). *Ave verum corpus* (female choir *a cappella*).

1953 Begins composition of opera *Dialogues des Carmélites*. Sonata for two pianos.

1954 *Bucolique* (orchestra, part of collective work *Variations sur le nom de Marguerite Long*). *Parisiana* (Max Jacob, voice and piano). 'Rosemonde' (Apollinaire, voice and piano).

1955 Death of Honegger, Adrienne Monnier.
21 October: death of Lucien Roubert.
Completes vocal score of *Dialogues des Carmélites*.

1956 Completes *Dialogues des Carmélites*. *Le Travail du peintre* (Eluard, voice and piano). *2 Mélodies 1956* (Apollinaire and Laurence de Beylié, voice and piano). 'Dernier poème' (Desnos, voice and piano).

1957 26 January: world première of *Dialogues des Carmélites*, in Italian, at La Scala, Milan.
21 June: first performance of original version, in French, at Paris Opéra.
Sonata for flute and piano. *Elégie* (horn and piano).

1958 February–June: composes *La Voix humaine* (Cocteau, tragédie-lyrique). 'Une Chanson de porcelaine' (Eluard, voice and piano). *Improvisations* (Nos. 13 and 14) (piano).

1959 6 February: première of *La Voix humaine* with Denise Duval (staged by Cocteau) at the Opéra-Comique.
27 May: 60th birthday concert at Salle Gaveau and final concert appearance of Bernac–Poulenc duo. Bernac retires from concert platform.
Improvisation (No. 15) (piano). *Laudes de Saint Antoine de Padoue* (male choir *a cappella*). *Novelette* (piano, based on theme by Falla from *El Amor brujo*). *Elégie* for 2 pianos. *Gloria* (soprano, mixed choir and orchestra). 'Fancy' (Shakespeare, from *The Merchant of Venice*, Act III scene 2; voice and piano).

1960 Tours USA with Denise Duval.
Begins to compose *Sept Répons des Ténèbres* (child soprano, mixed male

choir, and orchestra). *La Courte paille* (Maurice Carême, voice and piano).
Sarabande (guitar).

1961   Last visit to USA, for première of *Gloria* in Boston, 20 January.
La Dame de Monte-Carlo (Cocteau, monologue for soprano and orchestra).

1962   Completes *Sept Répons des Ténèbres*. *Renaud et Armide* (incidental music for play by Cocteau). Sonata for clarinet and piano. Sonata for oboe and piano.

1963   30 January: dies of a heart attack in his Paris apartment, leaving no unfinished composition.

Sources of Letters

TO FRANCIS POULENC:

Letters to Francis Poulenc, except those from Pierre Bernac, are in the collection of
Rosine Seringe.
Letters to Francis Poulenc from Pierre Bernac are copies held by Myriam Chimènes.

FROM FRANCIS POULENC TO:

Aragon, Louis. *Les Lettres françaises*, No. 759, 5–11 February 1959.
Audel, Stéphane. *Correspondance*.
Bakst, Léon. Bibliothèque de l'Opéra, Paris.
Beaumont, Comtesse Etienne de. *Correspondance*.
Bernac, Pierre. The following letters are in the Frederick R. Koch Foundation
Collection, on deposit in The Pierpont Morgan Library, New York: 152, 185, 189,
193, 229, 231, 233, 235, 237, 242, 250, 251, 252, 267, 275, 283, 287, 288, 291, 306, 312,
316, 319, 320, 325, 326, 337, 340, 344.
The following letters are in the Manuscript Department of the Bibliothèque
Nationale, Paris: 161, 164, 165, 166, 169, 180, 182, 183, 200, 213, 265, 304, 318, 323.
Bosredon, Marthe. *Correspondance*.
Britten, Benjamin. The Britten–Pears Library, Aldeburgh, Suffolk.
Casa Fuerte, Yvonne de. Collection of Flavie Alvarez de Toledo.
Cocteau, Jean. Harry Ransom Humanities Research Center, University of Texas at
Austin.
Collaer, Paul. *Correspondance*.
Conrad, Doda. Collection of Doda Conrad.
Dercourt-Plaut, Rose. Fred and Rose Plaut Archives, Yale University Music Library,
New Haven.
Diaghilev, Serge de. Letter 17: Frederick R. Koch Foundation Collection, on deposit
in The Pierpont Morgan Library, New York. Letters 48, 59, 97: Bibliothèque de
l'Opéra, Paris.
Duval, Denise. *Correspondance*.
Eluard, Paul. Harry Ransom Humanities Research Center, University of Texas at
Austin.
Esty, Alice. Collection of Alice Esty.
Falla, Manuel de. Fundacion 'Archivo Manuel de Falla', Madrid.
Girard, Simone. Collection of Hervé Bonnasse.
Gold and Fizdale. Collection of Robert Fizdale.
Gouverné, Yvonne. *Correspondance*.
Grey, Madeleine. Music Department of the Bibliothèque Nationale, Paris.
Hell, Henri. Collection of Henri Hell.

Hugo, Valentine. *Correspondance*.

Koechlin, Charles. Collection of Madeleine Li-Koechlin.

Leguerney, Jacques. *Correspondance*.

Lehmann, Maurice. Bibliothèque de l'Opéra, Paris.

Manceaux, Brigitte. *Correspondance*.

Milhaud, Darius. *Correspondance*.

Monnier, Adrienne. Bibliothèque Littéraire Jacques Doucet, Paris.

Munch, Charles. Serge Koussevitzky Collection, Music Division of the Library of Congress, Washington DC.

Pecci-Blunt, Contessa Mimi. *Correspondance*.

Peignot, Suzanne. *Correspondance*.

Polignac, Comtesse Jean de. *Correspondance*.

Rostand, Claude. *L'Avant-Scène Opéra*, May 1983.

Rouart, Paul. *Correspondance*.

Rouart-Valéry, Agathe. *Correspondance*.

Sauguet, Henri. *Correspondance*.

Schaeffner, André. Bibliothèque Musicale Gustav Mahler, Paris.

Sienkiewicz. Geneviève. *Correspondance*.

Stravinsky, Igor. *Igor Stravinsky Nachlass*, Paul Sacher Foundation, Basle.

Vidal, Pierre. Collection of Pierre Vidal.

Vilmorin, Louise de. Bibliothèque Littéraire Jacques Doucet, Paris.

Viñes, Ricardo. *Correspondance*.

Viñes Soto, Elvira. *Correspondance*.

Wiéner, Jean. Archives Jean Wiéner, Bobigny.

Index of Letters

Numbers refer to letters, not pages.
* indicates unpublished letters

<small>LETTERS FROM FRANCIS POULENC TO:</small>

LETTERS TO FRANCIS POULENC FROM:

General Index

Page numbers in *italic* indicate biographical details